PAST TIME

PAST
TIME

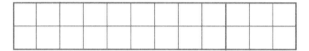

Baseball as History

JULES TYGIEL

OXFORD
UNIVERSITY PRESS

OXFORD
UNIVERSITY PRESS

Oxford   New York
Athens   Auckland   Bangkok   Bogotá   Buenos Aires   Calcutta
Cape Town   Chennai   Dar es Salaam   Delhi   Florence   Hong Kong   Istanbul
Karachi   Kuala Lumpur   Madrid   Melbourne   Mexico City   Mumbai
Nairobi   Paris   São Paulo   Shanghai   Singapore   Taipei   Tokyo   Toronto   Warsaw

and associated companies in

Berlin   Ibadan

Copyright © 2000 by Jules Tygiel

First published by Oxford University Press, Inc., 2000
198 Madison Avenue, New York, New York 10016

First issued as an Oxford University Press paperback, 2001

Oxford is a registered trademark of Oxford University Press

Library of Congress Cataloging-in-Publication Data
Tygiel, Jules.
Past time: baseball as history/Jules Tygiel
p. cm.
Includes bibliographical references references and index.
ISBN 0-19-508958-8 (Cloth)
ISBN 0-19-514604-2 (Pbk.)
1. Baseball—United States—History—19th century.
2. Baseball—United States—History—20th century.
I. Title.
GV863.AI T94 2000
796.357'0973 21—dc21   99-040106

Book design by Adam B. Bohannon

1 3 5 7 9 10 8 6 4 2

Printed in the United States of America
on acid-free paper

For Charlie and Sam

Contents

Introduction

This is a collection of essays about American history. I say that lest this be mistaken for a book about baseball. This would be a natural misconception. Baseball, after all, appears in its title. Each of its chapters revolves around baseball. The purpose of this book, however, is not to examine developments or events in the sport, but rather changes occurring in American society. The narratives rarely venture onto the field but concern themselves more with the broader baseball experience: how fans received and processed their baseball information; how they witnessed the games; what baseball symbolized in different eras; and how each generation reinvented the national pastime to fit its own material reality and ideological perceptions.

Many historians will recognize the subtitle, *Baseball as History*, as a play on Warren Susman's seminal collection of essays, *Culture as History*. "Each age has its special words, its own vocabulary, its own set of meanings, its particular symbolic order," wrote Susman. "A careful study of the conventions, the unassuming everyday acts, the rhetorical devices in speech and song, the unconscious patterns of behavior, all help to uncover . . . those fundamental assumptions that such cultures share."

Baseball, a constant in American life since the 1850s, reveals much about these "fundamental assumptions." I do not subscribe to Jacques Barzun's unfortunate and oft-quoted adage, "Whoever wants to know the heart and mind of America had better learn baseball." Remarkably, people with a total ignorance of baseball have written many fine books on American society and culture. Nor do I wish to over-intellectualize the game, ascribing hypo-

thetical meanings to rudimentary phenomena. Nonetheless, baseball, with its long, rich, well-documented history remains a powerful vehicle for exploring the American past.

If there is a unifying theme in these chapters, it is that, while
the game of baseball itself has changed minimally since its origins,
the context and format in which Americans have absorbed and
appreciated the game have dramatically shifted. In 1998 Americans
embraced the exhilarating quest by Mark McGwire and Sammy
Sosa to break Roger Maris's single-season home run record. They
did so in an environment markedly different from that in which
Americans in 1961 followed Maris's pursuit of Babe Ruth's record
and even further removed from the world of Ruth himself. When
Ruth set his first home run records in the early 1920s, he did so
in an age in which major league baseball was played in a few cities
in the Northeast and Midwest and daily newspapers remained the
dominant source of information. By 1927, when Ruth established
sixty home runs as a benchmark, the news could be relayed instantaneously to fans via the radio. Within days they could see the
feat in a newsreel. Thirty-four years later, baseball had begun its
westward expansion and a horde of newsmen from a variety of
media descended on Maris, challenging his powers of concentra-
tion as he approached Ruth's sacred record. Millions of fans, many
with mixed emotions, watched Maris dethrone Ruth, as it happened, on television.

The 1998 "media circus" dwarfed that which surrounded Maris.
Americans rejoiced in the friendly McGwire-Sosa competition in
a multitude of ways undreamed of by earlier generations. Twenty-
eight cities in all regions of the nation and two cities in Canada
now hosted major league teams. That Sosa hailed from the Do-
minican Republic gave the rivalry an international flavor. Fans
throughout the United States, Canada, and the Caribbean followed the chase on network and cable television and on the Internet, discussed it in e-mail chat rooms, and read about it in
national newspapers beamed to local communities via satellite. In
each era, different levels of technology facilitated different levels

of involvement and shaped the manner in which people responded.

I have organized these essays chronologically, but they need not be read in any particular order. Each stands alone as a separate inquiry into a particular age. The articles are designed to be suggestive, rather than definitive. Although I have done a substantial amount of primary research, the core analysis rests on secondary sources, the vast outpouring of writing on baseball history that has appeared in the 1980s and 1990s. I hoped to steer clear of two of the dominant themes in recent baseball writing: a heavy focus on the business side of the game and the ethereal, rhapsodic celebration of baseball and its special essence. These essays, with their emphasis on communications, team relocation, social mobility, and economic issues of supply and demand have drifted further into the realm of business than I had intended, but they nonetheless, I believe, approach these subjects from a fresh angle. I also make no grand claims for baseball beyond the obvious: that since its origins in the 1850s it has reflected broader changes in society and maintained a special place in American culture.

I am deeply indebted to my fellow historians, amateur and professional, scholarly and popular, who have offered new insights into the game and on whose work I have heavily relied. My fellow members of the Society for Baseball Research (SABR), both through their publications and SABR-L discussion list, have added significantly to my understanding of the game. John Thorn and Peter Palmer's *Total Baseball*, to which I am honored to contribute, was an irreplaceable source of information at every phase of this work. Unless otherwise noted, all information on attendance and player statistics is derived from *Total Baseball*.

My agent, Peter Ginsberg at Curtis-Brown, made this book possible. Dave Kelly at the Library of Congress and Scot Mondore at the Baseball Hall of Fame provided invaluable research assistance. Steve Appel helped out during a research trip to Cooperstown. Richard Zitrin, Ben Rader, John Thorn, Ron Story, Jeff Sammons, Don Spivey, Bill Issel, Barbara Loomis, Martha Tygiel, and Luise

Custer all critiqued portions of the manuscript. Bill Kirwin published earlier drafts of chapters one and two in *Nine: A Journal of Baseball History and Social Policy Perspectives*. I tested many of these ideas in "The History and Literature of Baseball," a course that I team-taught with the inimitable Eric Solomon. Both Eric and the students added greatly to my knowledge. I am, as always, grateful to my colleagues in the History Department at San Francisco State University for their collegiality and support. I also wish to thank Albright College, where I spent a delightful year as the National Endowment for the Humanities Visiting Professor as I completed the manuscript.

This is my third and final book written under the editorship of Sheldon Meyer, who has retired after almost a half-century of distinguished work at Oxford University Press. I thank Sheldon for his wisdom, kindness, patience, friendship, and support over the past two decades.

I thank my son Sam for developing an interest in baseball and making my springs and summers (and falls and winters) more enjoyable. As those who know him are well aware, my son Charlie cares less for baseball, but he enriches my life in innumerable other ways. Most of all, I thank my wife, Luise Custer. I cannot imagine a better and more loving traveling companion on life's unpredictable journeys.

I began work on *Past Time* during 1993 at a particularly foreboding moment in baseball history. Storm clouds were gathering, foretelling the onset of a major tempest: the devastating strike that resulted in the cancellation of the 1994 World Series. I conceived this book as an escape from these events, an inquiry into what was right about baseball, rather than an exposé about what was wrong with it; an examination of why baseball had appealed to different generations of Americans and how it had fit into and represented the fabric of their lives. I complete this book at a more upbeat moment. Although problems abound as salaries continue to rise and the imbalance between high- and low-income teams threatens its competitive structure, baseball, on the strength of a remarkable 1998 season, has largely recovered from the effects of the last strike.

Technological developments during the past five years have given us even more wondrous ways with which to access and enjoy the game. Above all, like the generations before us, we can still take ourselves to the ballpark, buy peanuts and cracker jacks (and garlic fries), suspend the present, and move past time, to bask in the unparalleled pleasures of "the old ball game."

PAST TIME

The National Game
Reflections on the Rise
of Baseball in the 1850s and 1860s

In November 1860 popular lithographers Currier & Ives depicted the results of the most significant presidential election in the nation's history in a most unusual fashion. The firm issued a print featuring the four leading contenders for the presidency—Unionist John Bell, northern Democrat Stephen A. Douglas, southern Democrat John Breckinridge, and Republican Abraham Lincoln—as baseball players. The three losing candidates each held baseball bats emblazoned with their political positions—"fusion," "non-intervention," and "slavery extension." Lincoln, holding a ball, his right foot planted firmly on "home base," fittingly held a long rail, labeled "equal rights and free territory." Each of the men discussed the outcome of the election using baseball jargon. Bell wondered "why we three should strike 'foul' and be 'put out.'" Douglas muses, "I thought our fusion would be a 'short stop' to his career." Breckinridge, shown slinking back to Kentucky with his fingers sealing his nostrils, complains "that we are completely 'skunk'd,'" a popular term for a rout or shutout. Lincoln warns his defeated opponents that should they choose to challenge him again, "You must have 'a good bat' and strike a 'fair ball' to make a 'clean score' & a 'home run.' " Currier & Ives entitled its editorial cartoon: THE NATIONAL GAME. THREE "OUTS" AND ONE "RUN."[1]

This print appeared at the very moment that the United States stood on the edge of defining for itself the meaning of terms like "nation" and "national." The "national game" illustrated here is not really baseball, but politics. Three years earlier, most Americans would have found this metaphor undecipherable. But Currier & Ives, a New York-based firm with a national clientele, felt confident that in 1860 its patrons not only would recognize the baseball imagery, but would understand the baseball language and be familiar with the notion that baseball had been anointed "the national game." Thus, the cartoon captures not just the profound political challenge confronting the United States, but also the extent to which a fledgling pastime had captured the imaginations of a significant segment of the American populace.

The question of why baseball appealed to the American people has evoked both treacly flights of romantic fancy as well as more serious scholarly analysis. Amherst College Professor Allen Guttmann attributes baseball's triumph, in part, to "the place of baseball in the cycle of the seasons." Yale President Bart Giamatti, shortly before he became baseball commissioner, lyrically explained, "The game begins in spring, when everything else begins again, and it blossoms in the summer . . . and then as soon as the chill rains come, it stops and leaves you in the fall alone." Philosopher Michael Novak invokes the "mysticism of baseball numbers," while Guttmann adds "the tendency of baseball toward extremes of quantification." Others have proposed theories of rural nostalgia, the folk-hero factor, and baseball as a compensatory mechanism for the travails of industrial life.[2]

Yet these explanations have a curiously ahistorical flavor. They describe values and attributes that Americans have grafted onto baseball after it became embedded in our culture. In 1860, when Currier & Ives felt comfortable in portraying baseball as "the national game," there was no clearly defined baseball season; statistical computations were in their barest infancy; few players or writers invoked rural imagery in their depictions; individual players remained anonymous rather than heroic; and industrial life had yet to cut the wide swath it would in the latter third of the nineteenth century. The key to baseball's appeal, therefore, rests not in the false nostalgia of the twentieth century, but in the culture of the United States in the years immediately preceding the Civil War.

The half-decade before the 1860 elections witnessed the clear elevation of the modern version of baseball in the consciousness of the influential mid-Atlantic states and, to a great extent, the nation as well. From the 1830s through the late 1850s Americans played an assortment of ball and bat games. Each city and region boasted its own variation. In New England, Philadelphia, and areas of Ohio and Kentucky, residents played versions of townball, in which squads of various sizes (up to fifteen men on a side) played on a square field with no distinction for foul territory and recorded outs by "plunking" base runners with a thrown ball. One out re-tired the side, and a fixed number of runs, usually 100, won the game.[3] One correspondent reported playing bat and ball games at midwestern barn raisings.[4] In many urban centers cricket flour-ished among British immigrants. In New York, the Knickerbocker game, which replaced the square with a diamond and "plunking" with the tag and force play, increasingly predominated in the 1850s.

Yet until roughly 1855 these games (other than cricket, which had been brought from England with a higher degree of organi-zation), while growing in popularity, appeared on a largely ad hoc basis. A handful of clubs structured regular practices and mostly intramural games. Most participants played ball games more in-formally. Games rarely pitted teams from rival regions, cities, or communities.

The next few years, however, featured both a startling explosion of organized baseball clubs, most playing the New York version of the game, and a growing assertion that baseball was now our national pastime. In 1855 the New York City area boasted a dozen clubs. The following year expansion began in earnest. *Porter's Spirit of the Times*, one of the first newspapers devoted to covering sport-ing events, reported that baseball players had converted every grassy lot within ten miles of New York into playing fields. Brooklyn, asserted the *Spirit*, was emerging as the "city of baseball clubs." The *Spirit* and the *New York Clipper* that year began to refer to baseball as the "national game." On December 5, 1856, the *New York Mercury* coined the phrase "the national pastime."[5]

These assertions might well be dismissed as wishful hyperbole. After all, the version of baseball being celebrated in 1857 was not a national, but a New York pastime. Even the *Spirit* qualified its initial 1856 designation, calling baseball "the National game in the region of the Manhattanese." In January 1857, when the first "national" convention of baseball clubs created a National Association of Baseball Players, all fourteen clubs represented came from New York and Brooklyn. As the *New York Clipper* noted after the second convention in 1858, the association was "a mere local organization, bearing no *State* existence even — to say nothing of a *National* one." A writer in *Harper's Weekly* in 1859 protested, "We see no evidence that . . . base-ball . . . is so generally practiced by our people as to be fairly called a popular American game."[6]

But the aptly named *Spirit of the Times* and others who asserted the national character of the new game had tapped into a deeply felt sentiment. Several commentators have argued, with considerable supporting evidence, that the wish to create a "national game" stemmed from, in Melvin Adelman's words, a "desire upon the part of Americans to emancipate their games from foreign patterns."[7] The *Spirit* called for a game "peculiar to the citizens of the United States, one distinctive from the games of the British like cricket or the German *Turnverein*." The *New York Times* in an 1857 article entitled "National Sport and Their Uses" argued that "To reproduce the tastes and habits of English sporting life in this country is neither possible nor desirable."[8]

The concept of nationalism, however, expresses not only distinctiveness from others but defines the disparate elements that unify a country. Improvements in transportation and communication in the antebellum era had begun to create a more truly national culture and fueled the ongoing sectional controversy over the meanings of federalism and republicanism. Indeed, this type of nationalism lay at the core of the political debates rending the United States in the 1850s. Northern soldiers fought for "union," a concept in which the needs of the nation transcended those of its component parts. Before the Civil War, the union, Carl Degler argues, was not yet a *nation*. American nationalism remained incomplete. The southern threat of secession challenged the assumptions of nationhood, threatening to fragment the United States, as James McPherson writes, "into several petty, squabbling autocracies" undermining the American experiment in democracy.[9]

This conviction did much to shape the demand for national attributes, particularly in the northern states, which facilitated the spread of baseball during the pre–Civil War years. Even by 1860, when the Currier & Ives cartoon appeared, baseball, particularly the New York version, had indeed become a more national pastime. The game had largely supplanted townball in both Massachusetts and Philadelphia. Baseball appeared in California and New Orleans in 1859. In 1860 the Brooklyn Excelsiors toured Philadelphia, Baltimore, and upstate New York, spawning new baseball clubs in their wake. Washington, D.C., and Lexington, Kentucky, also welcomed baseball in 1860, as did several cities in the Midwest, including St. Louis, Chicago, Milwaukee, Detroit, and Cleveland. Players in these cities adopted the rules published and printed by the National Association.[10] Songs like "Baseball Fever," "Baseball Polka," and, in 1861, the "Home Run Quick Step" celebrated the increasingly popular game.[11]

Ironically, throughout the 1850s, the British sport of cricket had a broader popularity than baseball. Cricket clubs appeared in at least twenty-two states and more than 125 cities and towns. At least in its organized forms, it attracted more participants, greater attention in the press, and larger crowds to its showcase events. In 1858, landscape architects for New York's new Central Park dubbed the land allocated for ball games the Cricket Ground, much to the chagrin of enthusiasts for the newer game. This has led several historians to posit a rivalry between the two games for the sporting soul of America, wherein "baseball vied with cricket for supremacy" and Americans ultimately "rejected" cricket, which "lost out" to baseball. Some engage in the dubious exercise of explaining how baseball appealed more to the American "character" or "spirit" than cricket. Others note the advanced institutional standardization of cricket, transplanted intact from England, and the unwillingness of British-American cricket players to adapt the game to make it more palatable to an American audience.[12]

This interpretation, however, misreads the tenor of the era. Cricket was rarely more than an immigrant game, one used, as George Kirsch points out, to allow the English community "to preserve its own ethnic identity."[13] Its popularity stemmed from the predominance of British immigrants in America among the white-collar and skilled occupations that employed most of those who participated in organized sports. There is no evidence that native-born Americans, who had always played indigenous varieties of ball and bat games, or non-British immigrants ever evinced much interest in cricket in any place other than Philadelphia, where the game had its greatest popularity. When crossovers occurred and choices had to be made, it was more likely to be the British-born cricketers, like Henry Chadwick and Harry and George Wright, who abandoned the immigrant game for that of their adopted homeland, rather than the other way around. Both games benefited from the same social forces that made organized sports possible in the 1850s, and baseball clearly borrowed from the institutional, statistical, and linguistic traditions of cricket. Nonetheless, baseball and cricket developed separately, rather than in any true competition with each other. Cricket remained contentedly confined to the British community, leaving a clear field for baseball to develop in its own manner.

The form that it assumed was the "Knickerbocker" or "New York" variation on townball. Both nineteenth-century commentators and some recent historians attributed the triumph of the New York game in the 1850s to its uncannily intuitive adherence to the American "temperament" or "character." In 1866 Charles A. Peverelly called it "a game which is pecularly suited to the American temperament and disposition," a sentiment echoed in the *Spirit of the Times* in 1867, which hailed it as "the pastime which best suits the temperament of our people." Twenty years later Mark Twain invested baseball as, "The very symbol, the outward and visible expression of the drive and push and rush and struggle of the raging, tearing booming nineteenth century."[14]

The fundamental difference between the New York game and most versions of townball and cricket lay in its configuration into a diamond, rather than a square or oval. In both townball and cricket the ball could be hit in any direction. The New York version of baseball designated a fair territory within the baselines established by the diamond, giving greater order and direction to the game. Indeed, the baseball diamond has assumed a mystical quality in the hands of romanticists. Allen Guttmann notes that, among team games, the movement in baseball is "uniquely circular" and wonders, "Is it wholly accidental that the four bases correspond numerically to the four seasons of the year?" Michael Novak writes, "To circle the bases is to traverse 360 feet, the precise number of degrees in a circle." The distance of ninety feet between the bases, contends Novak, repeating a frequently held fallacy, "leaves an almost exact balance between runners and fielders . . . another two feet in either direction might settle the issue decisively between them."[15] (In reality, any similar distance would produce a similar balance.)

Several recent commentators have performed metaphorical gymnastics to shoehorn the baseball diamond into the nineteenth-century American soul. David Lamoreaux sees the diamond as "an almost physical analogue of the country, an abstraction of the idea of the continent as it appeared to Americans in the mid-nineteenth century." The infield/outfield division parallels that between civilization and wilderness, with the infield "an abstract symbol of the civilized portions of the country." The outfield, "with its theoretically illimitable reach . . . suggests the frontier." Warren Goldstein, on the other hand, sees the diamond as an allegory of nineteenth-century urban life. "The game was a constant play of safety and danger," writes Goldstein, not unlike the daily journey through hostile urban neighborhoods. The tour around the bases required a passage through a territory "patrolled by the opposi-

tion," where one "could be put 'out' for the slightest error of skill
or judgement," in order to return home safely. Novak envisions
this same circuit as a "voyage" of "Yankee Clipper ships blown
silently across the sparkling seas, sails creaking in the wind (the
canvas that covers the diamond when it rains) . . . the silence and
isolation of each sailor at his post, encircling the world for trade."[16]

Stephen Gelber argues that baseball, appearing in "the formative
years of modern business" alongside large factories and commercial
enterprises, replicated the environment of the new urban workplace. "The highly structured, sequential nature of baseball" du-
plicated the modern urban work experience. Thus, baseball
"mark(ed) the transition from individual to corporate values . . .
subsuming the individual into the collective." Goldstein agrees
that the "baseball world had never been very far removed from
the world of work," but places its appeal within antebellum arti-
san culture, with its emphasis on manliness, self-control, and
self-discipline, rather than the incipient corporatism stressed by
Gelber.[17]

Melvin Adelman compares baseball to cricket, in which a batter
may hit indefinitely until put out. Adelman contends that "Baseball's structure expressed the American notion of individualism,
with its emphasis on independence, self-reliance and equality," ar-
ticulating the "American commitment to equal opportunity as each
batter is afforded roughly the same number of at bats regardless
of success." Novak carries the American analogy even further.
Baseball, writes Novak, "born out of the enlightenment and the
philosophies so beloved of Jefferson, Madison, and Hamilton," is
"designed as geometrically as the city of Washington . . . orderly,
reasoned, judiciously balanced . . . a Lockean game, a kind of contract theory in ritual form." Novak likens baseball to the U.S. Constitution, integrating a system of checks and balances, with the
umpire as judiciary, the batters as executives, and the fielders "a
congress checking the power of the hitters."[18]

Yet one need not dip into the murky depths of metaphor to
explain baseball's appeal. The sudden expansion and acceptance of

the New York game reflect several factors, not the least of which was the emergence of an increasingly national culture. The spread of the railroad and telegraph facilitated the spread of ideas and activities throughout the country. As George Kirsch has pointed out, the centrality of New York City in this emergent national culture helped to spread the game. The city's sporting weeklies, like *Spirit of the Times*, which enthusiastically promoted baseball, gained a limited but increasing circulation in other major cities. Businessmen traveling to New York, like George Beam who introduced baseball to Baltimore, discovered the game and brought it back to their home cities, while itinerant and migrating New York businessmen became missionaries for the game, founding clubs wherever they settled.[19]

Furthermore, the argument that baseball, the "New York" game in particular, suited the American or modern urban industrial character stands reality on its head. It would be more correct to say that the men who shaped baseball in the 1850s and 1860s fashioned it in their own image. As Adelman has noted, the originators of the game embraced the modern, rational, scientific worldview that had grown prevalent in mid-nineteenth-century America.[20] The appeal of the New York game lay not in its inherent attributes, but in the ability of its originators to incorporate emerging social attributes into the evolving game. Beginning in the 1840s, these athletes and, in the 1850s and 1860s, their supporters in the press consciously attempted to create a sport that suited their modern sensibilities. They replaced the chaos of townball—with its large teams, plunking, indefinite directional and time boundaries, and too frequent side changes—with a more ordered, rational variation. Limiting play to nine men on each side, imposing a diamond with foul lines radiating outward and confining play within that area, fixing the length of a game at nine innings, and replacing the "one out–all out" rule with a variation of three outs to allow more sustained play all reflected conscious decisions designed to make the game more attractive to those who played it. Baseball did not appeal to Americans, as many have suggested, because it took less time to play than cricket or townball. The architects of the game deliberately adopted an out and inning structure designed to compress play into the time available for games.

Nor were the New York arbiters averse to incorporating the best from other variations. At the early conventions of the National Association, delegates repeatedly debated rule changes designed to improve baseball. Fundamental elements of the game, like the distance between the pitcher's mound and home plate, the numbers of balls and strikes, and the meaning of a foul ball, would not be resolved for decades. In the 1880s baseball would incorporate overhand pitching from the Massachusetts game. The original New York game that spread through the nation in the late 1850s allowed players to be put out by catching the ball on a bounce. Both Massachusetts townball and cricket required the more difficult skill of catching the ball on the fly. Suggestions to adopt the fly rule were heard at the first national convention in 1857 in order to make the game "more manly and scientific." The debate over the fly rule lasted several years before the measure was ultimately adopted in 1863.[21]

The terms "manly" and "scientific" reflect the rhetoric of nineteenth-century modernism. Yet, there was nothing inherently manly or scientific about catching a ball on a fly (at least when compared to other athletic feats) or about the game of baseball. Players imbued the game with these desirable attributes so as to justify their participation and to make it more attractive to similarly minded men. Sportswriters and baseball publicists shared a similar worldview and described the game accordingly. By invoking this language, they gave the game of baseball a modern ethos.

These changes in the game largely reflected the desires of the players. Yet, it is surprising, given the absence of commercialized or for-profit matches in the 1850s, how prominently the concept and needs of spectators figured into these deliberations. As Harold Seymour argues, "The long process of rules refinement . . . was to make the game increasingly palatable to spectators." Part of the appeal of the Knickerbocker diamond configuration stemmed from its attractiveness to observers. The clear definition of fair and foul territory allowed those watching to get closer to the action without interfering with the course of play. Henry Chadwick, in defending the fly rule in 1860, invoked the demands of the fan, commenting, "Nothing disappoints the spectator . . . as to see a fine hit to the long field caught on the bound in this simple childish manner."[22] The growing demand for reports on baseball on the part of participants and nonparticipants alike led to expanded newspaper coverage. The first book catering to the baseball fan, *Beadle's Dime Base Ball Player*, appeared in 1860.

Yet, in the late 1850s and even the early 1860s spectators were not generally paying customers. Although sports entrepreneurs had charged for access to horse races, cricket matches, and prize fights for several decades, no record exists of an admission fee required at a baseball game until a New York–Brooklyn all-star contest in 1858. The need to recoup rental fees for the Fashion Course racetrack, rather than the quest for profit, led to a tariff variously reported as between ten and fifty cents. The practice of charging those wishing to attend games did not begin in earnest until 1862, when William H. Cannemeyer demanded a ten-cent fee to watch clubs at play at Brooklyn's new Union Grounds.[23] Others, particularly in the post-Civil War years, sought to emulate his success. By this time a ready baseball public had appeared without the lure of widespread commercial inducements.

The years immediately following the Civil War would witness, in the words of the *Chicago Tribune* in 1866, "the arrival of the Age of Baseball." The *Paterson (New Jersey) Press* described a baseball "frenzy" in the city. The nearby *Newark Advertiser* added in 1868, "People have baseball on the brain to an extent hitherto unequaled." The *Spirit of the Times* noted in 1867 that "Of all out of door sports, base-ball is that in which the greatest number of our people participate either as players or as spectators." Another national periodical conservatively estimated that 2,000 organized baseball clubs graced the nation that year. California alone boasted as many as 100 clubs.[24]

Baseball became a symbol of reunification. The *New York Clipper* in 1866 asserted that "the (baseball) fraternity should prove to the world that sectionalism is unknown in our national game." *Clipper* reporter Henry Chadwick, one of the most ardent advocates of a national game with standardized rules, expressed fears of regional variations leading to "four or five distinct styles of playing base ball," in which case "the term 'National Game' would have become a misnomer."[25]

By this time the leading clubs in many cities had evolved into professional teams, paying top players to represent them against other professional squads. These games, increasingly played before paying audiences, attracted large crowds. Harold Seymour estimates that 200,000 spectators attended games in 1868. The following year, the Cincinnati Red Stockings, the nation's first openly professional team, toured the nation. *Outing* magazine reported that 179,000 fans paid to see the Red Stockings play.[26]

Thus, by 1870 baseball's architects and promoters had invented a sport and established an ethos surrounding it that held a broad appeal to nineteenth-century Americans. They had rationalized the ball and bat games of preindustrial society and endowed the resulting amalgam with the language of modernism emphasizing order, science, and manliness. Baseball had become embedded in the culture on several levels: as a popular pastime for boys and men; a spectator sport; a centerpiece of national and local periodical reporting; a profession and form of entrepreneurial commercialized leisure; and increasingly as a source of national pride. The Civil War had defined the United States as a nation. In its aftermath, baseball truly reigned, as Currier & Ives had prematurely crowned it in 1860, as the "national game."

1	2	3	4	5	6	7	8	9	R	H	E

The Mortar of Which
Baseball Is Held Together
Henry Chadwick and the Invention
of Baseball Statistics

During the late nineteenth century, in the midst of a tour of England by American baseball players, a distinguished elderly gentleman approached one of the visiting athletes. The Englishman, Edwin Chadwick, was one of the most famous men in Great Britain. For almost a half-century he had reigned as that nation's "sanitary philosopher," the architect of its public health laws. In 1889 he would receive knighthood for his efforts. But on this day, Edwin Chadwick was concerned with celebrating the achievements of his younger American half-brother, Henry. Henry Chadwick, he reportedly boasted to the ballplayer, had "invented" the game of baseball. "Then you are the brother of a great man, Sir," responded the American.[1]

Edwin Chadwick's familial pride notwithstanding, no one, of course, not Abner Doubleday, or Alexander Cartwright, or Henry Chadwick, actually "invented" baseball. There is, however, more than an element of truth in the elder Chadwick's assertion. For Henry Chadwick, more than any other individual, created the game of baseball Americans have since celebrated and enjoyed. He invented not so much the game on the field, although through his continuous presence on the rules committee he significantly influenced its evolution. Rather, by his development of the box score, tabular standings, the annual baseball guide, the batting average, and most of the common statistics and tables used to describe baseball, Chadwick invented the game's historical essence. The ways in which Americans would absorb and analyze baseball from the late nineteenth century to the present emerged largely from Chadwick's vision, innovation, and reforming passion. In his lifetime, Chadwick was hailed as "Father Baseball." For more than a half-century, as a reporter for many of the major New York metropolitan newspapers and editor of, first, *Beadle's Dime Base Ball Player* and, later, the *Spalding Baseball Guides*, he was the most influential person in reporting the game and recording its early progress. He bequeathed to us a substantial archive of writings. Yet baseball historians have paid surprisingly little attention to Chadwick. There are no biographies, no major articles about him — only scattered accounts of his role in the rise of baseball in various histories of the sport.[2] The work of Henry Chadwick, however, and particularly his inspired decision to use statistics to chronicle and popularize baseball, illuminate not only the formative years of the national pastime, but the nation itself in the antebellum and post-Civil War eras.

Henry Chadwick was born in Exeter, England, in 1824. His grandfather, Andrew, an associate of John Wesley, had devoted his life to the promotion "of measures for the improvement of the condition of the population."[3] Henry's father, James, was a prominent figure in regional intellectual and cultural circles. A follower of Thomas Paine and a staunch adherent of the French Revolution, James Chadwick became an outspoken journalist and advocate of radical causes. At the time of Henry's birth James edited the *Western Times* in Exeter.[4] Half-brother Edwin, the product of an earlier marriage and twenty-four years older than Henry, had long since set out on his own.

In 1837, when Henry was twelve, James moved his second family to the United States and settled in Brooklyn.[5] Henry found America, and particularly its sporting activities, much to his liking. As a boy in England he had played rounders. Tall and athletic, he now became a skilled cricket player. He frequently accompanied friends to the playing fields of Hoboken, New Jersey, where he occasionally indulged in local variations on rounders, like townball. But Chadwick found these games juvenile and uninspiring. He particularly disliked the practice of "soaking" then prevalent in American baseball. "I remember getting some hard hits in the ribs, occasionally, from an accurately thrown ball," he later recalled with distaste.[6] James Chadwick encouraged his son to become a music teacher, but Henry was more attracted to his father's profession. As early as 1844, at age nineteen, he wrote articles for the *Long Island Star*. Four years later, he married and began to earn his living as a reporter, specializing in cricket and other sports coverage for a variety of New York and Brooklyn newspapers.[7]

In 1856 Chadwick rediscovered baseball. "On returning from the early close of a cricket match, I chanced to go through the Elysian Fields during the progress of a contest between the noted Eagle and Gotham Clubs," recalled Chadwick twelve years later. "The game was being sharply played on both sides and I watched it with deeper interest than any previous base ball match that I had seen. It was not long before I was struck with the idea that base ball was just the game for a national sport for Americans." From that day on, asserted Chadwick, he devoted himself to promoting and improving baseball.[8]

Meanwhile, Edwin Chadwick's career had blossomed in spectacular fashion.[9] In 1834, three years before Henry departed for America, Edwin had become a secretary to the royal commission on the reform of the poor laws. During the next decade Edwin Chadwick revamped the British system of administering poor relief. Like many reformers on both sides of the Atlantic, Edwin relied heavily in his work on the accumulation of accurate statistics. His 1842 *Report on the Sanitary Condition of the Labouring Population of Great Britain* became a sensation in England. A landmark of social research, the 1842 *Report* featured voluminous quantitative data supporting the opinions of doctors and public health officials. The primary author of the Public Health Act of 1848, Edwin became the Commissioner of the Board of Health from 1848 to 1854.

There is no evidence that the Chadwick brothers, separated by two and a half decades and later thousands of miles, had much contact during Henry's youth and adolescence, but Henry clearly followed, and gloried in, his brother's career.[10] In addition, through his radical father, young Henry was exposed to the same social ideals that had propelled his brother into the field of reform. These ideals meshed well with intellectual and political trends in antebellum America. As in England, urbanization led to growing concern about the impact of city life on American society and morality. Fears of crime, intemperance, prostitution, and vice inspired innumerable reform movements.[11]

Antebellum reformers worried about these most visible forms of urban pathology and also about the latent evils of the emergent order. City living exposed its residents to immorality, offered temptations that appealed to people's passion rather than reason, and also threatened their health. Severed from the invigorating countryside and bound by sedentary occupations, city-dwellers, especially young males, faced the prospect of physical as well as spiritual degeneration.

With the notable exception of the antislavery issue, on which Chadwick, who was married to a Virginian, apparently made no commentary, Chadwick fully embraced, and at times defined, the spirit and language of reform. In the middle decades of the nineteenth century, American health reformers and sportswriters evolved what Melvin Adelman has called a "new sports ideology" that justified baseball and other pastimes for their utilitarian benefits for the troubled urban social order.[12] Chadwick was a prime architect of this ideology. He publicized baseball as "a moral recreation" that would exert "a powerful lever . . . by which our people could be lifted into a position of more devotion to physical exercise and healthful out-door recreation."[13] Baseball, he wrote, merited "the endorsement of every clergyman in the country . . . (as) a remedy for the many evils resulting from the immoral associations [that] boys and young men of our cities are apt to become connected with."[14]

Chadwick's writings reverberated with the rhetoric of American reform. He sought to make baseball more "scientific" and "manly." He extolled team sports for their emphasis on "order" and "discipline." As Warren Goldstein notes, Chadwick's model baseball club constitution, first published in 1860, suggested fines for "profane language," "disputing the decision of the umpire," and "refusing obedience to the captain," offenses that exhibited a player's lack of self-control.[15] He continually favored strategies that emphasized displays of skill, control, and intellect over those reliant on unbridled power. "The true estimate of good pitching," he wrote in 1868, "is based on the chances offered fielders for outs. Striking out simply shows inferior batting, not superior pitching. . . . [A pitcher] would be more effective were he to depend less on mere speed."[16] Twenty years later he hailed the reduction in the number of called balls necessary for a walk from five to four, because "it would moderate the dangerous speed in delivering the ball to the bat."[17] Chadwick repeatedly rejected reliance on the home run over more "scientific" strategies for scoring.

Chadwick's passion for reform was most evident in his crusades against gambling and alcohol. Upon Chadwick's death, his friend and patron, Albert Spalding, celebrated the sportswriter's struggle with the "gambling and the pool-selling evils" as his greatest contribution to the game.[18] Chadwick repeatedly called for "prohibition planks" in player contracts. "The two great obstacles in the way of the success of the majority of professional ball players are wine and women," he wrote in 1889. "The saloon and brothel are the evils of the base ball world at the present day."[19] As Edwin Chadwick once joked, "While I have been trying to clean up London, my brother has been keeping up the family reputation by trying to clean up your sports."[20]

Chadwick's "ardent nature," bludgeoning language, and endless pontification were not always welcome. Chadwick dismissed those who disagreed with him "as old fogy individuals" and termed their arguments "absurd." "He made enemies by the hundreds; he received the personal abuse of unscrupulous newspapers and their correspondents," eulogized Spalding. In 1876 the *Chicago Tribune* dismissed him as the "Old Man of the Seas . . . a dead weight on the neck of the game." Even Harry Wright, who shared most of Chadwick's visions of sportsmanship, accused Chadwick of writing too much about "suspicious play" and "crooked players." Furthermore, chided Wright, Chadwick "also uses words he doesn't understand."[21]

But if Chadwick's zealous commitment to social reform offended his detractors, it also fed his inclination toward statistical analysis. As in England, antebellum social reformers were among the foremost adherents of statistical research. As early as 1816 prison, temperance, and school reformers in Boston and Philadelphia published statistical surveys to bolster their demands for reform. Temperance advocates in the 1830s compiled statistics of drunkenness and published almanacs detailing the dimensions of the problem. Antislavery advocates increasingly relied on numbers to sustain their arguments. As historian Patricia Cline Cohen has noted, "The statistical champions of the mid-nineteenth century were fairly clear about what they regarded as the effects of quantification on social thought. Enumeration focused concern on an issue, accurately described its dimensions and suggested the proper course of action to be taken."[22]

These statistical arguments found an ever more responsive and sophisticated audience. During the first half of the nineteenth century Americans were, as one English traveler noted in the 1830s, a "guessing, reckoning, and calculating people." According to Cohen, Americans in the Jacksonian and antebellum periods became a numerate people, "as things once thought of solely in qualitative terms became subject to quantification." The rise of a market economy, requiring more people to be competent in arithmetic, and the spread of mass education gave the public a growing familiarity with numbers.[23]

Statistical manuals and almanacs grew popular. In part the attraction of these almanacs stemmed from the same fervor that led Chadwick to envision the emergence of a "national sport for America." By statistics, wrote George Tucker in 1847, "we can trace the progress of society and civilization; or in other words measure a nation's moral and religious improvement; its health, wealth, strength, and safety." Newspapers, pamphlets, and journals included statistical sections. By the 1830s businessmen regularly employed double-entry bookkeeping, while pediatric advice manuals included tables of neonatal weights. The end of the decade marked the founding of the American Statistical Society.

This fascination with numbers was not a peculiarly American trait. A European historian has described the 1830s and 1840s as an "era of enthusiasm" for statistics.[24] Other industrializing nations like England, Prussia, and France demonstrated a greater sophistication in their collection and application of data and most of the major breakthroughs in mathematical theory occurred in Europe. But, as Cohen notes, "What struck foreign travelers in America was the extent to which ordinary inhabitants had incorporated and internalized a tendency to measure, count, and calculate." Thus, a compiler of statistics, "assured of an audience that would understand his numerical message and accord it a superior credibility, had only to choose the exact form his data would take."[25]

"It was not long . . . after I had become interested in baseball that I began to invent a method of giving detailed reports of leading contests," wrote Chadwick in 1868.[26] That these reports revolved around statistics reflected the temper of the times and Chadwick's reform inclinations. They also stemmed from his earlier experiences as a player and reporter of cricket. Methods for recording both individual cricket games and individual year-end statistics had long since appeared in England. Cricket box scores and other statistics appeared in American papers as early as the 1840s. In 1857 the *New York Clipper*, possibly at the urging of Chadwick, who joined the paper that year, attempted to compile its cricket data "in a systematic manner." As Chadwick himself later wrote, "I had been reporting cricket for years, and in my method of taking notes on contests, I had a peculiar plan of my own."[27] He sought to adapt these techniques to baseball.

For Chadwick, accumulating data not only provided a means of reporting on the games, but of reforming them as well. "From the time I first became an admirer of base ball," he wrote in 1868, "I have devoted myself to improving and fostering the game in every way . . . Seeing that everything connected with the game, almost, was new, its rules crude and hastily prepared . . . I began to submit amendments to the rules of the game."[28] Like his brother and other nineteenth-century reformers, Chadwick possessed a profound faith in the power of statistics to persuade. United States census official Joseph Kennedy eloquently expressed this vision in an 1859 address entitled "The Progress of Statistics." Statistics, he contended, could "ameliorat(e) . . . man's condition by the exhibition of facts whereby the administrative powers are guided and controlled by the lights of reason, and the impulses of humanity impelled to throb in the right direction." They were "the practical workings of an elevated Christianity."[29]

To Chadwick, for whom the promotion of baseball served a moral purpose, statistics were a means to this higher end. In a game that was still evolving, in his words, "step by step, little by little . . . from (an) almost simple field exercise . . . to (a) manly scientific game," the statistics gave him ammunition to support the changes he deemed indispensable to popularize the game. Disavowing "any egotistical spirit," he nonetheless confessed with the arrogance that infuriated his critics, "I have always proved . . . the correctness of my views, and, in this, I have, of course, been greatly assisted by facts and figures derived from actual observation and from a statistical analysis of each season's play."[30]

Chadwick defined his "main object" as "building up a national game."[31] The very conception of a "national game" had corollary ramifications. Baseball had to be made accessible not just to those who played the game, but to a broader audience of spectators and fans. A "national game," in order to be enjoyed and understood by those throughout the United States, must therefore have national standards: uniform rules, uniform scoring, and a means by which to measure its progress. Chadwick's first suggestion for improving baseball was thus "an innovation on the simple method of scoring then in vogue" based upon a system of shorthand reporting that he had devised. He invented a scoring system that used letters to designate each play. "The abbreviations of this system were prepared on the mnemonics plan of connecting the abbreviated words in some way or another with the movement to be described," he later recalled. Thus, "L" stood for a foul ball and "K," which Chadwick viewed as "the prominent letter of the word strike, as far as remembering the word was concerned," represented a strikeout. Over the years, numbers based on player positions replaced letters in this scheme. Only the unexpectedly lyrical "K" designation for strikeout has survived.[32]

Chadwick had created, according to Thomas Rice, "the simplest, most easily learned and most expressive of all the systems of shorthand ever invented,"[33] a form of double-entry bookkeeping in which plays on offense would balance out those on defense. To facilitate the widespread adoption of this scheme, Chadwick routinely included blank scoring forms and instructions for using his design in his annual guides. "It is requisite that all first nine contests should be recorded in a uniform manner," he insisted in *Beadle's Dime Base Ball Player* in 1861.[34]

With the practice of scoring games so thoroughly ingrained in baseball and other sports, it is easy to overlook the critical importance of Chadwick's vision and achievement. Even if one rejects Rice's effusive opinion that Chadwick's invention of baseball scoring "entitles him to a high position among the world's thinkers," the significance of Chadwick's contribution is evident. Scoring, as sportswriter Hugh Fullerton once observed, "is the process of transferring a baseball game from the field onto paper and the scorers are the recording secretaries and historians of the game." Economist Ralph Andreano adds, "Standardizing the rules of scoring was the equivalent of an industrial magnate's standardizing the weight, shape, and purity of a steel bar. If the statistics of performance were to have the meaning intended for them, it was absolutely essential that the playing situation for all teams and players be nearly comparable as possible."[35]

The end product of Chadwick's system of scoring and statistical analysis was his most artful and enduring creation, the box score. Branch Rickey has called the box score "the mortar of which baseball is held together." John Thorn and Peter Palmer have likened it to St. Peter's Book of Life. To Roger Angell it is "one of my favorite urban flowers . . . a precisely etched miniature of the sport itself."[36]

Like so many of Chadwick's innovations, the box score represented an adaptation of common cricket practice tempered by the spirit of reform. Box scores for cricket matches and, at least on one occasion an early baseball game, appeared in American newspapers as early as 1845. According to Adelman, after 1853, three years before Chadwick turned his attention to the new game, baseball box scores listing the batting order, outs made, and runs scored, the usual cricket categories, often appeared in the New York press.[37]

But the cricket box score was not readily adaptable to baseball. Cricket was a far simpler competition, despite its reputation as a more scientific game. A cricket match, although chronologically longer than baseball, lasted for only two innings. In cricket, which had only two bases, a hit and a run were synonymous. Reaching base meant running to the opposite wicket, which automatically scored a run. If the "striker" hit the ball and did not reach the opposite wicket, he was out. Thus, runs and outs were the only offensive possibilities, making the simple box score an accurate accounting of the game details.[38]

Baseball, however, had many more innings and offered many additional possibilities. Although runs remained the key to victory, a batter could reach base safely without scoring a run and he could reach base in a variety of ways: by hitting safely, by a walk (which did not exist in cricket), or through a fielder's error. In addition, hits had varying values. Some accounted for two bases, others three, and yet others four. Chadwick and others attempted to collapse this complexity into a capsule summary closely akin to the cricket box score. An 1858 *New York Tribune* box score of a Brooklyn–New York all-star game recorded a phenomenal amount of detail, including a delineation of "How Put Out," indicating whether batters were retired on a fly, bound, or foul catch or at which base they were tagged.[39]

Chadwick, who may have had a hand in the *Tribune* account, produced his first recorded baseball box score in 1859, documenting a contest in Brooklyn between the Excelsiors and the Stars. Chadwick's handiwork was strikingly similar to the modern box score. He did not list the traditional cricket categories of runs and outs, but instead runs and hits. He also listed three fielding statistics for each player: putouts, assists, and errors. Below the player information, Chadwick inserted another of his innovations, an inning-by-inning line score.[40]

For Chadwick, the reformer, however, box scores were not just game reports, but a series of mini-morality plays. Players should receive credit for their achievements and, through the category of errors, acknowledgment of their flaws. But just as reformers made distinctions between the "deserving and undeserving poor," Chadwick attempted to distinguish between positive achievements and those that befell a team or athlete as a result of opponents' misplays. In a summary section below the line score, Chadwick recorded "battery errors," which included walks as well as wild pitches or passed balls. More significantly, Chadwick introduced the concept of "earned runs," those that resulted from safe hits, "not by skillful base running and the fielding errors such running involves."[41] Chadwick apparently took this distinction, meant originally to measure batting, rather than pitching prowess, seriously. He charged the two teams with a total of sixteen errors. Out of twenty-nine runs scored in the game, he credited only five as "earned."

The issues raised in Chadwick's 1859 box score—how to adapt cricket measurements to baseball and the creation of a moral economy of baseball—would shape the evolution of baseball statistics. Ironically, Chadwick never really understood baseball and never fully appreciated the differences between baseball and cricket. He struggled (as have most serious baseball statisticians) with the significance of a hit and failed to incorporate events like the walk and the home run into his moral universe.

Despite the inclusion of hits in his 1859 box score, during the early 1860s Chadwick's box scores, which appeared with increasing frequency in the *New York Clipper*, reverted to traditional cricket categories, recording simply outs and runs. The remaining descriptive detail, including home runs, strikeouts, and "catches missed," appeared in a summary beneath the line score.[42]

Over the next decades, Chadwick expanded his reportorial and statistical horizons. The latter half of the nineteenth century was an extraordinary age of statistical innovation. In many industries and disciplines, writes historian Margo Cook, "The process of improving the data and statistical techniques was a slow and tedious one which took years of experimentation and analysis." In the 1860s insurance companies investigating mortality rates laid the foundation for gathering information on individuals, by recording details on individual cards, that could then be arranged in homogeneous groupings. The U.S. Census Bureau repeatedly revised its collection and reporting techniques, introducing both new statistics and innovative tabular reporting. Under the dynamic leadership of Francis Walker, the census bureau introduced calculating machines and revamped population reports to cross-tabulate occupational data by nation, state, and city as well as age, ethnicity, and sex. By 1870, the census reports had grown to five volumes; by 1880, twenty-two. The new social sciences of economics, anthropology, psychology, and sociology all increasingly utilized statistics.[43]

Chadwick's activities paralleled these broader developments. In the 1850s his reports had revolved primarily around providing accounts of individual games. In 1860, only four years after his baseball epiphany, Chadwick edited *Beadle's Dime Base Ball Player*, the first baseball annual. In this and subsequent volumes Chadwick's attention focused on how to present cumulative individual statistics and seasonal summaries

Historian Warren Goldstein associates the rise of individual statistics with the emergence of the professional game in the late 1860s. "Statistics were developed, employed, and promoted as measures of players' productivity on the ballfield," argues Goldstein, allowing "employers to measure the abilities of players they had never seen."[44] But it is telling how far Chadwick had advanced statistics prior to the widespread advent of professionalism. "In order to obtain an accurate estimate of a player's skill, an analysis both of his play at the bat and on the field should be made," Chadwick wrote in 1861. By 1867, at the dawn of the professional game, in addition to his annual guides and daily reports for the *Clipper* and *Eagle*, Chadwick edited a weekly *Ball Players' Chronicle*, which reported a wide array of statistics for the current year and made comparisons with past performances of preceding years as well.[45] Fans, not team owners, were Chadwick's primary audience.

Chadwick endlessly experimented with ways in which to evaluate and record player performance. In the spirit of reform, his reports stressed not just accuracy, but accountability. In the "matter-of-fact figures given at the close of the season," he argued in 1864, "we are frequently surprised to find that the modest but efficient worker, who has played earnestly and steadily through the season . . . has come in, at the close of the race, the real victor." Statistics thus had to distinguish and reward "the real victors," rather than the "dashing general player" with "a great deal of eclat in prominent matches."[46]

In 1865 Chadwick began to advance beyond simple counting of hits, runs, and outs into the realm of averages. Again borrowing from cricket, Chadwick printed runs per game figures in the *Clipper*. These figures appeared not as strict averages with decimal points, but rather as an "average and over." Dividing the number of runs scored by games played, a batter who scored twelve runs in five games had an average of two runs per game, with two left over. Two years later *The Ball Players' Chronicle* included outs per game and hits per game as well.[47]

As Chadwick expanded his statistical vistas, he became increasingly aware of the limitations of cricket statistics. In 1867 Chadwick finally reincorporated hits into his box scores. Characteristically, Chadwick now embraced hits wholeheartedly. "Outs and runs . . . is no criterion of a batsman's skill at all," he wrote in 1868. "We have known of dozens of instances in which batsmen have secured first or second base on their hits" but due to "the inferior batting of their successors, have had a large score of outs and no runs." Thus, concluded Chadwick, "There is but one true criterion of the skill at the bat, and that is the number of times bases are made on clean hits."[48] As Thorn and Palmer have demonstrated, the acceptance of hits as the key offensive statistic led inexorably to the computation of the batting average. In 1870 *Beadle's* began reporting hits per game in decimal rather than "over and under" form. In 1872 Chadwick's *Clipper* replaced games in the denominator with at bats, thus creating the modern batting average. When the National League began four years later, batting average was an official statistic and well established as the dominant measure of batting prowess.[49]

With the invention of the batting average, Chadwick, operating in his moral universe and obsessed with personal accountability, had begun to create what Thorn and Palmer have called "isolating stats . . . measure(s) of individual performance not dependent on one's own team."[50] But downgrading the significance of runs scored and elevating "clean hits" to the pinnacle of statistics nonetheless posed other problems. Not all hits were equal. *The Ball Players' Chronicle* compensated for this problem by reporting total bases and total bases per game (a forerunner of slugging percentage) as well. But, given the fielding deficiencies of the early baseball player, Chadwick felt uncomfortable placing too much credence in these statistics. "It is comparatively easy to judge whether (a player) was sure of his first base on his hit, but in running to second or third base on his hit, the errors of fielding, by which such base running is permitted, are multiplied five fold . . . and hence it is very difficult to decide impartially how often a batsmen is entitled to his second or third base on his hit," he maintained in 1868.[51]

This argument, of course, had limited applications to home runs, especially those that cleared the fence. But the home run offended Chadwick's reform sensibilities and never found favor with "Father Baseball." In the belief system of antebellum reform, science and control outweighed brute strength. Chadwick's assaults on the home run often veered into the irrational. Writing in 1868, Chadwick contrasted the "striker" who "hits a long ball and makes a clean home run" with four succeeding batters who each struck singles and later scored. "Now although the striker made four bases on his hit, he only secured one run, whereas the players who made but one base on their hits necessarily each secured a run."[52] A quarter of a century later Chadwick had not relented. The home run, he contended in 1894, was "the easiest hit . . . which the veriest novice at bat can make." Furthermore, "home run hitting . . . involves the costly expenditure of physical strength consistent upon running 120 yards at one's utmost speed, a test of strength . . . which ordinarily requires a good half-hour's rest to recuperate. . . . How much more effective is it, in the saving of strength, to earn single bases by hits." Chadwick also bemoaned that home runs deprived the opportunity "for all the attractive features of sharp in-fielding and active base running."[53]

Similarly, Chadwick, along with many of his contemporaries, experienced great difficulty locating bases on balls in the moral economy of baseball. Walks did not exist in cricket, and to Chadwick, according to later statistician Ernest Lanigan, "so long as a batter received one good pitch at which to swing, he rated no special consideration" in his personal accounting. Walks, reasoned Chadwick, were the result of poor pitching, not disciplined hitting. (Conversely, strikeouts were the product of bad hitting, and Chadwick never credited them to the pitcher in his scoring.)[54] In his earliest box scores, Chadwick recorded walks under battery errors; in his 1860s box scores he recorded them not at all. When Chadwick returned to the concept of earned runs in 1867, those runs scored as the result of bases on balls he deemed unearned by the offense.

By the mid-1870s bases on balls totals appeared in most box scores, but a debate raged as to how they should be counted in the scoring. In 1876, during the National League's inaugural season, walks counted as outs for the batter. Two years later league rules instructed scorers not to count walks as at-bats, an injunction ignored by the *New York Clipper* throughout the years that Chadwick was affiliated with its sports page.[55] In 1878, three years before Chadwick became its editor, the *Spalding Base Ball Guide* stated that a pitcher should be charged with an error for allowing a batter to reach base on called balls, "though there are times when a pitcher shows good judgment in doing so." This sanction appeared in the league rules as late as 1883. The 1885 rules restored the category of "battery errors."[56]

The debate reached its apogee in 1887. During the preseason the Joint Rules Committee of the National League and American Association, at the suggestion of star player and union leader John Montgomery Ward, decreed that bases on balls would henceforth be recorded as hits.[57] In modern parlance, on-base percentage had replaced batting average as the leading indicator of batting skill. Ward's innovation recognized that walks were as much the product of a batter's patience and skill as of a pitcher's wildness.

So entrenched had Chadwick's conception of batting averages become that the new rule met with widespread opposition, not just from Chadwick, but from others as well. Sportswriters in Boston and other cities boycotted the rule, failing to record walks as hits.[58] When the American Association's batting champion Tip O'Neill weighed in with a staggering .492 average, the die was cast. At the season's end the rules committee revoked the walk-as-hit rule. Batters who walked would again be exempted from an at bat. In addition, although walks would again be summarized as errors, runs scored as the result of walks would now be counted as earned runs.[59] Chadwick applauded the return of his original concept of batting average but dismissed the new policy on earned runs as "absurd," since it was possible to register an earned run without a single hit being made. "To estimate a pitcher's skill on such a basis is nonsense," he wrote in the 1889 *Spalding Guide*.[60]

If, however, Chadwick had lost this skirmish, he had won the broader war. Chadwick's batting average, defined as the number of hits per at bat, would henceforth prevail as the dominant, even sacred, measure of batting. The ability to reach base safely or to slug for extra bases, the two skills most essential to success in baseball, would be deemphasized in importance. Careers would be made or broken by the faithful adherence to the cult of the batting average.

As demonstrated by the great batting average debate of the late 1880s, Chadwick's role within the baseball universe had shifted. No longer the great innovator and shaper of a new national pastime, "Grandfather Chadwick," as *The Sporting News* called him in 1886,[61] had become the voice of the baseball establishment. Although clearly no less ardent or truculent than in the 1850s and 1860s, Chadwick's strident opinions now tended to be raised more on behalf of the status quo than with those seeking change. This may have represented a natural progression of age, but it also reflected his recognition that his personal livelihood and fortunes had grown dependent on those of professional baseball. In 1876, when William Hulbert and Albert Spalding of Chicago had staged the coup that created the National League, they had pointedly excluded the New York-based Chadwick from the venture. Chadwick sharply criticized the new league and for several years found himself excluded from the emerging baseball mainstream.[62] In 1881, however, Spalding, the dominant figure in the National League, welcomed Chadwick back into the fold, naming him editor of the annual *Spalding Baseball Guide*, the *ex-officio* voice of professional baseball. Chadwick, who edited the guide until his death in 1908, increasingly became the spokesperson for Spalding and the National League.

Chadwick's pronouncements on the growing rift between players and owners in the 1880s exemplified this role. In 1884 Chadwick attacked athletes for their "exorbitant" salary demands and defended the reserve clause that bound players to a single team and limited their earning power. According to David Voigt, when the players union rebelled in 1890 and formed a Players League, Chadwick was one of only a handful of major sportswriters who sided with the owners. Chadwick accused the union leaders of "a system of terrorism peculiar to revolutionary movements." Boston sportswriter Tim Murnane responded, "Anything more rabid than Chadwick's last effusion . . . would be hard to find . . . The older he gets, the worse he gets."[63]

Health problems dogged the aging Chadwick in the 1890s. He suffered from crippling inflammatory rheumatism for two years. Nonetheless, Chadwick continued to edit the *Spalding Baseball Guide*. As always, he amassed detailed statistics, and ranted against player dissipation, sloppy play, and the home run. He also received a series of honors. In 1894 the National League elected him an honorary member. In 1896 the league awarded him a $600 a year pension. In the new century President Theodore Roosevelt invited him to the White House, and he received a special medal at the 1904 St. Louis World's Fair.[64]

In 1905 a playful dispute with Spalding over whether Americans had invented baseball or it had evolved from British games like rounders resulted in the creation of the Mills Commission to "settle" the issue. Shortly thereafter, Spalding wrote to Chadwick suggesting that he write a book on "the origins and history of baseball." "Write as a baseball historian and not as a critic," Spalding advised the eighty-one-year-old Chadwick. "You are not going to live forever. Keep the book as free of statistics as possible."[65]

For the next two years Chadwick worked on his history, edited the guide, and continued to write on baseball in periodicals. In 1907 he edited the *Spalding Base Ball Record*, the first true baseball encyclopedia, which included players' statistics over four decades. The following spring, Chadwick completed work on the 1908 *Spalding Guide*, which featured the dubious report of the Mills Commission concluding that Civil War General Abner Doubleday had invented baseball.[66] On April 14, despite a "bitter east wind blow," Chadwick attended the 1908 home opener at Brooklyn's Washington Park. "Was at the game yesterday and caught a severe cold," he wrote to Jacob Morse, editor of *Baseball Magazine* on April 15. "Hurrah for Kelley and his men. No game today—rain." Typically, Chadwick added a critique of the fans. "The bleacherites behaved abominably," he noted. The following morning he rose early and at 6 A.M. wrote a poignant letter to Morse:

Please bear in mind, my old friend, that here I am, at 84 years of age, with lots of dear relatives to look after and working harder and for less than I did forty years ago. You are probably unaware that I live in a fourth flat of a four-story apartment house, and have no servant, two of my grandchildren serving us as housekeepers alternatively . . . Fortunately my mental powers have withstood the attacks of age and physical incapacity . . . blessed with a treasure of a wife I have been enabled to get along thus far on comparatively small means. So you see how necessary it is for me to avail myself of every chance to earn money by my pen.[67]

Chadwick's "severe cold" became pneumonia. Four days later, on April 20, 1908, Chadwick died at the age of eighty-four. At his funeral, Spalding, living in California, sent a floral arrangement of white immortelles in the shape of a baseball. The National League raised money to construct a cemetery marker decorated with crossed bats and a granite baseball. In his will, Chadwick left his voluminous collection of baseball writings, records, and memorabilia to Spalding, urging his patron to complete his unfinished history of baseball. The result was Spalding's classic volume, *America's National Game*.[68]

Over the decades critics have frequently recognized the shortcomings of some of Chadwick's statistical innovations, particularly the batting average. In 1919 future National League President John Heydler, arguing that "general reforms seem to be the order of the day almost everywhere and old established customs are falling down all around us," suggested changing the basis for batting averages. Ten years later sportswriter F. C. Lane, in an article entitled "The Faulty Foundations of Batting Averages," made a similar plea.[69] In recent years commentators have savaged the statistic. Thorn and Palmer dismiss it as "a bit of nostalgia," which will hopefully fade way.[70] But the batting average, rooted in the artifacts of cricket and crafted by the dictates of reform, has endured and survived its detractors.

If in this area Chadwick's handiwork has led us astray, however, the broader imprint of his grand achievement remains. Chadwick's incorporation of the modern passion for statistics into the core of the game, his invention of a scoring system and insistence on uniform standards, his innovation in forms of quantitative reporting and measurement, and the moral fervor with which he pursued these activities transplanted the enjoyment of baseball from the playing field to the parlor and beyond. Henry Chadwick invented the baseball experience, which makes him, as the American ballplayer told his brother, "a great man" indeed.

1 2 **3** 4 5 6 7 8 9 R H E

Incarnations of Success
Charles Comiskey, Connie Mack, John McGraw, and Clark Griffith

Few Americans in the early 1910s were more renowned or celebrated than a quartet of former baseball players who had come to symbolize not only the national pastime but also the contours of the American dream. Charles Comiskey, Connie Mack, and Clark Griffith, each an owner of an American League franchise, and John McGraw, who had left the ownership ranks for the more financially rewarding position of manager of the New York Giants, epitomized the promise of the nation. Sons of immigrants or dirt-poor southern farm folk, they now reigned as men of substantial prestige and wealth. Skilled baseball players who had achieved stardom on the field and played prominent roles in player rebellions against owner exploitation, they had risen through the ranks and become first managers and then owners. Each had played a key role in the ambitious creation of the American League in 1901, and each had reaped handsome rewards for his foresight. By 1913 Comiskey, Mack, and Griffith proudly bore the lofty mantle of "magnate," the pretentious designation by which major league owners identified themselves. McGraw reigned as the highest salaried man in the game and would rejoin the ranks of the magnates at the end of the decade.

The public knew the foursome by affectionate, honorific nicknames: Comiskey, the Old Roman; Mack, the Tall Tactician; Griffith, the Old Fox; and McGraw, the Little Napoleon. Sportswriters and commentators in national periodicals acclaimed them as exemplars of American virtues. *McClure's Magazine* hailed Mack, whose Philadelphia Athletics in 1913 became the first team to win three consecutive World Championships, as a man whose habits of "clean living and quick thinking" had "more influence with the youth of America than any man." Sporting goods magnate A. J. Reach celebrated Chicago White Sox owner Comiskey as "a great national heroic figure," who had achieved this status "by his own labor and effort in the face of many discouragements." As owner of the Washington Senators, Griffith hobnobbed with President William Howard Taft and U.S. senators, congressmen, and Supreme Court justices. He had "showed himself the real goods in every detail," wrote one national journalist, "one of the men who have made baseball of such commanding influence in the sporting world," added another. The feisty, controversial McGraw, whose Giants had won five pennants in his first decade as manager, elicited fewer accolades as a role model, but nonetheless as his biographer, Charles Alexander, writes, he was an international celebrity who "epitomized what a baseball manager should be."[1]

The quartet stood, as one writer had dubbed Comiskey in 1909, as "incarnation(s) of success,"[2] before a public for whom the celebration of success had been embedded in the national psyche. Yet even as Comiskey, Mack, Griffith, and McGraw basked in public acclaim, forces had been set in motion that would illustrate the limits of their achievements and how fleeting and fickle fame and fortune could be.

The four players cum magnates had emerged from strikingly similar backgrounds. Three—Comiskey, Mack, and McGraw— were the sons of Irish immigrants. Griffith alone came from native American stock. All came from large families and all, save Comiskey, the third of eight children of Chicago alderman John Comiskey, bore the scars of childhoods marked by the grinding toil and untimely family deaths that characterized the lives of the poor in late nineteenth-century America.

Connie Mack, born Cornelius McGillicuddy, was one of seven children born to Mike and Mary McGillicuddy. Contrary to baseball folklore, which has Connie's surname shortened to fit into box scores, the family always went by Mack, except on official papers, or "when we voted," according to Connie. At the time of Connie's birth in East Brookfield, Massachusetts, in 1862, Mike Mack was serving in the Union Army. After the Civil War, Mike supported his family by working in East Brookfield's factories and mills. An epidemic in the 1870s claimed the lives of two of Connie's sisters, thirteen-year-old Nellie and one-year-old Mary Augusta, who died in Connie's arms. Mike Mack died in 1879 at the age of fifty-two, leaving sixteen-year-old Connie, the oldest son, to support his mother and surviving siblings. Early deaths continued to haunt Mack into adulthood. William Hogan, who was Mack's best friend, the brother of his childhood sweetheart, and the pitcher who had recommended Mack for his first professional contract, contracted consumption and died during their first minor league season. Mack married Hogan's sister, Margaret, three years later. She bore him three children in five years, then died at age twenty-six, leaving Connie a thirty-year-old widower.[3]

John McGraw's childhood bore an unmistakable, if even darker, resemblance to Mack's. His father, John McGraw, Sr., had migrated from Ireland, served in the Civil War, then lost his first wife in childbirth, leaving him a young widower with a baby daughter. He settled in Truxton, New York, where he labored as a railroad construction worker and remarried. Ellen McGraw bore him eight more children, including John, Jr., the oldest. In the winter of 1884–85, when John was eleven years old, a diphtheria epidemic devastated the McGraw family. Ellen McGraw died within days of giving birth to her eighth child. Four of McGraw's siblings also succumbed to the epidemic. John McGraw, Sr., unraveled, taking out his anguish and rage on his oldest son, whom he flogged regularly. In fall 1885, less than a year after his mother had died, twelve-year old John fled his home to escape his father's violent onslaught and took up residence with Mary Goddard, a neighbor who ran a hotel. Like Mack, McGraw would suffer one additional tragedy in his early life. When he was twenty-six, his wife of two years, Minnie, died at age twenty-two, after surgery for acute appendicitis.[4]

Clark Griffith, the only non-Irishman in the group, passed his childhood in the country rather than the city, but suffered poverty and hardship nonetheless. The Griffith family lived on a farm at Clear Creek, Missouri. His father supplemented the meager family income by hunting and trapping. In 1871 a local boy mistook Griffith's father for a deer and shot and killed him, leaving two-year-old Clark, his four older siblings, and his yet unborn sister fatherless. Griffith remembered his early years in post-Civil War Missouri as braced by poverty and toil. "That must have been the poorest country in the world," he later recalled. "When I was growing up there was no such thing as money. The medium of exchange was apple butter." Griffith's mother "worked . . . and slaved," to provide for her brood and, he allowed, "all the neighbors were charitable." At age thirteen Clark barely survived a bout with malaria, prompting the family to move to a small town near Bloomington, Illinois, where his mother opened a boardinghouse.[5]

Their straitened circumstances, family tragedies, and customs of the day forced all of the future ballplayers into the labor force at a relatively early age. Griffith recalled earning money as a ten-year-old trapping skunks and red foxes. McGraw worked at Goddard's hotel, distributed newspapers, and sold magazines, fruit, and candies on the local railroad line. Mack spent his summers as a stock and errand boy at the local cotton mill from the time he was nine. Upon his father's death Mack left high school to work in a local shoe factory cutting sole leather. Even Comiskey, who had a far more comfortable childhood than the others, worked while a youth, first as an apprentice to a Chicago master plumber and later as the driver of a brick wagon.[6]

Baseball cast out a lifeline that rescued each of these youths. Three of the four had secured local reputations as teenage pitchers before launching professional careers at age seventeen. Comiskey abandoned the brick wagon when future major leaguer Ted Sullivan lured him to pitch for the semiprofessional Milwaukee Alerts in 1877. The following year he pitched for the Elgin Watch factory team before joining the Dubuque Rabbits of the Northwest League.[7] Griffith signed his first contract as a hurler for the local Bloomington club of the Central International State League in 1888. John McGraw rejected the advice of both Mary Goddard and his father, who urged him to take a steady job with the railroad and forget "this baseball foolishness." Just six days shy of his seventeenth birthday in 1890, McGraw convinced a New York–Penn League franchise located near Truxton in Olean, New York, to give him a chance, offering to play any position when the manager expressed doubts about his pitching abilities.[8]

Mack took a different route to professional baseball. Still supporting his mother and siblings at age twenty-one, Mack had worked his way up to a position as foreman in the East Brookfield shoe factory. Nonetheless, in 1884, when his local batterymate William Hogan secured him an offer to catch for Meriden in the Connecticut League, Mack leaped at the opportunity to escape the drudgery of factory life.[9]

Comiskey, Griffith, McGraw, and Mack each progressed relatively rapidly to the highest levels of baseball. Comiskey spent four years with the Dubuque Rabbits, who converted him from a pitcher into a first baseman, and then joined the St. Louis Browns of the American Association in 1882 when he was twenty-two. Clark Griffith spent three years in the minors before reaching the major leagues with the Browns (where Comiskey was manager) in 1891 at age twenty-one. The precocious McGraw survived a disastrous debut at Olean, where he made eight errors in his first game, to appear as a shortstop for the American Association's Baltimore Orioles, just sixteen months later, when he was only eighteen. Mack parlayed his maturity and catching skills to reach the Washington Nationals of the National League within two seasons of signing his first professional contract. He was twenty-three years old.

Although none of the four compiled records that would have automatically qualified them for the Baseball Hall of Fame as players, each carved out substantial major league careers. McGraw was most impressive. A master at fouling off pitches until he had either slashed a base hit or secured a walk, the five-foot-five-and-one-half-inch McGraw, who weighed as little as 121 pounds in his early playing days, compiled a lifetime batting average of .334. His .466 on-base percentage ranks third of all time, behind only Babe Ruth and Ted Williams. However, the relative brevity of his playing career (he appeared in over 100 games only five times during his career) and his woeful inadequacies as a fielder (in 1893 he made 66 errors in 127 games) diminish his ranking among the game's great performers. Like McGraw, Clark Griffith rates just below the best players of all time. As one of the standout pitchers of the 1890s, Griffith won twenty or more games seven times. Over his career he won 62 percent of his decisions. Comiskey and Mack, on the other hand, were below average hitters yet first-rate fielders. Other than 1887, when he batted .335 and scored 139 runs in 125 games, Comiskey had few good offensive years. His contemporaries, however, reportedly considered him the best fielding first baseman of the era. Mack, who distributed a scant 150 pounds into his wiry six-foot-one-inch frame, compiled a paltry .251 batting average in eleven seasons while gaining recognition as a wily catcher and handler of pitchers.

What is most striking about the playing careers of McGraw, Griffith, Comiskey, and Mack, however, is not their batting, fielding, or pitching skills but the uncannily parallel reputations they acquired for iconoclasm, rebelliousness, innovation, and leadership. Although they would come to represent authority and respectability in baseball, all typified the rowdy spirit that characterized baseball in the 1880s and 1890s. During these decades immigrant (primarily Irish and German) and working-class Americans predominated in the major leagues, bringing with them a more contentious manner of play than that which had characterized the earlier years of the game. The Irish, in particular, writes Benjamin Rader, "brought with them to the playing field far more physical and emotional explosiveness" than earlier players from native Protestant backgrounds.[10]

Comiskey, an early Irish star, helped to set the pattern in the 1880s with his constant heckling of the opposition, baiting of umpires, and win-at-all-costs style. In 1886 umpire Ben Young branded Comiskey "a most aggravating player," complaining that Comiskey used sotto voce conversations with players to berate the arbiters. Sportswriter Ban Johnson, destined to conspire with Comiskey to create the American League, protested two years later that Comiskey's St. Louis Browns "employed every means to win, using foul tactics when necessary." Another reporter went even further, calling the Browns "the toughest and roughest gang that ever struck this city . . . vile of speech, insolent in bearing . . . they set at defiance all rules, grossly insulting the umpire and exciting the wrath of the spectators."[11]

In the 1890s McGraw succeeded Comiskey as the personification of the unruly Irish player. His language, said reporter John B. Sheridan, "would burn holes in nickel twelve-inches thick." He "eats gunpowder every morning and washes it down with blood," complained umpire Arlie Latham. Future National League President John Heydler decried McGraw's Orioles as "mean, vicious, ready at any time to maim a rival player or umpire," singling out McGraw as the main perpetrator, necessitating "umpires (to) bathe their feet by the hour" after being "spiked . . . through their shoes."[12]

Among the non-Irish players of the 1890s, Griffith reigned supreme as a verbally abusive competitor. The *Chicago Record Herald* predicted in 1898 that he would be the game's first designated "rowdy." He was, according to another account, the "worst umpire baiter who ever lived." His "contemptuous air . . . riled the good hitters out of their composure," and "few batters came to the plate without being singed by his scathing tongue."[13]

The intense competitiveness of the four players materialized in other ways as well. "We got away with a lot back in the days when we played with only one umpire," recalled Mack, who admitted to being "kinda tricky" as a catcher. With catchers positioned far behind the batter and any foul ball caught on the fly an out, Mack perfected the practice of slapping his mitt when a batter swung and missed to simulate the sound of a foul tip. Umpires, thinking Mack had caught a foul ball, would call the batters out. "Of course the trick was found out eventually, and the rule was changed so that a foul tip had to go ten feet in the air . . . for the batter to be called out," Mack later told a reporter. When catchers moved directly behind the batter, Mack won a reputation for surreptitiously tipping the bat as the hitter swung, deflecting its course. While managing at Pittsburgh in the 1890s, Mack would freeze baseballs prior to the game, deadening them for hitting. He would slip the frozen balls into the game when his team was fielding, replacing them with a more temperate, livelier variety when his team was at bat.[14]

Griffith and McGraw likewise bore reputations for illicit chicanery. Griffith earned his nickname "the Old Fox" while still in his early twenties as a tribute to his sly pitching tricks. He "struck them out by stalling until they were nervous wrecks, by quick pitching them when they weren't ready, by scraping the ball against his spikes," wrote Ed Fitzgerald and Shirley Povich. "Griffith scuffed, scratched, cut and spit upon every pitch without hesitation," according to another account.[15] McGraw, the quintessential member of a Baltimore Oriole team that stretched the rules to their utmost limits, specialized in grabbing the clothes of base runners, crashing into fielders after they caught the ball, and obstructing his opponents in other ingenious ways. "He adopts every low and contemptible method his erratic brain can conceive to win a play with a dirty trick," complained one reporter.[16]

Their frequently crude competitive exteriors, however, also reflected keen, analytical minds that Comiskey, Mack, Griffith, and McGraw applied to the study and transformation of the game. Appearing at a formative time in baseball history, they, like others, regularly experimented with new strategies to enhance the level of play. In later years all four would claim, or be granted credit for, some of the game's most profound developments. Charles Comiskey, reported *American Magazine* in 1911, was "the great inventive genius of his day on the diamond" who "evolved scores of plays now in constant use." Comiskey perpetuated the notion that he had pioneered the practice of first basemen playing behind and to the right of the base, rather than anchored to the bag. "For a short time, his style was ridiculed," reported umpire/writer Billy Evans in 1917, "but he soon proved that it was possible to play a deep field yet have plenty of time to return to the bag to receive throws." All infield play reportedly evolved from this breakthrough, as Comiskey taught pitchers to cover first base on ground balls hit to the first baseman and pioneered the strategy of shifting fielders' positions depending on the game situation. Other accounts credit Comiskey with suggesting that the umpire move behind the pitcher to call balls and strikes, inspiring the creation of chalk-lined coaching boxes, and inventing the headfirst slide.[17]

Similarly, Mack, by one later account, "did much to fashion (baseball) rules, pioneering in the development of the torturous art of catching." Mack, reported Bob Considine, "was one of the first catchers to move up to a position just behind the batter and catch the ball before it bounced." A more far-fetched tale has Mack telling a minor league pitcher in the days of the underhand delivery to "try throwing the ball overhand," resulting in the modern style of pitching.[18] Clark Griffith claimed to have invented the screwball and the squeeze play and maintained that a lengthy duel between him and John McGraw, in which McGraw repeatedly fouled off his pitches, led to foul balls being counted as strikes. Some historians credit McGraw with perfecting the hit-and-run play, and, as a manager, inventing platooning.[19]

Most of these claims are either exaggerated or entirely bogus, a tribute to the quartet's longevity in the game and the powers of the mythmaking process. Recent historians, for example, have largely rejected Comiskey's fielding contributions, noting that first basemen had moved off the bag as early as the 1860s.[20] Nonetheless, their reputations as innovators formed an important part of the individual and collective mystiques of all four men. When one combines their penchants for trickery and alleged predilections for innovation, the resulting composite reveals players who were considered smarter, more adventuresome, and at least one step ahead of other athletes — the type of men, in short, who demonstrated leadership qualities early in their careers that predestined inevitable success.

Not surprisingly, given these attributes and the common practice of selecting managers from the ranks of the players, all four men guided major league squads at relatively early ages. The St. Louis Browns named Comiskey team captain after his first year and tapped him as manager one year later when he was twenty-five. McGraw first managed the Orioles in 1899 at age twenty-six. Griffith and Mack were thirty-one when they began managing. All except Mack, who failed to motivate the Pittsburgh Pirates during his two-and-a-half seasons as player–manager from 1894 to 1896, quickly demonstrated exceptional leadership talents. Comiskey's Browns won the American Association championship in four of his first five years as manager. McGraw led a decimated Baltimore Oriole team to a respectable fourth-place finish in 1899 and then won five National League pennants in his first ten years as manager of the New York Giants. Griffith's Chicago White Sox won the first American League championship in 1901.

Ironically, given their futures as major league magnates, Comiskey, Mack, and Griffith all played prominent roles in late nineteenth-century player rebellions. In the late 1880s, when major league athletes formed a labor union, the Brotherhood of Professional Baseball Players, both Comiskey and Mack enlisted in its ranks. Under the leadership of New York Giant shortstop John Montgomery Ward, the players demanded a limitation on the reserve clause, which bound players to one team and curtailed their earning potential, and an end to the blacklist that arbitrarily barred teams from signing troublesome players. When the owners adopted a classification scheme that would have limited salaries to $2,500 a year, the Brotherhood responded in 1890 by creating the Players League, a cooperative venture between the athletes and an alternative group of financial backers. The vast majority of the best players in the game, including Mack and Comiskey, jumped from their National League and American Association teams to the Players League.

For Comiskey, who already received the considerable sum of $8,000 as player-manager of the St. Louis Browns, the decision to join the Players League had to be a difficult one. He would later downplay his role in the revolt, attributing his support to loyalty to his fellow players. "I couldn't do anything else and be on the level with the boys," he explained. The Brotherhood, however, saw Comiskey as a pivotal figure. It lured him away from St. Louis by promising to meet his salary and naming him manager of a team in his hometown of Chicago, where Comiskey had always hoped to return.[21] Connie Mack needed no persuasion. He had been one of the first players to join the Brotherhood in 1886. Four years later he bolted from the Washington Nationals and led most of his teammates to the Buffalo franchise, in which he invested his life savings. Mack set a major league record that would last for several decades by catching 123 of his club's 132 games. Toward the end of the season he became de facto manager of the Buffalo team that, despite his efforts, finished a distant last in the pennant race — forty-six-and-one-half games out of first place.[22]

Although its games outdrew both of the established circuits, the Players League collapsed after one season when its backers, unprepared to face additional financial losses, abandoned the Brotherhood. Mack, who lost all of his money, remained surprisingly sympathetic to its memory. "The purpose of our Brotherhood was to protect the players," he wrote a half-century later in his autobiography, with no trace of irony. "The group which vigorously opposed us was interested in protecting the magnates." He credited the Brotherhood with starting "a new era in baseball" that awakened club owners "to the realization that ballplayers are human and must be given a fair deal or rebel."[23] Comiskey, on the other hand, never romanticized his experience. Although he believed that the Players League might have prevailed with better leadership and despite remaining hostile to the triumphant National League owners, Comiskey concluded that cooperative baseball was not feasible. He had learned, in the words of George Axelson, his authorized biographer, "that player and promoter could not travel in the same harness." He nonetheless vowed to return to Chicago with a team that would compete with the National League franchise.[24]

Neither Griffith nor McGraw had progressed to the major leagues by 1890, but the outcome of the Brotherhood War greatly affected their careers. Both took advantage of the chaos in baseball to jump their contracts in 1891 and improve their lot. Griffith, who had won twenty-seven games for Milwaukee of the Western League, abandoned the club to pitch for Comiskey, who had resumed his old post with the St. Louis Browns.[25] McGraw, just eighteen years old, signed contracts with as many as five different teams, precipitating at least one lawsuit, before landing with Cedar Rapids of the Illinois–Iowa league. In August McGraw bolted Cedar Rapids to join the Baltimore Orioles.[26]

If the short-term effects of the war had benefited McGraw and Griffith, the long-term consequences did not. The American Association collapsed after the 1891 season. The four richest clubs joined the National League to form one expanded twelve-team circuit. With the threat of the Brotherhood gone and no rival league to bid up player salaries, the owners proceeded to slash payrolls, setting a salary limit of $2,400. The nationwide depression of the 1890s also kept salaries down. Thus, although Griffith and McGraw emerged as two of the top stars of the decade, their earnings were limited. After an 1894 season in which he batted .340 and scored a remarkable 156 runs in 124 games, McGraw joined fellow Oriole standouts Hugh Jennings, Willie Keeler, and Joe Kelley in a holdout for higher salaries. Despite the stature of the four men (each had batted between .335 and .393, and all ultimately would be inducted into the Hall of Fame), they could not shake the salary cap. McGraw settled for $2,100.[27]

Clark Griffith emerged as a leading voice against the new owner tyranny. In 1897 Griffith, a star pitcher who had won ninety games in four years, began agitating for a resurgence of a players union and an increase in the salary ceiling from $2,400 to $3,000. One sportswriter, referring to the populist and socialist leaders of the age, labeled Griffith "the free-silver, politico pitcher . . . supporter of Bryan, Debs, and Tillman." When a new Professional Association of Baseball Players formed in 1900, Griffith became its vice president and spent the season recruiting players and urging them not to sign contracts for the 1901 season.[28]

Griffith's fortuitous appearance as a labor leader now merged with the ownership aspirations of Comiskey, Mack, and McGraw. The trio had already taken the first steps toward becoming major league magnates. On leaving the Browns after the 1891 season, Comiskey had played for and managed the Cincinnati Reds from 1892 to 1894. With his playing career at an end, he rejected what Axelson called an "attractive contract" to continue to manage the Reds and instead purchased a minor league franchise in the Western League. For the next five years Comiskey reigned as owner-manager of a team alternately called the Saints or Apostles in St. Paul, Minnesota.[29] Mack, meanwhile, after losing his initial investment in the Brotherhood League and faltering in his stint as player-manager at Pittsburgh, had become manager and part owner of the Western League's Milwaukee franchise.

McGraw also demonstrated an entrepreneurial spirit. Along with Oriole teammate Wilbert Robinson he had opened The Diamond Cafe in Baltimore. In 1900, after McGraw's first season as Oriole manager, the National League decided to eliminate four of its less profitable franchises and dropped Baltimore. McGraw and Robinson, desiring to stay in Baltimore, organized a group of investors, hoping to secure a team in a proposed new American Association. When that league died aborning, the pair reluctantly accepted assignment to St. Louis in the National League but harbored a continuing desire to return to Baltimore.[30]

Even Griffith, the union firebrand, clearly had his sights on future ownership. "When I wasn't pitching," he later related, "they used to have me serve as the club's representative at the gate, keeping track of how many admissions were paid. . . . It gave me a chance to learn something about the business end of the game, and it got me acquainted with all the executives and magnates in the league."[31]

Their personal ambitions notwithstanding, the four future owners shared a strong contempt for the men who ran the National League in the 1890s. The owners, who preferred to see themselves as "magnates" on a par with Rockefeller and Carnegie, were predominantly self-made men who, having amassed fortunes in other industries, had invested their profits into baseball clubs. A handful, most notably Albert Spalding of the Chicago White Sox, Al Reach of the Philadelphia Phillies, and Ned Hanlon of the Baltimore Orioles, had risen from the ranks of the players. For some like Spalding and Reach who had made fortunes in the sporting goods business, streetcar developers Frank and Stanley Robison who owned the Cleveland Spiders, New York real estate speculator Andrew Freedman, or brewers Harry and Herman von der Horst of Baltimore, investments in major league clubs were logical extensions of their other business interests. For other owners, like Cincinnati's John T. Brush, whose fortune came from his family's Indianapolis department store, or the Wagner brothers of the Washington Nationals, who had earned their money in meatpacking, ownership of a baseball team represented both an investment and an indulgence, an enterprise that would earn them a level of attention, if not acclaim, that their other businesses could not provide. "Convinced of their own importance . . . they even convinced themselves that they were as important to the fans as the players," writes historian David Voigt.[32]

In fall 1900 the careers and constellations of Comiskey, Mack, McGraw, and Griffith converged in a conspiracy to destroy the National League monopoly. The scheme to forge a new alliance had long gestated in the minds of Charles Comiskey and Ban Johnson, the former reporter whom Comiskey had recruited to be president of the Western League. The two men had discussed the possibility of transforming the Western League into a major circuit as early as 1893, but the depression years of the mid-1890s had not offered a promising time to launch such an ambitious venture. By the turn of the century, however, improved economic conditions and developments in baseball bode well for a bold move. After the 1899 season the National League had jettisoned its four weakest franchises in Cleveland, Washington, Louisville, and Baltimore, leaving these cities clamoring for teams and a surplus of talented players looking for jobs. In addition, during the summer of 1900 Griffith and other organizers for the Professional Association of Baseball Players had convinced many players not to sign contracts for the upcoming season until the owners made concessions on salaries, the reserve clause, and other issues.

Two weeks after the conclusion of the 1900 season Ban Johnson announced the reorganization of the Western League into a new American League.[33] The upstart association would field teams in the abandoned cities of Cleveland, Washington, and Baltimore and promote former Western League franchises in Detroit and Milwaukee to major league status. It would also challenge the National League directly in Chicago, Boston, and Philadelphia. Charles Somers, a Cleveland coal dealer, became the league's financial angel, providing initial underwriting for the Cleveland franchise and for those in Chicago, Boston, and Philadelphia as well.

Comiskey, Mack, McGraw, and Griffith constituted the core of the enterprise. Connie Mack enlisted as manager and part owner of the Philadelphia Athletics, which would compete for fans with the Phillies. Mack invested an estimated $5,000 to $10,000 for a 25 percent stake in the new club and recruited Ben Shibe of the A. J. Reach & Co. sporting goods firm as majority owner and primary financial backer. Shibe, called the "mechanical genius of baseball," had made his fortune by perfecting the machines that produced standardized baseballs.[34] In Baltimore John McGraw and Wilbert Robinson received exclusive rights to resuscitate the Orioles, with the twenty-seven-year-old McGraw serving as player and manager as well as minority owner.

The boldest initiative, however, unfolded in Chicago, where Charles Comiskey fulfilled his vow to return to his home city. Prior to the 1900 season Comiskey had secured the rights to move his St. Paul Western League franchise to the Windy City as a minor league team. He had agreed not to use Chicago in his club title, but nonetheless adopted the nickname "White Sox," hearkening back to the city's fabled first National League club. Thus, when the Western circuit metamorphosed into the American League the following year, Comiskey was already firmly ensconced in Chicago. Unlike Mack and McGraw, who became minority owners and managers of new American League teams, Comiskey assumed majority ownership of the White Sox, risking approximately $25,000 in the process. He also stepped down as field manager to run the administrative side of the organization on a full-time basis.[35]

Convincing players to bolt the established National League for the fledgling American posed the greatest challenge for the newcomers. In December 1900 a delegation from the Players' Protective Association, including Clark Griffith, presented National League owners with a uniform contract, which among other items gave players equal rights with owners to terminate any contract on ten days notice, effectively ending the reserve clause. A committee of National League owners brusquely rebuffed the athletes. Griffith, already working closely with Comiskey and Johnson and destined to become manager of Comiskey's White Sox, immediately wired the pair, "Go ahead, you can get all the players you want."[36] Johnson announced in January 1901 that his new league would honor the proposed Players' Protective Association contract. The new league also offered hefty salaries, obliterating the National League's maximum pay policy.

Griffith, Mack, McGraw, and other representatives of the American League (most notably Cleveland player-manager Jimmy McAleer, a less celebrated veteran of the Players League who would later become an owner of the Boston Braves) fanned out across the nation. They seduced National League players, most of whom, at Griffith's urging, had not yet signed contracts for the 1901 season, to abandon ship and seek shelter in the new port. "I never felt badly about going after the National League stars," commented Mack, who lured Napoleon Lajoie crosstown from the Phillies to the Athletics. "As a player I resented the $2400 rule . . . and I felt that a new major league would help the players."[37] The

American League raiders drew up a list of forty-six athletes whom they hoped to snare. Only Honus Wagner, the great Pittsburgh shortstop who remained loyal to the Pirates, eluded their net.

Thus, the American League bore many similarities to the abortive Players League of an earlier decade. It emerged, at least in part, as a result of player grievances over salaries and the reserve clause. It brought together an alliance of players, former players, and capitalists anxious to become baseball owners. Indeed, several of the key actors were veterans of the earlier venture. Most of the major stars, disgusted with the old regime, readily cast their fate with the new. Unlike the Players League, however, the American League was not a cooperative enterprise. Labor and management remained clearly distinct and separate. Financial backing for the league also seems to have been more substantial. Finally, the American League benefited from Ban Johnson's fine administrative instincts in its war against the establishment.

The American League scored an undeniable success in its inaugural season. Not surprisingly, the White Sox, carefully stocked by manager Griffith and paced by the Old Fox's own 24–7 record as pitcher, claimed the first pennant. "I signed players for the other clubs too," he later admitted, "but I managed to sign a championship club for Chicago."[38] Lajoie, playing for Mack's Athletics, batted .422 and paced the league in every major offensive category. Although the National League outdrew its new rival by over 200,000 fans, the American League attracted a healthy 1.6 million spectators, dispelling the fears that its investors, like those of the earlier Players League, would have to weather substantial losses. The new franchises in Chicago and Boston convincingly outdrew the more established teams in their cities.

Most significantly, the rivalry between the two leagues enhanced rather than detracted from interest in baseball. Unlike the catastrophic Brotherhood War that drove total baseball attendance down in 1890, overall attendance nearly doubled in 1901. Despite the competition from the new league, National League attendance actually rose. Nonetheless, the stunning inroads by the new league forced National League owners to abandon the $2,400 pay limit, touching off a bidding war that drove up team payrolls. When in 1902 each of the American League clubs in cities with teams in both leagues outdrew their National League counterparts at the gate and the American League attracted 2.2 million fans to the National's 1.7 million, the senior circuit agreed to recognize the new league. Ignoring most of the original demands of the Players' Protective Association, the two organizations negotiated the National Agreement of 1903, restoring the reserve rule without the salary cap and creating a three-man commission to rule the game.

The settlement crushed the hopes of union advocates, but the gamble to bolt organized baseball and establish a new league paid off handsomely for the four conspirators who had joined Johnson. Comiskey, Mack, and McGraw had achieved ownership status. Griffith had won recognition as a pennant-winning manager. Mack, who had experienced little previous success as a manager, guided his Athletics to the pennant in 1902. Nonetheless, the alliance among Comiskey, Mack, Griffith, and McGraw quickly unraveled. The experiences of the first two seasons had made clear to Ban Johnson that, while the nation's largest cities could easily support two major league teams, several of the original American League locales could not generate sufficient fan support.

Persistent rumors had McGraw's disappointing Orioles destined for New York to challenge the Giants. McGraw, whose investment in the Orioles had yielded no profit in 1901, hoped to lead the team into New York. However, relations between the fiery umpire-baiting Irishman and Johnson, who stressed order and discipline on the field, inevitably deteriorated. Before the inaugural season was three weeks old, Johnson had suspended McGraw for five days for mistreatment of umpires. The two men repeatedly clashed throughout the season and into the next. Convinced that Johnson would never allow him to manage in New York, McGraw staged a preemptive strike.

On June 28, 1902, McGraw provoked umpire Tom Connally and refused to leave the field when ejected from the game, resulting in an Oriole forfeit. Two days later, Johnson, proclaiming, "Rowdyism will not be tolerated in the American League," suspended

McGraw indefinitely. "No man likes to be ordered off the earth like a dog in the presence of his friends," responded McGraw righteously. "Ballplayers are not a lot of cattle to have the whip cracked over them." Noting that he had invested his own money to help create the American League, McGraw protested, "There is an end to self-sacrifice. A man must look out for himself." On July 8 McGraw negotiated the sale of his stock in the Orioles and resigned as team manager. The following day McGraw announced that he would henceforth manage Andrew Freedman's National League New York Giants.[39]

There is little doubt that McGraw orchestrated these events for his own benefit. His new contract, conceived as early as June 18, guaranteed him an annual salary of $11,000 for four years, more than any player or manager in the history of the game until that time. McGraw bitterly attacked "Czar Johnson" and the American League, which he said "is a loser and has been from the start." He called Mack's Philadelphia team a "big white elephant" and predicted its demise. Not satisfied with his enhanced fortunes, McGraw vindictively sought further revenge. He arranged for Andrew Freedman to covertly gain control of the Orioles. Freedman then released the Orioles' top stars. Four, including future Hall of Famers "Ironman" Joe McGinnity and Roger Bresnahan, immediately signed with the Giants. Johnson moved quickly to seize control of the Orioles and stock it with players from other American teams, allowing the club to finish out the season, albeit in last place. In August Johnson announced that the team would move to New York in 1903.

Clark Griffith, although still manager of the White Sox, determined that, like McGraw, he wanted to be in the potentially lucrative limelight of the nation's metropolis. After the 1902 season, with the war between the leagues still raging, Griffith convinced six players from the National League's pennant-winning Pittsburgh Pirates to jump to the New York team. He then dispatched a telegram to Ban Johnson: SIX PIRATE PLAYERS WILL JUMP TO THE AMERICAN LEAGUE ONLY ON CONDITION THAT I AM APPOINTED TO THE NEW YORK TEAM. Although Comiskey was reported to be "boiling mad" over Griffith's proposed desertion, Johnson, anxious to have a strong team to compete with the Giants, granted the Old Fox his wish.[40]

Thus, at the dawn of baseball's new age, the quartet had maneuvered themselves into positions far advanced from their humble origins. Comiskey and Mack were now full-fledged "magnates," owners of recognized and highly successful major league clubs. McGraw had eschewed ownership for the more remunerative and celebrated position of New York Giant manager. Griffith, although not as handsomely rewarded, also reigned as a manager in the nation's largest city.

Over the next decade, as baseball achieved an unprecedented popularity, Comiskey, Mack, and McGraw came to assume near-legendary status in the emergent mass American culture. Baseball attendance doubled between 1901 and 1909, topping 7.2 million at the end of the decade. General prosperity, increased leisure time, expanded newspaper coverage, and improved urban transportation contributed to the surge. The creation of the World Series in 1903, which pitted the champions of the two leagues in a season-ending competition, fueled further interest, producing an eagerly awaited national spectacle that appealed to fans and nonfans alike.

Comiskey, Mack, and McGraw were both the apostles and beneficiaries of baseball's ascension. Mack's Athletics and McGraw's Giants each won five pennants between 1902 and 1913. Three times their clubs met in the World Series. The two dissimilar Irishmen became familiar figures to the American public, as acclaimed and celebrated as any star player. Gaunt and lanky, Mack, the "Tall Tactician," managed calmly from the bench wearing a suit with a starched white collar, tie, stickpin, and derby or boater hat no matter how hot the weather, waving his scorecard to position players and rarely showing emotion. "He is not a dominant, driving manager of the McGraw type," wrote his star second baseman Eddie Collins in 1914. "He is the persuasive kind and his men would do anything for him." Off the field, Mack compelled the Athletics to wear business suits on road trips to present a better image.[41] McGraw, the "Little Napoleon," stood a half-foot shorter than Mack, and as the years passed his stocky frame filled out his Giants' uniform with added poundage. He remained ever the fiery baiter of umpires and intense motivator of players. Mack, a tee-totaler, "clean as a hound's tooth," according to *American Magazine* in 1910, symbolized the "lace-curtain" Irishman, who had risen from rags to respectability.[42] McGraw, a hard drinker and near-compulsive gambler, epitomized the rougher side of Irish working-class America.

Although his team did not fare as well on the field, Charles Comiskey had achieved far greater material success and an equal measure of acclaim. His White Sox, regardless of where they stood in the standings, usually led the American League in attendance. Numerous articles written in national periodicals between 1909 and 1917 portrayed Comiskey as an exemplar of the American success story, "the Prince of Magnates," "the self-made man of baseball." "Just as the Comiskey of the early 80's was different from other players, so Comiskey the millionaire baseball magnate is different from the other magnates of his time," wrote Hugh C. Weir in 1914. Comiskey, explained Weir, was the only owner who had risen from the ranks to sole ownership of a major league team devoid of entangling partnerships. In Chicago, he reigned as a beloved folk hero. "If the question were asked in the Windy City today, 'Who is the most popular man in town?' there would be a tremendous chorus of voices . . . shouting Comiskey," claimed sportswriter George C. Rice. Rumors constantly floated that the Old Roman would follow his father into politics and run for mayor.[43]

The construction of Comiskey Park in 1910, a few hundred feet from the site of the Old Brotherhood Park where Comiskey had managed in 1890, marked the crowning achievement of Comiskey's rise. Comiskey Park was the third of thirteen modern stadiums built or reconstructed by major league baseball teams between 1909 and 1915. These new ballparks, as several historians have noted, symbolized the maturity and permanency of baseball as a feature in American life. In addition, according to Benjamin Rader, "They were akin to the great public buildings, skyscrapers and railroad terminals of the day . . . edifices that local residents proudly pointed to as evidence of their city's size and achievements."[44]

Reflecting the philosophies of the City Beautiful Movement of the Progressive Era, Comiskey, like most of his fellow stadium builders, adopted a classical motif, designing Comiskey Park to reflect Rome's colosseum. If the appearance of these stadia harkened back to an earlier age, however, their planning and construction evoked the technology and style of the new century. The dramatic growth in attendance had rendered the older, primarily wooden ballparks seating no more than 10,000 to 20,000 people obsolete. The introduction of concrete reinforced by steel rods offered the possibility of building permanent stadiums with upper decks. Shibe Park in Philadelphia, built to house Mack's Athletics in 1909, became the first major league ballpark to capitalize on the new technology. Its double-decked stands allowed it to seat 23,000 people. An additional 7,000 crammed in as standees to celebrate its opening. Pittsburgh's Forbes Field, unveiled shortly thereafter, boasted three decks.[45]

Comiskey's Chicago edifice, which initially seated 28,500 people, was the largest ballpark yet built. Like Forbes Field and Shibe Park, its construction reflected elements of American modernity. The new arenas were fireproof, eliminating the danger of fires that had plagued the old wooden arenas. They featured elevators and telephones. Although Shibe Park had stairs to move the crowds from one deck to another, Forbes Field and Comiskey Park featured wide ramps that were safer and facilitated fan movement. Comiskey envisioned his ballpark as a "monument to the game."[46] Privately built at a cost of $700,000 and proudly bearing Comiskey's name, it was also clearly a monument to the Old Roman's personal achievements.

To this point Clark Griffith's accomplishments had been far less substantial. Since leaving Comiskey's employ in 1903, he had spent nine relatively undistinguished seasons managing the American League New York Highlanders and National League Cincinnati Reds. After the 1911 season he seized the opportunity to purchase a 10-percent interest in the Washington Senators of the American

League. As the manager and largest single shareholder, Griffith became the controlling figure on the club. When the old wooden National Park burned down during spring training in 1912, Griffith hastily constructed his own concrete and steel stadium. More modest than those built by Mack and Comiskey, the new arena eventually came to be known as Clark Griffith Park. The combination of the new ballpark, Griffith's opening day coup of handing President William Howard Taft a ball to throw out the first pitch, the emergence of Walter Johnson as the league's dominant pitcher, and the Senators surprising second-place finishes in 1912 and 1913 elevated Griffith to the heights of public acclaim enjoyed by Comiskey, Mack, and McGraw. Over the next decade Griffith would steadily increase his ownership share in the Senators. Griffith, wrote Frank C. Lane in 1912, "is one of those men whose unswerving faith in baseball has made possible some of its most pronounced successes. . . . There is no more shrewd, able and successful manager than he." "Everybody is strong for the Little Fox," added William A. Phelon in 1913.[47]

Everybody was even stronger for Mack and McGraw. In 1912 McGraw signed a five-year, $30,000-a-year contract with the Giants, securing his place atop baseball's salary structure. In 1913, after Mack's Athletics claimed their third World Championship in four years, defeating McGraw's Giants in the World Series, the New York Highlanders attempted to lure Mack away from the Athletics. Mack, still a minority owner of the Athletics, used the lucrative Highlander overture to leverage greater control over his club. Faced with the prospect of losing his celebrated manager, majority owner Ben Shibe lent Mack $113,000 to buy out the other minority interests and become an equal partner in the Athletics.[48]

The relationship between Shibe and Mack illustrated a critical point. Despite their pretensions, the fortunes of baseball's self-made magnates rested on fragile foundations. Comiskey, who favored recruiting former players as owners, might protest that "one more millionaire will break the American League" and Americans could extol baseball's "incarnations of success" as living symbols of the American dream. But, as umpire/writer Billy Evans noted, most major league owners who "boast(ed) of fat bankrolls" had "amassed their fortunes in other lines of endeavor."[49] Comiskey, Mack, and Griffith, who depended solely on team profits for their incomes, found themselves increasingly at a disadvantage.

The obvious way to overcome this obstacle was to drive down player salaries. Once they had donned the garb of management, the former players rapidly grasped the need for payroll constraints. Connie Mack's teams, which regularly finished high in the standings, usually ranked near the bottom of the salary scale. Both Mack's second-place 1903 club and his pennant-winning 1914 team reportedly had the lowest payrolls in the league. Some of Mack's players received less money playing for the Athletics than they had in the minor leagues.[50] Laudatory articles about Comiskey praised his fairness and generosity in dealing with players. Yet the gestures they described were often more of a charitable nature, keeping players as coaches after they retired or paying for children's education, rather than making wage concessions. Reports circulated that Comiskey was "free with his friends, but 'close' with his ballplayers." As early as 1902 White Sox manager Clark Griffith, just one year removed from the vice presidency of the Players' Protective Association, rationalized Comiskey's financial practices by arguing that reductions in salary during a player's reserve year did not constitute a pay cut. Ring Lardner, whose classic *You Know Me Al* stories first appeared in 1914, repeatedly depicted Comiskey fleecing naïve pitcher Jack Keefe in salary negotiations.[51]

As in 1890 and 1901 pecunious owner practices precipitated the creation of a new players' association and the formation of yet another new league. In 1913 lawyer David Fultz, a former major league outfielder who had played for Connie Mack's A's (for whom he led the American League in scoring in 1902) and Clark Griffith's Highlanders, organized the Fraternity of Professional Baseball Players. The following year a group of investors led by oil baron Harry Sinclair, ice magnate Phil Ball, and Brooklyn baking mogul Robert B. Ward launched the Federal League and began raiding National and American League rosters. As in the past, the end of major league baseball's monopoly triggered dramatic salary increases. Although few top stars jumped to the new league, most were able to negotiate more generous contracts with their old employers.[52]

For Griffith, just two years an owner and deeply in debt, the Federal League challenge drove home the realities of baseball economics. When Walter Johnson, his star pitcher, succumbed to the lures of the Chicago Whales, Griffith, the former contract jumper, union official, and league promoter lectured the "Big Train" on the virtues of loyalty. When this failed to sway Johnson, Griffith matched Chicago's salary offer. A chastened Johnson nonetheless lamented "That's all very fine, Griff, but we've already spent the $10,000 bonus they gave me." Griffith, his resources depleted, secured the money to pay back the bonus from Comiskey, who feared having Johnson pitching in Chicago for a rival team. Johnson remained with the Senators.[53]

The Federal League war proved far more devastating for Mack. His Athletics had won three World Series in four years and they opened a big lead in the American League race at the start of the 1914 campaign. But as the season progressed, the atmosphere around the team changed. "We had to write a lot of new contracts in the middle of the season," he later explained. "But the Feds kept raising their offers and a good many of our players became more and more dissatisfied." According to Mack, the team divided into two factions, one loyal to the Athletics and the other ready to jump to the new league.[54] The Athletics held on to win the American League pennant, but the Boston Braves embarrassed them, winning four straight games in the World Series.

"The Federal League wrecked my club by completely changing the spirit of my players," complained Mack. Before they had thought only of winning, he protested, now they were obsessed with money. But Mack had already begun to suspect the shortcomings of success. "When you win," he would later explain, "you have a general rise in all expenses. When a club is behind, salaries are low, so are expenses." As half-owner of the team, and personally burdened by his substantial indebtedness to Shibe, Mack decided to dismantle his championship squad. "If the players were going to 'cash in' and leave me to hold the bag, there was nothing for me to do but cash in too," he rationalized.[55]

Within weeks of the 1914 World Series Mack waived future Hall of Fame pitchers Eddie Plank and Chief Bender despite their combined 32–10 record. The team's best player, second baseman Eddie Collins, who in a recent *American Magazine* article had expressed the desire to play out his career under Mack (who "treated folks in a decent, white way"),[56] became the next to go. Mack shocked the baseball world by selling Collins to Comiskey's White Sox for $50,000. Over the next year selling shortstop Jack Barry, pitcher Bob Shawkey, third baseman Frank "Home Run" Baker, and others netted Mack an additional $130,000.[57] By the end of the 1915 season Mack had succeeded in slashing the already low Athletics payroll to an unprecedented level. He also transformed a pennant-winning squad that had won 65 percent of its games into a last-place club with an abysmal .283 winning percentage. Seven years would pass before the Athletics would climb out of the cellar.

Unlike Mack and Griffith, whose quest for ownership had left them deeply in debt at the outbreak of the Federal League challenge, Comiskey, who had "run a shoestring into better than a cool million,"[58] seemed to be one of the prime beneficiaries of the hostilities. His substantial resources enabled him to purchase Eddie Collins from the Athletics and "Shoeless Joe" Jackson from the Cleveland Indians. None of his White Sox players jumped to the Federal League as Comiskey met their escalated salary demands. His reconstituted White Sox would finish second in 1916 and win pennants in 1917 and 1919. Yet, in many ways, Comiskey would become the most profound victim of the Federal League war.

The Federal League collapsed after only two years, but the damage to major league baseball was considerable. National and American League attendance, which had peaked at 7.2 million in 1909, dropped to 4.4 million in 1914 and 4.8 million in 1915. At the same time player salaries rose dramatically. Major league owners sought to recoup their losses by freezing or cutting salaries. The 1916 season saw a substantial resurgence at the box office, but American entry into World War I in April 1917 erased most of the recovery.

In 1918 the two leagues played a 130-game schedule and total attendance barely topped 3 million. Planning another short season and fearing continued losses in 1919, many owners lowered salaries further and slashed expenses.

Although the aura surrounding Mack and Griffith, and to a lesser extent McGraw, had declined during these years, Comiskey's continued to shine. After his club won the 1917 World Series an article attempted to demonstrate how the "Old Roman" had "Won a Fortune and Whole Army of Personal Followers Through Enlightened Business Methods." Prior to the 1919 season Chicago sportswriter George Axelson authored *Commy*, a loving paean to the White Sox owner. Axelson portrayed Comiskey as a man of energy, daring, honesty, foresight, fairness, and generosity. Comiskey, in an afterword, cheered baseball as "the most honest pastime in the world," asserting, "Crookedness and baseball do not mix." His current Chicago White Sox team, declared Comiskey, "is the best bunch of fighters I ever saw. No game is lost until the last man is out." He predicted that 1919 would be "the greatest season of them all."[59]

Rarely does a book bristle so thoroughly with retrospective irony as does Axelson's *Commy*. In 1919 the sins of the reserve clause, shortsighted major league salary practices, and the consequences of the Federal League era came home to roost in Comiskey's White Sox. After winning the American League pennant several of the White Sox players conspired with gamblers to fix the World Series. Others with knowledge of the plot became complicit with their silence. Over the years, particularly since the 1963 publication of Eliot Asinof's *Eight Men Out*, the definitive history of the scandal, Comiskey has emerged as the arch-villain of these events. "What were the pressures of the baseball world, of America in 1919 itself, that would turn decent, normal, talented men to engage in such a betrayal?" asked Asinof. The answer he found rested largely with Comiskey, whose "ballplayers were the best and were paid as poorly as the worst."[60] Comiskey allotted the lowest subsidy in the league for meal money and alone among the owners deducted the costs of laundering uniforms from player wages. "He had no reason in the world not to deal fairly with his players," argues historian Bill James. "The White Sox drew the largest crowds in baseball in this period . . . yet the White Sox were one of the lowest-paying teams."[61]

Others have judged Comiskey more generously. "The idea that the White Sox were grossly underpaid doesn't really stand close scrutiny," writes Charles Alexander. Some players, like Eddie Collins and Ray Schalk, ranked among the best paid in the game and, although Joe Jackson was grossly undercompensated, other White Sox players had incomes commensurate with those on other teams. Nonetheless, as Robert F. Burk has pointed out, baseball salaries had largely stagnated since the collapse of the Federal League in 1915. Wartime and postwar inflation "severely eroded the real earnings of players."[62] In 1919, with the war over and Babe Ruth in ascendance, baseball attendance had mushroomed to record levels, generating dramatic profits for the owners without comparable rewards for the players. Comiskey's White Sox, as participants in the World Series, found themselves in a position to capitalize on their accumulated resentments.

In the end Comiskey's primary sin rested not so much with his employment practices, as abysmal as they may have been, but with his subsequent efforts to protect his team and investment by covering up the scandal and undermining the prosecution of the participants. Neither Comiskey nor the White Sox, at least during his lifetime, ever recovered from the devastation of 1919. Forty years would pass before the White Sox would win another pennant. Comiskey was, by all accounts, broken by the scandal. Although he died a wealthy man in 1931, his estate totaled far less than it might have had the Black Sox tragedy not occurred. The priest who delivered his funeral sermon attributed his death to "a broken heart."[63]

McGraw, Griffith, and Mack would all experience bright moments in the 1920s and early 1930s. McGraw rejoined the ownership ranks in 1919 when he joined the syndicate headed by Charles Stoneham that purchased the New York Giants. His Giants won four straight pennants and two World Series from 1921 to 1924.

For the next seven years his clubs always played winning baseball, but never again finished first. He stepped down as Giants' manager in 1932 and died in 1934. McGraw's opponents in his final World Series in 1924 were Griffith's Washington Senators, who had surprised the Babe Ruth Yankees to win their first American League pennant. The Senators topped the Giants in seven games. The Senators repeated as American League champs in 1925 and again in 1933. Mack's Athletics returned to championship form in 1929, 1930, and 1931, but, when the Great Depression threatened his profits, Mack again divested his roster of its high-priced stars and plunged his team into the second division.

Both Mack and Griffith continued as baseball owners into the 1950s. They became revered and honored grand old men of baseball, reminders of an age in which a player might become an owner and join the magnates of American industry. Their time, however, had clearly passed. Neither the Athletics nor the Senators ever again contended for pennants during their lifetimes. Attendance for the two clubs always languished near the bottom of the major leagues. Of greater significance, few former players ever again secured a significant ownership share of a major league club. In modern America success would assume different incarnations.

New Ways of Knowing
Baseball in the 1920s

The world broke in two in 1922 or thereabouts," wrote novelist Willa Cather.[1] Cather apparently had little interest in baseball—none of her numerous writings mention the game. Yet the 1922 World Series pitting John McGraw's New York Giants against Babe Ruth's New York Yankees, and particularly the manner in which Americans followed its progress, endorsed Cather's vision of a world suddenly divided between a more traditional culture and a modern technological sensibility.

Throughout the United States tens of millions of people gathered, as they had for decades, in town squares, city intersections, and indoor urban arenas to witness a pitch-by-pitch recreation of World Series games on large electrical and mechanical scoreboards. A "mammoth web" of 45,000 miles of telegraph wires brought the World Series to most corners of the nation, where it was transcribed into a public display.[2] Wilmer Thomson, a Chester, Pennsylvania, resident, described the modest scoreboard erected outside the local newspaper office when he was a boy. "When a ball was pitched they would show a yellow light," he reminisced almost three-quarters of a century later. "For a strike red lights would be turned on. Blue lights would show the number of outs. The bases would have lights to show the positions of runners. Whenever there was a hit they would ring a bell." About 150 men would gather each World Series day in Chester to share this communal experience, at once local and national in nature.[3]

In the New York metropolitan area, however, several million people enjoyed the 1922 World Series in a novel manner. In a promotion to encourage the sale of its new product, radio manufacturer RCA-Westinghouse arranged for WJZ, its pioneer radio affiliate, to broadcast the first two games of the series live from the Polo Grounds. Sportswriter Grantland Rice, sitting in a box seat near the Yankee dugout, described the action to what the *New York Tribune* called "the greatest audience ever assembled to listen to one man."[4] The *New York Times* marveled at the new technology. "Not only the voice of the official radio observer could be heard, but the voice of the umpire on the field announcing the batteries of the day mingled with the voice of the boy selling ice cream cones," reported the *Times* the next day. "The clamor of the forty thousand fans inside the Polo Grounds made the fans feel as if they were inside the grandstand. The cheers which greeted Babe Ruth when he stepped to the plate could be heard throughout the land."[5]

The rival transmissions of the 1922 World Series—one via telegraph, the other via radio—capture baseball at a crucial cultural turning point in American history. In the years following World War I, Americans underwent a dramatic transformation in the ways in which they assimilated information. There emerged what historian Warren Susman has called "new ways of knowing that stood in sharp contrast with the old ways of knowing available in the book and the printed word." Radio represented just one of these "new ways of knowing."[6] Media devoted to pictorial and visual display—movies, newsreels, tabloid newspapers, magazines, and advertising—revolutionized people's ability to vicariously participate in the world around them. "Photographs have the kind of authority over imagination today, which the printed word had yesterday, and the spoken word before that. They seem utterly real . . . and they are the most effortless food for the mind conceivable," observed Walter Lippmann in 1922. "In the whole experience of the race there has been no aid to visualization comparable to the cinema."[7] The addition of radio (and later talking pictures) added yet another dimension to this phenomenon.

Baseball became one of the foremost agents and beneficiaries of these changes. Fans who only a few years earlier could never have hoped to attend a major league game, yet who followed its progress assiduously through newspaper reports and scoreboard recreations, suddenly could see their heroes in motion picture theaters and dramatic photo displays. They could hear live radio broadcasts that placed them at the games. As these opportunities dramatically expanded the popularity of the national pastime, they also revolutionized people's perceptions and reshaped the baseball experience for millions of Americans.

The scoreboards themselves, of course, had already represented a grand advance into the modern era. Instantaneous telegraph transmissions allowed baseball fans to experience games as they transpired. What sportswriter H. G. Salsinger called an "invisible host of fandom"[8] thus shared in the exhilarating local communal experience of gathering for the games, while simultaneously participating in a national rite of autumn. As early as the 1890s communities began to translate these telegraphic reports of baseball games into visual recreations.[9] At the Atlanta opera house, young boys bearing the names of real players would run the bases on a baseball diamond laid out on the stage. In 1894 the "Compton Electrical System," a ten-by-ten foot board that featured lineups listed on either side of a diamond and lights to indicate which player was batting, the current baserunners, an up-to-the-minute ball/strike count, and other information appeared in many cities. After 1905, when the World Series became a permanent fixture on the national scene, scoreboard-watching became an equally entrenched annual ritual. Newspapers erected large displays in front of their offices, attracting crowds numbering in the thousands in large cities, often snarling traffic for many blocks.

In 1906 the *Chicago Tribune* began the practice of renting armories and theaters to hold the crowds. The indoor setting allowed scoreboards in the major cities to become increasingly more elaborate. In 1912 Madison Square Garden and other venues in New York City presented the Series on a display that moved the balls and players with magnets. Another model, "The Playograph," used a ball affixed to an invisible cord that emulated the course of the ball while white footprints illuminated the path of the baserunners. A Jackson Manikin Board employed for the 1915 World Series showed mechanical athletes that moved in and out of dugouts, swung the bat left- and right-handed, and even argued with the umpire.

For millions of baseball fans, these recreations seemed truly miraculous, enabling them to "attend" games played hundreds and thousands of miles away. "Before many of the thirty-six thousand spectators at the Polo Grounds were aware that the umpire had called a strike on the batter, fans in Denver, Colorado, and San Antonio, Texas, knew that the umpire had called a strike," asserted F. C. Lane. The fan, explained Salsinger, "visualized each man as he comes to bat. [He] 'sees' every pitched ball, closely follows the course of every batted ball." To Irving Sanborn, the crowds in the ballparks were no "more enthusiastically alive to every critical situation or more loudly appreciative of every fine play than those millions jammed into the various halls or thronging the streets in front of newspaper audiences." Some argued that the man in the street saw the game more clearly than fans at the stadium. The ballpark, after all, offered many distractions. Those watching the scoreboard, however, saw only the raw essentials of the game affording them, according to Lane, "a clearer view of what was happening at the Polo Grounds than was possible to a fraction of the fans who were actually present."[10]

This hyperbole notwithstanding, few Americans would actually have traded a seat at the ballpark for a space in front of a recreated display. Nor could the vicarious experience of scoreboard-watching compare to the new excitement offered by the radio in the 1920s. Commercialized radio began in 1920 when WWJ in Detroit broadcast local election returns. Three months later KDKA debuted in Pittsburgh, disseminating the results of the presidential election.

Since in its infancy radio emphasized news and information reporting, baseball proved a logical focus. In 1921, its first summer
on the air, KDKA began offering baseball scores. On August 5,
1921, Harold Arlin, the station's innovative engineer/announcer,
broadcast a Pirates' game live from Forbes Field.[11] That fall, WJZ
in Newark, New Jersey, offered a primitive recreation of the World
Series. A reporter for the *Newark Call* telephoned the play-by-play
to an announcer in Newark, who dictated the action over the air
to a limited host of listeners.[12]

The following year Grantland Rice's World Series broadcast attracted a broader audience. Local radio stations agreed to remain
silent to allow WJZ's transmission to be heard over as broad a
range as possible. Two additional stations — WGY in Schenectady
and WBZ in Springfield, Massachusetts — also picked up the signal.
Most listeners, in an audience generously estimated as high as five
million people, heard the games in a communal venue not dissimilar to the scoreboard-watchers in other parts of the country. They
gathered outside radio stores in groups large and small to listen to
the games over loudspeakers erected for the occasion. Those lucky
enough to own a radio, including many who had recently succumbed to Westinghouse newspaper advertisements heralding
Rice's broadcast, listened in the privacy of their homes.

The broadcast that they heard was quite primitive. WJZ, unable
to secure rights to use telephone lines for the transmission, dispatched the game over telegraph wires that diluted the voice quality and added a background hum. Rice had no idea what the role
of a radio announcer should be. He simply described what happened in a voice "a little flat, atonal, somewhat awkwardly mod-
ulated and unmistakably Southern." He contributed no additional
commentary, leaving dead space between the plays. "The broadcast
officials wanted me to keep talking. But I didn't know what to
say," he later revealed.[13]

The World Series returned to the air in 1923 with a greatly improved product. WEAF, owned by American Telephone and Telegraph, transmitted the game over telephone lines that enhanced

the reception. Seeking baseball expertise, the station once again turned to a reporter, W. O. McGeehan of the *New York Tribune*, to call the game. To assist him the station assigned Graham McNamee, a broadcasting veteran of all of four months, not to speak but, as McNamee explained, to coach McGeehan, "so that he would not crowd the instrument, sit too far away, or unduly raise or lower his voice." McGeehan apparently felt no more comfortable behind a microphone than had Rice. In the fourth inning of the third game McGeehan abruptly left and McNamee relieved him, broadcasting the balance of the six-game series.[14]

Graham McNamee was not a baseball expert, but, as a former concert singer, he understood the rudiments of pace, style, and performing for an audience, even one he could not see. Earlier reproductions of baseball action had focused on eliciting the facts. The Western Union operator who telegraphed World Series information was expected to remain, as F. C. Lane wrote in 1922, "perfectly cool and collected, no matter what happens. . . . He cannot yield to any enthusiasm of the moment . . . He must be above personal prejudice. . . . he is stationed at his responsible post to see facts and to narrate them without any mistakes and without any personal sentimental coloring."[15] Newsmen Rice and McGeehan had approached radio in the same way. McNamee, however, intuitively recognized that the new medium required a different approach. As he later explained,

The broadcaster must see to it that in his announcement that there are very few . . . "breaks on the air." For, with the breaks, the listener immediately imagines that something has gone wrong with his set. Besides, he did not buy it just to listen to dead silence. . . . I found myself more than ever falling back on general description. And that is where the imagination comes in. . . . You must make each of your listeners, though miles from the spot, feel that he or she, too, is there with you in that press stand, watching the movements of the game, the color, and flags; the pop-bottles thrown in the air;

the straw hats demolished; Gloria Swanson arriving in her new ermine coat; McGraw in his dugout, apparently motionless, but giving signals all the time."[16]

In the eighth inning of the sixth game of the Series, with the Yankees leading the series three games to two, but trailing in the game 4–1, Babe Ruth strode to the plate with the bases loaded. McNamee fully engaged his listeners into the action of the moment. "Here was the most advertised athlete in the game, one whose name appears in headlines more often than the President's," McNamee later wrote, capturing the drama that he had conveyed over the air. "Only one little crack—just a solid connection between ash and leather, and the series would be over. The chance that was the immortal Casey's was now the Babe's." Ruth "squared his shoulders and set himself menacingly enough," but like Mighty Casey, the Babe struck out, "making an ignominious exit . . . his face almost green now where before it had been white."[17]

"People who weren't around in the twenties when radio exploded can't know what it meant, this milestone for mankind," observed Red Barber, whose own career helped define the craft of sportscasting. "Suddenly with radio, there was instant human communication. . . . The world came into our homes for the first time. . . . We heard drama that we ourselves played a part in." McNamee, who reigned as voice of the World Series and many other events for the remainder of the decade, initiated millions of Americans into this experience. "When the nation heard him say, 'Good evening, ladies and gentleman of the radio audience, this is Graham McNamee speaking,' the nation hugged itself happily . . . waiting for something vital to come into the living room," recalled Barber. McNamee, according to Heywood Broun, "individualized and particularized every emotion. He made me feel the temperature and tension. The wind hit him and it deflected off to me . . . No mere ticker report could be comparable, because McNamee allowed you to follow the ball on the wing."[18]

Not everyone was as enamored of McNamee and the new technology. Several sportswriters expressed disdain for his "general description." "I don't know which game to write about," wrote Ring Lardner after one World Series contest, "the one I saw today, or the one I heard Graham McNamee announce as I sat next to him at the Polo Grounds." Unlike the telegraph operator who strove for accuracy, McNamee could and did make mistakes. "He mixed players and innings and teams," complained one reporter in 1927. "He made right handed batters left handed. . . . He put players on base where they weren't and left them off bases where they were."[19]

For the average listener, however, the medium, not the miscalls, provided the message. Raymond Francis Yates described McNamee's broadcast of the 1924 World Series as "one of the greatest heartbumping events of American sport. It made the game bigger" and gave the fans "almost as much of a thrill as though they were at the Polo Grounds." McNamee, wrote Yates, made every listener a spectator. He allowed them "to use their eyes—he painted word pictures that other minds could feast upon. . . . Very little imagination was required . . . especially when the announcer turned his microphone on the roaring, booing and cheering crowd. These little inserts of realism transplanted the atmosphere of the diamond to every nook and corner of the United States."[20] These nooks included a New York hospital where 800 patients, "a majority of whom are playing their last game and waiting for the exit gates to open," had listened to a McNamee broadcast. "Your colorful description made a hit here; and it was no ordinary bunt, but a powerful wallop that has had us talking ever since," wrote a hospital worker to McNamee. "Their little Main Street is quite narrow, and the radio is bringing the world to their feet."[21]

The popularity of McNamee's World Series extravaganzas encouraged several teams to experiment with regular season broadcasts. In 1924 WMAQ in Chicago transmitted all Cub and White Sox home games to local fans. Cubs' owner, William Wrigley, who believed that radio games increased interest in his team, allowed any station to broadcast Cubs games free of charge. In the late 1920s five stations carried the Cubs. In 1925 the two Boston clubs also began offering their games on the air. In general, however, teams in the eastern cities shied away from the radio, while those in the West embraced the new technology. By the end of the decade, St. Louis, Cleveland, Detroit, Cincinnati, Boston, and Chicago all featured regular broadcasts of home games, but none of the New York, Washington, D.C., or Pennsylvania teams followed suit.[22]

The opponents of baseball on the radio were numerous and adamant. Many feared that games delivered over the air would crimp attendance. Why, asked one owner, "should anyone pay between fifty cents and a dollar and a half for the entertainment that one could receive comfortably seated in an easy chair at home?" *The Sporting News*, in particular, waged sustained warfare against the medium. "Mr. Radio is going to butt into the business of telling the world all about the ball game without the world having to come to the ballpark to find out," warned the baseball weekly in 1922. Three years later it protested that "Baseball is more an inspiration to the brain through the eye than it is by the ear. . . . A nation that begins to take its sport by the ears will shortly adapt the white flag as its national emblem, and the dove as its national bird."[23]

The experiences in those communities that regularly broadcast games, however, confounded these predictions. In almost all these cities attendance rose in the 1920s. The radio stimulated interest not only within the urban confines, but, as reporter John Sheridan predicted in 1922, in surrounding areas as well. Sheridan noted that in towns of the Midwest crowds would gather around loudspeakers awaiting baseball scores. This prompted them to organize excursions to nearby cities to attend games. The combination of "radio communication, good roads, and the automobile" had expanded the radius of a team's fan territory from five miles at the turn of the century to 200 miles in the 1920s, argued Sheridan.[24]

The radio also encouraged the creation of a new type of baseball community that revolved around the local baseball announcer. "The announcers are stealing the glory which was once attached to the baseball writer," observed Frank Wallace of the *New York Post* after a swing through the Midwest.[25] In city after city the men who re-created the games developed devoted followings. In

Boston, Fred Hoey became, in the eyes of future announcer Ken Coleman, "a regional giant. The guy was loved. . . . On the air, Fred was Boston baseball." In Detroit Ty Tyson reigned supreme. "Ty was so vivid, he made games come alive," recalled one listener. "It was new, naturally, but it was his voice too—it was graphic . . . he had an urgency inside him and transmitted that to us . . . he made you feel like Gehringer, Cochrane and Goslin were right next door."[26]

The new community that emerged from radio, however, was profoundly different from that which had existed before 1922. For most fans major league baseball still entailed an act of imagination. But the process of fantasy had changed, transformed from belated newspaper coverage, to instant telegraphic recreations, to detailed broadcast descriptions. By 1929 one-third of all American families, and a majority of those who had electricity, owned radios. Increasingly they listened to the games in the privacy of their homes, rather than in the public spaces that had hosted the elevated scoreboards and loudspeakers of an earlier age. The arrival of radio, recalled Wilmer Thomson, marked "the end of the need for the scoreboard" in Chester.[27] The radio had, in a very important sense, democratized major league baseball, transmitting a more intimate sense of being at the game to millions who could never attend. Yet the process had become more familial or individualistic, replacing the communal experience with a more isolated one. Radio made baseball, more than ever, a national sport, but in a context far removed from earlier meanings of that term.

In whichever manner people in the 1920s experienced major league baseball—attending games, watching community scoreboards, listening to radio broadcasts, or perusing news stories, photographs, and newsreels—when they attempted to capture the essence of that experience, they invariably invoked the same image: that of Babe Ruth at the plate. Sportswriter F. C. Lane, wishing to convey the passion of scoreboard watchers during the 1921 World Series, described "the ninth and final" inning of the fourth game with Babe Ruth at bat. Young Wilmer Thomson, ringing the scoreboard bell that designated World Series hits, "felt like Babe Ruth." Graham McNamee, searching for "the most exciting experience I have ever had in broadcasting," selected Ruth striking out with the bases loaded in the 1923 World Series.[28] For Lane, Thomson, and McNamee, as for millions of others, Babe Ruth epitomized the national pastime.

"The Ruth is mighty and shall prevail," punned Heywood Broun.[29] The colossus that was Ruth prevailed not just in baseball, but throughout the national culture. He was arguably the most photographed of all Americans during the decade. A 1927 survey of the faces most likely to appear in the press concluded that Ruth's "phlegmatic, slightly puzzled expression peer[ed] out of the Sunday supplements" regardless of the season or setting. As early as October 1920 *Current Opinion* dubbed him "The Most Talked of American." The *Literary Digest* in 1922 captioned a photo of Ruth, "Everybody knows him," explaining that "backwoods citizens" and "darkies way out there in the wilderness and swamps" who might not know President Warren G. Harding would recognize Ruth.[30]

Richard Vidmer of the *New York Times* captured the essence of Ruth's passage through the South during spring training in 1927. On a rainy morning the Yankee train was scheduled to stop in a small Tennessee town.

All morning long the rain beat down in silver sheets. The little hamlet of Etowah, Tennessee was drenched and dripping . . . Etowah wasn't going to overlook the opportunity of seeing Ruth. The citizens searched the attic and closets, clothed themselves in garments best suited for the weather, and flocked to the station.

The train was an hour late, but when it finally arrived and passed, the platform contained all but four of the hamlet's inhabitants. Three were still looking for their rubbers, and the other had pneumonia already. Through the Babe's sweet, charitable nature they weren't disappointed. . . . The township of Etowah came to worship at the shrine of the king and left with a feeling of friendship. When the Babe grins, awe vanishes and he makes a pal.[31]

To many commentators, both contemporary and historical, the American fascination with Ruth represented the peculiar hungers of the Roaring Twenties. Westbrook Pegler, according to his biographer, saw Ruth as "an unequaled exhibition whose strength and accuracy with baseball were of a pace with the madness for crazy pleasure, unheard of speed, and aimless bigness convulsing the nation." John Sheridan equated the excitement of Ruth's home runs with "flapper thrills over her cigarette and still shorter skirt." Historian Benjamin Rader has labeled Ruth a "compensatory hero," who "assisted the public in compensating for the passing of the traditional dream of success . . . and feelings of individual powerlessness," while Warren Susman viewed him an ideal hero for the world of consumption emerging in the 1920s.[32]

Yet, to see Ruth as a particular product of the twenties, or even the modern age, seems to over-intellectualize a simple subject. It is hard to imagine any people, in any era, who would not have been enthralled by Babe Ruth. Ruth fascinated because he was fascinating. His life, as many have noted, had a mythical, almost godlike quality. He is, wrote biographer Marshall Smelser, "our Hercules, our Samson, Beowulf, Siegfried." Born in the slums of Baltimore, raised in the wilderness of reform school, he grew to become, in the eyes of Roger Kahn, "a real-life John Henry."[33] At the age of twenty-one he had already established himself as one of the game's greatest pitchers. Three years later he forsook the mound to revolutionize the art of hitting. He hit more home runs than anyone in history, and he hit them harder and farther and with an unparalleled majesty. He performed miracles on the baseball field, healed the sick, and was laid low by his own human frailties and hubris, only to achieve redemption and new heights of acclaim and worship.

Ruth dominated baseball as no other man ever had before or ever would again, and he did so with an infectious ebullience that characterized his personal life as well. Many contemporary observers understood this. People "will always idolize the man that can do something that no other man on Earth can equal," noted *Baseball Magazine*. "Other baseball champions excel competition by a slight margin," wrote F. C. Lane in 1921. "Babe Ruth excels all competition by a margin so wide that there is simply no comparison." For Lane and other sportswriters, Ruth was "a theme which never grows threadbare. . . . Familiar from every angle, there is yet something about him which is always new. . . . He is still forever doing something unexpected and novel."[34]

Remarkably, Ruth's off-the-field exploits matched his oversized athletic persona. In this arena he also elicited divine comparisons, evoking images of Bacchus and Dionysus, the gods of wine and sensual pleasure.[35] Although sportswriters of the 1920s rarely reported on Ruth's prodigious sexual appetites or his unattractive qualities, his profligate lifestyle and repeated conflicts with baseball officialdom were well known. Ruth might well have possessed, as American League President Ban Johnson protested, "the mind of a fifteen-year old," and he may have been "crude, uncultured, ill-educated, unrefined" and prone to "wild license . . . utter disregard of regulations . . . and coarse escapades," as the increasingly disillusioned Lane complained in 1925. This excess of humanity, however, endeared him to people all the more. "With Ruth they often loved him for his naughtiness," explained Fred Lieb in 1927. "He would go off the reservation and then try to regain favor by knocking a few more over fences which had never been cleared. And the regaining was never difficult."[36] Ruth's ability to rebound from self-imposed adversity, after suspensions, fines, and physical dissipation had led many to believe that he had squandered his talents, added to his appeal.

"Fortunately, the Bambino does not have to step out of character to be what he is—an appealing swashbuckling, roistering, boisterous figure who is as natural a showman as the late Phineas T. Barnum," explained New York *Times* sportswriter John Kieran in 1927.[37] These extraordinary aspects of the Ruthian character would doubtless have captivated Americans in the 1890s or 1950s as much as they did in the 1920s. Yet, while Ruth's appeal transcended chronological boundaries, it is impossible to imagine the Ruthian phenomenon reaching full flower in any previous generation. In the 1920s people across the nation could see Babe Ruth in pictures and newsreels, they could hear Babe Ruth (or at least descriptions of him) on radio, and they could experience the drama of Babe Ruth at the moment that it unfolded. In an age in which the modern ideal of celebrity was virtually invented, Ruth, along with a handful of Hollywood stars, personified that concept. Others might briefly eclipse his fame — Jack Dempsey on the eve of one of his infrequent heavyweight championship fights or Charles Lindbergh after his transatlantic flight in 1927 — but from 1919 until his retirement in 1935 the omnipresent Ruth alone appealed to the popular imagination on a day-in, day-out basis.

Ruth emerged as a national figure simultaneously with the new technologies and media forms transforming American communications. Nineteen-nineteen, the year that Ruth first captured the public fancy, witnessed the appearance of the *New York Daily News*, the nation's first successful tabloid newspaper; *True Story Magazine*, which would revolutionize popular periodical publishing; and the *Fox Movietone News*, which helped to bring newsreels into the modern age. Traded to the New York Yankees for the 1920 season, Ruth arrived in the nation's media center in the same year that the first radio stations took to the air. The advertising industry stood poised on the brink of an expansion that would more than double its revenues in less than a decade. Hollywood would also achieve its maturity in the succeeding years. Ruth thus stood at the hub of an unprecedented media crossroads. He could fully exploit the traditional opportunities open to players to increase their income and notoriety, but he also had a wide range of alternative vehicles to enhance his celebrity.

In an age in which most Americans lacked the opportunity to see major league baseball, players could earn considerable sums exhibiting themselves once the season had ended. Many formed teams that traveled across the nation playing games against local or other all-star competition. Ruth's presence elevated these time-honored tours to a new level. His 1927 barnstorming junket covered 8,000 miles and attracted 200,000 people, earning Ruth $30,000. Vaudeville also beckoned Ruth. In 1921 he signed a record $3,000-per-week, twenty-week contract to appear on the stage with song-and-dance man Wellington Cross, performing hokey magic tricks and delivering bad one-liners. Five years later his weekly fee for a vaudeville tour soared to more than $8,000.[38]

The new media, however, afforded Ruth his greatest exposure. Newspapers had dramatically expanded their sports coverage since the turn of the century, increasing the space afforded athletics by 50 percent. The fledgling tabloid newspapers, with their emphasis on what critic Silas Bent described as "bigger and bigger headlines . . . more and more pictures," the kind of pictures "a multitude of morons . . . like to see, and the kind of stuff they like to read," carried this trend further.[39] *Daily News* publisher Joe Patterson, wanting "very biff, bang, boom stuff," made Marshall Hunt the tabloid's year-round Babe Ruth correspondent. Wherever Ruth appeared, whether at ball games, nightclubs, or orphanages, Hunt was never far behind. When things slowed down, Hunt would create news opportunities and file exclusive coverage to the *Daily News*.[40]

The tabloids, Sunday rotogravure sections, and weekly magazines of the 1920s stimulated the demand for pictorial images. The sports photograph, long a staple of the press, became even more prevalent. Modern cameras "geared to take a picture in a thousandth of a second or less recorded breathless base slidings and fierce lunges at the ball by energetic batters" observed Lane.[41] Few subjects appeared as often as Babe Ruth. His distinctive physiognomy and insatiable hunger for attention rendered him a natural target for photographers both on and off the field. Ruth's face appeared on the covers not just of major periodicals, but on such arcane journals as *American Boy, Strength*, and *Hardware Age*. Photos of Ruth posing with children, chimpanzees, and celebrities and garbed in an astounding variety of outfits permeated the press. Silas Bent suspected that Ruth was striving for a "pictorial frequency record" to complement his baseball marks.[42]

The Babe had also alighted into an age of motion pictures. The first newsreel for American audiences had surfaced in 1911. By 1919, when *Fox Movietone News* made its debut, four major companies produced news films for exhibition in the nation's theaters. With new features appearing twice each week, the newsreels reached an audience in excess of 30 million people. For major stories the filmmakers rushed footage to the theaters almost as quickly as newspaper coverage. Sports coverage accounted for the largest single category of film, arising at its peak to as much as 25 percent of the program.[43] As with radio, the availability of filmed images invited speculation as to their impact on baseball. Walter Lippmann, anticipating the onset of instant replay, predicted that "the last vestige of dispute could be taken out of the game . . . if somebody thought it worth while to photograph every play." Ruth naturally appeared frequently in these film clips. In 1920 Educational Pictures of New York, an enterprising movie company, collated available newsreel footage into a series of *Babe Ruth Instructional Films*, including "How Babe Ruth Hits a Home Run" and "Play Ball With Babe Ruth."[44] He was a familiar figure in Fox Movietone, Pathe, Hearst, and Paramount newsreels. Americans could thus see the Babe in action almost as often as they went to a movie theater.

Inevitably, given the public's unflagging desire to see Ruth, offers to star in feature films also came his way. Even before he arrived in New York City, Ruth was reported under contract to make several movie shorts. The proposed titles included both the predictable (*Home Sweet Home* and *Touch All Bases)* and the improbable (*Oliver Twist.)* The films were mercifully never made. During the 1920 season, Ruth's first with the Yankees, Ruth skipped batting practice for a week and arrived at the Polo Grounds each day wearing makeup to star in *Heading Home*, a silent feature that bombed at the box office.[45] This failure temporarily stalled Ruth's acting career as plans to shoot a film with director Raoul Walsh were cancelled. In 1926 Ruth traveled to Hollywood where he filmed *The Babe Comes Home*. Reviews of the movie proved less than flattering. "There is no reason for John Barrymore or any other thespian to become agitated about the matter," commented one reviewer. Ruth, observed another, "was never built for romance under the kliegs." The assessment by Ruth's teammate Mark Koenig was even more blunt. "He couldn't act worth crap," said Koenig. Like its predecessor, *The Babe Comes Home* flopped.[46]

The failure of Ruth's movies to attract an audience spoke less to a lack of interest in the Yankee star than to the inability of a scripted venue to capture his natural exuberance. He came across as stiff rather than animated, shy rather than rambunctious. This often proved true of his adventures in radio as well. In 1921 Harold Arlin at KDKA, pioneering the practice of interviewing famous personalities, naturally sought out Ruth for a broadcast. Taking precautions, Arlin wrote out a speech for Ruth to deliver. The Babe, confronted by a brand-new medium and unfamiliar script, froze in front of the microphone. Arlin quickly grabbed the speech and pretended to be Ruth. Since few people knew the sound of Babe's voice, the ruse worked. Letters to KDKA praised Ruth's surprisingly rich tones.[47]

In later years, Ruth grew more comfortable on the radio but was never at his best with a prepared text. On one occasion he appeared with Graham McNamee on a national broadcast. He had rehearsed his role until he had his timing down perfectly, but when the show began, according to Grantland Rice, Ruth abandoned the script and "was off and running." A line designed to refer to the Duke of Wellington's adage that the Battle of Waterloo had been won on the playing fields of Eton, came out, "As Duke Ellington once said, the Battle of Waterloo was won on the playing fields of Elkton." The listeners and the network, wrote Rice, "got a load of Ruth at his purest that night."[48] Only an unstructured, spontaneous setting could bring out the unalloyed Babe.

The vast dimensions of Ruth's celebrity propelled him into yet another emergent field of the modern era, public relations. The profession had emerged in the first decade of the twentieth century, when business leaders, hoping to offset the adverse images propagated in the muckraking press, began to hire specialists to plant news items portraying them in a more favorable light. In the

1910s John D. Rockefeller employed Ivy Lee to transform the millionaire's negative reputation. Numerous individuals, businesses, and enterprises followed suit. On the eve of American entry into World War I, the Newspaper Publishers Association listed 1,200 people working as publicity agents in New York City. By the mid-1920s an estimated 5,000 agents practiced in New York, 2,000 in Washington, D.C., and presumably similar numbers in other great cities. In Hollywood, studio press agents had grown legion.[49] "The great corporations have them, the banks have them, the railroads have them, all of the organizations of business and social and political activity have them," wrote Frank Cobb in 1919.[50] Two years later Babe Ruth had one as well.

The demands of Ruth's fame and his own natural naivete in business matters made it inevitable that Ruth would need someone to manage his affairs. Promoters approached Ruth with a wide variety of endorsement opportunities and business propositions. In his early years in Boston Ruth employed a friend, Johnny Igoe, to attempt to coordinate his affairs. Igoe, however, could neither rein in Ruth's impulsive instincts and spendthrift ways nor secure or collect adequate compensation for the slugger's efforts. Ruth was never fully paid for his starring role in *Heading Home* (the check from the producers bounced) and at the peak of his home run prowess accepted a paltry five dollars per homer for a syndicated account of each clout.[51] Fortunately for Ruth, in 1921 he fell into the enterprising and benevolent clutches of Christy Walsh.

Walsh was, by his own description, one of "thousands of young dreamers anxious to escape the smaller hometown and hie for the city." He had worked as a sports cartoonist for the *Los Angeles Herald* and in 1919 served as a ghostwriter for World War I hero Eddie Rickenbacker describing the running of the Indianapolis 500. He moved to New York City and worked at an advertising agency until the recession of 1921 led to his dismissal. "I was out of a job in the biggest city in the world and didn't have money for rent," he wrote in his autobiography, *Farewell to Ghosts*. "I was blocking traffic on this great highway to fame." Recalling his experience with Rickenbacker, Walsh decided to form a ghostwriting syndicate, which would offer articles written by professional writers under the byline of celebrities, whose names and thought would attract readers, but who had neither the time, talent, nor inclination to write.[52] Walsh did not invent this concept. Ghostwriters had invaded baseball as early as the 1911 World Series. What Walsh did, according to sportswriter Joe Williams, was "to put the proposition on a sound systematic basis."[53]

In early 1921 Walsh lined up a few clients, including Rickenbacker, but he felt that he needed the biggest celebrity in New York to establish his credibility. Walsh found it amazing that "such a gift from the gods (as Ruth) should be on the loose." The Babe, wrote Walsh, "was pursued by every glib talker in town." Walsh established an outpost outside the Ansonia Hotel, where Ruth made his home, but could never corner the Yankee star. Walsh wisely cultivated an acquaintance with the corner bootlegger, who, in the face of Prohibition, illicitly supplied Ruth with his beer. One evening, Ruth called while the regular delivery boy was on another errand. Walsh volunteered to transport Ruth's order. Ruth, never a man to notice details, did not realize that the gentleman in coat and tie was not the usual emissary. When Walsh informed him of his identity, Ruth laughed appreciatively about the ruse and listened to Walsh's pitch. Walsh promised that, if Ruth would sign an exclusive contract with him, he would increase his earnings from writing from $5 a home run to thousands of dollars a year. He pledged to pay Ruth the first installment of $1,000 within ninety days.[54]

Ruth was no stranger to ghosted stories. In addition to his home run sagas, he had already "written" several articles (including "Why I Hate to Walk" ghosted by Westbrook Pegler) and one book, *The Home Run King—Or How Pep Pindar Won His Title.* He might have just wanted to get rid of the pesky Walsh. For whatever reason, Ruth impulsively agreed to sign a contract naming Walsh as his exclusive representative. On opening day Walsh approached the Babe at the Polo Grounds and handed him a check for $1,000, more than a month ahead of schedule. "I shall never forget the expression on Babe Ruth's face when I handed him a check," recalled Walsh. "Here was a fellow who had been skinned so many times by strangers that I felt the way to win his confidence was to pay in advance."[55]

With Ruth in the fold, Walsh was able to sign up dozens of other top athletes. Although he had originally conceived of a syndicate representing all types of celebrities, Walsh now began to specialize in sports. He became, according to Joe Williams, "the literary godfather of the athletes . . . who harnessed this literary Niagara of writing genius and turned it into artistically useful channels." Thus, "the reading public was assured the best thoughts of the best athletic minds in the best manner."[56]

Walsh's syndicate expanded and prospered, but he retained a special relationship with Ruth. He consolidated Ruth's literary enterprises, raising his writing income from $500 in 1920 to $15,000 in 1921. Walsh also took command of all of Ruth's moneymaking activities, emerging, in Dan Parker's words, as "the man behind the Bam, the man who relieves Babe of his burden of thinking." Before his relationship with Walsh, wrote Parker, "Babe didn't know how to make use of his by-products. But what Armour did for the cow, Christy did for Babe."[57] Walsh lined up Ruth's 1921 vaudeville tour and negotiated Ruth's contract with the Yankees that called for Ruth to receive, on top of his record salary, 10 percent of the gate for all exhibition games. He took charge of Ruth's public appearances, booking him to materialize at various functions, like banquets and county fairs, and arranging for photo opportunities and publicity for Ruth's charitable activities. He hired Ruth out to "guest edit" newspaper sports pages.[58]

Most significantly, Walsh capitalized on the growing market for advertising that surfaced in the 1920s. Newspaper, magazine, and billboard advertising quadrupled between 1917 and 1929. Although copywriters had discovered the power of testimonials long ago, endorsements "gained a new popularity during the 1920s as advertisers searched for a personal approach," according to Roland Marchand.[59] Few figures were as sought after or as willing to endorse products as Babe Ruth. Ruth appeared in advertisements for cigarettes, men's clothing, sporting goods, milk, appliances, kennels, pajamas, underwear, and innumerable other items. He endorsed Cadillacs in New York, Packards in Boston, and Reos in St. Louis. Ruth also became one of the first celebrities to lend his name to an extraordinary variety of products, including Babe Ruth sweaters, Babe Ruth caps, Babe Ruth Gum, Babe Ruth Home Run Shoes, and Bambino Smoking Tobacco.[60]

As Ruth's business manager/publicity agent, Walsh found that he had inadvertently "detoured right smack into the main stem, a grand adventurous thoroughfare of imagination, invention, and high pressure competition." And Ruth, in danger of drowning in a sea of con artists and swindlers, had luckily latched onto a sound life preserver. Walsh combined the proper blend of honesty and chicanery that characterizes the best publicity men. In operating his ghostwriting syndicate, Walsh espoused a flexible code of ethics. "There is a wide difference between illusion and deceit," he averred. Walsh "never knowingly released copy that was 'fake'," although he admitted that emergency circumstances sometimes forced him "to distribute a signed article that had neither been discussed with, nor approved by the author." Walsh never claimed that the athletes wrote their own copy, simply that the article "was written by a man who enjoyed the author's confidence and understood his views on the subject." To cover Ruth, Walsh employed four different ghostwriters, most frequently Bill Slocum, whom Ruth allowed innocently, "writes more like me than anyone I know."[61]

Walsh's early dealings with Ruth embraced the same benign ethical code. Unbeknownst to Ruth, the $1,000 that Walsh paid Ruth on opening day 1921 came not from writing income but rather from a bank loan borrowed at 6 percent interest. Walsh, who undoubtedly collected more than the standard 10 percent agent's fee, earned enough to retire in 1937 at age forty-six. "He had grown rich showing Babe how to get rich," noted Dan Parker. But, avowed Parker, the Ruth/Walsh axis "is the most equitable partnership ever established in athletics." Walsh "steers him away from the phony investments that formerly lured Babe and his lucre. He has taught him that there is a rainy day ahead and it behooves even a demigod to lay aside an odd penny for that evil day."[62]

Walsh battled desperately and usually in vain to get Ruth to curb his spending. Despite Ruth's dogged resistance ("You never have any fun outta life," Ruth would complain), Walsh managed to channel a small fraction of the slugger's immense earnings into an irrevocable trust fund. He placed the money in annuities, rather than stocks, thus cushioning Ruth from the impact of the stock market crash. "They will not have to hold benefit games for the Babe, though he has been the most profligate athlete since John L. Sullivan," predicted Parker in 1927. When Ruth retired, the trust, amounting to a quarter of a million dollars, allowed him to live comfortably for the remainder of his life.[63]

Walsh also helped to steer Ruth's popular image away from a Rabelaisian bad boy of the early 1920s to the beloved benefactor of charities and children celebrated in countless photographs. Although Ruth appeared at hospitals and orphanages willingly and often without fanfare, Walsh guaranteed that these visits would not be forgotten, cementing the saintly side of Ruth's persona.[64] Assisted by Walsh's keen instincts, Ruth became the first true celebrity of the modern era, recognized as much for his fame as for his audacious feats. He symbolized not only the exuberance and excesses of the 1920s, but the emergent triumph of personality and image in a modern America suddenly positioned to glorify these attributes. Lavishly chronicled on radio and in print, memorialized in photos and film, elevated to a new form of adoration in testimonial advertising, and molded by shrewd public relations, Ruth fulfilled people's fantasies and embodied their new reality.

Baseball itself rode the coattails of the public's fascination with Ruth and the new media that brought him to their doorsteps. Baseball fans relished their expanding universe, and so the national pastime prospered in the 1920s as never before. Yet baseball's brain trust, never the most farsighted of thinkers, saw potential gloom on the distant horizon. The ever-vigilant, ever-pessimistic, but nonetheless prescient *Sporting News* posited a dark vision of the technological future: "When Ruth hits a homer . . . a film will catch him in the act, wireless will carry it a thousand miles broadcast and the family sitting in the darkened living room at home will see the scene reproduced simultaneously on the wall. Then what will become of baseball?"[65]

Adjusting to the New Order
Branch Rickey, Larry MacPhail, and the Great Depression

The Great Depression ensnared baseball slowly, but inexorably. In 1930, as the nation slid into a deep recession, baseball flourished. Major league hitters, led by Chicago Cub Hack Wilson, who hit a National League record 56 home runs and drove in an astonishing 190 runs, and Babe Ruth, who again led the American League in home runs, treated fans to an unprecedented offensive outburst. A heart-stopping four-team pennant race in the National League further stimulated attendance. Thus, despite the economic downturn, attendance in 1930 topped ten million for the first time and major league profits soared to almost $2 million, more than triple the 1929 surplus. The season seemed to uphold the conventional wisdom that "poor business years are good baseball years." In past recessions, baseball had found that unemployed workers, many with savings to tide them over, had ample time and adequate funds to attend games. The latest economic slump, reasoned baseball owners, would be no different.[1]

The year 1931, however, hinted at a disturbing reality. Attendance fell by more than 15 percent and income plummeted. Although the major leagues as a whole showed a $217,000 profit, most teams lost money, and several others barely edged into the black. In 1932, as the Depression dragged into its third year with no end in sight, baseball finally felt its full brunt. Attendance dropped below 7 million for the first time since 1919. All but four clubs ran deficits. Total losses exceeded $1.2 million. The *Literary Digest*, in an article entitled "Hard Times Hit the Majors," observed, "Whereas in July 1930 it was a case of scaring up four bits for a bleacher seat at the Stadium, [now] it [was] a matter of getting enough for a cheap meal." The hemorrhaging escalated in 1933 as the major league deficit grew to $1.65 million.[2]

Thus, in the early 1930s the baseball industry confronted the dilemma shared by a multitude of American businesses during the Great Depression. Faced by declining revenues and a reduced demand for their product, what was the appropriate strategy for survival? Commissioner Kennesaw Mountain Landis, echoing the classic conservative reaction to the Depression, preached patience. "The American people love baseball," commented Landis. "They will return as paying customers as soon as they have money." Washington Senator owner Clark Griffith agreed. "Our business has held up at least as well as any other. We're just going on the way we are," he cautioned those calling for change. Others, however, argued that the response to the Depression necessitated, in President Franklin D. Roosevelt's words, "bold, persistent, experimentation." The Great Depression, warned *The Sporting News*, required baseball officials to "adjust themselves to the new order, or make way for others not so shackled by precedent."[3] Rather than passively endure the storm, baseball might seize the opportunities offered by economic stringency to restructure and rationalize its operations or develop new ways to stimulate interest in the game.

As was true for most businesses, the solutions to baseball's problems lay in the realm of supply and demand. Alone among baseball officials, Branch Rickey and Larry MacPhail, two very disparate men, stepped forward to accept these challenges. Rickey, the veteran baseball man, attacked the supply side of the equation, creating the farm system to streamline the player development process. MacPhail, a newcomer more attuned to the dictates of twentieth-century consumer culture, addressed the question of demand. Rickey and MacPhail were, according to Gerald Holland, "as far apart as their favorite drinks," martinis for MacPhail and root beer and milk for Rickey. They began as allies and ended as bitter personal enemies. Yet, asserts Holland, they did "more to change the face of baseball than any other two men or two hundred men ever connected with the game."[4]

The prosperity of the 1920s had obscured several fundamental weaknesses in baseball's economic foundation. The industry had, in effect, achieved horizontal integration, defeating or absorbing all of its rivals in the decades before World War I. Yet its haphazard relationship with the minor leagues, its primary source of players, precluded any true vertical integration, preventing teams from controlling the process and cost of player development. Furthermore, as G. Edward White has observed, baseball leaders maintained a limited vision of the potential audience for major league games. Attendance had boomed in 1920 but then remained relatively static throughout the remainder of the decade. As an industry, baseball had been slow to recognize the emerging consumer society and reluctant to incorporate new technology into its domain. It had never fully embraced radio as an ally, and it had totally ignored the possibility of night baseball.[5]

In the face of the Depression most baseball men demonstrated minimal imagination. They refused to lower ticket prices, reasoning, probably correctly, that the impoverished masses could not afford games at any price. Instead, faced by plummeting revenues and staggering financial losses, the baseball industry followed the path of most American businesses, "adjusting to the new order" by driving down labor costs. At the December 1931 winter meetings, owners agreed to pare down the active rosters from twenty-five to twenty-three players. Teams hired fewer coaches and front-office employees. A growing number of clubs turned to player-managers, eliminating one more slot from the payroll. The greatest savings came from slashing player salaries. The 1932 winter meetings produced a formal resolution to roll back these expenses.[6] "The problem of the top-heavy payroll is the true cause of much

of the financial difficulty that now embarrasses Major League Baseball," explained *Baseball Magazine* editor Frank C. Lane. "Salaries
and wages elsewhere have been drastically reduced. Boom time
salaries are no longer defensible in baseball."[7]

The new policy spared few. Commissioner Landis voluntarily
accepted a reduction in pay from $65,000 to $40,000. Babe Ruth,
despite again "having a better year than the President," saw his
salary drop $28,000 below his $80,000 peak. The cuts trickled
down throughout the major leagues as owners reduced their payrolls by an estimated $800,000. Philadelphia Athletics owner Con-
nie Mack replicated his 1914 purge. In that year, faced by higher
salaries inspired by the upstart Federal League, Mack had broken
up his championship team and sold off his stars. After more than
a decade in debasement Mack rebuilt another dynasty, winning
three consecutive pennants from 1929 to 1931. In 1932, however,
the Athletics dropped to second place and attendance fell to less
than half its 1929 levels. Faced by a high payroll and declining
income, Mack again divested his team. Between October 1932 and
December 1935, Mack sold the contracts of Al Simmons, Lefty
Grove, Mickey Cochrane, Jimmy Foxx, and others, garnering
$590,000 while returning his club to the bottom of the standings
in the process.[8]

Not all members of the baseball establishment advocated inaction and retrenchment. Chicago Cubs president Bill Veeck, Sr.,
suggested scheduling interleague play during July and August to
stimulate attendance. Some clubs sought to attract more fans by
scheduling doubleheaders on Sundays, a variation on the increasingly common business practice of offering premiums. The two
leagues adopted a livelier ball to inflate offensive production for
the 1934 season, hoping, in the words of sportswriter John E.
Wray, that "The new deal baseball will act like the New Deal dollar
is supposed to—it would stimulate business."[9] It is probably also
not coincidental, as historian Bill James has noted, that baseball's
three greatest honors—the Most Valuable Player Award, the All-
Star Game, and election to the Hall of Fame—emerged from the
maelstrom of depression as a psychological and financial boost for

the troubled game. "Baseball needed to show that it was not in a state of decadence," argued *Chicago Tribune* writer Arch Ward in proposing the annual all-star exhibition, the proceeds of which would provide a charity fund for indigent former ballplayers. National League President Ford Frick also recognized the broad economic value of a baseball Valhalla, when he threw his support behind promoters from Cooperstown, New York, who wished to establish a Hall of Fame in baseball's alleged birthplace.[10]

St. Louis Cardinal General Manager Branch Rickey adopted a broader view of the opportunities offered by the Great Depression. Raised in the late nineteenth century on a midwestern farm, Rickey instinctively saw the challenge in terms of production. As general manager of the St. Louis Cardinals, the products that Rickey planted, harvested, and ultimately sold to the public were the men who played the game. From the beginning of his career in baseball management Rickey had focused his energies on the recruitment, development, and training of these athletes. He maintained close contacts with college baseball programs to identify top prospects at an early stage. He hired and encouraged the efforts of scouts, most notably his brother Frank, who scoured the nation for talented youngsters. As a field manager with the St. Louis Browns, Rickey stressed the importance of drills and fundamentals to perfect his output. "He is a Professor of Baseball," wrote a sportswriter in 1914. "His efficiency courses in sliding, baserunning, and batting mark a new departure in the game."[11] Throughout his career Rickey focused on devising new training techniques and technology to further refine his product.

When Rickey became the general manager of the St. Louis Cardinals in 1916, he felt the problem of player development even more acutely. Operating in one of the smallest markets in the major leagues and competing against the crosstown Browns, Rickey lacked the financial resources to compete with more prosperous teams for players. In the early decades of the twentieth century minor league teams tended to be independent operations with the right to sell their players to the highest bidder. Knowledge of Rickey's interest in a prospect often allowed these club owners to drive up the price or to sell the player to another club. In 1919 the cash-poor Cardinals paid $10,000 to purchase the contract of pitcher Jesse Haines. Unable to sustain this level of expenditure, Rickey needed an alternative method to produce his players more cheaply and efficiently. He knew that he could "find them young . . . develop them . . . and keep them until they were ready for the Cardinals." But he "needed . . . the place to train them," beyond the reach of other clubs.[12]

"Good farmer that he was," observed Harold Seymour, "Rickey decided to grow his own crop on his own land." The invention of the farm system, Rickey contended, was "the result of stark necessity," a desperate solution to meeting "a question of supply and demand for young players."[13] In the past some major league clubs had owned minor league affiliates or had entered into working agreements with them. Rickey, however, was the first to envision a vertically integrated network of teams owned by the parent club, ranging from the lowest to the highest levels of Organized Baseball through which players might be trained, sifted, and selected en route to the major leagues. In 1919, around the time of the Haines purchase, the Cardinals bought a half-interest in the Fort Smith, Arkansas, franchise. Over the next decade, the Cardinals secured control of four other teams as well.

The system, although still modest, worked exceptionally well. Although the Cardinals had ranked among the laggards in league attendance during the first half of the 1920s, by 1926 the team had built a squad that would win four pennants in six years. Attendance doubled and Rickey supplemented the team's profits by selling off his surplus—players who did not make the Cardinals—to other teams. Despite the limited size of its market, the Cardinals became the most profitable franchise in the major leagues. Because Rickey collected 10 percent of all profits on top of his $40,000 a year salary, he shared handsomely in the rewards of the farm system.[14]

The onset of the Depression enabled Rickey to dramatically expand and perfect his organizational pyramid. Minor league operators, struggling to make ends meet, welcomed affiliation with a major league club that would underwrite payroll costs and other expenses. With salaries dropping as low as $300 a month, the burden on the Cardinals of assuming these obligations also declined. Between 1929 and 1936 the Cardinals added twenty-three clubs to their empire. By 1940 they owned thirty-two teams and had working agreements with eight more. The majority of these clubs were at the lowest, or D level, of the minors. To fill out their rosters, Rickey expanded his scouting system and established three-day tryout camps that attracted thousands of young men anxious for a chance to play professional baseball. The Cardinals selected the most promising of these athletes and signed them to contracts. Baseball's reserve clause guaranteed that these "green peas," as one sportswriter dubbed them, would be bound to the Cardinals as long as that club had a use for them. They could remain on the farm, as Rickey would say, until they "ripened into money."[15]

"Out of quantity comes quality," preached Rickey, expounding his own version of Darwinian selection.[16] The Cardinals finished in first or second place fifteen times in twenty seasons between 1930 and 1949. Players developed in the Cardinal farm system appeared on rosters throughout the major leagues. Other teams attempted to emulate the Rickey model in the 1930s, but only the Yankees approached his level of success.

Commissioner Landis watched the expansion of Rickey's empire with growing horror. Landis feared that a relationship in which major league teams moved players at will, without regard to the fortunes of their minor league affiliates, would make a mockery of competition at the lower levels and destroy the independence and fabric of minor league baseball.[17] Revealingly, Landis and other critics likened Rickey's system not to a farm, which still possessed a certain sanctity in American folklore, but to the modern chain store movement, a bête noire of twentieth-century populism. The chains, which replaced local businesses with affiliates of national corporations, had attracted a growing opposition from small businessmen in the 1920s and 1930s. Yet, as Rickey understood, they also reflected the incorporation of small-town America into a national culture. Radio, newsreels, and advertising had blurred the boundaries between national and local. The problems of minor league baseball stemmed more from a lack of fan support than a lack of independence.[18]

During the early 1920s veteran owners Barney Dreyfuss of the Pittsburgh Pirates and Frank Navin of the Detroit Tigers had convinced Landis that Rickey's scheme was impractical and that his pyramid would ultimately implode. Thus, Landis, although ruling that a major league club could not own stock in more than one team in a league, initially did nothing to block Rickey's broader design. By 1930, however, Landis had seen enough. He openly accused Rickey, whom he privately referred to as "that sanctimonious so-and-so," of "raping the minors."[19] Rickey defended himself in a speech to the national 1930 Minor League Convention. Rickey noted that thirteen minor leagues had failed in the preceding years. None of those leagues had major league affiliations. Those teams aligned with the Cardinals, he pointed out, "had not suffered at all in comparison with those who are unable to continue." Taking aim at Landis, seated nearby, Rickey assailed the do-nothing approach to the Great Depression. "I deplore the philosophy of indifference that is going on," he asserted. In 1933, the owners, defying Landis, unanimously approved a rule allowing the establishment of farm systems. In later years Rickey argued that dependence had brought stability to the minor leagues. "The farm system," he maintained, "was the savior of (minor league) baseball."[20]

In addition to raising fundamental issues about the growing incursions of the national economy into the local marketplace, Rickey's strategies also revealed an often callous exploitation of labor during the hard times of the Depression. Rickey was notorious for his parsimony in salary negotiations with major and minor league players alike. "It was easy to figure out Mr. Rickey's thinking about contracts," said Chuck Connors, who played for Rickey before moving on to an acting career. "He had both players and money—and just didn't like to see the two of them mix." Enos Slaughter, who played his way up through Rickey's Cardinal system, commented, "When you talked money to him you could get none of it. He was always going to the vault to give you a nickel's change." That Rickey received a percentage of team profits made these one-sided negotiations all the more galling. "He knocked down everyone's salary," recalled minor league catcher Lou Kahn, "and he put the difference between what they got and what they should've got, in his own pocket."[21]

Rickey justified his treatment of ballplayers in the time-honored tradition of the nineteenth-century capitalist entrepreneur. Work agreements were contracts entered into by individuals as equals, extending opportunity, rewarding the worthy, and uplifting all participants. "I offered millhands, plowboys, high school kids a better way of life," he stated. "They rose on sandlots to big city diamonds. And no young man who signed a contract with me has ever suffered educationally or morally. . . . When he quit the Cardinal chain, he had learned the lesson 'clean living' and 'moral stamina.' "[22] But in light of the youth of the players, the desperate economic times, and the one-sided ironclad guarantees provided by the reserve clause, Rickey's practices could hardly be called equitable. Many viewed Rickey's labor policies in a less flattering light. Lou Kahn complained, "I was just a number to Branch Rickey. He ran baseball factories and he screwed his players every way but right side up." Jim McLaughlin, later a major league scouting director, described Rickey and "the way he manipulated people and then made those pious speeches" as an "ethical fraud."[23]

Although not a baseball player, Larry MacPhail first entered Branch Rickey's orbit via the Cardinal farm system. Unlike Rickey, who had settled on a career in baseball at an early age, the peripatetic MacPhail had, at age 40, already tried his hand in a variety of businesses. The son of a Michigan banker, MacPhail practiced law with a Chicago firm and ran a department store in Nashville, Tennessee, before enlisting in the army in World War I at age twenty-seven. A combat veteran of two major campaigns, Mac-Phail barely escaped court-martial for his participation in a quixotic attempt to kidnap the Kaiser at the war's end. He mustered out to a life in Columbus, Ohio, in which he owned first a glass company, then an auto dealership, and finally a construction firm. He also refereed college football games and was active in the Ohio Golf Association. Although many of his business ventures were successful, the failure of a building project left him broke at the dawn of the Depression.[24]

In search of a new enterprise, MacPhail acquired an option to purchase the Columbus Senators of the American Association. Knowing that the Cardinals were looking for minor league affiliates, MacPhail telephoned Rickey, who expressed an interest in acquiring the team. According to MacPhail's biographer, Don Warfield, when MacPhail asked Rickey for an appointment, Rickey, assuming a day's train travel between Columbus and St. Louis, told MacPhail to be there at three o'clock, expecting to see him on the morrow. MacPhail dashed to the airport, caught a plane to St. Louis, and appeared at Rickey's office that afternoon. Duly impressed by MacPhail's industriousness, Rickey agreed to purchase the Columbus franchise and installed MacPhail as the club president.[25]

The circumstances of their first meeting demonstrate a critical difference between the two men. Although they were only nine years apart in age — Rickey born in 1881 and MacPhail in 1890 — the two men reflected the generational divide of the centuries. Rickey represented the world of the impoverished nineteenth-century agricultural producer, MacPhail the affluent twentieth-century modern. Both men were known for their verbosity, but reporters depicted Rickey as a traditionalist preacher, MacPhail as an expansive blusterer. Rickey, who also became an avid flyer, was not averse to innovation, but he was rarely as quick as MacPhail to understand the potential of new technology. Whereas Rickey viewed the baseball business from a perspective of containing costs, MacPhail embodied the consumer component of modern capitalism. Revealingly, while MacPhail frequently spoke of "what the customers want" and the "fellow who sits out there in the bleachers," Rickey, the most quoted man in baseball history, left no remembered adages about fans.

MacPhail's stint with the Columbus team (renamed the Red Birds on its affiliation with the Cardinals) proved a dress rehearsal for his future baseball enterprises. He took over a floundering operation at the worst possible moment. Columbus had not won a pennant in twenty-three years and had landed in the second division for fifteen straight years, including a sixth-place finish in 1930. The club had lost $500,000 during the prosperous 1920s and now faced the Great Depression with dim prospects. MacPhail, however, believed that he could convince local fans to come out to the games. With Rickey and the Cardinals providing the players and in essence handling the supply side, MacPhail focused on stimulating demand. Refashioning ramshackle Neil Park into a more attractive place became his first priority. MacPhail surrounded his Columbus Red Birds in a sea of bright red, with large red birds painted on the outfield fence, a bright red flagpole in centerfield, and ushers, vendors, and ticket sellers bedecked in red fedoras and neckties. He added distance markers down the foul lines and piped in music over the loudspeaker system. Boys under sixteen could attend games for free five days a week, while women could buy a season ticket for three dollars.[26]

The 1931 season wreaked devastation across the minor leagues, but in Columbus attendance increased by 50 percent. The Red Birds were the only team in the American Association to turn a profit. MacPhail's success convinced Rickey and Cardinal owner Sam Breadon to build a new ballpark in Columbus. On opening day 1932, 18,000 fans turned out to celebrate MacPhail's new showcase. For those who could not attend, MacPhail had the game broadcast over the radio—a Columbus first.

On June 17 MacPhail unveiled yet another twist: night baseball. The technology for night games had longed existed, but Oganized Baseball, displaying its usual wisdom, had been slow to adopt it. Although night games promised an opportunity for working people to attend games and a relief from the heat of the summer, baseball officials dismissed it as "unnatural." Clark Griffith called it " "bush league stuff . . . just a step above dog racing."[27] As early as 1929 the Kansas City Monarchs of the Negro National League had equipped themselves with a traveling lighting unit enabling them to play night games. In 1930 several minor league teams introduced night baseball. On April 18 Independence, Kansas, hosted the first night game in the minor leagues, using a portable lighting system. In Des Moines, Iowa, the hometown Demons installed permanent floodlights and on May 2 drew national attention and a live NBC radio broadcast to its first night game. Other minor league teams followed suit.[28]

Columbus's 1932 entry into the ranks of teams offering night baseball secured the club's success. With a new stadium, night games, and radio broadcasts, the Red Birds drew a record 310,000 fans, outdrawing the parent Cardinals. Yet if MacPhail's ability to draw crowds pleased Rickey, their divergent personalities and inclinations inevitably led to discord. Rickey, the archetype of nineteenth-century Protestant morality, believed in a world of frugality, moderation, and temperance. MacPhail dressed in bold, garish clothes (a "municipal eyesore," according to one Columbus colleague) and swaggered boldly through life, employing a voice likened by one sportswriter to "the call of an adult male moose" and another as "a living loudspeaker in human form."[29] His physical appearance with bright red hair and a face freckled to a similar shade enhanced his impact. MacPhail spent lavishly, entertained frequently, and, Prohibition notwithstanding, drank to excess. Rickey blamed MacPhail for cost overruns at the new stadium and particularly bristled at his lavish office appointed with walnut paneling and Oriental rugs. On one occasion MacPhail became embroiled in a drunken dispute with a hotel manager and uprooted his team in the middle of the night. In May 1933, after a controversy arose over the handling of players sent by Rickey to the Red Birds, Rickey forced a reluctant MacPhail from the club presidency.[30]

Yet the apparent rift between the two men was misleading. MacPhail possessed the irrepressible, uninhibited type of persona that alternately exasperated and captivated Rickey. Despite his prohibitionist leanings, Rickey often surrounded himself with talented but intemperate employees. He once described his famed Cardinal "Gas House Gang" as "a high class team with nine heavy drinkers," among them the tempestuous Leo Durocher who later managed

Rickey's Brooklyn Dodger teams. MacPhail likewise felt a kinship to Rickey. "He thinks the world of you," wrote MacPhail's brother Herman to Rickey after the 1933 dispute. "And he never tackled anything as wholeheartedly as he did baseball in Columbus. If there is any way possible for you to sponsor him . . . I wish you would because nobody had the influence over him you seem to have." Later that year, the Cincinnati Reds approached Rickey about taking over the club. Rickey declined, but recommended MacPhail for the job. "He has great imagination and is completely fearless," Rickey reportedly told the team's directors. "He has ideas enough to revive baseball enthusiasm in your city. He's a wild man at times, but you've got to stay with him."[31]

The Reds had finished in last place for three consecutive seasons. Only 218,000 fans had paid their way into the ballpark in 1933. But MacPhail had what Roger Kahn would call a "passion [for] salvaging wrecks." He officially took control of the club in December 1933 and within a month was hailed as "a revelation" in the baseball world. "He thinks baseball needs promotion and he is ready to promote," commented the *New York Evening Post*.[32] Recognizing the need for more substantial financial backing, MacPhail approached Powel Crosley, Jr., one of Cincinnati's wealthiest citizens. Crosley manufactured radios and refrigerators. More significantly, he owned and operated several radio stations. Major league owners were still leery of radio, many of them blaming it for their attendance woes during the Depression. The Cardinals prohibited broadcasts of all games in 1934, and the three New York teams agreed to a five-year radio blackout. MacPhail, on the other hand, convinced Crosley that radio and baseball offered a perfect marriage of interests. Not only would game broadcasts stimulate interest in the Reds, they would also enhance the popularity of his radio station. In February 1934 Crosley purchased a controlling share of the Reds. Among the assets he brought with him was a young radio announcer already in his employ named Walter "Red" Barber, whom Crosley assigned to announce the Reds' games in 1934.[33]

Crosley promised MacPhail ample capital to spruce up the local stadium, create a farm system, and purchase players for the Reds. As at Columbus, MacPhail immediately painted the ballpark, now renamed Crosley Field, outfitted the ushers in sprightlier uniforms, and brought in young women to peddle cigarettes in the stands. Always interested in setting precedents and garnering publicity, MacPhail chartered two airplanes to fly the Reds to Chicago, a major league first. Although several players opted for a train, MacPhail generated excitement by placing a shortwave transmitter on board and having Barber send live reports back to Cincinnati.[34] Yet no amount of hoopla could have rescued the Reds in 1934. The team lost twenty-three of its first twenty-eight home games, sank quickly into last place, and actually drew fewer fans than the preceding year.

MacPhail sought salvation in lights. At the winter meetings in December he asked the National League to lift its ban on night baseball. "Young man, you can write this down. Not in my lifetime or yours will you ever see a baseball game played at night in the majors," Commissioner Landis warned him before the meeting. Opposition by any single club could doom his proposal, and Giants owner Charles Stoneham vowed, "I'll never vote for night baseball." MacPhail, who had prepared a forty-page brief on the virtues of night games, spoke for three hours to convince his National League rivals. In the end seven teams voted approval and Stoneham abstained, thus allowing the plan to go forward.[35]

MacPhail enlisted General Electric to design the best possible illumination system and recruited President Franklin D. Roosevelt to switch on the lights via telegraph from Washington, D.C. On May 24, 1935, more than 20,000 fans, perhaps ten times the usual weekday crowd, descended on Crosley Field to attend the Reds' first night contest. Drum and bugle corps, high school bands, and fireworks enlivened the occasion. The new Mutual Broadcasting System featured the game as its first national sports event. Red Barber, announcing for both Cincinnati and Mutual, later described the evening:

A silence fell over the crowd as the magic moment of 8:30 approached. Precisely on time, President Franklin D. Roosevelt pressed a telegraph key in the White House. . . . A mighty roar went up from the crowd. . . . There was light—tremendous, almost blinding light.[36]

Other major league officials remained unimpressed. Yankee General Manager Ed Barrow dismissed it as a fad that "will never last once the novelty wears off." Detroit Tigers owner Frank Navin foresaw "the ruination of baseball." Night games, he protested, "change the players from athletes to actors."[37] MacPhail, always more attuned to fan desires, recognized the sport's inherent theatricality. "Sure, night baseball is a spectacle with a lot of hoopla," MacPhail countered his critics, "but that's what the customers want. Baseball under the lights looks more glamorous, colorful . . . the uniforms look better, the players look faster and bigger, and the fans react accordingly." They "loved the brilliantly lit park set against a background of darkness," recalled Barber.[38]

The Reds played seven night games in 1935, attracting almost 124,000 people to these contests. Special excursion trains brought people from cities and towns throughout the Ohio Valley to witness the spectacle.[39] Total Cincinnati attendance more than doubled, and the club turned a profit for the first time in years. The Reds even climbed out of the cellar, attaining sixth place, the club's highest finish since 1928.

The team continued to improve in the standings and at the gate in 1936. But MacPhail's alcoholic self-destructiveness again began to surface. "It seemed he couldn't live without success," as Harold Parrott observed. "Worse yet, he couldn't live with it." MacPhail seemed increasingly unable to control his temper or moderate his booming voice. "We were slightly afraid of our father. When he was angry he was formidable," remembered his son Lee. The senior MacPhail often humiliated his employees, who bore the brunt of his volatility. During the 1936 season he punched and broke the jaw of a policeman during an altercation at a downtown Cincinnati hotel. "Boy, isn't that great publicity," he allegedly commented when confronted by Crosley. As the season drew to a close in mid-September, MacPhail left the Reds, voluntarily by some reports, fired according to others.[40]

"There is a thin line between genius and insanity," Leo Durocher would later say of MacPhail, "and in Larry's case it was sometimes so thin you could see him drifting back and forth." In 1936 MacPhail himself clearly recognized that he was treading perilously close to a psychological brink. He had developed a nervous facial tic and allowed his drinking to get out of hand. According to Rickey's friend and biographer Arthur Mann, after leaving Cincinnati MacPhail stopped in St. Louis to see Rickey. He told Rickey that he was heading back to rest with his family in his native Michigan and wouldn't "drink another drop for a year." Rickey responded, "Why a year? Why put a time limit on it at all?"[41]

MacPhail remained out of baseball for the 1937 season, but another wreck in need of salvage soon beckoned. The Brooklyn Dodgers had lost over a half-million dollars in three years. The Ebbets and McKeever families, who shared club ownership, were at constant loggerheads. The Brooklyn Trust Company, the bank that had underwritten the team's losses, now declined further financial support for the feuding regime. As at Cincinnati in 1934 the Dodgers' Board of Directors unsuccessfully attempted to woo Rickey away from the Cardinals. At this point, depending on which tale one believes, either Rickey or National League President Ford Frick or both suggested MacPhail as the Dodger savior. MacPhail requested and received absolute control over all operations and a virtually unlimited credit line from Brooklyn Trust.[42]

MacPhail attacked the Dodger debacle with his usual energy. As always, he made the ballpark his first priority. Neglect had plunged Ebbets Field into a severe state of disrepair. MacPhail resurfaced the infield, replaced broken seats, renovated the dugouts, clubhouses, and restrooms, and repainted the entire facility an eye-catching turquoise blue. To create a more hospitable atmosphere, MacPhail imported ushers from Chicago to instruct the infamously surly Brooklyn employees in courtesy. He introduced the Knothole

Club, which offered free admission to thousands of children. He also hatched plans to install lights for night baseball.[43]

MacPhail recognized, however, that no amount of renovation could overcome a bad team. "People won't come to see us play day or night if we are lousy," he barked. Without the luxury of an established farm system and instinctively inclined to purchase what he needed, MacPhail bolstered the Dodgers' lineup by buying players from other teams. He paid the Phillies $50,000 for first baseman Dolph Camilli and made innumerable lesser acquisitions. He also began building a farm system and bolstered the Dodgers' scouting staff, laying the groundwork for the future. "I don't know how to make money without spending plenty of it," he explained.[44]

Despite MacPhail's best efforts, the Dodgers started poorly on the field and at the gate. As in the past, MacPhail responded with night baseball. Remarkably, despite the success of his Cincinnati experiment three years earlier and the extensive use of lights in the minors, no other major league team had dared brave the darkness. The American League had unconditionally banned night baseball. Over the protests of the Yankees and Giants, MacPhail installed a $72,000 six-tower lighting system and scheduled the first game on June 15 against his former squad, the Cincinnati Reds. He supplemented the festivities with fireworks, marching bands, and a race featuring Olympic legend Jesse Owens. Cincinnati hurler Johnny Vander Meer rose to the occasion by hurling his second consecutive no-hitter, a feat unmatched in baseball history.[45]

Three days later, with people still buzzing about the historic evening, MacPhail staged another coup, signing Babe Ruth, who had been out of baseball since his retirement in 1935, to coach at first base. Twenty-nine thousand fans turned out for Ruth's debut, and 50,000 more attended a series of exhibition games designed specifically to showcase the Babe. "Keep the customers awake and you'll keep 'em coming," MacPhail explained his philosophy.[46]

When the dust had settled on the 1938 season, although the Dodgers finished in seventh place, they had drawn almost 200,000 more fans than in 1937. MacPhail, reported *The Sporting News* in

August, used these "profits of his successful debut as Brooklyn's baseball boss to strengthen the Dodgers for the future," buying five players from other clubs.[47] Although MacPhail had laid out hundreds of thousands of dollars for ballpark improvements, lights, and players, the Dodgers posted an operating deficit of only $11,000, a vast improvement over earlier years.

MacPhail stepped up the pace in 1939. He released Babe Ruth and hired shortstop Leo Durocher as player-manager. When the five-year New York City blackout on radio broadcasts expired, MacPhail and the Dodgers refused to participate in an extension. He contracted with 50,000-watt station WOR to carry the games, signed an agreement with General Mills as a sponsor, and brought in Red Barber from Cincinnati to handle the games. "I'll have the most powerful station and the best sponsor and the world's greatest announcer at the mike," boasted MacPhail.[48] The Dodgers broadcast both home and away games to their growing mass of devotees.

"There was little he wouldn't try," recalled Barber. "The dead hand of tradition never gripped him. . . . One of the things he dearly loved was to be first . . . particularly . . . in something new and constructive." Thus, when NBC, flush with the success of live television demonstrations at the New York World's Fair, suggested televising a Dodger game, MacPhail jumped at the chance. MacPhail, the team board of directors, and a handful of writers watched in the press box as Barber, working without a monitor and unaware of where the cameras were pointed, announced the game from an upper deck seat behind third base. "The players were clearly distinguishable, but it was not possible to pick out the ball," reported Harold Parrott in *The Sporting News*. Nonetheless, recognizing the potential of the new technology, MacPhail initiated weekly telecasts of Dodger games in 1940.[49] That year MacPhail also reintroduced air travel to baseball, flying the Dodgers home to Brooklyn after a western road trip. Thirty thousand fans flocked to Floyd Bennett Field to greet the team.[50]

The 1939 version of the Brooklyn Dodgers finished in third place, trailing only the pennant-winning Cincinnati Reds, a team that MacPhail had resuscitated and largely assembled, and Rickey's St. Louis Cardinals. Attendance approached the million mark and club profits exceeded $140,000. The Dodger improvement continued in 1940, when the team finished second to Cincinnati.

By the start of the 1941 season MacPhail had become an institution in Brooklyn. His wardrobe, nearly scandalous in Columbus and Cincinnati, grew even more garish in Brooklyn. "He wears loud check suits and ties with stripes two inches broad," wrote Robert L. Taylor in a *New Yorker* article entitled "Borough Defender." "He likes color contrasts, when wearing a pair of pale green trousers with a jacket of yellow plaid. Most of his shirts are custom made and silk." Although he had his critics among the press (Dan Parker translated his initials L. S. to stand for "Lucifer Sulphurous"), he had won over most of the sportswriters by building a new press box with an adjoining club room equipped with a bar, affectionately dubbed "Larry's Saloon."[51] When the Dodgers edged past Rickey's Cardinals to win the pennant in 1941, drawing 1.2 million fans and ushering in the golden age of Brooklyn baseball, MacPhail became a local hero.

The Dodger triumph in 1941, following so closely on the heels of two Cincinnati pennants, elevated MacPhail alongside Branch Rickey to the pinnacle of the baseball world. Their approaches still differed dramatically. Rickey's Cardinals, who depended on player sales for the bulk of their income, had not bought anyone since Jesse Haines in 1919. By contrast, MacPhail's favorite activity, as Taylor noted, was buying ballplayers. "His main belief in building up the Brooklyn club," observed Taylor, "has been that in order to make a dollar you have to spend as much as fifty cents." By the start of the 1941 season he had purchased three catchers, twelve pitchers, six infielders, and eight outfielders at a cost of a million dollars.[52] MacPhail, despite his relative inexperience in baseball, proved a shrewd judge of talent. His spending spree brought standouts Pee Wee Reese, Dixie Walker, Billy Herman, and Whitlow Wyatt to the Dodgers.

Throughout the early years in Brooklyn MacPhail retained a strong relationship with Branch Rickey. In 1939 MacPhail hired

Branch Rickey, Jr., who had been laboring in his father's shadow at St. Louis, to direct and build the Dodger farm system. Rickey returned the favor, promising MacPhail's son Lee a job in the Cardinal organization when he graduated from college and later offering him a position as a general manger with Toronto in the high-level International League.[53] In 1938, after Commissioner Landis, in his strongest attack on Rickey's farm pyramid, ordered seventy-four Cardinal farmhands released from their contracts, Rickey had entrusted Pete Reiser, the best of those players, into MacPhail's safekeeping. MacPhail promised that the Dodgers would hide Reiser in the low minor leagues until the Cardinals could legally buy back his contract after the 1940 season.[54]

By the early 1940s, however, relations between the two men had begun to sour. Their first conflict stemmed from the Reiser deal. MacPhail, despite the best of intentions, could not keep the talented twenty-year-old hidden. Leo Durocher, unaware of MacPhail's promises, had spotted the player at spring training in 1939 and inserted him into the Dodger lineup in three games, coincidentally against the Cardinals. Reiser hit four home runs and reached base eleven consecutive times. Durocher bragged about his "find" to sportswriters, who nicknamed Reiser "Pistol Pete" in their dispatches. MacPhail ordered Durocher not to play Reiser again and sent the young player to the Eastern League. The damage, however, had been done. When Reiser tore up the Eastern League in 1939 and again in the early months of 1940, MacPhail informed Rickey that any attempt to return him to St. Louis would bring down the wrath of the Brooklyn fans and press. "Branch, they'd lynch me," MacPhail reportedly cried. Knowing that his archenemy Commissioner Landis was closely monitoring the situation, Rickey acquiesced.[55]

In June 1940, perhaps as partial compensation for Reiser, MacPhail sent four fringe players and, more significantly, $125,000 to the Cardinals for all-star outfielder Joe Medwick and pitcher Curt Davis. MacPhail justified the high price in the belief that the acquisition of Medwick would secure a Dodger pennant. On June

19, however, just one week after Medwick had joined the club, Cardinal pitcher Bob Bowman beaned him with a fastball. As Medwick lay unconscious on the ground, MacPhail, doubtless under the influence of alcohol, exploded onto the field. "Waving his arms and roaring in his vibrant moose voice, he galloped across the diamond to the pitcher's box," according to one account, challenging Bowman and other Cardinals to a fight. Some, including Red Barber, believe that MacPhail had convinced himself that Rickey had ordered the beaning.[56]

MacPhail's inebriated excursion onto the field was one of several signs that he had once again begun to unravel. As his son Lee recalled, "After a couple of martinis," his father would grow "insulting and pugnacious." In 1939 he punched *Brooklyn Eagle* reporter Harold Parrott in the nose for leaking a potentially damaging story. He repeatedly fired and instantly rehired manager Leo Durocher. According to Rickey biographer Murray Polner, reports reached Rickey of the oppressive and unpredictable atmosphere that permeated the Dodger offices. As Harold Parrott later wrote, "There was no doubt that when [MacPhail] roared in the Dodger office, everybody jumped." Another reporter called MacPhail's tenure the "reign of terror." Dodger farm director Branch Rickey, Jr., told a friend that he "hated to enter the office every morning." Another friend informed the senior Rickey that his son "is really getting himself worked up more and more about the thought of quitting the Brooklyn organization immediately." Office politics grew more difficult when MacPhail left his wife of three decades to take up with a much younger Dodger switchboard operator.[57]

In 1942 MacPhail added yet another innovation to his repertoire. At his daughter's urging he had installed an organ in the park and hired Gladys Goodding to serenade the fans and play rally music.[58] Meanwhile, the Dodgers won a club record 104 games, but lost the pennant to the Cardinals on the last day of the season. After the final game MacPhail called a press conference. "The five years I have spent in Brooklyn," he announced tearfully, "have been the happiest years of my life." His reign, he proclaimed, had ended. With war raging in Europe and Asia, MacPhail, now fifty-two years old, had reenlisted in the army as a lieutenant colonel.[59]

MacPhail departed with a flourish of patriotism, but other factors were also at work. He had grown characteristically restive, the five years in Brooklyn exceeding his tenure in any previous position that he had held. The challenge of rebuilding had ended. Nor were the Dodger directors and shareholders necessarily disappointed to see him go. MacPhail had worked miracles with the team, converting a perennial second division finisher into a pennant winner and paying off almost a million dollars in debts while generating a surplus of $300,000. In the process, as Gerald Eskenazi has noted, he had "made America Brooklyn Dodger conscious," making the team synonymous with the nation during the war years. Yet MacPhail's behavior and endless spending had alienated some of his employers. Most of the Dodger revenues had been funneled back into operations, leaving little in the way of realized profits. Some have speculated that the Dodgers did not plan to renew his contract. When MacPhail asked the team to establish an interim management in his absence, the Board of Directors declined this offer and instead accepted his resignation.[60]

Nor did the Dodgers hesitate in naming MacPhail's replacement. On November 1 they announced that they had lured Branch Rickey away from the Cardinals. Rickey, whose relationship with Cardinal owner Sam Breadon had frayed badly, welcomed the opportunity to be reunited with his son and to assume leadership of a pennant-contending club.

The transition from MacPhail to Rickey did not go smoothly. MacPhail no doubt resented being replaced by his old mentor and rival, especially after Rickey acquired an ownership interest in the team, a goal that had eluded MacPhail. According to Harold Parrott, when Jack MacDonald, MacPhail's former secretary, transferred his allegiance to Rickey and authored a mildly critical article in the *Saturday Evening Post*, provocatively entitled "The Fall of the House of MacPhail," the former general manager responded angrily with a message quoting a biblical verse. Rickey immediately recognized the passage as a reference to Judas. "Our egomaniacal friend is appointing himself as Christ Almighty in that telegram," commented Rickey. The exchange, wrote Parrott, now a Rickey assistant, "was the first inkling I had of a real falling out between these two giants."[61]

Rickey also apparently still bore ill feelings toward MacPhail over the abortive Reiser transaction. Reiser had more than fulfilled his promise, leading the National League in hitting in 1941. The next season he had injured himself crashing into a fence, only to be allowed by MacPhail to continue playing against doctors' orders, compounding his maladies. "That character should have never been entrusted with anything so fine," a bitter Rickey reportedly told Parrott.[62]

MacPhail's drinking buddies among the press dreaded Rickey's ascension. At the annual New York writers show, Louis Effrat sang "Will the lights go on again . . . in Larry's Saloon?"

Will Branch serve Ruppert's beer
Or Seven-Up on draft?
It seems a shame to waste the gin,
And serve us Rickey Finn.

Many mercilessly attacked Rickey for both his handling of players and his pontificating style, labeling him "El Cheapo" and dubbing his office "The Cave of the Winds." They began to call his son Branch, Jr., the "Twig."[63]

Rickey's approach to building a team remained diametrically opposed to MacPhail's. Rickey vowed to end the practice of buying players and moved to dispose of some of the older high-salaried players whom MacPhail had accumulated. He traded fan favorites Joe Medwick and Dolph Camilli. Since the club also lost Pee Wee Reese, Pete Reiser, and Hugh Casey to the military, the Dodgers won twenty-three fewer games during Rickey's first year at the helm than they had in 1942 and slipped to third place. Nineteen forty-four proved even worse. The Dodgers finished in seventh place, forty-two games behind the Cardinals. Reporters and fans blamed Rickey for the club's decline. Rickey, however, had already shifted Dodger priorities. With his eye firmly focused, as always, on player development, Rickey expanded the farm system that MacPhail and Rickey, Jr., had started. He also launched two behind-the-scenes initiatives that delivered little immediate assistance to the Brooklyn club but would yield significant long-term results. Unlike other teams who curtailed their scouting efforts during the war years fearing to lose players to the war, Rickey, gambling on a relatively short conflict, stepped up his recruitment efforts and signed players too young for the draft. In addition, Rickey secretly began scouting the Negro Leagues and the Caribbean for African-American players. These strategies would make the Dodgers a dynasty in the postwar years.[64]

MacPhail, meanwhile, plotted his return to baseball. Even as he worked at the Pentagon, MacPhail nonetheless found time to peruse the baseball horizon for postwar opportunities. He found one literally in Rickey's backyard where ownership of the New York Yankees had become available. While still in the military, MacPhail lined up Dan Topping, an heir to Anaconda Copper, and construction magnate Del Webb to underwrite his purchase of the Yankees. In February 1945 MacPhail left the army to become a co-owner and general manager of baseball's most fabled franchise.[65]

With the two now hostile rivals competing in the same city, conflict was inevitable. The controversial issue of racial integration became their first battleground. Pressures were building on all three New York clubs to add African-American players to their rosters. In April 1945 *Amsterdam News* reporter Joe Bostic brought two Negro League players to the Dodger training camp demanding a tryout. A second confrontation occurred ten days later in Boston when Wendell Smith of the *Pittsburgh Courier* coerced the Red Sox into staging a workout for future major leaguers Jackie Robinson and Sam Jethroe. On April 24 major league baseball created a Committee on Baseball Integration. Rickey, MacPhail, and *Baltimore Afro-American* reporter Sam Lacy were named to the panel. The group never met because "MacPhail always had some excuse," remembered Lacy. Later that summer, New York Mayor

Fiorello La Guardia formed his own Committee on Baseball, with Rickey and MacPhail again represented.[66]

In October 1945 MacPhail publicly expressed his views on the race issue. He condemned "political and social minded drumbeaters" for their efforts on behalf of integration and called for a strengthening of the Negro Leagues. This might allow a few African Americans of "ability and character" to move into Organized Baseball. A few weeks later MacPhail's opinion became moot.[67] On October 23 Branch Rickey announced that Jackie Robinson had been signed to play for the Dodgers' top farm club at Montreal, marking the beginning of the end of baseball's color line.

MacPhail believed that in acquiring Robinson, Rickey had "double-crossed his associates for his own personal advantage." He made no public criticism, but almost a year later he found the opportunity to vent his rage at the man who had succeeded him in Brooklyn. In July 1946 the major leagues created a steering committee to define the challenges facing Organized Baseball. MacPhail headed the committee and wrote its report, including a lengthy section on the "Race Question." As before, he attacked advocates of integration "who know little about baseball and nothing about the business end of its operation." Tellingly, MacPhail questioned the ultimate consequences of increased black attendance at the ballparks. Noting that Robinson's presence in the International League had attracted thousands of black fans, MacPhail worried that "a situation might be presented . . . in which the preponderance of Negro attendance . . . could conceivably threaten the value of Major League franchises." MacPhail concluded his report with a coldly calculated attack on Rickey. "Your committee does not desire to question the motives of any organization or individual who is sincerely opposed to segregation," wrote MacPhail. However, "The individual action of any one club may exert tremendous pressures on the whole structure of Professional Baseball," threatening the stability of several clubs.[68]

The differences between Rickey and MacPhail on this matter reflect the growing personal animus between the two men and a number of more substantive issues as well. MacPhail, unlike

Rickey, clearly had little sympathy for integration. Furthermore, MacPhail's Yankees drew a considerable income from the rental of Yankee Stadium and their minor league ballparks in Newark and Kansas City to Negro League teams. Most significantly, their attitude toward desegregation sprang naturally from their approach to baseball. Although religion and morality played critical roles in Rickey's historic undertaking, labor considerations were never far from his thinking. "The greatest untapped reservoir of raw material in the history of the game is the black race!" he told his family. Furthermore, since Rickey, with his distaste for buying players, had no intention of paying the Negro League teams for this "raw material," he had uncovered a remarkably cheap source of talent. MacPhail, on the other hand, had his eye on the box office. "I've always believed that the ball club belongs to the fellow who goes out there and pays his way in," he told a reporter when he purchased the Yankees. "I've always tried to keep faith with the fans and I believe I've been fairly close to the fellow who sits out there in the bleachers."[69] These fellows, he believed, would not want to sit next to Negroes. The resulting decline in attendance, MacPhail feared, would be devastating.

As the Jackie Robinson drama played itself out in 1946 and 1947, both the Dodgers and the Yankees and Rickey and MacPhail headed on a collision course. The New York club acquired by MacPhail was not in any sense a wreck, but by Yankee standards the team had fallen on hard times. After winning seven pennants in eight years, the Yankees finished third in 1944 and fourth in MacPhail's first season at the helm. Wartime attendance had remained modest. MacPhail arrived too late to institute significant changes in 1945, but for the 1946 campaign he inaugurated his trademark makeover. He ordered lights installed at Yankee Stadium and undertook a major renovation of the ballpark itself. He created baseball's first Stadium Club, a members-only restaurant for season ticket holders. He also expanded the general catering facilities. Amid the postwar euphoria attendance shot upward throughout the major leagues in 1946, but nowhere more so than in the Bronx. Despite a third-place finish, the introduction of night games and other MacPhailian promotions brought a major league record 2,265,512 fans to Yankee Stadium, almost doubling the previous club best.[70] In 1947 the Yankees returned to form, running away with the American League pennant, while again drawing over 2 million fans. MacPhail also sold the television rights to Yankee home games, allowing millions more to enjoy the club's resurgence.

Rickey's Dodgers had also experienced a rebirth. With the war over, the return of Reese and other stars and the harvest of Rickey's well-stocked Dodger farm system returned Brooklyn to pennant contention. In 1946 the team finished two games behind the Cardinals and attracted almost 1.8 million fans to Ebbets Field. The addition of Jackie Robinson would drive the team to the National League Championship and new attendance highs in 1947.

Robinson's debut, however, was almost overshadowed by a bizarre offshoot of the growing Rickey–MacPhail feud. During spring training in 1947 Rickey and Leo Durocher had protested the presence of gamblers in MacPhail's box seats in a game in Havana. MacPhail, complaining that he had been slandered and libeled, filed charges against the Dodgers with Baseball Commissioner Happy Chandler. Chandler held hearings to investigate the allegations. In a baffling decision, handed down just days before Robinson's scheduled debut, Chandler fined both the Yankees and Dodgers for irregularities and, most significantly, suspended Dodger manager Leo Durocher for the 1947 season.[71]

Many believed that Chandler and MacPhail had conspired to punish Rickey for signing Robinson. Others dismissed the Robinson angle, but nonetheless saw Chandler, whom MacPhail had handpicked for the commissioner's job in 1945, as a tool of the Yankee owner. When MacPhail charged that Rickey himself had orchestrated Durocher's dismissal, Rickey exploded with rage. "I've taken all I can stand. I'm suing MacPhail for a million dollars," he raged.[72] Rickey never followed through on this threat, but tensions continued to simmer as the Yankees and Dodgers headed for a showdown in the 1947 World Series.

Few World Series in baseball history match the drama and excitement of that 1947 classic. Five of the seven games were settled by two runs or less. In the fourth game Yankee pitcher Bill Bevens carried a no-hitter into the ninth inning only to lose when Cookie Lavagetto doubled with two outs and two on. In the sixth game, Dodger outfielder Al Gionfriddo robbed Joe DiMaggio of a game-tying three run home run with one of the most memorable catches in baseball history, allowing the Dodgers to tie the Series at three games apiece. The Dodgers grabbed an early lead in the seventh game, but the Yankees prevailed to win the World Championship.

The victory should have marked MacPhail's ultimate achievement. He had restored the Yankees to dominance, breaking attendance records in the process. The four World Series games at Yankee Stadium had attracted an average of over 70,000 fans. He had triumphed over his former team and his archrival. MacPhail embraced the moment with an orgy of alcoholic self-destruction. "That's it! It's all over! I'm through. No more pressure! I'm retiring from baseball and resigning as president of the Yankees," he screamed into the microphone at the postgame celebration, tears running down his inflamed cheeks. He berated his former secretary John MacDonald, then punched him in the eye and knocked him down. He unceremoniously fired George Weiss, who had built the Yankee farm system. Seeing Rickey in the crowd, he put one arm around the old man's shoulder and extended the other for a handshake. Speaking in a voice so low as to be almost inaudible, Rickey told him, "I am taking your hand only because there are so many people watching. But don't you ever speak to me again!" By the next day Topping and Webb had purchased MacPhail's interest in the Yankees, and he had severed all relations with the club.[73]

MacPhail's fourth, final, and most ferocious exit from baseball largely brought his tempestuous relationship with Rickey to an end. The two men would clash again briefly in February 1948 when Rickey charged that other baseball owners had unanimously voted against his decision to bring Robinson to the majors. MacPhail denounced Rickey's statements as "false and inflammatory," adding, "Churchill must have had Rickey in mind when he said, 'There but for the grace of God goes God.' " Ten years later a still bitter

This 1860 Currier & Ives lithograph using baseball as a metaphor for politics in the aftermath of Abraham Lincoln's election to the presidency demonstrates how rapidly baseball had grown in popularity and familiarity in the pre–Civil War years. (LIBRARY OF CONGRESS)

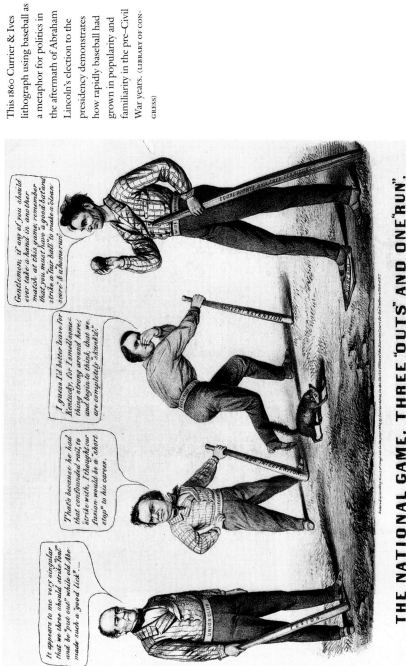

THE NATIONAL GAME. THREE "OUTS" AND ONE "RUN".
ABRAHAM WINNING THE BALL.

FIRST NINE OF THE

CINCINNATI

(RED STOCKINGS) BASE BALL CLUB.

The 1869 Cincinnati Red Stockings, baseball's first all-professional team, toured the nation, attracting a reported 179,000 fans and ushering in a new age for the sport. (LIBRARY OF CONGRESS)

Henry Chadwick, "The Father of Baseball,"
invented baseball scoring, the box score, and
many of the statistics still in use today. (NATIONAL
BASEBALL HALL OF FAME)

Albert Spalding, star pitcher, manager,
owner, founder of the National League,
and sporting goods magnate, played a
critical role in the development of the
national pastime in the nineteenth century. (TRANSCENDENTAL GRAPHICS)

Spalding Baseball Guide, 1884, edited by Henry Chadwick. (TRANSCENDENTAL GRAPHICS)

Four future owners as young baseball players: Charles Comiskey as player-manager of the St. Louis Browns in 1886; Connie Mack, a catcher with Meriden in the Connecticut League in 1884; Clark Griffith as pitcher for Milwaukee in the Western League in 1889; and a slender John McGraw, third baseman for Olean in the New York Penn League, 1890. (LIBRARY OF CONGRESS; NATIONAL BASEBALL HALL OF FAME; LIBRARY OF CONGRESS; NATIONAL BASEBALL HALL OF FAME)

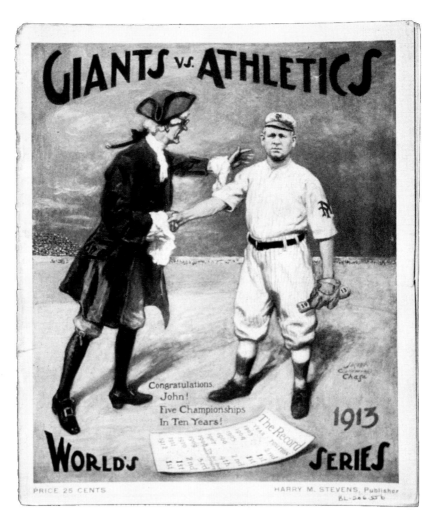

The 1913 World Series pitted Connie Mack's Philadelphia Athletics against John McGraw's New York Giants, who were in the series for the fifth time in ten years. (TRANSCENDENTAL GRAPHICS)

Connie Mack and John McGraw as grand old men of the game in the 1930s. (NATIONAL BASEBALL HALL OF FAME)

Above: Crowds gather in front of a Play-O-Graph Scoreboard to follow World Series action. (NATIONAL BASE-BALL HALL OF FAME)

Left: Graham McNamee broadcasting the World Series in the early 1920s. "He painted word pictures that other minds could feast upon." (NATIONAL BASEBALL HALL OF FAME)

Above: A scene from the 1926 movie *The Babe Comes Home* starring Babe Ruth and Anna Q. Wilson. "He couldn't act worth crap," said New York Yankee teammate Mark Koenig. (NATIONAL BASEBALL HALL OF FAME)

Left: "The most equitable partnership ever established in athletics," Babe Ruth and his agent/manager Christy Walsh. (NATIONAL BASEBALL HALL OF FAME)

Branch Rickey confers with Larry MacPhail, whom he replaced as Brooklyn Dodger general manager, at the 1943 all-star game. MacPhail is wearing his army uniform. (NATIONAL BASEBALL HALL OF FAME)

Branch Rickey, in a familiar pose, signs a young prospect to a contract. The prospect, Duke University all-American basketball and baseball star Dick Groat, will become an All-Star shortstop for the Pittsburgh Pirates. (CORBIS-BETTMAN/NATIONAL BASEBALL HALL OF FAME)

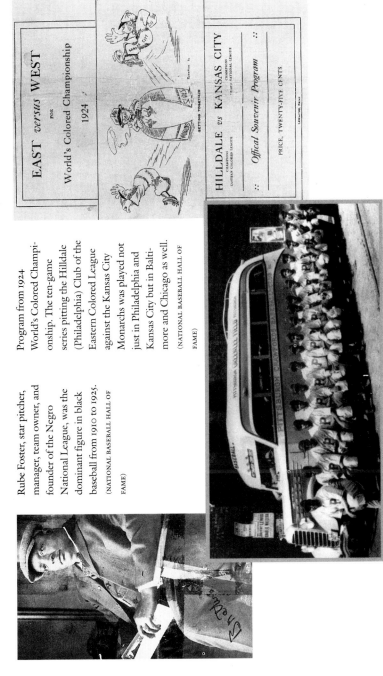

Rube Foster, star pitcher, manager, team owner, and founder of the Negro National League, was the dominant figure in black baseball from 1910 to 1925. (NATIONAL BASEBALL HALL OF FAME)

Program from 1924 World's Colored Championship. The ten-game series pitting the Hilldale (Philadelphia) Club of the Eastern Colored League against the Kansas City Monarchs was played not just in Philadelphia and Kansas City but in Baltimore and Chicago as well. (NATIONAL BASEBALL HALL OF FAME)

The 1935 Negro National League Champion Pittsburgh Crawfords were not only one of the greatest teams ever assembled, they were also one of the few Negro League teams to play in their own stadium. Here they pose in front of the team bus parked outside the ballpark, built by the team's owner, Pittsburgh numbers king Gus Greenlee. (NATIONAL BASEBALL LIBRARY/TRANSCENDENTAL GRAPHICS)

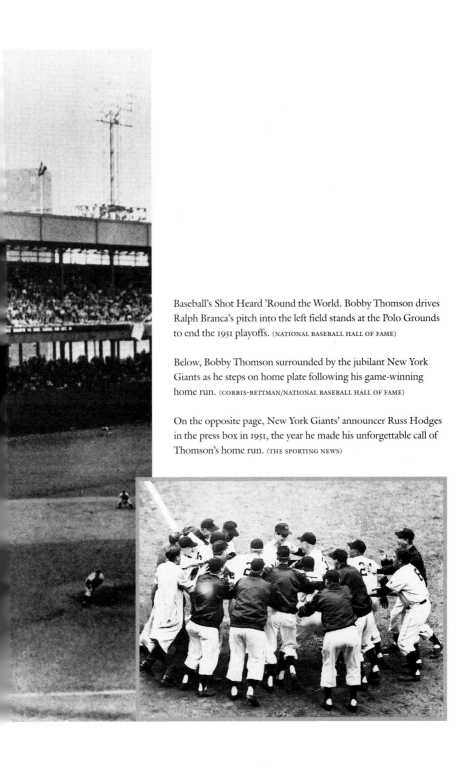

Baseball's Shot Heard 'Round the World. Bobby Thomson drives Ralph Branca's pitch into the left field stands at the Polo Grounds to end the 1951 playoffs. (NATIONAL BASEBALL HALL OF FAME)

Below, Bobby Thomson surrounded by the jubilant New York Giants as he steps on home plate following his game-winning home run. (CORBIS-BETTMAN/NATIONAL BASEBALL HALL OF FAME)

On the opposite page, New York Giants' announcer Russ Hodges in the press box in 1951, the year he made his unforgettable call of Thomson's home run. (THE SPORTING NEWS)

Milwaukee celebrates the Braves' National League pennant in 1957 in a ticker-tape parade complete with Indian braves. (AP/NATIONAL BASEBALL HALL OF FAME)

Throngs of excited San Franciscans welcome the Giants and their star center fielder, Willie Mays, on the day before the 1958 season opener pitting the Giants against the Los Angeles Dodgers in the first major league game played on the Pacific Coast. (AP/NATIONAL BASEBALL HALL OF FAME)

A major league record 78,672 fans attended the Dodgers' first home game at the Los Angeles Coliseum on April 18, 1958, but most sat far from the action in the cavernous, misshapen arena. (AP/NATIONAL BASEBALL HALL OF FAME)

In 1998 Sammy Sosa and Mark McGwire rejuvenated interest in baseball with their pursuit of Roger Maris's single season home run record. Fans followed this historic chase via Internet, cable television, and satellite transmissions, symbolizing a new age in baseball communications. (ED NESSEN/THE SPORTING NEWS)

MacPhail told reporter Gerald Holland, "Branch Rickey never did a damn thing for me except to fire me at Columbus."[74]

In the end, their personal differences had overwhelmed their common love for the national pastime. Yet together, Rickey and MacPhail had prepared baseball for the economic realities of post–World War II America. Rickey, in his ceaseless attempts to find better ways to "put the dollar sign on the muscle," had perfected the farm system and rationalized player development. All teams would emulate this model in the 1940s and 1950s. In signing Jackie Robinson, Rickey had positioned baseball in the forefront of American social progress and identified new sources of players to sustain and expand baseball's talent pool. MacPhail, focusing his efforts on "the fellow who digs down in his jeans and clicks the turnstiles," had ushered baseball into the consumer age. National League President Warren Giles once dismissed MacPhail as a "sensationalist . . . whose only contribution to baseball consisted of painting the seats at Cincinnati, Brooklyn and New York red or yellow instead of green."[75] But MacPhail, in his startlingly brief thirteen-year period as a baseball executive, had dramatically enhanced the vistas for baseball attendance and profitability. His profound faith in the ability of radio to simultaneously generate interest and revenue streams, his unswerving commitment to night baseball, and his experiments with television had restored baseball's popularity and redefined the ways in which millions of fans experienced the game. His interest in air travel paved the way for expansion beyond the eastern and midwestern states.

These lessons of supply and demand derived by MacPhail and Rickey from the scarcity of the Great Depression would prove even more valuable in the affluent society of the postwar years. Their visible hands had reshaped the baseball marketplace, establishing a new order for a modern age.

1 2 3 4 5 **6** 7 8 9 R H E

Unreconciled Strivings
Baseball in Jim Crow America

Andrew "Rube" Foster epitomized African-American pride. A tall, imposing, right-handed pitcher, he had migrated from his native Texas to Chicago in 1902 to play for the Chicago Union Giants. When warned that he might face "the best clubs in the land, white clubs," he announced, "I fear nobody." Over the next decade he established himself as perhaps the outstanding pitcher in all of baseball. In 1911 he formed his own team, the Chicago American Giants, and won a reputation as a managerial genius equal to his friend, John McGraw. Nine years later Foster, seeking to "keep colored baseball from control of the whites" and "to do something concrete for the loyalty of the Race," created the Negro National League. Foster criticized white owners for not letting African Americans "count a ticket [or] learn anything about the business," and called for a league dominated by black men. "There can be no such thing as [a black baseball league] with four or five of the directors white any more than you can call a streetcar a steamship," he asserted. Foster urged black fans: "It is your league. Nurse it! Help it! Keep it!" Yet Foster's intense racial pride notwithstanding, he also made his ultimate goal clear. "We have to be ready," he proclaimed, "when the time comes for integration."[1]

Rube Foster—and indeed, the entire experience of blacks in baseball in early twentieth-century America[2]—exemplifies elements of Booker T. Washington's call for the development of separate economic spheres so that his race might prepare itself for ultimate inclusion in American life. Yet black baseball also captured what Washington's rival, W.E.B. Du Bois, labeled the "twoness" of the African-American experience. "One ever feels his twoness—an American, a Negro," wrote Du Bois, "two souls, two thoughts, two unreconciled strivings; two warring ideals in one dark body, whose dogged strength alone keeps it from being torn asunder." The architects of black baseball embodied this dualism. They strove to create viable enterprises that served their communities and simultaneously might win a measure of respectability in the broader society. These ventures would prepare them for the day on which, according to Du Bois's vision, it would be "possible for a man to be both a Negro and American, without being cursed and spit upon by his fellows, without having the doors of Opportunity closed roughly in his face."[3]

The essence of black professional baseball is far more elusive than that of its white counterpart. The major leagues always constituted the epitome and cultural core of mainstream baseball, but the formal Negro Leagues represented no more than a segment of the black baseball experience. No leagues existed until 1920, and even during their halcyon days official contests never constituted more than perhaps a third of the games played. Some of the strongest black teams and best players performed outside the league structure. Top teams often boasted names like the Homestead Grays, Bachrach Giants, or the Hilldale Club, reflecting affiliations not to major cities but to people and smaller communities. The most popular attractions often involved exhibitions against white semiprofessional and professional teams. In all of these many guises and varieties, black baseball constituted a vital element of African-American culture, while also dramatizing the contradictions and challenges of survival in a world dominated by whites.

Within the African-American community, the officials, players, and teams of black baseball symbolized pride and achievement while creating a sphere of style and excitement that overlapped with the worlds of black business, politics, religion, and entertainment. During the baseball season Negro League teams constituted a constant presence in the black community. Placards announcing the games appeared in the windows of local businesses, along with advertisements featuring player endorsements and commands to "get those pretty clothes" for the "opening day . . . Fashion Parade."[4] In Kansas City fans could purchase tickets in a number of locales where African Americans congregated, including the Monarch Billiard Parlor, Stark's Newspaper Stand, the Panama Taxi Stand, and McCampbell's and Hueston's Drug Store. The Elbon and Lincoln movie theaters would show pictures of the players, advertisements for the games, and newsreel footage of the lavish opening day ceremonies.[5]

Local businesses rallied around the teams. Some, like Herman Stark's clothing store in Detroit, offered prizes to the first player to hit a home run or get a hit in a Sunday or opening day contest.[6] Several cities featured booster clubs, like the Hilldale Royal Rooters and Baltimore's Frontiers Club, that supported their teams. The Kansas City Booster Club, the most lavish of these organizations, included both black and white merchants whose stores served the black community. Formed in 1926, the Kansas City Boosters organized the opening day parade, sponsored banquets for the players, and staged beauty contests at the ball game.[7] These businesses profited, in turn, from black baseball. "The cafes, beer joints, and rooming houses of the Negro neighborhoods all benefited as black baseball monies sometimes trickled, sometimes rippled through the black community," writes Donn Rogosin. After the 1944 East-West all-star game in Chicago, reported Wendell Smith, "Hot spots were all loaded, and so were most of the patrons."[8]

African-American baseball also provided one of the most popular features of black newspapers. As early as the turn of the century the *Indianapolis Freeman* had discovered that baseball coverage attracted readers. Sportswriter David Wyatt, who had played for the Cuban Giants and Chicago Union Giants from 1896 to 1902, reported on news of black baseball from all over the country. The Indianapolis ABCs and other teams would arrange matches by placing ads in the *Freeman*.[9] Other black weeklies began covering the game more seriously after 1910. The *Philadelphia Tribune* forged a close alliance with Ed Bolden's Hilldale Club. Bolden advertised games in the *Tribune* and provided press releases and game results. Beginning in 1914 the *Tribune* began to print box scores and in 1915 published Bolden's weekly column, "Hilldale Pickups."[10] Black newspapermen, led by Wyatt, played key roles in the creation and promotion of the Negro National League in 1920. "Behind this opening should be the concentrated support of every race man in Detroit," asserted the *Detroit Contender*. "If the league succeeds your race succeeds; if the league fails, the race fails. . . . Our ability to put over large projects will be measured largely by the way we handle this one."[11]

Nonetheless, reporting in the African-American journals was frequently sketchy. Black newspapers could not afford to send writers to accompany clubs on the road and depended heavily on reports submitted by the teams. This source proved highly unreliable, as the traveling squads often failed to call in or refused to reveal losses. In addition, since many of the black weeklies appeared on Saturday, they tended to focus on previews of the following day's contests, rather than results of the previous week, making it difficult for fans to follow a team with any consistency. Nonetheless, by the 1920s and 1930s all the major black weeklies had substantial sports sections with regular coverage and standout columnists like Frank A. (Fay) Young of the *Chicago Defender*, Wendell Smith of the *Pittsburgh Courier*, and Sam Lacy of the *Baltimore Afro-American*. The black press played a critical role in promoting the East-West all-star game, the showcase event of Negro League baseball. The newspapers printed ballots and lists of eligible players and by 1939 top performers received as many as 500,000 votes. "The success of the game was made by Negro newspapers," commented Fay Young. "It was the Negro press that carried the percentages, the feats of the various stars all through the year, and it was the readers of the Negro newspapers who had knowledge of what they were going to see."[12]

Owners and officials of black clubs often ranked among the most prominent figures in the African-American community. Club officials participated actively in local business, fraternal, and civil rights organizations. Ed Bolden, owner of the Philadelphia-based Hilldale Club in the 1920s, belonged to local black fraternal groups and the Citizen's Republican Club. Kansas City Monarchs' secretary Quincy J. Gilmore was the guiding force behind the local Elks Club and the Negro Twilight League that brought together industrial, youth, and semiprofessional teams in the Kansas City area. Homestead Grays owner Cum Posey served on the Homestead school board.[13] Bolden, Posey, Rube Foster, and others wrote regular columns for local black newspapers.

Several team owners figured prominently in civil rights activities. Olivia Taylor, who inherited the Indianapolis ABCs from her husband, became president of the Indianapolis NAACP chapter in 1925.[14] Newark Eagle owner Effa Manley was an indefatigable campaigner against discrimination. In the years before she and her husband Abe purchased the ball club, Manley had achieved prominence in New York City as the secretary of the Citizen's League for Fair Play, which waged successful campaigns against Harlem businesses that refused to employ African Americans. In Newark Manley served as the treasurer of the New Jersey chapter of the NAACP and on several occasions held ballpark benefits for the organization. At one event the Eagles sold NAACP "Stop Lynching" buttons to fans. Manley also joined the "Citizen's Committee to End Jim Crow in Baseball Committee" created by the Congress of Industrial Organizations in 1942.[15]

Black teams hosted numerous benefit games for African-American charities and causes, raising funds for churches, hospitals, youth groups, and civil rights bodies. The Kansas City Monarchs staged benefits for the Negro National Business League and the Red Cross. The Newark Eagles regularly raised money to purchase medical equipment for the Booker T. Washington Community Hospital. During World War I the Indianapolis ABCs and Chicago American Giants played games on behalf of the Red Cross, and in the 1920s Hilldale played fund-raisers for war veterans. The first black baseball game at Yankee Stadium pitted the Lincoln Giants and Baltimore Black Sox in a 1930 benefit for the Brotherhood of Sleeping Car Porters. The outbreak of World War II prompted additional efforts.[16]

The players themselves often had close ties to the cities in which they performed. Many teams recruited from the local sandlots and discovered some of their best players literally perched on their doorsteps. Hall of Fame outfielder Oscar Charleston, who grew up on Indianapolis's East Side, served as a batboy for the ABCs before joining the squad as a player. He performed alongside Frank Warfield, "the pride of Indianapolis's West Side." The Homestead Grays discovered Josh Gibson playing semiprofessional baseball in Pittsburgh's Hill district. Memphis Blues pitching ace Verdell Mathis grew up within a short walk of Martin Field. Effa Manley's Eagles frequently found their best players—including Monte Irvin, Larry Doby, and Don Newcombe—in the Newark area.[17] The Birmingham Black Barons snatched the fifteen-year-old Willie Mays from a local high school.

The players often made the Negro League cities their year-round homes and became fixtures in their communities. In Detroit in the 1920s players found winter jobs in the local automobile plants. Turkey Stearnes and other Detroit Stars worked in factories owned by Detroit Tigers co-owner Walter O. Briggs, glad to hire them in his legendarily grimy and unsafe paint shops, but not on his baseball team. In Pittsburgh many of the Crawfords found work as lookouts for owner Gus Greenlee's gambling operations.[18] Some athletes stayed on in the cities where they had won their fame, opening up bars or other small businesses. John Henry "Pop" Lloyd, who had played for, among other teams, the Bachrach Giants of Atlantic City, settled there on retirement and reigned as "a

sort of foster father" to the city's children. Lloyd became the commissioner of the local little league and had a neighborhood ball
field named in his honor.[19]

Those who did not have homes in the city often resided during
the season at the finest black hotels. In an age when most mainstream hotels even in northern cities barred African Americans,
each major city featured a showplace hotel where traveling athletes,
entertainers, and members of the black elite lodged and congregated. These were the places, as poet Amiri Baraka describes Newark's Grand Hotel, where "the ballplayers and the slick people
could meet."[20] In Detroit the players stayed at the Norwood,
which also housed the Plantation nightclub. In Baltimore the Black
Sox lived at the Smith Hotel, owned by the city's black Democratic
political boss. Street's Hotel in Kansas City, located at Eighteenth
and Vine Streets, was the place, according to its manager, that
"everybody that came to KC stopped at."[21]

As a teenager in Newark, Baraka reveled in mixing with the
postgame throngs at the Grand Hotel, where "Everybody's super
clean and high-falutin'." Monte Irvin recalls, "To the fans, the hotel
presented an opportunity to join the ballplayers' special circle."[22]
This circle often included not just ballplayers, but the entertainment royalty of black America—jazz musicians, dancers, actors and
actresses, theater and movie stars, and boxers like Jack Johnson
and Joe Louis. Indeed, a close bond formed between the itinerant
athletes and performers. Entertainers often could be found at the
ballparks, rooting for their favorite clubs and clowning around
with their favorite players. The Mills Brothers loved to don Pittsburgh Crawford uniforms and work out with the club. When they
appeared at team owner Gus Greenlee's Crawford Grille, Satchel
Paige, a talented singer, would return the favor, joining them on
stage for impromptu jazz sessions. In Memphis, where Martin
Park bordered the Beale Street music district, bluesman B. B. King
would set up near first base and sing as the fans filed in. Lena
Horne, whose father was Gus Greenlee's right-hand man, appeared
frequently at Negro League games. The New York Black Yankees,
co-owned by dancer Bill "Bojangles" Robinson, attracted a parade

of celebrities to games at Dyckman's Oval in Harlem. When Count Basie was in Kansas City on a Sunday, he headed out to see the Monarchs, "because that's where everyone else was going on a Sunday afternoon."[23]

The games themselves, particularly season openers and Sunday games, were festive occasions in the black community. As the *Chicago Defender* reported in 1923, fans would turn out for the first home game "like a lot of bees hidden away all winter . . . getting active when the sun shines."[24] The contests often marked the culmination of daylong celebrations. David Wyatt, a former player turned sports reporter, described the scene in Indianapolis in 1917:

The big noise, the mammoth street parade, swung into motion promptly at 10 o'clock upon Saturday. There were something like one hundred conveyances of the gasoline, electric or other propelling types in the line . . . occupied by persons of both races, some internationally known to fame. . . . [We] jammed the downtown district and went on our way rejoicing.[25]

In Kansas City the Monarchs' Booster Club organized an annual parade that snaked through the city's black district and arrived at the park in time for the opening ceremonies.[26] These ceremonies in most cities featured high school bands, color guards, prominent black celebrities, or black and white politicians to throw out the first pitch.

Indeed, as the African-American citizenry in northern cities expanded in numbers and influence, baseball stadiums became a prime location for politicians courting the black vote. In Atlantic City in the 1920s the Bachrach Giants were named for Mayor Henry Bachrach, who had brought an African-American team up from Florida to entertain the resort town's growing population of black hotel workers. Playing at a converted dog track near the Boardwalk, the Bachrach Giants became a popular fixture and an advertisement for the mayor for the remainder of the decade. Indiana Governor Harry Leslie, hoping to rebuild black support for the Republicans in the wake of the party's flirtation with the Ku Klux Klan, threw out the first pitch at the ABCs home opener in 1930.[27] Although attendance by governors proved rare, in the 1930s and 1940s big-city mayors routinely kicked off the local black season. When Pittsburgh Crawfords' owner Gus Greenlee unveiled his new stadium in 1932, the mayor, city council, and county commissioner all attended. In 1935 Mayor Fiorello La Guardia performed the first-pitch honors at a Brooklyn Eagles–Homestead Grays game, and Cleveland Mayor Harry L. Davis joined 8,000 fans at a match between the Crawfords and American Giants honoring Ohio State track star Jesse Owens. The mayors of Baltimore, Kansas City, and Newark all frequently appeared at opening games. The mayor of Newark, recalls Jerry Izenberg, could avoid the Eagles' home opener only "if he chose not to be re-elected."[28]

Opening day and Sunday contests attracted a wide cross section of the African-American community, dressed in their finest clothes. A white writer who attended a Sunday game in Detroit in 1922 reported, "All the youth, beauty, and chivalry of local African aristocracy is there to see and be seen. The latest 'modes and the most advanced fashions in "nobby suitings for young men" are on view'. . . . Gallons of perfumery and tons of powder are expended on this great social event." The tradition continued into the 1940s. Memphis blues/soul singer Rufus Thomas recalls: "They put on their best frocks, the best suits, the best everything they had and went to the ballgame and when they would sit up there watching the game, it looked like a fashion parade." For a rookie pitcher, like Newark's James Walker, the intimidating scene "looked like a big cloud of flowers of different colors."[29]

The Sunday spectacle, according to Newark resident Connie Woodruff, represented "a combination of two things, an opportunity for all women to show off their Sunday finery" and "a once a week family affair." People would arrive, according to Woodruff, "with big baskets of chicken, potato salad, all the things you would have on a picnic . . . it was the thrill of being there, being seen, seeing who they could see."[30] For recent arrivals from the South, Sunday games often served as reunions. Lena Cox, the sister of

Homestead Grays' star Buck Leonard, had migrated from Rocky Mount, North Carolina, to Washington, D.C. "You would see everyone from home when you went to the ball game," she recalled. Many people went directly from church to the ballpark. Clubs often played benefit games for churches and gave free passes to ministers, who, in return, urged their flocks to accompany them to the games. In Washington, D.C., where Elder Michaux operated a popular church across the street from Griffith Stadium, his parishioners would cross Georgia Avenue to catch the Homestead Grays in action during the 1940s after the service.[31]

The Sunday games, asserted Black Yankees outfielder Charlie Biot, "were THE event of the week." Teams capitalized on the popularity of these contests by throwing their star pitchers and scheduling four-team doubleheaders. According to an intimate of Rube Foster, Foster commanded Negro National League affiliates in the 1920s that "no star twirler was used to the limit before a small Saturday crowd with the prospects of a good Sunday attendance." In Memphis in the 1940s ace Verdell Mathis became known as the "Sunday Feature," because he almost always hurled the first game of the scheduled doubleheader.[32]

This emphasis on Sunday games, however, also revealed the limitations of black baseball. The black professional game depended, as Janet Bruce has written, "on an impoverished people who had too little discretionary money and too little leisure time."[33] As most blacks who could afford to attend games worked or searched for casual work six days a week, Sunday was often the only day they could attend games. Sunday matchups usually attracted between 4,000 and 8,000 fans; weekday contests drew a few hundred. As Foster noted, "There are only twenty-seven Sundays and holidays in the playing season. It is a proven fact that on Sundays only have clubs been able to play at a profit. The weekdays have on many occasions been a complete loss."[34] Since several states, most notably Pennsylvania, had "blue laws" prohibiting Sunday games, teams like the Hilldale Club lost these lucrative home dates. Teams that shared facilities with white major and minor league squads could only schedule home Sunday dates when the host club was on the road. A few Sunday rainouts could devastate a team's narrow profit margin.

Attempts to stage a World Series between the champions of the Negro National League and the Eastern Colored League in 1924 illustrated the problem. Since black fans in any city could not be expected to afford tickets for more than a few consecutive games, the ten-game series pitting the Hilldale Club against the Monarchs was played not just in Philadelphia and Kansas City, but in Baltimore and Chicago as well. Three Sunday dates attracted an average of almost 7,000 fans a game. Two Monday games, including the finale to a tightly contested series, attracted crowds of 534 and 1,549. This pattern continued into the 1930s and 1940s. The Newark Eagles, for example, averaged 4,293 Sunday admissions in 1940, but only 870 on other days.[35]

These realities of black baseball exposed a great deal about the complex racial dynamics of America. As early as 1911 David Wyatt pointed out that "baseball can not live or thrive upon the attendance of colored only," and noted the necessity of scheduling weekday games against white teams. As Neil Lanctot demonstrates, the success of the Hilldale Club in the early 1920s stemmed from the availability of white opponents. Hilldale played almost two-thirds of its games against white semiprofessional and industrial teams.[36]

White baseball fans across the nation attended games that pitted black teams against white semiprofessional and professional squads, but most whites had minimal exposure to top-level competition between black athletes. The daily press in most cities rarely covered constructive black activities of any kind. When several white papers deigned to mention the 1924 Negro World Series, the *Kansas City Call* observed, "Negro sport has done what Negro Churches, Negro lodges, Negro business could not do . . . shown that a Negro can get attention for a good deed well done, and that publicity is no longer the exclusive mark of our criminals." In the 1930s and 1940s Effa Manley discovered that "it was next to impossible to get much space in the white metropolitan dailies."[37] Reports of games that found their way into the white press often lampooned the fans and festivities or referred to the players as "duskies" and other racist terms.

White fans appear to have been more likely to attend all-black games in the early years of the century. In 1907 a three-game series in Chicago between the Indianapolis ABCs and Lincoln Giants attracted 30,000 fans of both races. "There was no color line anywhere; our white brethren outnumbered us by a few hundred, and bumped elbows in the grandstands . . . the box seats and bleachers," reported Wyatt. The ABCs, Monarchs, Hilldales, and Lincoln Giants (who played in Harlem) all reported substantial white attendance during these years.[38] During the 1920s, however, perhaps due to the more rigid segregation arising in response to the Great Migration and 1919 race riots, white attendance dropped to 10 percent or less. Efforts to bolster profits by attracting more whites inevitably proved unsuccessful. In 1939 Effa Manley made a strong effort to lure whites to Newark Eagles' games, but the *Philadelphia Tribune* reported in 1940 that "Up in Newark . . . [one] would have seen 95 colored faces for every five white ones." Chicago reporter Fay Young frequently criticized attempts to get more whites to the games. Although the leagues had employed white promoters to bolster attendance at all-star games in Chicago and New York in 1939, observed Young, the 32,000 fans in Chicago included only 1,500 whites, and "the white people in New York didn't give a tinker's damn about Negro baseball." Two years later, Young noted, the crowd of 50,000 people who attended the East–West game "didn't have 5,000 white people out."[39]

Although whites rarely attended Negro League games, blacks in many cities frequented major and minor league ballparks. Many African Americans, particularly those who read only mainstream newspapers, were more aware of white baseball than the black alternative. "Scores of people in Harlem . . . do not know there is a colored baseball club in the city," alleged the *Amsterdam News* in 1929. The *Philadelphia Tribune* reported that black children attending a Hilldale game in the 1920s "had heard of Cobb, Speaker, Hornsby and Babe Ruth and other pale-faced stars, but knew not that they had players of their own group who could hold their

own with any stars of any league." Buck O'Neil recalled that as
children in Florida he and his friends, unfamiliar with black baseball, emulated the intensely racist Ty Cobb and other major league
players in their imaginary games.[40]

African-American newspapermen repeatedly chided blacks for
supporting organized baseball. "It is bad enough to ride on Jim
Crow cars, but to go into ecstasies over a Jim Crow sport is un-
forgivable," admonished the *Chicago Whip* in 1921. Two years later
a sportswriter in Washington, D.C., where African Americans av-
idly rooted for the Senators, asked, "Why then should we continue
to support, foster and fill the coffers of a national enterprise that
has no place or future for men of color, although they have the
ability to make the grade?"[41] Wendell Smith offered a scathing
critique of black fans in 1938:

> Why we continue to flock to major league ball parks, spend-
> ing our hard earned dough, screaming and hollering, stamp-
> ing our feet and clapping our hands, begging and pleading
> for some white batter to knock some white pitcher's ears off,
> almost having fits if the home team loses and crying for joy
> when they win, is a question that will probably never be set-
> tled satisfactorily. What in the world are we thinking about
> anyway?
>
> The fact that major league baseball refuses to admit Negro
> players within its folds makes the question just that much
> more perplexing. Surely, it's sufficient reason for us to quit
> spending our money and time in their ball parks. Major
> league baseball does not want us. It never has. Still we con-
> tinue to help support this institution that places a bold "Not
> Welcome" sign over its thriving portal and refuse to patronize
> the very place that has shown that it is more than welcome
> to have us. We black folks are a strange tribe![42]

The presence of black fans at white games grated for many reasons. As a Kansas City minister commented about the patronage
of white-owned businesses, "All of that money goes into the white

man's pocket and then out of our neighborhood." The prevalence of segregated seating provoked additional irritation. In St. Louis, where fans had to sit in a separate area behind a screen, a black newspaper condemned fans who ignored the St. Louis Stars, but chose to "fork over six bits to see a game at Sportsman's Park . . . and get Jim Crowed in the bargain." In Kansas City blacks faced segregated seating at minor league Blues games throughout the 1920s. When former major league catcher Johnny Kling bought the team in the 1930s, he ended this policy, but when the Yankees purchased the club in 1938, the organization reinstituted Jim Crow. Other ballparks, like Griffith Stadium in Washington, had no formal policy dividing the races, but African Americans always sat in specific areas of the outfield. "There were no signs," remembered one black Senators fan. "You just knew that was where you would sit."[43]

Many of these same ballparks regularly hosted Negro League and other black contests. After 50,000 fans attended the all-star extravaganza at Comiskey Park in 1941, Fay Young protested, "The East versus West game ought to make Chicago folk get busy and have a ballyard of their own. Why is it we have to 'rent' the other fellows belongings?" But the cost of constructing a stadium fell beyond the limited resources of most team owners. Only a handful of teams—the Memphis Red Sox, the Pittsburgh Crawfords in the 1930s, and the Nashville Elite Giants—owned the stadiums they played in.[44] Most leased or rented facilities usually controlled by whites, often in white neighborhoods, and governed by the unpredictable racial mores of the era.

The thorny issue of acquiring a place for black teams to play further illustrated the complex American racial dynamics. For the independent clubs of the early twentieth century, the ability to secure reliable access to a playing field often elevated the team from sandlot to professional level. After 1907 the Indianapolis ABCs held a lease to play at Northwestern Park, a small black-owned stadium in the city's African-American district. The club advertised itself as one of the few black teams to "own their own park" and its ability to guarantee playing dates attracted a steady stream of frontline opponents. In the 1910s Ed Bolden obtained the use of Hilldale Park in Darby, Pennsylvania, just outside Philadelphia. Connected by trolley to Philadelphia's African-American area, Hilldale Park seated 8,000 fans, providing Bolden's Hilldale Club with a steady following.[45]

Hilldale Park was a curious affair, with several trees and tree stumps scattered through the outfield and a hazardous depression that ran across center field. Indeed, many of the ballparks left much to be desired as playing fields. Early teams in Newark performed at Sprague Stadium, hemmed in on one side by a laundry building so close to the infield that balls hit on its roof became ground-rule doubles. The Baltimore Black Sox played in what the *Afro-American* called "a sewer known as Maryland Park, which featured broken seats, holes in the roof, nonworking toilets and weeds on the field."[46]

As the popularity of black baseball increased, however, teams began renting larger and better white-owned facilities from recreation entrepreneurs or major and minor league teams. Some parks were located in black neighborhoods, but others brought players and fans across town into white districts. When the White Sox abandoned 18,000-seat South Side Park in Chicago's Black Belt for the new Comiskey Stadium, Charles Comiskey's brother-in-law, John Schorling, refurbished the arena and offered it to Rube Foster's American Giants. After 1923 the Kansas City Monarchs leased Muehlebach Stadium, home of the Kansas City Blues of the American Association, another ballpark located in a black section. The Detroit Stars, on the other hand, played at Mack Park, situated amid a German working-class neighborhood. After Mack Park burned down in 1929 the Stars moved to a field in Hamtramck, a Polish community.[47]

Playing in a white-owned facility raised numerous problems for black teams and players. Many stadiums refused to allow African-American players to use the locker rooms. When the Pittsburgh Crawfords or Homestead Grays played at Ammons Field or Forbes Field, the players had to dress and shower at the local YMCA. Some ballparks, like American Association Park in Kansas

City, where the Monarchs played from 1920 to 1922, insisted on segregated seating, even for Negro League games.[48] The shift from a small black-owned arena to a larger white-owned one also raised the specter of racial betrayal. The 1916 move by the ABCs from Northwestern Park to Federal League Park posed a familiar dilemma. Switching to the new park placed the ABCs in a modern facility, comparable to many major league fields. However, as the *Indianapolis Freeman* complained, the relocation would transfer rent and concession money as well as jobs from blacks to whites.[49] When the Lincoln Giants moved their games from Olympic Stadium in Harlem to the more distant, but attractive Protectory Oval, the *New York Amsterdam News* protested, "To see a good baseball game in which colored men engage you now have to travel miles out of the district."[50]

By the late 1930s and early 1940s several major and minor league teams had discovered that renting their stadiums for Sunday Negro League doubleheaders could be a lucrative proposition. In 1932 the New York Yankees began scheduling four-team doubleheaders at Yankee Stadium when the Yankees were on the road. In 1939 the Yankees even donated a "Jacob Ruppert Memorial Cup," named after the team's late owner, to the black club that won the most games at the stadium that year. By the end of the decade the Yankees also rented out the ballparks of their Kansas City and Newark affiliates to the Monarchs and Eagles.[51] In 1939 the Baltimore Orioles, who had previously refused to allow the Elite Giants to use Oriole Park, accepted several Sunday dates. The Homestead Grays played regular Sunday dates at Griffith Stadium starting in 1940, averaging better than 10,000 fans a game. Even Shibe Park in Philadelphia, where blacks had rarely played previously, began scheduling Negro League games in the 1940s.[52]

These bookings marked important breakthroughs. They demonstrated the economic potential of black baseball fans and their respectability as well. As the *Kansas City Call* commented in a 1949 editorial, "From a sociological point of view, the Monarchs have done more than any other single agent to break the damnable outrage of prejudice that exists in this city. White fans, the thinking class at least, can not have watched the orderly crowds at Association Park . . . and not concede that we are humans at least, and worthy of consideration as such."[53]

Perhaps the most significant area of racial controversy revolved around the white owners and booking agents who profited from black baseball. In 1917 David Wyatt derided "the white man who has now and in the past secured grounds and induced some one in the role of the 'good old Nigger' to gather a lot of athletes and then used circus methods to drag a bunch of our best citizens out, only to undergo humiliation, with all kinds of indignities flaunted in their faces, while he sits back and grows rich off a percentage of the proceeds."[54] Yet, as Wyatt well knew, few African Americans in the early twentieth century had the resources to underwrite a baseball enterprise. As *Pittsburgh Courier* columnist Rollo Wilson observed in 1933: "Mighty few teams have been entirely financed by Negro capital. . . . There have been many instances of so-called Negro 'owners' being nothing but a 'front' for the white interest behind him."[55] Before the 1930s, when the urban "numbers kings" began bankrolling Negro League franchises, economic survival almost always required either partial or complete white ownership or an alliance with white booking agents who controlled access to playing fields.

Both contemporaries and historians have frequently portrayed white booking agents as the Shylockian villains of black baseball. Operating in a universe in which few African-American teams owned playing fields, these baseball entrepreneurs controlled access to the best ballparks and many of the most popular opponents. Nat Strong personified these individuals. A former sporting goods salesman, Strong, like the men who founded vaudeville, had glimpsed an opportunity to profit along the fringes of American entertainment. Recognizing the broad interest in semiprofessional baseball in the 1890s, Strong gained control of New York-area ball fields like Dexter Park in Queens that hosted these games. He rented out these facilities to white and black teams alike and gradually expanded his empire to include a substantial portion of the East Coast. In 1905 Strong formed the National Association of

Colored Professional Clubs of the United States and Cuba, which booked games for the Philadelphia Giants, Cuban X Giants, Brooklyn Royal Giants, and other top eastern black squads.[56]

Any team hoping to schedule lucrative Sunday dates at a profitable site had to deal with Strong, who systematically attempted to secure a monopoly over black professional baseball. Teams that defied Strong found themselves barred from the best bookings. When John Connors, the black owner of the Royal Giants, obtained a playing field in 1911 and attempted to arrange his own games, Strong blacklisted teams that dealt with Connors. Within two years Strong had wrested control of the rebellious franchise from Connors.[57] Black teams also resented the fact that Strong paid a flat guarantee rather than a percentage of the gate, allowing him to reap the profits from large crowds. Behavior like this led former player and organizer Sol White to remark in 1929, "There is not a man in the country who has made as much money from colored ballplaying as Nat Strong, and yet he is the least interested in its welfare."[58]

The creation of the original Negro Leagues in the 1920s occurred against this backdrop. Historians have usually accepted Rube Foster's descriptions of his Negro National League (NNL) as a purer circuit than the rival Eastern Colored League (ECL). Black owners predominated in the NNL; white owners, particularly Strong, prevailed in the ECL. Foster vehemently dismissed the ECL as a tool of Strong. Yet, the reality of the two leagues was more complex.

As Neil Lanctot has demonstrated, the key figure of the ECL was not Strong, but its president, Ed Bolden. Bolden, a black Philadelphia-area postal worker, had elevated the Hilldale Club of Darby, Pennsylvania, from a sandlot team into a frontline independent competitor. In 1918, when Strong had attempted to gain control of the Hilldale Club, Bolden sent an open letter to the *Philadelphia Tribune*, proclaiming, "The race people of Philadelphia and vicinity are proud to proclaim Hilldale the biggest thing in the baseball world owned fostered and controlled by race men. . . . To affiliate ourselves with other than race men would be a mark against our name that could never be eradicated."[59] Yet, five years later Bolden allied with Strong to form the ECL. Bolden, heavily dependent on scheduling nonleague games at locales like Dexter Park, owned or controlled by Strong, recognized the benefits of amalgamation. "Close analysis will prove that only where the color line fades and co-operation instituted are our business advances gratified," wrote Bolden in 1925.[60]

If, as Foster and black sportswriters alleged, Strong "was the league and ran the league," his conduct certainly belied this accusation. The ECL failed, in no small measure, because Strong's Brooklyn Royal Giants refused to adhere to the league schedule. A traveling team with no home base, the Royal Giants frequently bypassed games with league opponents if offered more lucrative bookings. In 1924 the league commissioners voted the Royal Giants out of the ECL, but relented when Strong promised his team would play all scheduled games. His failure to adhere to this pledge greatly weakened the league.[61]

As Bolden noted, however, the Negro National League also had a "few [white] skeletons lurking in the closet."[62] The most visible white presence in the NNL was league secretary J. L. Wilkinson, the owner of the Kansas City Monarchs. Wilkinson represented the best in Negro League ownership, white or black. As Wendell Smith later saluted, he "not only invested his money, but his very heart and soul" in black baseball. But Wilkinson always remained conscious of the need to portray the Monarchs as a black institution. African Americans Dr. Howard Smith and Quincy J. Gilmore became the public faces of the Monarchs, attending league meetings and riding in the lead car at the opening game festivities.[63] In Detroit, first Tenny Blount and later Mose Walker fronted for white businessman John Roesink as owner of the Stars. Most significantly, Foster himself was not the sole owner of the Chicago American Giants. John Schorling, owner of Schorling Stadium, the team's home grounds, underwrote the American Giants and split all profits evenly with Foster. After the *Chicago Broad Ax* protested in 1912 that Schorling received proceeds that "should be received by the Race to whom the patrons of the game belong," Foster concealed Schorling's role. Nonetheless, other NNL owners remained suspicious of Schorling's influence and, when Foster became ill in 1926, Schorling assumed sole ownership of the team.[64]

Nor was the NNL free from the tyranny of booking agents. In this instance, however, the key figure was Foster. As early as 1917 Foster had seized control of scheduling in the Midwest. As president of the NNL, Foster booked all league games and received 5 percent of the gate. Critics leveled charges against Foster's domination similar to those directed at Nat Strong in the East. St. Louis Giants secretary W. S. Ferrance protested Foster's profits, noting, "There was not a man connected [with the league] that was not in a position to book his own club and had been doing so for years." Others charged that Foster guaranteed lucrative Sunday home games for his American Giants. One black writer charged that Foster's "Race baseball league" was designed to "extend his booking agency," just as Foster accused Strong of manipulating the ECL.[65]

Racial controversies also arose in the operations of both leagues, most notably over the issue of employing white umpires. Fay Young protested in 1922, "It isn't necessary for us to sit by the thousands watching eighteen men perform in the national pastime, using every bit of strategy and brain work, to have it all spoiled by thinking it is impossible to have any other man officiating but pale faces."[66] Many owners believed that white arbiters could exercise more authority and better control player rowdiness. They also argued that few blacks had the requisite experience to offer competent officiating. "The colored umpire does not have the advantage that the white umpire has, in passing from sandlot ball to the minor leagues and then to the majors," contended Baltimore Black Sox owner George Rossiter. "As a result of his inexperience he is not able to deliver the goods." Nonetheless, many fans and sportswriters agreed with the verdict of the *Philadelphia Tribune*, which argued, "Regardless of the reason for colored ball games having white umpires it is a disgusting and indefensible practice" and "a reflection on the ability and intelligence of colored people."[67]

The very presence of white owners also continued to rankle many in the African-American community. After a tragic fire injured 219 black fans at Mack Park in Detroit in 1929, some blacks organized a boycott protesting white owner John Roesink's "failure to advertise in 'shine' newspapers, his arrogant, insulting attitude toward patrons of the game" and "his failure to compensate, or visit or even speak kindly to any of the persons injured in the catastrophe at Mack Park." The boycott reportedly "brought Roesink down from his 'high horse' " and elicited a promise that he would stay away from the park and allow his black assistant Mose Walker to operate the Stars.[68] That same year the *Baltimore Afro-American* attacked the local Black Sox on the umpire issue. Ignoring the fact that both white-owned and black-owned teams employed whites, the *Afro-American* maintained, "If the Sox management were colored, we'd have colored umpires tomorrow."[69]

Both the NNL and ECL collapsed with the onset of the Great Depression. By this time a group of unorthodox, but highly successful, black businessmen wealthy enough to finance black professional baseball had arisen in many cities. Cuban Stars' impresario Alessandro (Alex) Pompez pioneered this new breed of owner in the 1920s. Pompez, a Cuban American born in Florida, reigned as the numbers king of Harlem. The numbers game was a poor man's lottery. For as little as a nickel, individuals could gamble on hitting a lucky combination of three numbers and winning a payoff of 600 to 1. Since the true odds of winning were 999 to 1, considerable profits awaited a resourceful and reliable man who could oversee the operation. Pompez reportedly grossed as much as $7,000 to $8,000 a day from his organization. In the 1920s Pompez purchased Dyckman's Oval, a park and stadium in Harlem, and staged a variety of sports events including boxing, wrestling, and motorcycle racing. Pompez, who had strong connections in Cuba and a keen eye for baseball talent, formed the Cuban Stars to play at Dyckman's Oval. In 1923 they joined the ECL, one of only two black-owned clubs in the league. During the 1930s he owned the New York Cubans. Pompez imported top Cuban players like Martin Dihigo and Luis Tiant, Sr., to perform for his teams.[70]

The numbers operations run by Pompez and others were illegal but widely accepted in black America. In a world in which African Americans had few legitimate business opportunities, many of the most talented and resourceful entrepreneurs, men who, according to novelist Richard Wright, "would have been steel tycoons, Wall street brokers, auto moguls had they been white,"[71] entered the numbers racket. Some, like Jim "Soldier Boy" Semler of New York or Dick Kent of St. Louis, were ruthless gangsters, prone to violence and intimidation.[72] Others, like Pompez and Gus Greenlee of Pittsburgh, although not averse to using strong-arm methods to expand and defend their empires, won reputations as community benefactors. Often these numbers kings turned a portion of their profits back into the black community through loans, charity, and investments.[73]

In the 1930s black gambling barons throughout the nation began to follow Pompez into baseball. In Pittsburgh Gus Greenlee, a Pompez friend and protégé whose peak income has been estimated at $20,000 to $25,000 a day, launched the Pittsburgh Crawfords. In Detroit Everett Wilson, numbers partner of John Roxborough who managed Joe Louis, bought the Detroit Stars from John Roesink. Abe Manley, a retired numbers banker from Camden, owned first the Brooklyn and then the Newark Eagles. Semler ran the New York Black Yankees and Rufus "Sonnyman" Jackson supplied needed capital for Cum Posey's Homestead Grays. When Greenlee united the eastern teams into a new Negro National League in 1933, league meetings, according to Donn Rogosin, brought together "the most powerful black gangsters in the nation."[74]

Their wealth, power, and influence within the black community notwithstanding, the numbers kings still had to make their way in a white-dominated world. Of the Negro National League teams of the 1930s and 1940s, only the Pittsburgh Crawfords owned and operated their own stadium. All teams still relied heavily on white booking agents for scheduling. Nat Strong had died in the early

1930s, but William Leuchsner who ran Nat C. Strong Baseball Enterprises in the New York area, and Eddie Gottlieb, who operated out of Philadelphia, now ruled Strong's domain.[75] In the Midwest, where a new Negro American League formed in 1937, Abe Saperstein, better known as the founder of the Harlem Globetrotters, had succeeded Rube Foster as the preeminent booking agent. Saperstein even received 5 percent of the substantial gate at the East-West showcase.[76] These arrangements were not without benefits for Negro League teams. Gottlieb, for example, coordinated ticket sales and newspaper and poster publicity for events he booked, enabling teams to reduce their overhead and maintain fewer employees. The booking agents also negotiated reduced rental, operating, and insurance fees from major and minor league ballparks. The Homestead Grays reported that Gottlieb's intervention with the New York Yankees saved league owners $10,000 in 1940.[77]

Nonetheless, many owners bridled at the influence of white booking agents and repeatedly sought to be free of them. According to Effa Manley, who owned the Newark Eagles with her husband Abe, "[We] fought a . . . war against the booking agents from the first day [we] entered the picture . . . but [we] fought a losing battle. The tentacle-like grip of the booking agents proved impossible to break." Their resistance cost the Eagles their Yankee Stadium playing dates in 1939 and 1940. At the 1940 league meetings, the Manleys demanded the removal of Gottlieb as booking agent for Yankee Stadium. According to *Baltimore Afro-American* sports editor Art Carter, Effa Manley "assumed the position that the league was a colored organization and that she wanted to see all the money kept within the group." When Posey defended Gottlieb, Manley (who, although she lived as a black woman, later claimed to be white) denounced the Gray's owner as a "handkerchief head," a street-slang variation on "Uncle Tom."[78] That same year black sportswriters at the East–West game organized the American Sportswriters Association to protest Saperstein's domination of that event and the Negro American League removed Saperstein as its official booking agent. The fact that Strong,

Leuchsner, Gottlieb, and Saperstein were all Jewish injected elements of anti-Semitism into these disputes.[79]

The race issue also reared its head in hiring decisions. On several occasions teams hired whites to handle publicity in hopes that they might be able to better attract more whites to the games, much to the chagrin of black sportswriters. In the 1920s, when Ed Bolden hired a local white sportswriter as the ECL umpire supervisor to garner attention, John Howe of the *Philadelphia Tribune* called it inappropriate to hire whites in a league "of . . . for . . . and by Negroes." Greenlee employed Saperstein to publicize the East-West game in the 1930s, but the move brought out few white fans.[80] Even the Manleys, who demanded black control, had, in the words of sportswriter Ed Harris, "the temerity to hire a white press agent to do their work," evoking widespread criticism. One columnist noted, "Speaking of unholy alliances, how about the one between . . . the Negro owner of a Negro baseball team who hires a white press agent." Oliver "Butts" Brown of the *New Jersey Herald News*, protested: "No white publicity man could be of much assistance to you in the many things you hope to do to improve the condition of Negro baseball. In fact he would be a detriment."[81]

These conflicts and debates over the role of whites in black baseball revealed not just the racial tensions that always existed in the age of segregation, but the stake of African Americans in successful black-owned and -operated institutions. "Who owns the Grays?" reflected the *Washington Afro-American* in 1943. "It is a pleasure to inform the fans of Washington that the Washington Homestead Grays are owned and operated by three colored gentleman."[82] A scene at the opening game of the 1946 Negro League World Series captured this sense of pride. When heavyweight champion Joe Louis threw out the first pitch, he tossed a silver ball that had been awarded to the Cuban Giants, the first great black professional team, for winning a tournament in 1888. As James Overmyer writes, "With a sweep of his right arm, Louis, the greatest black athlete of his day, symbolically linked the earliest era of Negro baseball with its most recent high point."[83]

The World Series ceremony occurred at a critical juncture in the history of black baseball. In September 1946 Jackie Robinson was completing his successful first season in Organized Baseball. The response to Robinson revealed the fragile hold that all-black baseball held on the African-American psyche. From its earliest days, the promoters of the African-American game had made its transitional nature clear. In *The History of Colored Baseball* in 1906, Sol White advised the black ballplayer to take the game "seriously . . . as honest efforts with his great ability will open an avenue in the near future wherein he might walk hand-in-hand with the opposite race in the greatest of all American games." In a remarkably prescient passage, White added, "There are grounds for hoping that some day the bar will drop and some good man will be chosen out of the colored profession that will be a credit to all, and pave the way for others to follow."[84] Rube Foster had another vision, wherein an all-black team would pierce the ranks of the white professional leagues, but the model of ultimate integration remained. *The Crisis*, the journal of the National Association for the Advancement of Colored People, left no doubt as to the ultimate purpose of the Negro Leagues. "It is only through the elevation of our Negro league baseball that colored ballplayers will break into white major league ball," avowed *The Crisis* in 1938. Even as strong an advocate of "Race baseball" as Fay Young who railed against white umpires, publicity men, and booking agents, joined the chorus. "We want Negroes in the major leagues if they have to crawl to get there," wrote Young in 1945.[85]

Most people involved with black baseball had few illusions as to what the impact of integration would be. Asked about the prospect of blacks in the major leagues in 1939, Homestead Grays Manager Vic Harris replied, "If they start picking them up, what are the remaining players going to do to make a living? . . . And suppose our stars—the fellows who do draw well—are gobbled up by the big clubs. How could the other 75 or 80% survive?" Black sportswriters like Sam Lacy "knew [that integration] would have a devastating effect on black baseball."[86] Joe Bostic wrote in 1942:

Today, there are two Negro organized leagues, just on the threshold of emergence as real financial factors. . . . To kill [them] would be criminal and that's just what the entry of their players into the American and National Leagues would do.

Nor should money from the byproducts be overlooked such as the printers, the Negro papers and the other advertising media, which get their taste: the officials, scorekeepers, announcers, secretaries and a host of others. These monies are coming into Negro pockets. You can rest assured that we'd get none of those jobs in the other leagues, *even with a player or two in their leagues*.

In sum: From an idealist and democratic point of view, we say "yes" to Negroes in the two other leagues. From the point of practicality: "No."[87]

But for Lacy, Bostic, and others, "the idealistic and democratic point of view" won out. Less than three years after issuing his admonition, Bostic ardently pursued the policy he had condemned, confronting Branch Rickey with Negro League players Terris McDuffie and Dave Thomas and demanding a tryout with the Dodgers during spring training in 1945. Wendell Smith might criticize black fans for attending white games, but, working alongside Rickey, he became one of the key architects of baseball integration. Sam Lacy acknowledged, "After Jackie, the Negro Leagues [became] a symbol I couldn't live with anymore." For these sportswriters, as James Overmyer points out, "covering baseball integration [was] the biggest story of their lives" and they pursued it wholeheartedly.[88]

Throughout black America the focus shifted from the Negro Leagues to the major leagues. The African-American press reduced its coverage of the Negro Leagues to make room for updates and statistics about Robinson and other black players in Organized Baseball. Advertisements appeared for special rail excursions to National League cities to see Robinson play. Even the Negro Leagues themselves attempted to capitalize on Robinson's popularity. The cover of the 1946 Negro League yearbook featured Robinson rather than one of the established league stars. A program for the Philadelphia Stars in the late 1940s pictured Robinson in his Dodger uniform.[89]

Negro League fans voted with their dollars decisively in favor of integration. In 1946 Effa Manley found that "our fans would go as far as Baltimore" to see Robinson play for the Montreal Royals.[90] Once he joined the Dodgers and New York-area fans could see Robinson in eighty-eight games at Ebbets Field and the Polo Grounds, attendance plummeted for the Newark Eagles and New York Black Yankees. Other teams also felt the pinch. "People wanted to go to see the Brooklynites," recalled Monarch pitcher Hilton Smith. "Even if we were playing here in Kansas City, people wanted to go over to St. Louis to see Jackie."[91]

Occasionally critics raised their voices to protest the abandonment of black baseball. "Around 400 players are involved in the Negro version of the national pastime," warned Dan Burley in *The Amsterdam News* in 1948. "If there are no customers out to see them, they don't earn a living. In enriching the coffers of the major league clubs, we put the cart before the horse for no purpose."[92] But most commentators were less sympathetic. In response to Manley's complaints about declining fan support, the *Kansas City Call* cajoled, "The day of loyalty to Jim Crow anything is fast passing away. Sister, haven't you heard the news? Democracy is a-coming fast."[93] The Manleys sold the Eagles after the 1948 season. By the early 1950s all but a handful of the Negro League clubs had disbanded.

As Burley, Manley, and others had predicted, the end of segregation would mean that fewer, rather than more, African Americans would earn their living from baseball in the latter half of the twentieth century. The failure of major league teams to hire black managers, coaches, and front-office personnel compounded this problem. The nearly universal celebration of Jackie Robinson's triumph notwithstanding, integration would produce negative as well as positive consequences.

Cultural critic Gerald Early sees the demise of the Negro Leagues as the destruction of "an important black economic and cultural institution" that encompassed many of the best and worst elements of African-American life. Blacks, writes Early, "have never gotten over the loss of the Negro Leagues because they have never completely understood the ironically compressed expression of shame and pride, of degradation and achievement that those leagues represented."[94] In the final analysis, the black baseball experience captured the "twoness" in the "souls of black folk" as well as the "dogged strength" that kept them "from being torn asunder."

The Shot Heard
'Round the World

At 3:58 P.M. on October 3, 1951, New York Giants third base-man Bobby Thomson launched the most famous home run in baseball history. With two men on base in the bottom of the ninth inning of the third and final game of a playoff series between the Giants and their interborough rivals, the Brooklyn Dodgers, Thomson drove Ralph Branca's second pitch into the left field stands, lifting New York from a 4–2 deficit to a 5–4 victory, cap-ping perhaps the most dramatic pennant race ever staged. The feat instantly entered the nation's folklore, a symbolic signpost for a generation of Americans. "It was likely the most dramatic and shocking event in American sports and has since taken on the tran-scendent historic character of Pearl Harbor and the Kennedy As-sassination," observed journalist George W. Hunt in 1990. "Any-one alive then and vaguely interested can answer with tedious exactitude the question: 'Where were you when you heard it?' " Roger Angell calls it "baseball's grand exclamation point." Novelist Don Delillo used it to introduce *Underworld*, his fictional inquiry into the meaning of modern America. "Isn't it possible," mused Delillo, "that this midcentury moment enters the skin more last-ingly than the vast shaping strategies of eminent leaders, generals steely in their sunglasses—the mapped visions that pierce our dreams?"[1]

On the day after the home run, the *New York Daily News*, recalling Ralph Waldo Emerson's patriotic hymn, called Thomson's hit "the Shot Heard 'Round the Baseball World." A *New York Times* editorial invoked the same imagery, dubbing it "the home run heard 'round the world."[2] The two similar phrases merged in the popular memory, forever celebrating Thomson's triumph, in Emerson's exact phrase, as "the shot heard 'round the world."

Labeling Bobby Thomson's home run in this manner endowed the moment with several enduring, yet unintended ironies. In one sense it reflected American postwar arrogance about the country's centrality in world affairs: that people across the globe cared about all things American, including its idiosyncratic national pastime. Yet it also reflected Cold War reality. Hundreds of thousands of American military personnel stationed " 'round the world," in Europe and Asia, heard "the shot" via Armed Forces Radio. Millions of others who experienced the event as it occurred also literally *heard* it on radio broadcasts beamed not merely across the New York metropolitan area, but throughout the nation. Significantly, still others *saw*, rather than *heard* the shot in homes, in bars, or standing on the street outside store windows with television sets, many of them watching their first televised baseball game. Thus, Thomson's home run, the last great moment of radio sportscasting, simultaneously offered the first nationally televised sports highlight. These radio and television witnesses included untold numbers of African Americans drawn to a contest pitting the National League's two most racially integrated teams—the Jackie Robinson Dodgers and the Willie Mays Giants. Thus, baseball's "home run heard 'round the world"—stroked against Cold War and civil rights backdrops, situated at a crucial communication crossroads, and occurring at a juncture of critical changes in both baseball and society—offers a revealing glimpse of mid-century America.

For many fans and historians the 1951 playoffs mark the premiere highlight of a golden age of baseball that extended from the arrival of Jackie Robinson in 1947 to the uprooting of the Dodgers and Giants from New York to California a decade later. To a great extent, the retrospective romance of the era reflects the centrality of New York in both the baseball and American universe at mid-century. Although perhaps not as dominant as its provincial residents believed, and increasingly challenged by developments in Washington, D.C., Los Angeles, and other large cities, New York City at that moment remained the center of radio, television, publishing, and recording and theatrical culture. Events taking place in New York assumed an often-exaggerated significance. Furthermore, in no other era would New York baseball teams achieve the success they had over these eleven seasons. Between 1947 and 1957 a New York team appeared in the World Series every year but one. Seven of the eleven World Series pitted the Yankees against either the Dodgers or the Giants. The 1951 playoffs possessed a particular resonance. Despite baseball folklore about the great Giant-Dodger rivalry, the two teams had rarely battled for a pennant. Only in 1920, when the Dodgers finished first by seven games, and 1924, when the Giants edged the Brooks by a game and a half, had the teams finished in the top two slots in the National League. Played against the backdrop of the Jackie Robinson experiment, these matchups proved a formative signpost for an entire generation of New Yorkers.

There remains much to commend this idealized view. The game in 1951 seemed, both figuratively and literally, closer to the fans than later editions. Baseball still maintained the limited geographical configuration established a half-century earlier. Ten cities, none further south or west than St. Louis, hosted sixteen teams. Teams played in stadiums largely built in the teens and early twenties, located amid urban neighborhoods, within walking distance or streetcar and subway rides of most fans. The ballparks, most of which, like Ebbets Field, held between 30,000 to 40,000 fans, brought fans close to the action.

The players themselves were less remote and more accessible. Bobby Thomson and Ralph Branca, the two pivotal figures in the final game's final play, epitomized this link. Both came from large immigrant working-class families; both had been raised and lived in the New York area, and, according to legend, had kissed their mothers good-bye when they left for the game that morning. Thomson, born in Scotland, had come to the United States at the age of two. His family had settled in Staten Island, where he still lived. On the day of the game he commuted to Manhattan on the Staten Island Ferry. Branca, one of thirteen surviving children of an Italian father and Hungarian mother, had been born and raised and resided in Mount Vernon, New York. A local boy who made good, Branca was even engaged to marry the boss's daughter (Ann Mulvey, whose father owned 25 percent of the Dodgers) at the end of the season.[3]

Other Dodgers and Giants also had direct links with the metropolitan area. The Dodgers routinely scouted local prospects at the Parade Grounds, a complex of twenty-six baseball diamonds not far from Ebbets Field. As a goodwill gesture the Dodger club routinely signed about ten Brooklyn boys a year to play in its farm system. Although few of these aspirants ever made the Dodgers, those who did became local heroes. Reserve outfielder Cal Abrams, a graduate of James Madison High School and veteran of the Parade Grounds, was a particular favorite among the Jewish fans who honored him on a special "night" during the 1951 season.[4]

Even those who did not hail from the New York metropolitan area often seemed a part of the community. Players tended to live during the season, and sometimes all year, in the cities in which they appeared, rather than in affluent suburbs. Their salaries, although higher than the average workingman, rarely elevated them out of the working class. Most sought off-season employment to supplement their incomes. Physically, as well as financially, they weighed in only slightly above average. Relatively few exceeded six feet in height or 200 pounds in weight. Reporters described former Cleveland third baseman Al Rosen at five feet ten inches and 175 pounds as "big and burly."[5]

Like Thomson and Branca, the athletes on the 1951 Dodgers and Giants captured the polyglot makeup of postwar urban America. In addition to the distinctive racial mix, the teams included players representing a wide variety of ethnicities. A majority of the players hailed from the American South and Midwest. But the Giants' lineup—with Whitey Lockman, Don Mueller, and Larry Jansen—had a substantial contingent of German extraction. Sal Maglie, Carl Furillo, Branca, and Roy Campanella were the sons of Italian immigrants. Clem Labine was of French-Canadian heritage; Andy Pafko, Hungarian; Ray Noble, Cuban. Along the bench sat players with ethnic surnames like Abrams, Hermanski, Palica, Miksis, Koslo, and Podbielan. Many had served in the military during World War II. Several, like Gil Hodges, Monte Irvin, Billy Cox, and Furillo, had experienced active combat.

Yet the roseate glow adhering to these seasons obscures other more sobering truths. It is telling that the third game of the 1951 playoffs, despite the massive hype surrounding it, attracted only 34,320 fans, filling just two-thirds of the seats at the Polo Grounds. Threatening weather and the last-minute availability of tickets partially explain the attendance shortfall. But the less than capacity crowd also reflected baseball's new economic reality. At least when measured at the box office, baseball experienced a staggering decline in the early 1950s. From 1947 through 1949 the major leagues had drawn approximately 20 million fans a season. In 1951 the sixteen teams barely topped the 16 million mark (a figure that would further sag to 14.3 million in 1953.) The New York teams were not immune to the plague. Whereas 5.6 million people had attended Yankee, Dodger, and Giant games in 1947, in 1951, despite the great pennant race, only 4.3 million fans went through the turnstiles. Crowds were surprisingly small at several key junctures of the season. On August 28, after the Giants had won sixteen straight games to propel them back into contention, only 9,000 fans appeared at the Polo Grounds to see if they could extend this streak. At the home finales for the two clubs on September 22, only 19,000 people appeared at Ebbets Field; a scant 6,000 at the Polo Grounds.[6]

Commentators have advanced many explanations for baseball's mid-century attendance woes. Suburbanization drew fans away from the old ballparks, with automobiles replacing streetcars for many as the primary mode of access. With few stadiums equipped with adequate parking (Ebbets Field had only 750 spaces)[7] and most games now played at night and often televised, suburbanites found a trip to the ballpark a chore rather than an escape. Historian Ben Rader also attributes the decline to a "fundamental shift in urban leisure patterns," in which the suburban home, revolving around the television set, "became a self-sufficient recreation center," and the rapid growth of the suburbs drew people not just distant from inner-city ballparks, but into rival leisure pastimes. Charles Alexander notes that while urban Americans spent two-thirds of their recreation dollars on baseball in 1948, just two years later baseball accounted for less than half of these expenditures.[8]

Often lost in these discussions is the uniqueness of the post–World War II baseball boom. Before 1945 major league teams had never drawn consistently large crowds. Game attendance during the boom years of the 1920s averaged only 7,531 fans. During the Depression years it dropped to 6,578. In 1945, as the war drew to a close, the 10.8 million fans who attended games established a new record. In 1946 baseball, a symbol of the euphoric postwar celebration, nearly doubled its attendance as 18.5 million people flocked to ballparks. The figure rose to 19.8 million in 1947 and 20.8 million in 1948. Average game attendance between 1946 and 1949 jumped to an unprecedented 16,027.[9]

In retrospect, this bulge, which created new standards for major league attendance, was clearly an aberration rather than a new yardstick. The decline of the 1950s represented a correction to baseball's postwar bull market. Nor did this drop necessarily mean a corresponding decline in devotion. As Roger Kahn has noted, "The crowds watching television baseball multiplied and grew. Interest as opposed to attendance never flagged."[10] Even in 1953, when fan support slipped to its lowest level in the postwar era, attendance hovered almost one-third higher than in 1945 and 50 percent higher than most wartime and prewar seasons.

Yet major league owners drew several lessons from the attendance dip: most cities could not maintain more than one team; many of the older stadiums needed to be replaced, preferably with arenas with easier access to the suburbs and adequate parking; and cities outside the sacred circle of the Northeast and Midwest could offer new markets and larger crowds. In 1953 the Braves migrated from Boston to Milwaukee launching an era of relocation and expansion that would transform not just the map of baseball, but the game itself. By 1958, both the Dodgers and Giants would be in California. Although they did not realize it at the time, the fans watching and listening to the final game of the 1951 playoffs were bearing witness to the end of an era.

Two memorable artifacts of Thomson's shot have left the game indelibly etched in the nation's soul. The first is the remaining newsreel footage of the game, showing Branca's pitch, Thomson's swing, Dodger outfielder Andy Pafko standing at the wall looking up, and Thomson exuberantly romping around the bases, stomping on home plate into the jubilant arms of his Giant teammates. The second is a recording of Giants' radio announcer Russ Hodges's famous home run call:

> Branca throws again . . . there's a long fly . . . it's gonna be . . . I believe . . . the Giants win the pennant . . . the Giants win the pennant . . . the Giants win the pennant . . . the Giants win the pennant.

This description has been replayed so often as to create the illusion that most Americans who experienced the Thomson home run did so through Hodges's impassioned exclamations. In reality, if not for the improbable actions of a Dodger fan, Hodges's broadcast would long since have been forgotten. Neither teams nor radio stations routinely taped or preserved broadcasts in the early fifties. Thus, no full record of Hodges's work in the radio booth on October 3, 1951, has survived. However, Lawrence Goldberg, a Dodger fan listening to the game in Brooklyn, confident of a Dodger victory, decided to record Hodges's call of the final half-inning so that he could relive Hodges's anguish in defeat. Placing a primitive tape recorder next to his radio, Goldberg instead captured the classic home run call. A lesser man, or a more devious

Dodger diehard, might have destroyed the tape, but Goldberg called Hodges the next day. "I want you to have this tape," explained Goldberg, unwittingly creating a piece of Americana.[11]

If not for Goldberg's recording, our memories of Thomson's home run would be quite different. Only a small proportion of those experiencing the game did so via Hodges's broadcast. Indeed, Americans in general, and New Yorkers in particular, had an unprecedented range of options for partaking in the playoffs. The *New York Times* called the decision about which version of the game to tune in on, "the great schism of 1951. . . . The metropolis went quietly mad trying to figure out which radio station to listen to."[12] In New York City the playoffs were broadcast by Hodges and Ernie Harwell on WMCA, the Giant station, while Red Barber and twenty-three-year-old Vince Scully handled the Dodger accounts on WMGM. A group of radicals at CCNY heatedly debated the issue of Barber v. Hodges, finally compromising by alternating stations after each inning. Those opting for neutrality could settle for national broadcasts on the Mutual Network with "Brother Al" Helfer, a former Dodger and Giant announcer.[13]

Television offered yet another alternative. The Dodgers had televised the first playoff game, played at Ebbets Field, on Channel 9. The second and third games, at the Polo Grounds, were televised on Channel 11, the Giant station. Hodges and Harwell alternated the radio and television announcing chores. As the senior announcer, Hodges covered the middle three innings on television, allowing him to deliver the more crucial first and last three innings on the radio.[14]

As Yankee announcer Mel Allen later noted, the early fifties were an experimental era for radio and television. "In '51 and '52 they were both giants—both hating each other's guts, and the competition was conducive to baseball because they were both great vehicles for the game," commented Allen.[15] For those in the New York area, television had lost some, though not all, of its uniqueness by 1951. Many, if not most, New York homes possessed televisions. Others could partake in the "World Series special" offered by General Electric, allowing them to buy a seventeen-inch television for just $299.95 with weekly payments as low as $2.72. Those who did not own sets could watch with neighbors or relatives or in a variety of other venues. Bars and restaurants had long since discovered that televisions broadcasting sports events attracted patrons. As early as 1947 an estimated 3,000 New York City bars and grills had added televisions, prompting *Newsweek* to observe "Television is the best thing to happen to the neighborhood bar since the free lunch." Many watched the game in small crowds around televisions placed in windows of appliance and other stores. One twelve-year-old New Jersey boy later recalled watching the Thomson game on a television set up in a local Passaic bank.[16]

Nor was televised baseball a novelty. New Yorkers had watched the World Series on television since 1947. All three New York teams broadcast many of their home games during the regular season. In August 1951 the Dodgers had even experimented with color television. Ten thousand viewers received color wheels, allowing them to convert the images on their screens. Red Smith, who watched the game at CBS headquarters, found "the reproduction . . . excellent, striking, and only faintly phony." Gil Hodges's well-muscled arms "were encased in a pelt of somewhat lovelier tone—about the shade of medium roast beef—than Gil wears in real life." Dodger Manager Charlie Dressen's white uniform appeared "as immaculate as a prom queen's gown," until when walking along the grass, "he turned green, like cheap jewelry."[17]

Outside New York City fans had fewer options, but a nonetheless impressive array of choices. The dramatic expansion of television in the postwar era obscures the corresponding boom in radio broadcasting. The number of local radio stations in the nation doubled between 1945 and 1950. Baseball became a major staple of radio programming on the local, regional, and national levels. Several major league clubs, including the Dodgers and Giants, had established regional networks to carry their games. The St. Louis Cardinals, whose network encompassed over 120 stations in nine states, dispatched Harry Caray to the Polo Grounds to call the game live. The Giants network broadcast games over thirty-eight stations to an estimated audience of 3 to 4 million people.[18]

The Dodgers, in addition to a local regional network that reproduced Barber's broadcasts, had established a second innovative Dodger Network in 1950. This network broadcast Dodger games recreated by announcer Nat Allbright in a Washington, D.C., studio. It primarily targeted the South, where the Dodgers as the pioneers of baseball integration attracted a wide audience, primarily, although not solely, among African Americans. "They were . . . even in the South almost a matter of life and death," recalled Allbright. "You had whites who were praying for Big Newk (Don Newcombe) and Jackie Robinson to lose. You had blacks who wanted them to win." In Washington, D.C., broadcasts over the Dodger Network reportedly garnered higher radio ratings than Senators games.[19]

On the national level most fans absorbed their baseball on one of two networks: the Mutual Broadcasting System and the Liberty Broadcasting Network. In 1949 Mutual, the nation's largest network with 350 affiliates, contracted with major league baseball to air a Game of the Day every afternoon of the baseball season except Sundays. During the 1951 season Mutual carried 145 major league games over 520 stations, many of which had signed on specifically to carry its baseball programming.[20] Liberty was the creation of Texan Gordon McClendon. Beginning in 1949 McClendon, who dubbed himself "the Old Scotchman," bypassed major league licensing by purchasing game transcripts from Western Union and recreating his own games of the day from his studio in a Dallas suburb. By 1950 McClendon had established a network of 430 stations, mostly in the South and Southwest. Unlike Mutual, Liberty aired games on Sundays, and in 1950 added a "Game of the Night."[21]

McClendon became an institution in the postwar American South. Author Willie Morris, who grew up in Yazoo, Mississippi, recalled, "By two o'clock almost every radio in town was tuned in to the Old Scotchman. His rhetoric dominated the place. It hovered in the branches of the trees, bounced off the hills, and came out of the darkened stores." One out of four weeks each month, Liberty would broadcast live from a major league ballpark. In 1951

the *Sporting News* named McClendon its broadcaster of the year.
By that time his empire had grown so large that McClendon had
begun to limit his own on-air time to major events, turning over
the daily broadcasts to young announcers like Lindsay Nelson,
Jerry Doggett, and Buddy Blattner. On October 3, however,
McClendon manned a mike at the Polo Grounds, broadcasting live
to his devoted following. Indeed, more Americans may have heard
McClendon's home run call than either Hodges's or Barber's or
Helfer's on Mutual. Like Hodges, McClendon barked out, "The
Giants win the pennant!" Then after several moments of crowd
noise, the Old Scotchman added, "Well, I'll be a son of a mule."[22]

Television, not radio, however, had emerged as the major media
issue facing baseball in 1951. Four years earlier New York Yankee
General Manager Larry MacPhail, who had pioneered radio and
television broadcasts, had unsuccessfully attempted to block the
sale of television rights to the 1947 World Series, fearing that telecasts would drive down attendance. World Series attendance nonetheless remained high, but Dodger President Branch Rickey con-
curred in his arch-rival MacPhail's assessment of the impact of
television on the gate. When offered $150,000 to televise Dodger
games, Rickey rejected the proposed deal. "Radio stimulates interest. Television satisfies it," pronounced Rickey, predicting an ero-
sion of the fan base. Yet within a short time both the Yankees and
Dodgers (as well as the Giants) had capitulated to the lure of television revenues. From a business standpoint the choice was not
hard to make. By the mid-fifties the Dodgers earned more than
$750,000 for television and radio rights, a figure that exceeded the
player payroll by $250,000. "We were in the black before Opening
Day," allowed Dodger executive Buzzie Bavasi.[23]

Yet baseball, at least in the short run, had entered into a Faustian
bargain. Many observers blamed television for the decline in attendance in the early fifties. Veteran sportswriter Grantland Rice
opened the 1951 season with a *Sport* magazine broadside entitled
"Is Baseball Afraid of Television?," identifying television as "by all
odds the greatest problem baseball has faced in these 75 years." The
following season prompted articles by St. Louis Browns owner Bill

Veeck and sportswriter Dan Daniel, both of whom had advocated baseball telecasts in 1948, entitled "Don't Let TV Kill Baseball" and "TV Must Go—Or Baseball Will." "All we've got to sell are seats," argued Veeck. "If our ballparks are empty, what good does a TV sponsor's fee mean." Veeck also presciently predicted that "television would help widen the inequality that has existed for too long in baseball . . . the rich are getting richer and the poor are getting poorer."[24]

The 1951 Dodger-Giant playoffs added a new dimension to these debates. Prior to 1951 television shows could not be transmitted live from coast to coast. Programs produced in New York were filmed and then flown to California for western distribution. This hardly diminished the appeal of most early television, but it proved a poor substitute for live sports events. Several months prior to the playoffs, however, American Telephone and Telegraph had installed a coaxial cable allowing nationwide broadcasts. The 1951 World Series, scheduled to begin on October 2, was to be the first nationally televised sports event. Taking advantage of the new technology, the Dodger-Giant playoffs supplanted the Series as the pioneer programming. This development was so unexpected that CBS televised the regular Dodger broadcast of the first playoff game from Ebbets Field on October 1 nationally without a commercial sponsor. For games two and three from the Polo Grounds, however, Chesterfield cigarettes, the Giants' regular sponsor, agreed to pay the coast-to-coast transmission costs in exchange for commercial rights over NBC.[25]

The playoffs thus found a ready national audience. *Time* reported that in Los Angeles, where people "never used to get excited about the World Series," television purchases skyrocketed. Denver, according to *Time*, was experiencing not only its first live World Series, but its first television of any kind. Denver's Grand Palace Department store installed sets in its show windows and hotels placed televisions in their lobbies for the week. Other cities replicated the pattern found in earlier years in New York. When the Series began, "TV watchers . . . clotted around dealers' show windows, jockeyed cunningly for position at bars, ate with their eyes upraised in restaurants which had a video screen." Police erected barricades to control crowds watching the games.[26]

It is difficult to gauge how many people in the United States watched the third game of the 1951 playoffs on television. Many people still lived in areas that could not receive television transmissions, and most Americans outside the New York metropolitan area probably did not own televisions. Media reports focused primarily on the World Series, rather than the playoff television experience. *Look*, in an article entitled "The World Series Stare," estimated that 70 million people watched the first game of the 1951 World Series.[27] A lesser, but nonetheless unprecedented number probably saw Bobby Thomson instantaneously dash the Dodger pennant hopes, undoubtedly whetting their appetites for more televised baseball.

The phrase "shot heard 'round the world" possessed yet another irony. Although the vast majority of people in the world paid no heed to the events at the Polo Grounds, baseball, like the nation as a whole, seemed unusually focused on world affairs. The entire 1951 season had been played out against the backdrop of Cold War and Korean War tensions. The season opened on the day that General Douglas MacArthur, recently relieved from his command in Korea by President Harry S. Truman, arrived in the United States for his triumphal farewell tour. Thomson's home run coincided with President Truman's acknowledgment that the Soviet Union had detonated a second atomic bomb, confirming the end to the American nuclear monopoly.

These concerns never seemed far removed from the baseball diamond. MacArthur delivered his famous "Old soldiers never die" speech on April 19, the third day of the baseball season. He then faded not away, but into the midst of the first Dodger–Giant series of the season. On April 20, as President Truman threw out the first ball in Washington, D.C., to a chorus of boos, New York City held a massive ticker-tape parade honoring MacArthur. At the Polo Grounds the Giants delayed the starting time for their first game against the Dodgers by one hour to accommodate parade goers and recruited a marine wounded three times in Korea to throw out the first ball. MacArthur, who on arrival in the United States after a two-decade absence had listed baseball among the things he missed most, made a well-publicized appearance at the Polo Grounds on April 21. Forty-six thousand fans watched the general's son Arthur, seated alongside the general, throw out the first ball.[28]

MacArthur became a familiar figure at New York City ballparks, attending games at Yankee Stadium and Ebbets Field as well as the Polo Grounds. In May Dodger publicist Irving Rudd orchestrated MacArthur's Brooklyn debut with a lavish ceremony, featuring the World War II Nisei "go-for-broke" battalion and MacArthur materializing in full-dress uniform out of a limousine driven through a gate in the right field fence. MacArthur told the crowd, "I have been told that one hasn't really lived until he has been to Ebbets Field. I am delighted to be here." Nor was this mere rhetoric. The deposed general returned to Ebbets Field twelve more times in the course of the season and attended the playoff series as well. Major league owners joined the MacArthur mania, floating his name as a replacement for Commissioner Happy Chandler, who, like MacArthur, had been dismissed when he failed to please his superiors. When MacArthur declined, the owners offered the job to his colleague, Major General Emmett "Rosey" O'Donnell. President Truman, however, refused to release O'Donnell from active service.[29]

Cold War themes reverberated throughout the 1951 season. Sportswriters took to calling Giant second baseman Eddie Stanky, who in 1949 had set a National League record for walks, "Gromyko" for the Russian diplomat who had stormed out of the United Nations. When Dodger Manager Charlie Dressen chastised pitcher Irv Palica for lacking guts, a *New York Post* editorial challenged this "unfortunate statement." "The public does not readily associate courage with a game that children can play, especially when they turn the page and read the latest casualty lists from Korea," commented the *Post*. Dressen later blamed the Dodger collapse, in part, on the shortage of reserves created by the Korean War draft that had claimed 190 players out of the Dodger system. Those recalling the playoffs often did so within the context of the war. One group of Dodger fans watched the first game on TV while waiting to give blood for American combatants. A group of antiwar protesters at CCNY unanimously voted to adjourn their strategy meeting to listen to the third game.[30]

The *New York Times* also joined the Cold War chorus. The *Times* lead editorial on October 4 dealt with "The Russian Bomb," calling "it news of gravest import in the whole world." The *Times* immediately followed this dire pronouncement with an editorial beginning, "Well, the Giants exploded a bomb, too," invoking the image of a "home run heard 'round the world."[31]

The notion that events in baseball might have bearing on the Cold War had already been introduced by the game's unfolding racial drama. Only four years had passed since Jackie Robinson's historic breakthrough and major league desegregation had progressed grudgingly. Only three teams in each league fielded black players in 1951. Yet many observers grasped on the imagery of an integrated game as a potent propaganda weapon. In 1949 when Paul Robeson had questioned whether African Americans would participate in a war against the Soviet Union, the House Un-American Activities Committee recruited Robinson to rebut his charges.[32] A group of promoters proposed a world tour by the Brooklyn Dodgers and the Cleveland Indians, the most integrated team in the American League. They considered it "most important that the Negro race be well represented, as living evidence of the opportunity to reach the top which America's No. 1 sport gives all participants regardless of race."[33]

The 1951 Dodgers and Giants symbolized baseball's, and America's, impending racial revolution. The two New York squads accounted for all but one of the black players in the National League. (Sam Jethroe, the 1950 Rookie of the Year, whom the Boston Braves had acquired from the Dodgers, was the sole black player on the remaining six teams.) Both the Dodgers and Giants fielded several African Americans, almost all of whom had played critical roles in the pennant drive. During spring training both clubs toured the South, breaking down color barriers in many cities, while attracting overflow crowds of both black and white fans. It was not lost on contemporary observers that the two most integrated teams in the National League had finished in a dead heat for the pennant.

According to most accounts, racial harmony prevailed on both clubs. But the unique element of race always percolated just beneath the surface of the Giants and especially the Dodgers. The Giants began the season with four Negro League veterans: Monte Irvin, who would emerge as the team's leading slugger; Hank Thompson, the erratic, alcoholic third baseman; backup shortstop Artie Wilson; and journeyman Cuban catcher Ray Noble. Several key Giant performers including team leaders Stanky, Alvin Dark, and Whitey Lockman hailed from the South. Nonetheless, maintains Irvin, "We got along with those guys just fine . . . there was absolutely nothing racial on the ball club."[34]

Several incidents, however, illustrated the uncertain dynamics of the newly integrated game. Announcer Ernie Harwell claimed that the "fun-loving" Stanky took to calling Noble "Bushman." The catcher warned manager Leo Durocher, "I'll kill him if he calls me that again."[35] Giant personnel decisions raised the specter of a quota system limiting the number of blacks on the team. In late May the Giants management promoted African-American sensation Willie Mays to the major league club. The Giants had purchased Mays' contract from the Birmingham Black Barons of the Negro American League in 1950, and Mays had advanced through the Giants farm system at an unexpectedly rapid rate. Assigned to the Minneapolis Millers in 1951, just one step below the major leagues, Mays assaulted American Association pitching at a .477 rate while astounding eyewitnesses with his spectacular fielding. Giant Manager Durocher demanded that Mays be added to his squad. When the promotion came on May 27, the Giants demoted Artie Wilson, one of the four other African Americans, to make room for Mays. Several weeks later, the Giants sent slumping third baseman Hank Thompson to the minor leagues. For the third straight year they bypassed Negro League great Ray Dandridge as a solution to their perennial third base problem. The Giants left Dandridge stranded on their Minneapolis farm club and instead shifted outfielder Bobby Thomson, who had never played the position, to third.[36]

Had the Giants imposed a quota preventing them from keeping too many African Americans on the team? Many observers at the time and subsequent chroniclers of the 1951 Giants believe they had. "They'll deny it," Irvin later commented, "but I'm sure there was a quota system. . . . My feeling is they didn't want more than two or three blacks playing then."[37] Dandridge, arguably the greatest third baseman in baseball history and the American Association's Most Valuable Player in 1950, never made it to the majors.

The promotion of Mays injected yet another element into the racial mix. The twenty-year-old phenom captivated nearly everyone with his skills and exuberance. But responses to Mays, whose southern mannerisms and youthful naivete often reinforced racial stereotypes, revealed much about attitudes and assumptions of the time. The Giants assigned Irvin to room with Mays and, in Irvin's own words, to "look after him." Announcer Russ Hodges recalled that Irvin, "a man of quiet dignity and great pride . . . realized at once that Mays, as a potential national figure, must also be a credit to his race." Leo Durocher delighted in his own relationship with the young Mays, who always called him "Mr. Leo." Yet, as Roger Kahn notes, "There was always an Uncle Tom in Durocher's view of Mays. . . . He was the straw boss and Mays the plantation hand." Newspapers endowed Mays with a Stepin Fetchit discourse. One 1951 cartoon depicted Mays in action exclaiming, "Ah gives base runners the heave ho!" and "Ah aims to go up in the world."[38]

Revealingly, the three most important cogs of the 1951 Dodgers—Roy Campanella, who won the National League Most Valuable Player Award; twenty-game winner Don Newcombe; and Jackie Robinson—were the squad's only black players. Four years after Robinson's debut, all the reserves, other starting pitchers, and relief pitchers on the pioneer team of baseball integration were white. As always, the race issue on the Dodgers coalesced around Robinson. Robinson reigned at the peak of his playing prowess— batting .338, hitting a career-high nineteen home runs, scoring 106 runs, and setting National League records for second basemen in fielding percentage and double plays. On the final day of the regular season Robinson's heroics, including a game-saving catch in the eleventh inning and a game-winning home run in the fourteenth (prematurely dubbed by *New York Post* writer Arch Murray the "shot heard 'round the baseball world"), had forced the playoff series. In the aftermath of Thomson's home run a *New York Times* editorial addressed Robinson's almost supernatural mystique, acknowledging that "even the great Jackie Robinson must bow to miracles."[39]

Robinson was also at the peak of his talent for generating antagonism and controversy. On May 2 National League President Ford Frick chastised Robinson for his aggressive baserunning. When Robinson defiantly defended himself, Frick responded angrily, "I'm tired of Robinson's popping off. I have warned the Brooklyn club that if they don't control Robinson, I will." According to John Kiernan, Robinson, still unintimidated, countered, "And I'm getting tired of being thrown at. Let Mr. Frick change the color of his skin and go out and hit against Maglie." Three weeks later in Cincinnati Robinson received three letters threatening his life. After a close call at home plate and the ejection of Campanella in the ensuing argument cost the Dodgers a critical September contest against the Braves, newspapers falsely accused Robinson of smashing in the door to the umpire's dressing room. As Robinson later complained, the report led "millions of baseball fans to believe . . . that I am a foul-tempered character."[40]

One particular episode involving the Giants and Dodgers illustrates the pent-up racial undertones of the campaign. At Ebbets Field only a thin wall separated the clubhouses between the home and visiting teams. Losing players could hear the revelry in the other locker room. After one Dodger victory over the Giants, Robinson deliberately taunted his arch-rivals, tapping his bat against the wall and yelling insults. The enraged Giants began cursing back. Stanky shouted, "Stick that bat down your throat, you black nigger son of a bitch," only to find his teammate Irvin standing next to him. For Irvin it was a delicate situation. He had never been close to Robinson, and the Dodger-Giant rivalry rather than any racial solidarity dominated his thoughts. Angered by Robinson's tirade and anxious to retain harmony on the Giants, Irvin reassured his teammate. "That's just fine with me, Eddie," he told Stanky, later explaining, "I could have gone along with anything they said, I was that mad."[41]

The presence of Robinson, Irvin, Mays, and other black players reflected not just a social transition, but a profound change in the game on the field as well. As one sportswriter has noted, "Baseball in 1950 stood at the end of the era built by Babe Ruth," who had died two years earlier. It poised on the brink of an age forged by Robinson and, especially significant in 1951, by Willie Mays. Mays, with his indisputable excellence, convinced all but the most stalwart resisters to integration of the need to recruit African Americans. The Ruthian game had been characterized by what Bill James has described as a "one-dimensional offense . . . the baseball of the ticking bomb."[42] Black players would transform major league play. Led by Mays, they added the speed and flair that had characterized the Negro Leagues without sacrificing the power introduced by Ruth.

Indeed, in the fall of 1951 baseball, like America, seemed poised on the brink of change in many areas. In the nation's capital a House subcommittee launched the first congressional investigation into baseball's monopolistic practices, ending the game's isolation from government scrutiny. The season marked the first in which Walter O'Malley, who would emerge as the dominant personality of baseball's elite, guided the fortunes of the Dodgers. He had wrested control from Branch Rickey, architect of both baseball integration and its minor leagues, the symbol of an earlier era. The game also had a new commissioner, Ford Frick, named to the post just one week before the playoffs began. Frick, unlike his predecessors Kennesaw Mountain Landis and Happy Chandler, was a man drawn from the ranks of the game, not a politician. He would restore command over the game to the owners. In one of his first actions Frick limited unauthorized radio recreations of the game, dooming McLendon's Liberty Network. "Tonight, a chapter in the life of the American dream closes," lamented McLendon in his farewell broadcast.[43]

Another more subtle challenge to the traditions of the game was in evidence at the third game of the 1951 playoffs, though few people realized it at the time. Baseball, for all its fascination with statistics and recordkeeping, had always pursued a stalwartly unscientific and unsystematic course. Field managers guided the destinies of their teams "by the book," an unwritten compendium of arcane strategies and intuitive impulses. The two colorful, controversial managers at the Polo Grounds on October 3, 1951 — Leo Durocher of the Giants and his former protégé, Charley Dressen of the Dodgers — personified this approach. Dressen, renowned for taking credit for victories but blaming his players for losses, summed up his leadership philosophy as, "Stay close to 'em. I'll think of something."[44]

Dressen rarely paid attention to an innovative young Canadian who had labored for the Dodgers since 1947. Allan Roth had approached then Dodger president Branch Rickey with a hobby he had developed as a child, tracking the game pitch-by-pitch and keeping detailed records of each player's strengths and weaknesses. Rickey, always attuned to the scientific approach, employed Roth and encouraged his efforts. With pencil and paper, Roth began to compile the most detailed analysis of baseball ever undertaken. "Back then my system was unique," he later explained. "I would record the types of pitches and location. I even had averages for players when they were ahead or behind on the count. My system showed the record for a hitter against a pitcher for the year and over his career." Roth's efforts, especially with the introduction of computers in the 1970s, would provide the basis for modern baseball statistics. Unfortunately, in 1951 his was a craft in the wilderness. "Charley Dressen didn't want to see it," said Roth. "The man didn't want help from anybody. He thought he could do it all himself."[45]

In the bottom of the ninth inning, with two men on base, the Dodgers leading 4–2 and Bobby Thomson scheduled to bat, Dressen made a pitching change. He called in Ralph Branca. Dodger publicist Irving Rudd turned to Roth. "Allan, Allan, what are the statistics on Ralph Branca pitching to Thomson?" asked the anxious Rudd. Roth did not even have to check his numbers. Branca, who had allowed just seven home runs to the rest of the league, had surrendered ten to the Giants. Five of his eleven losses had come against the Giants. Thomson had stroked two of those homers including one two days earlier in the first game of the playoff series. Roth, staring out at the field, just shook his head sadly.[46] Moments later, Thomson struck "the shot heard 'round the world."

The Homes of the Braves
Baseball's Shifting Geography, 1953–1972

On April 14, 1953, Warren Spahn took the mound for the Braves' home opener against the St. Louis Cardinals. One month earlier Spahn had expected to be pitching at Braves Field, an aging, decaying ballpark in the heart of Boston. Instead, the lefthander unexpectedly found himself in Milwaukee County Stadium, the sparkling new home of the Braves. Spahn peered in at his catcher, kicked up his right leg, and fired a strike past the Cardinal leadoff man. "A tremendous roar went up," Spahn recalled. "I looked up to see what was going on, and then I stepped off the rubber and looked behind me." Everywhere he gazed Spahn saw not the empty seats that had grown commonplace at Braves Field, but wildly ecstatic baseball fans. A veteran of five all-star games and the 1948 World Series, Spahn was nonetheless stunned by the boisterous crowd reaction. "I realized that all they were screaming about was the first pitch. I have never experienced anything like it in an All-Star or in a crucial World Series game," marveled Spahn. "Those fans were welcoming our team as no team has ever been welcomed."[1]

The roar that greeted Warren Spahn and the Milwaukee Braves

proclaimed a new era for Organized Baseball. Fifty years had passed since the last franchise shift, the 1903 transfer of the Baltimore Orioles to New York City, where they would ultimately become the Yankees. In the interim, the nation's population had more than doubled and major urban areas had developed far beyond the traditional Northeast/Midwest industrial core. Yet baseball, as one executive later noted, had "stood still . . . while the country's population changed and baseball's market changed."[2] The number of major league ballplayers held steady at 400. The sixteen major league teams—the Boston Braves, Boston Red Sox, Brooklyn Dodgers, Chicago Cubs, Chicago White Sox, Cincinnati Reds, Cleveland Indians, Detroit Tigers, New York Giants, New York Yankees, Philadelphia Athletics, Philadelphia Phillies, Pittsburgh Pirates, St. Louis Browns, St. Louis Cardinals, and Washington Senators—remained anchored to ten metropolitan outposts. Four cities had two teams each; New York City had three; and St. Louis stood as both the westernmost and southernmost outpost of the "national" pastime. The spectacular success of the Braves in Milwaukee, however, launched a dramatic reconfiguration of the baseball map. In less than a decade six of the original sixteen teams would be playing in different cities. Within two decades expansion and additional franchise shifts would bring major league baseball to eight more communities. California hosted four teams, Texas two. Atlanta and Montreal expanded baseball's southeastern and northeastern boundaries.

Ironically, many remember this era as one of abandonment, rather than delivery, as cause for lamentation rather than celebration. Mayor John B. Hynes called the loss of the Braves "a body blow to Boston." Local fans labeled team owner Lou Perini "the Benedict Arnold of baseball."[3] The protests were even louder four years later when the New York Giants and Brooklyn Dodgers departed for California. New York City Council President Abe Stark condemned San Francisco Mayor George Christopher as a "pirate." Dodger fans like Doris Kearns Goodwin still denounce the club's exodus as "an invidious act of betrayal."[4] Yet, viewed from the perspective of those cities receiving teams, the franchise shifts, at least in their initial phase, provoked widespread jubilation. The acquisition of a major league team marked a sense of maturity, arrival, and acceptance, an acknowledgment of an elevated status in a newly emergent American constellation. These transfers reflected the broader changes affecting the nation as the country's economic and population base shifted from the Northeast and Midwest into the South, Southwest, and Far West. As with all dramatic transformations, the results were unpredictable and often disappointing, revealing a mosaic far more complex than any simple model of progress and loss might have augured.

The demographic shifts accelerated by World War II and its aftermath prompted a reexamination of baseball's limited geography in many quarters. In 1947 Californian H. D. Robins prepared a 115-page monograph, complete with diagrams, charts, and tables, analyzing baseball's increasingly irrational status quo. The sport, protested Robins, "had not responded to shifts in population or other pertinent changing factors." Given population increases and improved standards of health, he argued, "the number of men of major league caliber must not be twice but several times the number of men as were available at the turn of the century." Robins noted that although Cincinnati, the twentieth largest city in the United States, Canada, and the Caribbean, had a major league team, and St. Louis, the tenth largest city, had two teams, Los Angeles and San Francisco, the third and ninth ranking cities, had none. Montreal, Baltimore, Toronto, Buffalo, Havana, and Milwaukee, all larger than Cincinnati, also lacked representation, as did the burgeoning metropolises of Kansas City, Houston, and Minneapolis. Robins proposed a radical solution: the establishment of four eight-team major leagues, with a "Great Southern League" and a "Great Western League," joining the National and American Leagues, thus creating a truly national pastime.[5]

Although few embraced the bold scope of Robins's expansionist vision, he was not alone in reevaluating the baseball map. Both major and minor league turnstiles clicked at a record pace in the immediate postwar years, emboldening the baseball dreams of cities throughout the United States, most especially in California.

Pacific Coast League attendance nearly doubled between 1941 and 1946. Both the San Francisco Seals, who established a new minor league attendance mark, and the Oakland Oaks drew more fans than the St. Louis Browns and Kansas City Athletics. The Los Angeles Angels and Hollywood Stars combined to attract more than a million fans. "Is the West Coast Ready for Big League Baseball?" wondered a 1947 *Sport* magazine article. Pacific Coast League (PCL) President Clarence "Pants" Rowland, long an advocate of a third major league, proposed a new classification for the PCL, placing it above the triple-A level as a preliminary to big league status.⁶

The major leagues responded coolly to the PCL bid. Everyone recognized that both Los Angeles and San Francisco possessed legitimate major league potential, but many discounted PCL attendance figures as inflated by a long 186-game season and the practice of counting women and children who received free admission. Furthermore, Seattle, Portland, Oakland, and San Diego, saddled with inadequate ballparks and smaller populations, seemed dubious prospects. Baseball Commissioner Happy Chandler proposed that, rather than add an entire league, the two existing circuits should be expanded to ten teams each. The National League unanimously endorsed Chandler's suggestion, but the American rejected it, placing all expansion plans on hold.⁷

This lack of initiative and foresight on the part of the major league establishment was not surprising. None of the aspiring cities had viable major league facilities and, while all major league stadiums were privately built and owned, increased costs made new ballpark construction a daunting challenge unless underwritten by public funds. In addition, as David Voigt has noted, the traditional eight-team configuration produced a "marvelously balanced" 154-game schedule. Each team played the other twenty-two times, and Pullman trains easily accommodated "western" excursions.⁸ Despite dramatic improvements in air travel, few owners could envision an alternative to this arrangement. In 1946 United Airlines had introduced the DC-6, capable of traveling 300 miles an hour and carrying more than fifty passengers; larger and faster planes were in development. As Dan Daniel noted in *Baseball Magazine*, a team could now travel from New York to Los Angeles in half the time it took to get to St. Louis by train. Larry MacPhail, always far ahead of his colleagues, signed an exclusive contract with United to transport the New York Yankees on most of their road trips. Most major league executives, however, some fearing the possibility of losing an entire squad to an air disaster, resisted plane travel.[9]

The unwillingness of the major leagues to expand or recognize a third major league left just one alternative for cities hoping to achieve major league status: to lure an existing team away from its long-standing home. But, the postwar attendance boom had seemingly secured the profitability of all franchises, save the lowly St. Louis Browns, and Organized Baseball had strict restrictions on the shifting of franchises. Any proposed transfer had to be approved by a unanimous vote of both leagues. Thus, as it approached mid-century, the baseball establishment seemed poised, as usual, on the brink of inaction.

By 1951, however, the pressure to change had intensified. The attendance bubble had burst, threatening the financial viability of not just the Browns, but the Boston Braves and Philadelphia Athletics, the other weak franchises in two-team markets. In addition, a congressional subcommittee, headed by Emmanuel Celler, launched an investigation of baseball's business practices. With Los Angeles Congressman Patrick J. Hillings leading the way, the committee challenged baseball's restrictions on rewarding and relocating franchises.[10] In response, National League President Ford Frick produced a report on "the Pacific Coast and its baseball potentialities," halfheartedly suggesting that while expansion was "the most practical solution," the major leagues had to tread carefully lest they violate minor league interests. The following year major league baseball, while still evidencing little interest in expansion, greatly eased its restrictions on franchise shifts. Instead of requiring a unanimous vote in both leagues, a move could be approved by a vote of the affected league.[11] This series of decisions guaranteed that baseball's adaptation to modern America would occur not in a planned or orderly manner, but rather in haphazard style, pitting city against city in a quest for major league status.

The carousel began spinning in spring 1953, not in Boston or Milwaukee but in St. Louis. Browns' owner Bill Veeck had struggled to make his perennially cellar-dwelling club into a viable rival to the more popular St. Louis Cardinals. A series of inspired promotions, including sending midget Eddie Gaedel to bat in a ball game, had doubled Browns attendance in two years, giving Veeck hope that he might seize the local initiative. In February 1953, however, the Annheuser-Busch brewery purchased the Cardinals, dashing any possibility that the team might ultimately be driven out of St. Louis. Veeck, taking advantage of the newly liberalized relocation rules, announced his intention to immediately move the Browns. Although many suitors savored his franchise, only Baltimore and Milwaukee, both of which had built publicly funded stadiums hoping to lure a big league team, had adequate facilities to host major league baseball. Veeck, who had once owned the minor league Milwaukee Brewers, favored the Midwestern city.[12] However, Boston Braves owner Lou Perini now controlled the Brewers and the territorial rights to baseball in Milwaukee. On March 3, 1953, Milwaukee fans learned that while proclaiming he would never stand in the way of the city getting a major league franchise, Perini had refused to allow Veeck to move the Browns into Milwaukee.[13]

The decision enraged the local populace. Milwaukee officials threatened to terminate the lease that allowed Perini's Brewers to play in County Stadium in 1953. Fans threatened to boycott the team. The local congressman vowed to reopen an investigation of baseball. Perini, whose Braves had drawn only 281,278 fans in 1952, had hoped to relocate the following year, but he had set his sights on larger cities with greater attendance potential. Faced now with the possibility of substantial financial losses in both Boston and Milwaukee, Perini caved in. On March 13, just ten days after rejecting Veeck's bid, Perini called for an emergency meeting of baseball owners to request a move to Milwaukee. On March 18, less than a month before the season was to start, the National League voted unanimously to approve the transfer.[14]

Perini was far from enthusiastic about the sudden and unexpected change. Although Milwaukee boasted a brand new stadium with 12,000 parking spaces and the city had offered him an extraordinarily generous lease, Perini expected no great bonanza. In Milwaukee he found himself in the second smallest city in the majors; the minor league Brewers had drawn fewer than 200,000 fans in a pennant-winning season in 1952. Privately, Perini confessed that he anticipated attendance reaching no more than 750,000. Seeking to protect his gate receipts, Perini refused to televise any games.[15]

Milwaukeeans, however, responded with what the *New York Times* described as an electric enthusiasm. Cheers rang out in downtown bars and restaurants. The news dominated the front pages of the Milwaukee newspapers under the headlines—WE'RE BIG LEAGUERS, and WE'RE HOME OF THE BRAVES. The Association of Commerce and others passionately endorsed the latter phrase as a promotional device. The city of Milwaukee cancelled its mail with a metered stamp reading, "Milwaukee, the home of the Braves." The local Photo Engravers Union stamped the slogan with an Indian head on its envelopes. Schoolchildren reportedly ended their daily national anthems, singing, "And the home of the Braves." Fans flocked to the stadium to sit in the stands and watch the final stages of construction, causing Sunday traffic jams in the weeks leading up to the season.[16]

On April 8 the Braves arrived to play an exhibition game against the Red Sox. Thirty models wearing Indian headdresses and 12,000 fans greeted the team at Milwaukee Station, where a red carpet had been laid out from the train shed to the street. An additional 50,000 fans lined Wisconsin Avenue as the players drove by in open cars, accompanied by marching bands and Native Americans on horseback. When the convoy reached the Shroeder Hotel, according to W. C. Heinz, "Every church bell, fire siren, factory and tugboat and railroad whistle in Milwaukee and vicinity let loose." In the hotel the players found a Christmas tree, decorated with

bats and balls, and laden with gifts. A large banner read, YOU
BROUGHT US CHRISTMAS IN APRIL.[17]

Civic leaders made no secret of the psychological impact of the
Braves' arrival. Since the end of the war the Greater Milwaukee
Committee for Development had laid out plans for over $200 mil-
lion in public projects including highways, airport improvements,
and a new zoo, library, museum, and war memorial. The stadium,
built at a cost of $4,000,000 and viewed as the first phase of this
program, had produced dividends within a few short years. "Once
in the life of a city . . . there comes that wonderful golden opportunity for greatness," explained Mayor Frank Zeidler. "Milwaukee
had its chance at greatness and it grasped and made splendid use
of the opportunity."[18]

The phrase "big league" reverberated in the city's discourse. Visiting reporter Al Hirschberg discovered that the sudden appearance
of the Braves had given Milwaukee a long-sought-after sense of
identity. "Something happened to the ego of the people," reported
Hirschberg. "They threw out their collective chest, looked the
world squarely in the eye, and proclaimed, 'We're big league.' " A
campaign to build a new public library succeeded on the platform,
"We're a big league town, we have to have a big league library."
Striking brewery workers lofted signs stating, "We're a big league
town. We want big league wages." Milwaukee's "whole inferiority
complex is gone," exclaimed a longtime resident.[19]

Sportswriter Shirley Povich attributed the commotion to a
"mass brainwashing," in which "other values are replaced by a
baseball hysteria."[20] The ferment escalated throughout the season.
The Milwaukee Braves required only thirteen home games to sur-
pass the previous season's attendance in Boston. The club passed
one million paid admissions on July 31. The team's surprising performance fueled the passion. After finishing in seventh place in
1952, the Braves began the new season like pennant contenders.
Behind the bats of second-year third baseman Eddie Mathews and
newly acquired first baseman Joe Adcock, the glove of rookie cen-
terfielder Billy Bruton, and the pitching of Warren Spahn and Lew
Burdette, the Braves seized first place for a giddy twelve days in

June. Local fans embraced the team with an unprecedented ardor. "I've just seen a World Series in May," marveled a veteran Pittsburgh sportswriter. "Braves fans are the most rabid the game has ever seen." Milwaukee, stated a *New York Times* correspondent, is "more Brooklyn than Brooklyn."[21] Supporters swamped the players with affection and gifts. Milwaukee's heavily ethnic population regularly honored players of their respective nationalities. According to one report,

> Jews put on a night for Sid Gordon and Germans for Warren Spahn; Italians gave one for Sibbi Sisti; Negroes for (Bill) Bruton, Jim Pendleton and George Crowe; Iowans for (Jack) Dittmer. Lutherans turned out 10,000 strong to see Andy Pafko; Poles gave a birthday party at home plate for Max Surkont.

Gifts of cheese, pork sausage, and kielbasa descended on the clubhouse. "I've got to watch out they don't smother us with kindness, beer and sauerbraten," joked Manager Charlie Grimm.[22]

The excitement extended beyond the boundaries of Milwaukee. The Braves, located in the northwest reaches of the major leagues, tapped into a vast regional following. "Thousands of fans flocked to the games not only from all over Wisconsin, but from Minnesota, Milwaukee, Illinois, Iowa, the Dakotas and more distant points," reported *Business Week*. Trains and buses from all over the Midwest materialized at County Stadium. The Milwaukee Railroad built a passenger platform at the ballpark but frequently had to turn down excess requests for special trains. At a June night game 150 buses arrived overflowing the forty-slot bus parking lot.[23]

Even after the Braves dropped from the pennant race the frenzy continued. On the final day of the season Braves' attendance surpassed 1.8 million, establishing a new National League record. The total more than doubled the city's population. Only the limited seating capacity of County Stadium, which held only 33,000 fans, prevented the club from topping two million. The Association of Commerce boasted that the team had pumped between $5 million and $8 million into the local economy in increased taxi, restaurant, hotel, and retail revenues. "This is the greatest thing that has happened to Milwaukee since beer," crowed one merchant.[24]

Major league baseball had inadvertently stumbled into a gold mine. In a year in which attendance for all but two other clubs had sharply declined, the Braves had drawn 1.5 million extra fans. The Braves' triumph created a new blueprint for success. Teams suffering from poor attendance could reinvent themselves by moving to one of the many communities desperate for major league baseball. The Milwaukee experience also awakened baseball owners to the possibilities of regional franchises and the Braves second-place finish raised the chimera of new surroundings enhancing on-field performance. For cities aspiring to big league status, netting a major league team hooked with the lure of a publicly funded stadium meant profits and prestige, financial rewards and spiritual benefits.

The euphoria in Milwaukee obscured the potential downside lessons of the transfer. Much of the vaunted economic impact involved not a stimulus, but a shifting of spending patterns. Some local merchants, notably restaurants, complained that business fell on game days, as fans hovered near home and office radios to hear the action.[25] Money brought into Milwaukee was drained from nearby communities. Indeed, both the Chicago Cubs and Detroit Tigers saw sharp attendance drops in 1953, possibly related to the Braves' relocation. (Nor did the Boston Red Sox benefit from the Braves' departure; patronage declined by 8 percent.) Furthermore, the "Milwaukee Miracle" established an important precedent. "Any city that wants to get a big-league team nowadays is going to have to provide a stadium," commented a baseball executive.[26] Cities seeking teams would have to spend tax dollars to build stadiums, subsidizing private enterprises from the public coffer. Finally, the abandonment of Boston raised the issue of a team's responsibility and relationship to a community. If the Braves could leave Boston, where they had drawn over a million fans just four years earlier, couldn't they also leave Milwaukee when the novelty of major league baseball wore off and attendance declined?

Few observers raised these questions in 1953. The path had cleared for additional franchise shifts. In 1954 the St. Louis Browns migrated to Baltimore, where they became the Orioles. The Maryland seaport seemed an ideal solution to the Browns' perennial attendance woes. Baltimore was the ninth largest city in the United States, able to draw on a metropolitan population of 1.5 million people. The city had a long-standing baseball tradition and had ardently supported its minor league Orioles. In 1947 voters had approved a $2.5 million bond issue to build Memorial Stadium. Three years later they authorized the addition of a second deck, raising the seating capacity to 50,000. City officials surrendered the showcase ballpark to the Orioles for a minimal rent and promised free office space and stadium maintenance, while allocating all parking and food revenues to the team.[27]

Both local politicians and baseball officials ignored the scattered protests accompanying the move. The arrival of the Orioles threatened to further weaken the struggling Washington Senators, less than an hour's drive to the south. In addition, civil rights leaders questioned whether Baltimore, a segregated city, deserved major league status. The Orioles did little to allay these fears when the club failed to resign Satchel Paige, its only black star, and cut pitcher Jesse Heard, the only black player on the roster, during spring training. Nor did the Orioles support Governor Thomas McKeldin's plea for local hotels to welcome visiting black players on other teams.[28]

These drawbacks notwithstanding, the 1954 season opened with visions of a replication of the Milwaukee scenario. "We stand on the eve of the Great Day we have anticipated so keenly," crowed the *Baltimore News-Post*. In 1953 the local Association of Commerce had hailed the promise of a major league team as "a development of great importance to our economic and community progress and a proper and overdue recognition of our city's national stature." With the Birds in hand, the Association celebrated "the amazing amount of favorable publicity—the kind that can't be bought," and predicted a buoying of "all aspects of the city's economy." An early flood of ticket orders boosted hopes that the Orioles would match or exceed Milwaukee's attendance figures. "I believe we'll come close to 2,000,000 admissions for the season," forecast club president Clarence Miles.[29]

Baltimore, reported the *New Yorker*, "was going slightly wacky" amid a recurrent theme of "Back in the Big League." Throughout the city, "the orange and black colors of the team floated everywhere, like the banners of the ancient artisans' guilds."[30] The town greeted its new club with a parade described by *Life* magazine as the "most exuberant demonstration since the Civil War." A half-million people joined Vice President Richard Nixon and baseball's last remaining links to Baltimore's earlier major league incarnation, ninety-one-year-old Connie Mack and eighty-five-year-old Clark Griffith, to welcome the team. The procession featured marching bands, women garbed as Orioles and baseballs, and a twelve-foot papier-mâché float of Baltimore native Babe Ruth rotating on a pedestal. The ballplayers threw 20,000 plastic baseballs into the cheering crowd.[31]

The Orioles played before a sellout crowd on opening day and attracted 43,383 fans to the first night game, creating "the most glorious traffic jam in the history" of Memorial Stadium. After the first five home games the Orioles had drawn 130,506 fans.[32] Unlike the Braves in Milwaukee, however, the change of scenery failed to improve the club's fortunes on the field. In 1953 the Browns had won fifty-four games, lost 100 and finished in last place, forty-six-and-a-half games behind the pennant-winning Yankees. The Orioles posted an identical record in 1954 and trailed the high-flying Cleveland Indians by fifty-seven games. Only the woeful performance of the hapless Philadelphia Athletics kept Baltimore out of the cellar. By midseason fans began to lose interest in the inept performance. Attendance tailed off far below preseason expectations. Nonetheless, the Orioles attracted 1,060,910 paid admissions. The total more than tripled the Browns' 1953 season and exceeded the highest figures ever recorded by the Browns, Senators, or Athletics. An economic survey reported that more than one in four patrons had come from out of town and spent an average of $30 each in Baltimore each time they attended a game, pumping $5 million into the local economy. Echoing the conventional wisdom, *U.S. News and World Report* would conclude, "A big league team is a financial asset to a city."[33]

In 1955 the scene shifted to Kansas City, where *Kansas City Star* sports editor Ernie Mehl had long waged a campaign for a major league team. Mehl approached Chicago businessman Arnold Johnson, who owned the local minor league stadium, and, according to Arthur Mann, assured Johnson "he could write his own ticket if he brought a big league team to Kansas City." The city would buy his ballpark for a generous price, raze it, and build a major league arena on the foundations. Johnson could rent back the new arena for a nominal fee.[34] Johnson, a business associate of New York Yankee owners Del Webb and Dan Topping, then offered to buy the Philadelphia Athletics from the Mack family and move the team to Kansas City. Connie Mack had reigned in Philadelphia since 1901 and his family had strong ties to the community, but team attendance had dropped to 362,113 in 1953. "The last thing we want to do is move the team out of Philadelphia," stated his son Roy. "But we can't afford another year as bad as last year." A "Save the A's" campaign ignited but quickly extinguished in Philadelphia and attendance plummeted to 304,666.[35] The Macks sold out to Johnson, who brought the Athletics to Kansas City.

For Kansas City baseball fans, the acquisition of a major league team, even one as lowly as the Athletics, inspired what one writer recalled as "an emotional binge of pride and optimism." Ernie Mehl explained, "The important thing is that we've gone big league, you've got to take the best you can get. The successful ball clubs aren't on the market." Voters approved the stadium bond issue by a five-to-one margin, and builders completed the reconstruction in only twenty-two weeks. In April 1955 Kansas City staged its own version of the ritual welcoming parade, with 200,000 "applauding, cheering, beaming friends" lining the streets to cheer the players. Governor Fred Hall of Kansas, Lt. Governor James T. Blair of Missouri, and a host of mayors from nearby cities joined the festivities. Regional enthusiasm for the team surfaced immediately. "Baseball fans swarmed in on the city like set-

tlers bound for a house raising in pioneer days," reported Gerald
Holland in *Sports Illustrated*. "They came by car, bus and plane,
and by excursion trains. . . . They came from Arkansas, Oklahoma,
Texas, Colorado, Nebraska and from deep into what used to be
St. Louis Cardinal Missouri territory."[36] Moving up to sixth place,
the Athletics drew 1,393,054 paid admissions, trailing only the Yankees in American League attendance.

From the perspective of 1955 the revamping of the major leagues
seemed an unqualified success. The Braves had drawn in excess of
two million fans to an enlarged Milwaukee County Stadium in
both 1954 and 1955 and, although attendance in Baltimore had
dropped to 852,039 in the Orioles' second year, this still marked
a dramatic improvement over the St. Louis years. As Charles C.
Euchner has commented, baseball had "replaced three over-
saturated markets with six well-served markets." Yet this trio of
transfers had scarcely broadened the boundaries of the national
pastime. Although Kansas City was a few hundred miles west of
St. Louis, notes G. Edward White, all the newly relocated clubs
fit comfortably into the established train-travel networks.[37] With
the logical candidates for transplantation accounted for, the West
Coast metropolises of Los Angeles and San Francisco remained
outside the major league orbit.

These early transfers had each involved money-losing franchises,
the weaker club in a two-team market. Other teams, however, even
profitable ones, shared the problems that had driven the Braves,
Browns, and Athletics from their homes—declining patronage and
aging stadiums with minimal parking spaces for a suburban population increasingly inclined to drive to games. New York City's
two National League clubs, the Dodgers and Giants, both remained remunerative ventures, but each had experienced dramatic
drops in attendance and required new ballparks to attract more
fans. The Giants had drawn more than 1.1 million fans during their
pennant-winning season of 1954, but in 1956, despite the attraction
of Willie Mays, only 653,923 people came to the venerable Polo
Grounds. Games against the Dodgers accounted for a third of this
total, leaving them heavily dependent on their interborough rivals.

Television revenues virtually guaranteed an annual profit, but, rebuffed in his efforts to build a new stadium or share Yankee Stadium with the Yankees, Giant owner Horace Stoneham decided to move his club. Stoneham chose Minneapolis, where he owned the minor league franchise and the city had built a new stadium.[38] In Brooklyn, owner Walter O'Malley presided over the most profitable franchise in the major leagues, but New York City politics had frustrated his attempts to secure land rights for a new downtown ballpark. O'Malley also cast a fearful eye in the direction of Milwaukee, where the Braves had drawn more than twice as many fans as the Dodgers in 1954 and 1955. "I want to produce winning ball clubs and to continue to do so, I must be able to compete, dollar-for-dollar, with the Braves," O'Malley worried openly.[39]

In 1956 public officials in Los Angeles and San Francisco began to court the New York clubs. Los Angeles City Supervisor Kenneth Hahn, attending the World Series in hopes of luring the Washington Senators to Los Angeles, discovered that the Dodgers might be available. Shortly thereafter, O'Malley stopped in Los Angeles to meet with city officials.[40] San Francisco Mayor George Christopher began a secret weekend shuttle to New York to convince Stoneham that his city offered a preferable alternative to Minneapolis. "Getting a major league team into San Francisco is a crusade with us," confessed Christopher.[41] On February 21, 1957, the Dodgers purchased the Pacific Coast League Los Angeles Angels from the Cubs, securing territorial rights to the city. The following day Stoneham announced that if the Dodgers headed West, the Giants would also depart. Shortly thereafter Stoneham acquired the San Francisco Seals from the Red Sox.[42]

These actions notwithstanding, neither team had made a firm commitment to move to the West Coast. Both continued to negotiate with the California cities over proposals to build new stadiums. Stoneham announced on July 17 that the Giants would definitely leave New York, but left their ultimate destination open. O'Malley meanwhile continued to insist that a new stadium in Brooklyn would keep the Dodgers at home. On August 9 San Francisco formally offered to build a 40,000- to 50,000-seat stadium with 12,000 parking spaces for the Giants. Nine days later the Giants' Board of Directors approved the move to San Francisco. "Whether or not the Dodgers move to Los Angeles," stated Stoneham, "the Giants are definitely going—even if we have to go it alone." The fate of the Dodgers seemed almost assured, but not until October 7, when the Los Angeles City Council formally agreed to turn over 300 acres to O'Malley, where he could build a new ballpark, did the Dodgers officially confirm the move.[43]

Most New Yorkers conceded the inevitability of the Giants move. When asked how he felt about depriving New York's children of their beloved Giants, Stoneham commented, "I feel bad about the kids, but I haven't seen many of their fathers lately."[44] Few could fault his logic. The flight of the Dodgers, however, was another thing. "It's no laughing matter," wrote sportswriter Dick Young. "Yank this ball club out of Brooklyn where the people have been living and dying with it for three generations, and you tamper seriously with the fabric of their lives. What of the ball club's responsibility to the fan?"[45] The abandonment of Brooklyn secured O'Malley a permanent mantle of villainy in local folklore.

Across the continent, the arrival of major league teams set off the celebrations already familiar from Milwaukee, Baltimore, and Kansas City. The Giants instantly carved out a place in the hearts of San Franciscans. Billboards reading "Welcome San Francisco Giants. Swat those Bums" greeted the team. Mannequins in downtown store windows appeared in Giants' uniforms and the welcoming ticker-tape parade down Market Street attracted hundreds of thousands of people. "Major league ball . . . has taken its place alongside the famous fogs and the earthquake of '06 as a prime topic of conversation," asserted a longtime resident. Local baseball legend Lefty O'Doul opened a new restaurant near Union Square, anticipating a boom in baseball-related business. The Dimaggio Brothers doubled the size of their Fisherman's Wharf eating establishment. Newspaper columnist Charles McCabe observed, "The Giants . . . have given us all a notable civic strut. San Francisco has been saying for decades that it is big league. In its secret heart it has never been quite sure. These days it is."[46]

The Dodgers evoked the same sense of exhilaration and affir-
mation, offering "the first focal point on which everyone can
unite." The team, claimed the *Los Angeles Times*, made Los Angeles
"a great city, with common interests, and the civic unity which
gives a city great character." Two months into the 1958 season,
sportswriter Jim Murray proclaimed the Dodgers, "quite clearly a
part of Los Angeles and Los Angeles a part of baseball."[47]

Before the 1958 season began, the general consensus held that
the Dodgers, landing in the more populous city, had attained a far
better deal than the Giants. As Tim Cohane explained the popular
perception, "O'Malley, regarded as masterfully shrewd, planned
the move west for both teams. He sold the idea to Stoneham who
is supposed to be less shrewd." Yet, from the moment the season
opened and the Giants trounced the Dodgers 8–0 at San Francisco's Seals Stadium, the opinion began to spread that the Giants
had stumbled into Nirvana, while the Dodgers, according to Cohane, had "wandered into the original Valley of Migraine."[48] The
Dodgers, perennial pennant contenders and third-place finishers in
1957, immediately sank to the bottom of the standings. The Giants,
expected to duplicate their sixth-place status, unexpectedly rose to
the top. Los Angeles fans watched fabled Dodger stars Gil Hodges,
Pee Wee Reese, Duke Snider, and Carl Furillo on the decline. In
San Francisco, rookies Orlando Cepeda, Jim Davenport, and Willie Kirkland joined twenty-seven-year-old Willie Mays as a promising core for the future.

The contrast extended beyond the playing field. Both teams had
been promised new stadiums, but in 1958 they settled into temporary headquarters. The Giants moved into Seals Stadium in the
city's Mission District, one of the nation's finest minor league ballparks. Although Seals Stadium seated only 23,000 fans, it offered
convenient access and an intimate charm for players and fans alike.
The Dodgers, forced to choose between the old Angels' home of
Wrigley Field, which seated 10,000 fewer fans than Ebbets Field
and offered no parking, or the Los Angeles Coliseum, described
by Arthur Daley as "a huge oval with plenty of room for customers
but no room for a playing field," opted for the latter. The result

was a ballpark like no other that irredeemably distorted the games played within its confines. The right-field fence lay a distant 390 feet from home plate; centerfield a daunting 435 feet away; and the asymmetric left field stood only 250 feet deep. To compensate for the difference, the Dodgers erected a forty-foot high "queer-looking meshed" screen in left field. The configuration had a devastating effect on left-handed power hitters like Dodger star Duke Snider. Of the 193 home runs hit at the Coliseum in 1958, only eight were hit to right field and two to center. Snider's home run output fell from forty in 1957 to fifteen in 1958.[49]

The Giants seemed to have gotten the better of the political wars as well. After Stoneham rejected a downtown location for a new ballpark, San Francisco had promised to build a stadium at Candlestick Point, just south of the city. Although visiting newsmen like Arthur Daley complained about the cold weather at Seals Stadium ("This reporter froze to death . . . during the first night game of the season in San Francisco. He was wearing an overcoat too," recounted Daley), they were reassured that "the new Giant park . . . is being hollowed out of a hill that will serve as protection from both fog and winds." Candlestick Park, promised Mayor Christopher, would be located at a site where fog would not be "troublesome." The new $15-million arena, constructed entirely with public funds, constituted a massive giveaway to a private corporation, but despite a short-lived taxpayer suit, San Franciscans voiced minimal opposition. Construction began on schedule, and the Giants would have their new home in time for the 1960 season.[50]

The situation in Los Angeles evolved in a diametrically opposite fashion. Unlike Stoneham, Dodger owner Walter O'Malley proposed building a new ballpark with his private funds. The City Council agreed to turn over Chavez Ravine, a 315-acre site near downtown Los Angeles and its central freeways, to the Dodgers for this purpose. Once the home of an impoverished but thriving Mexican community, Chavez Ravine was the largest undeveloped parcel of land close to the downtown area. Most residents had left in the early 1950s when the federal government had acquired the land for public housing. In 1952, however, Los Angeles voters blocked this project, so the land reverted to the city under the stipulation that it must be used for an appropriate public purpose. This requirement had left the land not only undeveloped, but also seemingly undevelopable. The Council traded the problematic gulch to the Dodgers in exchange for the less valuable Wrigley Field property, promising to use public funds to grade the canyon and build access roads.[51]

Opposition to the Chavez Ravine deal arose immediately. Several City Council members protested awarding the Dodgers land and services worth millions of dollars. Professional baseball, they contended, was not an appropriate public purpose. Underwritten with monies provided by John A. Smith, who owned the Pacific Coast League San Diego Padres and feared the arrival of the Dodgers would weaken his franchise, opponents placed an initiative on the June 1958 ballot seeking to reverse the City Council's agreement with the Dodgers. The action took O'Malley by surprise. "I never anticipated a referendum," he observed. "In fact, I was completely unaware of the thing they called a referendum because they never had that in New York." O'Malley grew even more concerned when polls began to show voters, especially those in outlying districts, tilting against the land deal. In desperation, Los Angeles Mayor Norris Poulson suggested a "scare campaign," portraying the election as an unalterable "yes-or-no vote for baseball." Hollywood celebrities, headed by comedian Joe E. Brown, formed a city's committee for "Yea on Baseball." The committee staged a telethon shortly before the balloting. The cast included George Burns, Groucho Marx, Jack Benny, and Debbie Reynolds. The highlight came when Ronald Reagan, an actor en route to a political career, derided the argument against the Chavez Ravine deal as "One of the most dishonest documents I ever read in my life." O'Malley, observed the future president, was getting a good deal, but so was the city.[52]

The June 3 balloting proved remarkably close. "On the day of the vote we were uncertain of the outcome until about midnight," recalled Dodger executive Buzzy Bavasi. The voters approved the

stadium contract by a narrow margin of 51.8 percent to 48.2 percent. According to Charles Alexander, African Americans, loyal to
the Dodgers since the days of Jackie Robinson, may have cast the
decisive ballots.[53] The Dodgers experienced only fleeting jubilation. Opponents had filed a taxpayers' suit seeking to prevent the
transfer of Chavez Ravine. Three days after the election, a superior
court judge issued a preliminary injunction blocking consumma-
tion of the agreement. One month later another judge declared the
contract "an illegal delegation of the duty of the City Council, an
abdication of its public trust, and a manifest gross abuse of discre-
tion." The decision dealt the Dodgers and the prospect of a ballpark at Chavez Ravine a severe blow.[54]

The Dodgers drew consolation from the team's splendid showing at the box office. Despite the bizarre dimensions of the Coliseum and the poorest Dodger finish since World War II, the team
attracted 1,845,268 fans. Dodger radio broadcasts featuring the extraordinary Vince Scully became a staple of Southern California
listening, receiving the highest local radio ratings since the advent
of television. The Dodgers had outdrawn the Giants, whose attendance had been limited by the lesser capacity of Seals Stadium, by
more than a half million fans. Nonetheless, the move had proved
a financial success for both clubs. The Giants, behind a strong
third-place finish, had doubled their New York draw. "I'm positive
that I picked the better city," Stoneham told *New York Times*
sportswriter Arthur Daley. Daley "fully" agreed with Stoneham.
"He's more set than O'Malley is because his stadium is already in
the process of construction," affirmed the reporter.[55]

The travails of the Dodgers began to lift in 1959. In January the
California Supreme Court issued a writ of prohibition, which in
effect overruled the superior court ruling on the Chavez Ravine
controversy. In April the state supreme court declared the original
contract constitutional, allowing the Dodgers to proceed with construction. The Dodgers, however, would suffer one further humiliation. In May they proceeded to remove the last remaining
residents of Chavez Ravine. Only twenty families were left of the
hundreds who had once shared the gullies and hillsides. Most de-

parted willingly, but the Arechiga family, who had lived in the arroyo for thirty-six years and had turned down a $10,500 federal buyout in 1951, refused to leave. Police deputies forcibly evicted the recalcitrant squatters, with the women kicking and screaming, and bulldozed their home. Television news cameramen reported and repeatedly rebroadcast the scene, provoking an outpouring of sympathy, particularly in the Mexican-American community. The Arechigas, claiming that they now had no place to live, pitched a tent nearby and continued their defiance for ten days. Public sympathy, and the family's resistance, collapsed when a local newspaper revealed that far from being destitute, patriarch Manuel Arechiga owned at least nine houses, including one vacant property.[56] The Dodgers were finally free to move ahead with their Los Angeles pleasure palace.

The Dodgers also experienced an on-the-field rebirth in 1959. A mild reconfiguration of the Coliseum, bringing in the right-field fence, and a rejuvenation of the lineup produced an unlikely National League pennant and a World Series Championship. Attendance soared over 2 million. Crowds exceeding 92,000 fans also turned out for three World Series contests and a Dodger–Yankee exhibition game honoring paralyzed Dodger catcher Roy Campanella. A Chicago reporter decried the spectacle of the World Series at the Coliseum as a "travesty." But in Los Angeles, wrote Sid Ziff, where people had "grown to enjoy their weird ball park . . . [t]he whole community has gone Dodger nuts." "Who will have the effrontery to tells us now," crowed the Los Angeles Times, "that the movement to supply the Dodgers with a decent playing yard was against the public interest. Their triumph is that they have created one of those centers of attachment that the metropolitan area of Los Angeles has needed so desperately."[57]

The Giants also continued to prosper. In 1959 attendance jumped to 1.42 million. Candlestick Park debuted in 1960. Built entirely with reinforced concrete, it became the first stadium without a single obstructed seat. However, it quickly became apparent that Candlestick's deficiencies far outweighed its virtues. A June 1960 report in the Californian criticized the cold, harsh winds blowing in off the bay, the smell of sewage, and "Cardiac Hill," the long climb from the parking lot to the ballpark, which it claimed had already caused six deaths from heart attacks.[58] Nonetheless, just under 1.8 million people visited the 'Stick during its inaugural season.

The Dodgers finally unveiled Dodger Stadium in 1962. The only privately funded stadium built in the postwar era, Dodger Stadium proved to be, in the classically hyperbolic words of Jim Murray, "not just any baseball park, but the Taj Mahal, the Parthenon, and Westminster Abbey of baseball." Two million seven hundred thousand fans attended Dodger games in 1962 and Dodger profits exceeded $4 million. The Dodgers had become what economist Roger Noll would later call "baseball's answer to the Denver Mint."[59]

The 1958 transcontinental migration of the Dodgers and Giants whet the appetites of other communities for major league baseball. New York City formed a committee to secure a team to replace the departed franchises. With few of the original clubs still candidates for relocation, the only hope for most major league aspirants was the expansion of the existing leagues, but organized baseball stubbornly refused to abandon its sixteen-team tradition. "If baseball owners ran Congress," observed Bill Veeck, "Kansas and Nebraska would still be trying to get into the union."[60] The solution, according to William Shea, chairman of the New York baseball committee, was to revive the idea of a third baseball league. On November 13, 1958, he announced the creation of a new Continental League with franchises in Houston, Dallas–Fort Worth, Atlanta, Denver, Toronto, Minneapolis–St. Paul, and second teams in New York and Detroit. Representatives from each of these cities posted $50,000 to indicate their sincerity.[61]

The league gained added credibility when Shea introduced Branch Rickey as the commissioner. Rickey, long an advocate of expansion, argued that a third circuit was preferable to piecemeal expansion of the National and American Leagues. Rickey argued that expansion teams would be overmatched in the existing leagues. "It may seem illogical and paradoxical that you can't get manpower for four extra clubs but you can for eight," reasoned Rickey. "New ones can't compete on a basis of equality with old ones. But eight teams can compete equally while recognized as a third major league. Our new league would not pretend to be major the first year. But by the end of the third year that would not be unthinkable."[62]

The Continental League, seeking to neutralize opposition from Organized Baseball, lobbied Congress to pass legislation eliminating baseball's antitrust exemption. Senator Estes Kefauver introduced a bill in the Senate placing baseball under the purview of the Federal Trade Commission and the Sherman and Clayton Antitrust Acts. The Kefauver bill also proposed to outlaw any efforts "preventing, hindering, obstructing, or adversely affecting the formation and operation of a new major league," a proscription that might be construed to include baseball's treasured reserve clause. Kefauver's measure failed to pass by only four votes.[63]

The Continental League may have been no more than a grand bluff. As Houston advocates admitted, "What fans in Houston and every other expansion city wanted was their team playing the Dodgers or the Yankees, Red Sox or Pirates."[64] The aggressive third league threat, however, crushed Organized Baseball's stubborn resistance to expansion. Several days after the perilously close Senate vote, Commissioner Ford Frick announced that the American and National Leagues would each add two new franchises in the near future. To ensure the collapse of the Continental League, the majors offered National League franchises to New York and Houston. In addition, the American League allowed Clark Griffith to move the Washington Senators to Minneapolis–St. Paul and awarded the nation's capital an expansion team. Hoping to cash in on the vast Southern California market, the American League created a second team for Los Angeles.

The fiery enthusiasm inspired by relocated teams burned less brightly for the expansion squads. As Rickey had predicted, none of the squads proved competitive with the older clubs, dampening fan enthusiasm and attendance figures. The American League introduced its new ten-team format in 1961. The Senators finished tied for last with the Athletics, and the Angels landed in eighth place. Both franchises recorded disappointing attendance. The Angels, playing in tiny Wrigley Field, attracted just over 600,000 patrons. The new Senators fared worse than either the Angels or their 1960 Washington predecessors, drawing only 597,000 fans. On the other hand, the transplanted Senators became the success story of 1961. To avoid alienating the citizens of either Minneapolis or St. Paul, owner Clark Griffith christened the club the Twins and named his team after the state of Minnesota rather than one of the cities. The appellation captured the regional attraction of the team. Fans reportedly came from seven states and three Canadian provinces to see the Twins, arriving by the busload and trainload from as far away as Billings, Montana. Fans sang a special fight song, *We're Going to Win, Twins* and, although the team failed to comply, the club drew 1,256,723 fans.[65]

National League expansion arrived in 1962. The bonanza attendance figures that had rewarded the relocated teams did not automatically carry over to the expansion clubs. Both of the new clubs were shackled with inadequate stadiums and neither reached the million mark in attendance during their first year. Houston, now the seventh largest city in the majors, had waged a six-year campaign for big league recognition. Voters had repeatedly approved bills to build a big league ballpark, but public officials had hesitated to start construction before the city secured a team. To accommodate the new Colt 45's, the city hastily built a temporary open-air stadium seating 32,000 people. The heat of the day forced most games into the nighttime, the hunting hours for the city's voracious mosquitoes. Colts Pitcher Hal Woodeschick recalled: "We'd get to the ballpark and watch it rain every day between four and five in the afternoon. Then the groundskeepers would go through the stands with an insecticide fogger to kill the mosquitoes. The ballplayers would have to be sprayed before every game. If we didn't have the stuff on our bodies, they would eat us up in the bullpen."[66] A healthy but unspectacular 924,456 fans braved the heat and mosquitoes to watch the eighth-place team play.

In New York, the fledging Mets, playing in the decaying Polo

Grounds, erected a monument to ineptitude. The team, managed by the inimitable Casey Stengel and stocked with aging former all-stars like Gil Hodges and Richie Ashburn and soon-to-be legendary underachievers Marv Throneberrry and Choo Choo Coleman, staggered out of the gate, losing their first nine games. They improved only minimally, triumphing in only forty of 160 games to post the worst winning percentage in major league history. "The youth of America," as Stengel referred to the dedicated and surprisingly rabid fans, turned out to see the team, but in less than stellar numbers. The Dodgers and Giants in their last year of residence had drawn a total of almost 1.7 million fans. Only 922,530 paid to see the Mets in 1962, fewer than had watched the Dodgers in 1957. Games with the prodigal Dodgers and Giants accounted for a disproportionate percentage of the Mets' draw.

Having reluctantly created four new franchises, three of them in cities that already or previously had teams, Organized Baseball evidenced no inclination to further enlarge its domain. The major league hopes of other cities once again rested with snaring an existing franchise by building a new stadium and promising greener pastures. Ironically, the teams most available for relocation were the Braves and Athletics, two of the clubs that had begun baseball's reconfiguration less than a decade earlier. Astonishingly, the Braves had fallen on hard times in Milwaukee. The Braves had won pennants in 1957 and 1958 and attracted two million fans for four consecutive seasons. In the early 1960s, however, the enthusiasm evaporated when the Braves dropped from contention. Ownership policies exacerbated the situation. The team converted general admission seats into higher-priced reserve seats and, perhaps more offensive to Milwaukeeans, barred fans from bringing their own beer into the ballpark.[67] In 1961 attendance dropped to 1.1 million; in 1962 it fell to 766,921.

Meanwhile, the situation in Kansas City had degenerated into farce. The Athletics had finished in sixth place during their inaugural 1955 season, but only reached that less than dizzy elevation once over the next decade. Baseball expert Bill James, who grew up rooting for the Athletics in those years, laments, "It would be very difficult, if not impossible for any team to become as bad as the Kansas City Athletics were. . . . The A's never had a winning record. . . . They very rarely had a winning *month.*" Before acquiring the Athletics, Kansas City had hosted a New York Yankee farm club. During the late 1950s the Athletics appeared to maintain that role. Whenever the club developed a good player like Roger Maris or Ralph Terry, it traded him to the Yankees, where he blossomed into a star. Many fans blamed owner Arnold Johnson, who had close ties to the Yankee owners. However, the situation did not improve after Johnson died in 1960 and the team fell into the hands of eccentric Chicago insurance man Charles O. Finley. Finley discontinued trading with the Yankees, but the team continued to flounder on the field. The irascible Finley feuded with his players, sportswriters, the league office, and Kansas City itself. Under these circumstances Kansas City fans gave the Athletics surprisingly strong support, but attendance nonetheless fell precipitously during the Finley years.[68]

By 1963 both the Braves and the Athletics had begun to cast about for new homes. Finley, as James notes, "spent his entire time in Kansas City threatening to move." In 1961 he eyed Dallas–Ft. Worth. He considered Denver, New Orleans, Phoenix, and Seattle as well.[69] The American League repeatedly turned down his requests to move. In Milwaukee Lou Perini, who had moved the team in 1953, sold the Braves to a Chicago-based syndicate. Reports circulated that the new owners planned to relocate the team. "We didn't buy the franchise to move it. . . . How do those rumors get started?" asserted Braves Board Chairman William Bartholomay. Shortly thereafter he secretly hired a firm to find a new home for the Braves.[70]

Both the Braves and the Athletics honed in on Atlanta as a potential market. Although the Georgia community had fewer residents than either Milwaukee or Kansas City, it had other charms. A growing metropolis far distant from any major league town, Atlanta boasted the entire South as its hinterland. Revenues from a seven-state television and radio network promised to more than make up for any attendance shortfalls. The Atlanta-based Coca-

Cola Company reportedly was prepared to purchase extensive advertising time. Civic boosters hoping to justify public expenditures to entice a big league team echoed a now familiar refrain. "The true worth of a major league team is what it does for the posture of a city," explained Arthur B. Montgomery of Coca-Cola. "You're either a first-rate or a second-rate city." Atlanta's aggressive Mayor Ivan Allen cited the "national prestige" that he hoped his city would earn. "Is there any other area of activity where a city gets as much national publicity as sports?" asked Allen. With the civil rights movement growing, Allen also saw the acquisition of a big league team as evidence of a new era in southern race relations. Atlanta, the home of Martin Luther King, billed itself as a city "too busy to hate." "Major league sports here are a by-product of equal rights," explained Allen. "The Negro's full citizenship was one reason we (are) looked on with favor and the Negro population swells our potential."[71]

Finley visited Atlanta in 1963 and promised Mayor Allen that if Atlanta built a stadium, he would move his team there. The American League, however, refused to grant Finley permission to move and forced him to sign a four-year lease guaranteeing that he would remain in Kansas City. Mayor Allen nonetheless secured approval for the construction of a downtown stadium and began negotiations with the Braves, whose owners registered at Atlanta hotels under false names to hide their involvement. In March 1964, Bartholomay and Allen shook hands on an agreement to move the Braves to Atlanta. One month later Bartholomay, amid a concerted season-ticket selling push designed to save the team for Milwaukee, again blatantly lied about his intentions. "We are positively not moving," he told reporters. "We are playing in Milwaukee, whether you are talking of 1964, 1965 or 1975. I hope this is the last time anyone tries to link us with Atlanta or any other city."[72]

The Sporting News exposed Bartholomay's chicanery in July 1964. Milwaukee exploded with livid anger. The *Milwaukee Journal* decried the "greed, ingratitude, deception, and betrayal" that characterized the Atlanta coup. Baseball, charged Mayor Henry W.

Maier, had become "a traveling flea circus." The city feared losing the $3.5 million that major league baseball purportedly added to the economy, explained *Sports Illustrated*, and furthermore it did not "relish the colossal loss of face it would suffer. Milwaukee, scornfully called Bushville when the Braves arrived in 1953, would be right back where it started."[73] One letter writer captured the controversy in a parody of classic baseball verse:

This is the worst of all possible deeds,
From Boston to Bushville to South. . . .
Hopping around where the outlook's more sunny,
Clutching and grasping for big TV money,
Changing their names till it ain't even funny,
From Boston to Bushville to South.[74]

Both Milwaukee County and the state of Wisconsin filed antitrust suits to block the Braves' flight. The city, they argued, had expended millions of dollars to construct the stadium and support the team. The Braves would be the first team to abandon a publicly funded stadium and Milwaukee would be the first major league city to be left entirely without a baseball franchise. "How a ball club is permitted to come into a city like this, milk it for a dozen years and then jump elsewhere, I can't understand," protested Milwaukee County Executive John Doyne. Under these circumstances, argued the city attorney, "The denial of major league baseball . . . constitutes a denial of a substantial and significant right to the city."[75] Milwaukee won an injunction preventing the Braves from moving in 1965, but the National League granted the team permission to switch to Atlanta in 1966.

The Braves played three exhibition games in their new Atlanta stadium ("the happiest occasion since we got General Sherman headed back north in 1864," stated Mayor Allen) and then settled in for an unhappy lame-duck season in Milwaukee. The Wisconsin Supreme Court dashed any hopes of permanently blocking the move when it declared itself "powerless" to act against a major league team.[76]

In 1966 the Braves opened the season in Atlanta, where they drew 1.5 million fans in their inaugural season. More significantly, the Braves collected $2.5 million in television and radio revenues, five times what they had earned in Milwaukee. Georgia sportswriter Furman Bisher hailed these developments, without any sense of irony, as the "Miracle in Atlanta." *The Sporting News,* on the other hand, called them a "sorry chapter in baseball history."[77]

The loss of Atlanta to the Braves infuriated Charlie Finley. When his lease to play in Municipal Stadium expired in 1967, Finley announced that he would move the Athletics to Oakland, California, where the city had built a new ballpark, and threatened to sue the American League if they again blocked his plans.[78] The people of Kansas City expressed mixed reactions to the departure of the Athletics. Although bitter over the abandonment, they seemed relieved to see Finley leave. "The loss of the A's is more than recompensed by the pleasure of getting rid of Mr. Finley," commented U.S. Senator Stuart Symington, "Oakland is the luckiest city since Hiroshima."[79]

Both Kansas and Milwaukee now called for another expansion to win back their major league status. "We can't steal a team from another city after what we've been through," explained one potential Milwaukee investor. A group called Teams, Inc., headed by local Ford dealer Bud Selig, set out to convince Organized Baseball to add more teams. In Kansas City an advertisement in the local newspaper congratulated the community on losing the A's, predicting, "the real excitement, the real fun that comes with solid, year-in, year-out major league baseball is just around the corner. . . . In two years we will be back and will field a team that will truly represent Kansas City."[80]

The major leagues, arguing that the available talent pool would not support expansion, targeted 1971 as the earliest possible date to add new teams. The delay infuriated Missouri's Senator Symington. Symington, reportedly using "picturesque language similar to dock hands," convinced baseball owners to accelerate their timetable rather than succumb to a new congressional investigation.[81] Big league officials agreed to a new expansion for the 1969 season. When announced, the lineup of new teams included Kansas City, Seattle, San Diego, and Montreal. Baseball had bypassed Milwaukee, the erstwhile home of the Braves.

The latest round of reshuffling again yielded disappointing results. Although the Atlanta Braves drew well in the late 1960s, the Athletics did not catch on in Oakland. Finley had brought with him to California not the sad sack Athletics who had demoralized Kansas City, but a squad of exciting young players destined for greatness. The 1968 roster included Reggie Jackson, Rollie Fingers, Jim "Catfish" Hunter, Bert Campaneris, Sal Bando, and Joe Rudy. The Athletics won more games than they lost for the first time since 1952. But after 50,000 fans turned out for the home opener, the crowds never materialized. Finley, writes Norman Macht, "gave them fan appreciation days, but very few came out to be appreciated." The Athletics drew only 111,000 more fans in Oakland than they had in Kansas City.[82]

If the Athletics' invasion of Northern California failed to significantly improve Finley's financial fortunes, it nonetheless shattered the idyll of the crossbay San Francisco Giants. When Horace Stoneham had moved the Giants to San Francisco, he had assumed he would maintain a monopoly in the region. "We thought there'd always be one club in the vicinity and we'd be it," he explained. The arrival of the A's "certainly . . . will hurt us," predicted Stoneham. "It is a question whether both of us can survive."[83] From 1958 to 1967 the Giants had been one of baseball's great success stories, averaging almost 1.5 million patrons a year, despite playing in the ill-conceived Candlestick Park. In 1968 Giant attendance dropped to 837,220. With the exception of 1971, when the team won a division championship, the Giants failed to attract over 900,000 fans until 1978. The Athletics, meanwhile, became the best team in baseball, winning the World Series in 1972, 1973, and 1974, but only once drawing over 1 million people to the Coliseum.

Of the four expansion teams added in 1969, only the Montreal Expos drew particularly well. The Expos attracted 1.2 million fans while winning fewer than a third of their games, but Kansas City fans displayed lukewarm affection for their replacement team. Only

902,414 turned out to watch the new Royals play. In San Diego the Padres lost 110 games and drew a meager 512,970 people. The Seattle Pilots, who, according to *Sports Illustrated*, "charged some of the highest prices in baseball to watch one of the sport's worst teams," declared bankruptcy after one season.[84] The American League hastily moved the Pilots to Milwaukee, where, under the stewardship of Bud Selig, they became the Brewers.

Since 1961 expansion teams had demonstrated a mixed record. Before 1969 none of the teams, with the exception of the third-place 1962 Los Angeles Angels, fared well in the standings. Nonetheless, the National League teams, thanks to the construction of new stadiums, had flourished at the box office. In Houston the 1965 opening of the Astrodome, baseball's first indoor arena, lured 2.1 million people to see the recently renamed Astros finish in ninth place. Dubbed the "Eighth Wonder of the World," the Astrodome continued to be an attraction even as the club foundered. The New York Mets moved to Shea Stadium in 1964, where they regularly drew in excess of 1.7 million fans a year despite their perennial last-place finishes. Suddenly, in 1969, the Mets, behind a young pitching staff bolstered by Tom Seaver, miraculously won the World Championship. Mets fans, jubilant in defeat, grew ecstatic in victory. Attendance climbed to over 2 million fans.

One final shift would close out baseball's era of movable franchises. In Washington the second incarnation of the Senators had proven no more successful than the first. Other than in 1969, the American League expansion team had finished repeatedly at or near the bottom of the standings. Attendance had only occasionally topped 700,000 fans. Team owner Robert Short blamed the lack of support on the proximity of the Orioles, Washington's high crime rate, and the District's predominantly black population. But the Senators' perpetually laggard performance and the highest ticket prices in baseball kept even willing fans at bay. Short, wrote Arthur Daley, had "bought a franchise that was overpriced. He was underfinanced. Acting as his own general manger, he was hornswoggled in every trade."[85]

But, as Daley observed, "There is a reward for mismanagement in modern baseball. . . . The delinquent is given permission by the lodge brothers to seek instant prosperity elsewhere." After the 1971 season Short moved the Senators to Dallas–Ft. Worth, where city fathers promised him a new stadium and a $7.5 million radio-television deal. Many people suspected that Short had deliberately orchestrated the Senators' failure. Short had previously owned the Minneapolis Lakers of the National Basketball Association. After a few years he had moved the Lakers to Los Angeles, where he sold the team for a substantial profit. He had repeated a similar scenario in Washington. "Bob Short committed the perfect crime. He stole our team," complained one Senator fan.[86]

The Senators, renamed the Rangers, debuted in Texas in 1972. Nearly two decades had passed since the Braves had left Boston. The baseball map now bore little resemblance to the traditional contours that had defined the pre-1953 era. Expansion had introduced eight new teams; nine cities had lost teams to other communities. Washington, D.C., had lost two teams. The result was a truly more national pastime, played in many more cities and regions. Yet a sense of restiveness, resistance, and skepticism had replaced the enthusiasm that had greeted the earlier franchise shifts. "Now, as never before," commented Congressman Emanuel Celler after the second flight of the Senators, "there is growing recognition that the owners . . . occasionally exhibit precious little concern for the community welfare." The owners, complained Senator Sam Ervin, "demonstrate a 'public be damned' attitude."[87]

Nor had baseball's haphazard, unplanned approach to franchise placement necessarily benefited the game. Total major league attendance had jumped from 14.4 million in 1952 to 27 million in 1972, but average team attendance in 1972 was less than it had been in the post-World War II boom years, despite a dramatic national population increase and a longer season. Several teams appeared poised to move yet again. The San Francisco Giants seemed destined for Toronto. Charlie Finley began eyeing New Orleans. The Twins reportedly had soured on Minnesota, and Washington, D.C., hoped to fill its baseball void with the San Diego Padres. The outward path, however, would be strewn with legal barriers.

Ever since the Braves had left Milwaukee, noted *The Sporting News*, "No club has moved without facing political heat, legal action, or the threat of lawsuits. Now the penalty for moving a team in distress is a multimillion dollar damage suit."[88]

The impending chaos that seemed so imminent in the 1970s never came to pass. The 1972 exodus of the Senators marked the last franchise shift of the twentieth century. Baseball would add six more teams through expansion, extending its domain into Florida, Colorado, Arizona, Toronto, and returning to Seattle, but the teams that existed in 1972 remained in place. An age of stability replaced an era of uncertainty, and fans rewarded the teams with a new outpouring of support that would drive baseball attendance to unprecedented heights. Although few realized it in the mid-1970s, baseball stood on the brink of a new golden age.

Populist Baseball
Baseball Fantasies
in the 1980s

Baseball's postmodern era began fittingly in a French restaurant on Manhattan's East Side in January 1980. Thirty-one-year-old writer Dan Okrent assembled a group of friends at La Rotisserie Français to suggest a way to make the upcoming season "a little more fun." Okrent's proposition was a simple one. "It wasn't enough to watch baseball, or to study it in the box scores and leaders list," he told his colleagues. "We all [wish] in some way to possess it, to control it." As lifelong baseball fans, they had honed the skills necessary to run a baseball team. "Hadn't we been appraising talent all our lives?" asked Okrent. Can't we run a team better than Al Campanis, the general manager of the Los Angeles Dodgers, or Tal Smith of the Houston Astros? But as Okrent knew, "Lacking twenty million bucks, memberships in the right country clubs, and a pair of plaid pants, I was clearly never going to own a major league baseball club." Okrent suggested that the group create its own major league: form teams, draft real major league players, and keep track of the progress of their squads based on how the players performed in several statistical hitting and pitching categories. Unlike the real majors, each team would have an identical amount of money to spend, thus leveling the playing field. They dubbed their creation the Rotisserie League and over the next several weeks hammered out a league constitution and rules. By the start of the season, the group had grown to eleven—ten men and one woman—and on the first Sunday of the season they gathered to hold an auction, placing dollar values on players from the rosters of the National League.[1]

The game began as a whimsical lark. The owners, predominantly writers and advertising executives, thought up clever names for their teams. Okrent called his club the Okrent Fenokees, after the swamp in the Pogo comic strip; Michael Pollet's charges became the Pollet Burros; Rob Fleder's team, the Fleder Mice. But the competition quickly took a serious turn. The Rotisserie League came to dominate their lives. "Each morning, all of us ran to the box scores, manically searching the agate type for news," reported Okrent. The "owners" made daily calls to major league teams to check out the health of their players. Bruce McCall began publishing a newsletter about his McCall Collects. Okrent, the commissioner of the league, compiled the weekly standings from statistics in *The Sporting News*. Unable to wait for the journal to arrive in the mail on Friday, he would drive twenty miles each way to a newsstand that received the paper on Thursday.[2]

The owners developed a schizophrenic rooting style that transcended traditional baseball loyalties. They might root in one inning for a batter on the Mets, in the next for a pitcher on the Dodgers. The Rotisserie League had, in effect, deconstructed baseball, breaking down the game from its normative team emphasis, and reconstituting it on an individual statistical basis. This fantasy now assumed its own reality. "You could say these teams are imaginary," wrote Rotisserie Leaguer and *Sports Illustrated* reporter Steve Wulf, "but we prefer to think of them as real and the Chicago Cubs as imaginary." The Rotisserie Leaguers made trades, waiver moves, and placed players on the disabled list. They teased, bantered, argued, and bonded. "They're animals, thieves, liars, and cheats. And I don't say that lovingly," charged Valerie Salembier, the league's only woman owner, who clawed her way to a fourth-place finish. At the start of the season many of the owners hardly knew each other, but, as Steve Wulf later wrote, they had learned that solid friendships could be "formed out of knowing Biff Pocoroba's vital statistics." By the end of the season, most agreed with Glen Waggoner's repeated cry, "This is the best thing that ever happened to me."[3]

During the 1980 season Okrent had formed a second circuit, the Bush League, based in New England and drafting players from the American League. In Spring 1981 Okrent published an article in *Inside Sports* chronicling the Rotisserie League's inaugural season. A second feature, "How To Own A Baseball Team" by Conn Nugent of the Bush League, appeared in *Harvard Magazine.*[4] Both pieces included rules for playing the game. Suddenly Rotisserie Leagues and other fantasy loops began popping up throughout the nation. By 1984, when Okrent and the other founding fathers and mother published *Rotisserie League Baseball*, an "official how to play guide," the game had become, according to *People* magazine, "the hottest craze to hit the national pastime since trading cards." Soon hundreds of thousands of people played Rotisserie League baseball and its variants. Celebrity participants included Congressman Fred Gandy, New York Governor Mario Cuomo, and *Today* Show host Bryant Gumbel, who when in China regularly called New York to monitor his team's progress. The term Rotisserie League became a part of the national sports language. "I'm convinced," joked Okrent, "that if I bring about world peace and find a cure for cancer, the headline on my obituary will still be, 'Okrent Dies—Invented Rotisserie.' "[5]

Writing in 1981, Nugent referred to his Bush League as "populist baseball." "We have reinvented baseball," boasted original Rotisserie League member Lee Eisenberg.[6] Indeed, the Rotisserie League was only one manifestation of an explosion of vicarious fan participation in the 1980s. Fans not only rediscovered baseball, they attempted to redefine and reclaim it in their own image. The Rotisserie creators had inadvertently tapped into several broad currents of change coursing through the game and nation in the 1980s: resentment over soaring baseball salaries, the binding of the nation's psychological wounds after the divisive 1960s, the maturity and affluence of the postwar baby boom generation, and the emergence of a new information age triggered by the personal computer, satellite communications, and cable television. Many baseball fans perceived an opportunity to indulge themselves in an illusory form of empowerment. They flocked to ballparks in record numbers. They rejuvenated childhood dreams by becoming owners of fantasy teams and players at "fantasy camps," where aging baby boomers worked out with and played against the baseball heroes of their youth. They reconstructed baseball statistics, devising new ways to measure player productivity and assess conventional strategies. Many invested the game with a new baseball romanticism. Intellectuals wrote scholarly articles and books and penned soppy paeans to baseball's ethos. Filmmakers evoked the game's mystique in movies like *The Natural, Bull Durham*, and *Field of Dreams*. These efforts were neither coordinated nor necessarily conscious, but Americans in the 1980s attempted, in Okrent's words, to "possess" and "control" baseball, to reshape it to fit the contours of the computer and consumer age of late twentieth-century America.

Baseball attendance had remained relatively static during the 1960s and early 1970s. Despite infusions generated by franchise shifts and expansion, average game attendance hovered between 14,000 and 15,500, well below the post–World War II peak. In the mid-1970s patronage began to rise. Some have attributed this surge to the remarkable 1975 World Series that pitted the Cincinnati Reds against the Boston Red Sox. Five of the seven contests were decided by one run. In the sixth game, regarded by many as the greatest ever played, the Red Sox staved off elimination with Bernie Carbo's game-tying three-run home run in the eighth inning and then won it in the twelfth on Carlton Fisk's majestic home run down the left-field foul line. Amid protests from traditionalists, most World Series games had been shifted from afternoon to evening to accommodate the television audience. On the night of the seventh game a record 76 million people tuned in to watch the grand finale.[7] The Reds came from a 3–0 deficit to tie the game in the seventh and win it, 4–3, in the ninth. The following year major league attendance soared over the 30-million mark for the first time in baseball history. Real growth escalated, however, in 1977, when total attendance (sparked in part by expansion into Toronto and Seattle) jumped to 38,709,780 and the game average reached an unprecedented 18,380. In 1979 teams averaged over 20,000 patrons per game. Ten years later the figure topped 26,000, as over 55 million people turned out for major league games.

Baseball's sudden prosperity, achieved in an unstable economic environment, reflected several factors.[8] New stadiums with easier automobile access attracted suburban fans. A series of close divisional races invigorated interest. Perhaps most significantly, the vast postwar generation, raised in the 1950s, the last era in which professional baseball would reign as the nation's undisputed favorite sport, had reached maturity and returned to its roots. Moving into their thirties and settling down with jobs and families, male baby boomers, many of whom had allowed their baseball allegiances to ebb during the tumultuous sixties, once again appeared at games. With the Vietnam War over in 1975 and the countercultural impulse on the wane, many former protesters staged a symbolic homecoming through baseball. The sheer numbers and growing affluence of the postwar cohort fueled baseball's resurgence.

Ironically, the new interest in baseball coincided with a controversial transformation of the baseball industry. Beginning in the late 1960s the Major League Baseball Players' Association, led by veteran union organizer Marvin Miller, had steadily chipped away at baseball's venerable reserve clause, the contract stipulation that bound players to one team and prevented them from selling their services to the highest bidder. In December 1975, as baseball basked in the afterglow of the Reds–Red Sox World Series, a federal arbitrator ruled that players could only be reserved for one year at the end of their contracts, after which they would become free agents. The decision transformed baseball's economic structure and sent team payrolls skyrocketing. The average salary jumped from $45,000 in 1975 to $144,000 in 1980 and $891,000 in 1991.[9] A new breed of high-spending team owners, symbolized by George Steinbrenner of the New York Yankees and Ted Turner of the Atlanta Braves, fueled the bidding frenzy. Attempts by team owners to stem the rising tide led to a long player strike in 1981 and a shorter work stoppage in 1985. Fans grew increasingly frustrated by the constant labor-management warfare and alarmed by the escalating player incomes.

The economic strife, however, failed to deter people from going to the ballpark. Indeed, free agency stimulated attendance by ending the age of baseball dynasties. In earlier decades a few teams, most notably the New York Yankees, had dominated competition. The new baseball marketplace allowed teams to quickly rebuild and contend, ushering in an era of competitive balance. Between 1976 and 1991 nine different teams won the National League pennant and eight triumphed in the American League.[10] Six other teams won divisional titles. Not even the bitter seven-week shutdown in 1981 seriously dented fan enthusiasm. Attendance in 1982 established a new major league record.

Okrent's Rotisserie League captured both the upsurge in enthusiasm and the growing resentment over rising player salaries and overbearing owners. In the fantasy league competitors bid for players in much the same way that the modern baseball magnate did. Okrent entitled the 1981 *Inside Sports* article that launched the phenomenon "The Year George Foster Wasn't Worth $36," a pointed contrast to the hundreds of thousands of dollars a player of Foster's stature might draw as a free agent. "There being no Marvin Miller present, we quickly agreed to a form of price fixing," explained Okrent of the decision to cap spending at $250 per team. Although Okrent in 1981 focused on the challenge of being a general manager, subsequent accounts more frequently emphasized the fantasy of ownership. *Playboy* called the competitors "Armchair Steinbrenners," a sentiment shared by Jim Battles of the Pacific Ghost League. "I feel like an owner, like George Steinbrenner," commented Battles in 1983. " 'I paid good money for you guys,' I feel like saying, 'and you're dogging it.' "[11]

The illusion of ownership, however, paled before the fantasy of playing in the major leagues. Former Chicago Cubs catcher Randy Hundley and longtime Cubs fan Alan Golding ran summer baseball camps for children. Why not, they wondered, a camp for "middle-aged kids," where men over thirty-five could practice and play against Hundley and his former teammates? Their 1982 brochure promised, "We won't just take you out to the ball game. We'll put you in it—against the 1969 Chicago Cubs." The price tag was a hefty $2,195 plus meals for a one-week camp, but sixty-three aspiring, if over-the-hill, athletes, ranging in age from thirty-six to fifty-six, responded. They included a corn farmer, a jet pilot, an engineer, a psychiatrist, a Chicago policeman, a law professor who canceled his classes to attend, and a host of other professionals. In January 1983 they traveled to the former Cubs spring training facilities in Scottsdale, Arizona, where they were greeted by the stars of the 1969 Cubs, including Hall of Famer Ernie Banks, future Hall of Famers Billy Williams and Ferguson Jenkins, all-star third baseman Ron Santo, and Hundley. The real Cubs ushered the Cub-wanna-bes into the locker room where they donned genuine Cubs uniforms. "Most of us would have been willing to die at that point," reported camper and *Sports Illustrated* writer Roy Blount, Jr.[12]

The novices received instruction from the former ballplayers. "Williams showed me that I'd been holding a bat wrong all my life," revealed Blount. "I've [also] been holding the glove wrong all my life. [Jim] Hickman and Jenkins also explained to me that I'd been holding the ball wrong all my life."[13] The faux-Cubs dressed, showered, and sat in the whirlpool with the real Cubs who regaled them with tales of their legendary manager Leo Durocher and the team's storied collapse in 1969 before the oncharging Miracle Mets. After a week of training, the middle-aged pretenders played a game against the Cubs, batting and pitching against their onetime heroes, in front of a crowd of 4,200 people, including Durocher himself.

Like all fairy tales this one had its dark side. The campers pulled hamstrings and discovered aches in deltoids, quadriceps, and other muscles they had never known existed. "The only part of me that doesn't hurt is my fingernails," moaned one amateur. A thirty-eight-year-old real estate developer required knee surgery. And the play on the field could leave one feeling, in Blount's description "overpowered" and "lost." "It was never my boyhood dream to miss a pop-up in front of thousands of people," confessed Blount. The 1969 Cubs crushed the upstarts 23–6 in the final contest. Nonetheless, the uncommon venture proved an outrageous success. Television networks glorified these "historic first middle-aged campers" on national news reports. Blount's raucous *Sports Illustrated* article, entitled, fittingly, "We All Had a Ball," glamorized the "fantasy camp" for millions of potential participants. "The reality," affirmed *New York* Magazine, was "better than the fantasy."[14]

Other entrepreneurs moved quickly to sate the reawakening of adolescent baseball hormones. In 1984 a company called Baseball Fantasies Fulfilled offered a Los Angeles Dodgers camp. Another packaged a Yankees/Dodgers version, wherein "you play the game with your heroes and against your enemies." By 1985 a half-dozen promoters ran operations featuring players from fifteen different teams, including baseball idols Willie Mays and Mickey Mantle. Several major league clubs sponsored their own camps. The training junkets became popular gifts from wives on their husband's fortieth birthdays. Acquisitive child-men carted home baubles and souvenirs: camp T-shirts, replica big league contracts, videotaped highlights of the week's play, group camp photos, personalized bats, baseball trading cards with their photos and personal information, and uniforms bearing their names. Costs soon soared as high as $3,400, but the high price did not diminish the ardor of the affluent clientele. In 1990 the Big League Sports Medicine Conference in Reno staged a physicians' baseball camp, where doctors interspersed medical seminars with workouts led by former San Francisco Giants Orlando Cepeda and Vida Blue, while receiving twenty credit hours of continuing medical certification.[15]

The popular camps allowed aging fans to indulge a variety of baseball fantasies. "This is one place where I can completely immerse myself in a fantasy world and not think of anything else but baseball," observed a Canadian corporate president. The men could "think, smell, and eat baseball for seven days," noted one of the rare female participants.[16] With few exceptions the camps were a male preserve. Grown men revived childhood visions and aspirations long since left behind, though not forgotten. The play actors imagined themselves as their boyhood heroes. "I'm on third base, dancing down the line like Jackie Robinson," marveled a Dodger camp partisan, moments before stealing home. Others spoke of dashed hopes. "My dream was to be a professional baseball player," confessed one participant. "I had to settle for being a doctor."[17] Most endured considerable physical agony to complete the camps. An Arkansas neurosurgeon broke two ribs diving into second base. He wired himself with an electronic device to block the pain and played out the week. A lawyer pitched two innings with a broken hand. A fifty-two-year-old from Los Angeles discovered on returning home, "Both of my shoulders had self-destructed . . . but I didn't realize it at the time. I was on an emotional high all week." Nonetheless, he confessed, "I am ready to go back to Dodgertown again and go through the paces one more time."[18]

The chance to fraternize with real baseball players, with whom, observed a pair of sociologists, the campers had "sustained imaginary social relations since adolescence" proved the most satisfying fantasy. "These guys represent the best years of our lives," remarked a nostalgic neurosurgeon. As Blount noted, "Take away the Cubs and the camp would have degenerated into middle-aged doctors, lawyers, brokers and businessmen, rolling around on the ground fighting over whose bat it was."[19] Meeting the heroes of one's youth could at times be less than exhilarating. Financial consultant Robert Grossman described meeting the always-charming Enos Slaughter at a Yankee camp. As Grossman walked to the plate, bat in hand, Slaughter called him over as if to give him a batting tip. "He stops six feet in front of me and deposits a gallon of tobacco juice on my right cleat," Grossman recorded in his diary. "The guy scares me." But when Grossman met former Yankee first baseman Bill "Moose" Skowron in the hotel lobby, Skowron asked to join him for dinner. "He would like to join *me?*"

marveled Grossman. "I spend two hours talking to the Moose. . . . This is one of my main heroes. . . . Just me and the Moose. . . . Who is going to believe this? He pays for dinner over my objections. I would have bought him a car for those two hours and he pays for my dinner." If that was not enough, Grossman later found himself "nose to nose" with Mickey Mantle. "I walk into the elevator and turn to jelly. . . . I drool and twitch. My voice is strangely high-pitched and hoarse at the same time," wrote the adoring acolyte. Mantle also awed a White Plains attorney. "I hope my wife understands this," said the lawyer after meeting Mantle. "I can die now and go to heaven."[20]

The onset of a new information age further enhanced the ability of baseball fans to vicariously participate in the game. The emergence of computers had generated a fascination with numbers not unlike what had swept the nation in the era of Henry Chadwick. Baseball, with its rich statistical heritage and ongoing analytical possibilities, became a showpiece and testing ground for the new technology. Computers offered the possibility of amassing data and generating simulations to establish probabilities based on large numbers of occurrences. As early as 1959 statisticians used early mainframe computers to construct models of play based on thousands of theoretical games. In 1965 General Electric demonstrated a new computer model by analyzing American League clutch hitting. Two years later Macmillan Publishing employed Information Concepts, Inc. (ICI) to create a massive database of baseball records. Under the guidance of David Neft, a professional statistician, ICI researchers painstakingly compiled a player-by-player, season-by-season accounting of the game's history. ICI entered the information into a computer data bank and Macmillan typeset the resulting volume entirely by computer—the first such book ever prepared in this manner. *The Macmillan Baseball Encyclopedia* appeared in 1969 and established a milestone in baseball and computer applications. Its hundreds of pages of minute statistical information placed the answers to myriad baseball questions at any fan's fingertips and opened new vistas for serious researchers.[21]

Others also grasped the potential of the computer for baseball analysis. Brothers Eldon and Harlan Mills recorded every play from the 1969 and 1970 seasons into a computer in order to determine the possible outcomes of each batter's plate appearance. A Canadian statistician simulated 200,000 games to determine a team's best possible batting order. Pete Palmer embarked on an even more ambitious project. Palmer created a computer model based on all major league games played since 1901, incorporating the result of every at bat, enabling him to measure the significance of every possible offensive event.[22]

In the 1960s and early 1970s only those with access to powerful mainframe computers could engage in this level of inquiry. But a growing number of fans, with and without computers, became interested in challenging baseball's antiquated reliance on traditional statistics. In 1971 Bob Davids gathered sixteen fellow baseball enthusiasts at Cooperstown, New York, to form the Society for American Baseball Research (SABR). Dedicated to promoting the study of both baseball history and statistics, the organization grew slowly but steadily. SABR's committee on statistical analysis, chaired by Pete Palmer, attracted a core of partisans who questioned the sanctity of batting average as the dominant measure of baseball prowess and devised new methods to gauge performance. They exchanged ideas about baseball statistics and published their results in SABR's *Baseball Research Journal*.[23]

Among the new breed of rebels was a shy, intensely curious Kansan named Bill James. A baby boomer born in 1948, James had developed a facility for numbers and a fascination for baseball undimmed by his boyhood allegiance to the woeful Kansas City Athletics. At the University of Kansas in the 1960s, James majored in English and economics, learning mathematical modeling techniques and the rudiments of graceful writing. Upon graduation he served in the army and then briefly as a high school teacher. But James's true passion remained baseball. In the mid-1970s he abandoned the classroom and took a job as a boiler room attendant at a food packing plant. The pay was poor and the prospects dim, but the position allowed James to "spend five minutes an hour making sure the furnaces didn't blow up and 55 minutes working on my numbers."[24]

His numbers came from the *Macmillan Baseball Encyclopedia* and daily box scores. James counted them, reconfigured them, recalculated them into new statistics, and recorded his findings in endless notebooks. He worked without a computer or even a calculator. A self-confessed "eccentric" and "stat freak," James counted "all kinds of stuff that lots of people are sort of interested in, but nobody in his right mind would actually begin to count." He tallied the number of stolen bases recorded against each catcher and pitcher. He recorded how many people paid to see each starting pitcher. James considered himself a "baseball agnostic," making "it a point to never believe anything just because it is widely known to be so." He developed a technique of "listening very carefully to the things that baseball people said and then asking the question: If this is true, what would be the consequences of it? If it was false, what would be the consequences of that?" Sportscasters might comment that a ballplayer had his prime years between the ages of twenty-eight and thirty-two or a manager might credit a defensive player with saving his team 100 runs a year. James would spend tedious hours poring over box scores, checking out these assertions. He had also learned to doubt many of the statistical assumptions that had governed the game since Chadwick's day and sought to develop new measurements of batting, pitching, and fielding.[25]

Standing tall and darkly bearded, James bore a cursory resemblance to the nineteenth-century father of baseball statistics. He also shared Chadwick's crusading zeal, if not in the direction of social reform, at least regarding the uses and abuses of baseball numbers. To James, baseball statistics had "the powers of language" constituting "a literature and poetry accessible to millions." Some numbers evoke power, others speed. They "define skills, they draw limits," wrote James. Furthermore, baseball possessed an unparalleled historical record, compiled across the decades to allow a level of analysis and interpretation unavailable in almost any other field. Yet commentators relied on unverified traditional wisdom and oft-repeated clichés. Sportswriters, protested James, used baseball statistics selectively not to understand baseball, but to "decorate their articles" and force conclusions by "arranging . . . evidence so that it points in the direction desired." James, on the other hand, wanted to develop tools and measures to establish the validity of these assertions, "to teach people . . . to cut toward the truth."[26]

James discovered kindred spirits in SABR and dubbed the work of the upstart statisticians "sabermetrics." He wrote articles based on the new science for *Baseball Digest* and authored a regular column for the small-circulation *Baseball Bulletin*. Although he believed that an audience existed for his work, most editors did not agree. "The articles I thought were really good, the articles that made a contribution toward one's understanding of the subject, would not sell," he learned.[27] In 1977 James decided to self-publish his work, offering unorthodox statistics unavailable anywhere else. Operating out of "a tiny bedroom in one of the tiniest houses" in Lawrence, Kansas, James calculated monthly records for batters and pitchers, counted the stolen bases allowed by individual catchers and pitchers, and introduced the concept of range factor (counting all the plays each defensive player successfully participated in) as a replacement for fielding average. He photocopied, collated, and stapled the sixty-eight-page typewritten manuscript between two cover pieces and tossed in instructions for a table baseball game. James entitled his effort the *Baseball Abstract*, priced it at four dollars a copy, and advertised in *The Sporting News* and other baseball publications. Seventy-five people responded.[28]

James's first *Abstract* relied heavily on numbers interrupted only occasionally by exposition. He lacked, he later explained, "the self-confidence to write about the material." With his second *Abstract*, published in 1978, James began to hit his stride. Weighing in with 115 pages, James introduced a team-by-team format and supplemented his statistics with lengthy analytical essays.[29] A graceful and often witty writer, James adopted an informal conversational style. His *Abstracts*, as he later wrote, had "no true beginning, no middle or end, no natural order, any more than a series of conversations that you might have with a friend would have a beginning, a middle, or an end." He encouraged his readers to follow his thought processes and engage in their own analysis. He introduced new statistics as "tools" to equip them to explore these issues on their own. He aimed his writing not at the average baseball supporter, but at the intense, intelligent, educated elite at the peak of the fan pyramid. The 1978 edition sold 325 copies.[30]

By 1981 James had emerged as a cult figure to a small but growing group of followers who shared his disdain for conventional baseball wisdom. His early subscribers included Roger Angell, the *New Yorker's* popular baseball writer nonpareil, novelist Norman Mailer, baseball agent Randy Hendricks, and Rotisserie League creator Dan Okrent. Through Okrent's intervention James became a regular contributor to *Esquire*. In 1980 Angell recounted an afternoon at the ballpark with James in the *New Yorker*, describing the *Abstract* as "invaluable" and James's use of statistics as "dazzling." In 1981 Okrent made James the focus of a long, laudatory feature in *Sports Illustrated*. "He finds things in [baseball statistics] that most people don't know are there," crowed Okrent. That year, the *Abstract*, still self-published, but now a bound volume complete with graphics, sold 2,200 copies.[31] In 1982 Ballantine Books began producing *The Bill James Baseball Abstract* for a mass audience.

The years in the wilderness had allowed James to hone his craft and emerge on the national scene as a polished talent. The first *Abstract* introduced several fundamental concepts that underscored James's work: batting averages overrated players like Bill Buckner, who rarely walked or hit home runs, and underrated others like Gene Tenace, who had low batting averages, but nonetheless reached base frequently and hit for power; hitter-friendly ballparks like Fenway Park inflated offensive statistics, while Shea Stadium and others favored pitching, resulting in statistical illusions in judging players; and, most significantly, players could be evaluated using "Runs Created," a formula that James had developed that combined "all of the known elements of a player's batting record" into a reliable measure of offensive production. James presented his "tool shack," a collection of a dozen original measures of player performance with esoteric names like "Isolated Power," "Value Approximation Method," and "Pythagorean Method." He promised that forty more tools lay waiting to be unveiled in future editions. James also evaluated teams, managerial strategies, and, in what would become his most popular and controversial feature, ranked major league players at every position.[32]

James's sharp wit and pungent opinions elevated the *Baseball Abstracts* from a technical treatise into an entertaining excursion. "The starting eight of the Phils has nearly 100 years of professional experience, which would be wonderful if they were in the real estate business," he wrote in 1980. "There is a tunnel at the end of the light, and it is not far off." He described Cleveland second baseman Duane Kuiper as "a pathetically inept offensive player," commenting, "It's absolutely incredible that a player this bad could be given 3,000 at bats in the major leagues." His engaging digressions into relatively meaningless topics like the "Birthday effect" (batters hit better on their birthdays) and Reggie Jackson's performances before large crowds further spiced the *Abstracts*. When Joe Morgan, one of James's favorite performers, stated that "I don't think that I've ever had a bad September," James checked it out and concluded, "I think I've finally found Joe's weakness. The man has no memory. He has probably had more bad Septembers than any great player in history."[33]

The *Baseball Abstract* took off. The 1982 and 1983 editions sold a total of 150,000 copies. His eighth annual *Abstract*, published in 1984, rose to number four on the *New York Times* best-seller list. Articles featuring James appeared in nonsports journals like *Atlantic Monthly*, *Psychology Today*, and *Discovery*. *Sport* magazine hailed James in 1984 as "arguably the most influential baseball writer in America."[34]

James remained, however, a "designated outsider." His sudden success, blunt assessments, and inevitable miscalls offered ample ammunition for critics. "I think we—the media—have created a monster," worried sportswriter Tracy Ringolsby in 1984. "James has gotten carried away with himself. He sets himself up as a godlike figure. . . . He's trying to make absolute judgments in a game that has no absolutes." After James described Detroit Tiger utilityman Enos Cabell as a player who "can't play first, can't play third, can't hit, can't run and can't throw," Cabell responded, "I think he knows as much about baseball as I do about writing." Cabell's manager Sparky Anderson, a frequent James target, added, "I don't think anyone in baseball takes him very seriously."[35] Others noted that James's forecasts were often erroneous. The eloquently disparaged 1980 Phillies, after all, won the World Series.

Far more important than the accuracy of James's predictions was his impact on baseball statistics and reporting. By 1984 James had become the central figure in a virtual baseball revolution in which fans wielding personal computers and sophisticated and often complex new statistics sought to wrest control of baseball's numerical soul from the sport's traditional record keepers. The introduction of the personal computer in the late 1970s and its rapid proliferation in the 1980s empowered thousands of people to engage in a type of analysis previously available to a select few. By 1985 SABR itself had grown to almost 6,000 members. The success of the *Abstract* opened the doors of publishing houses to scores of books on baseball statistics. These works ranged from the truly significant, like *The Hidden Book of Baseball* by John Thorn and Pete Palmer, which became the basis for *Total Baseball*, the definitive compendium of the game's history and statistics, to the superficial and inconsequential.

Major league baseball and the people who reported on the game were characteristically slow to recognize the potential of the computer and the rising statistical sophistication of its fans. "Computers are coming. They are ready for us, but we are not quite ready for them," commented Cleveland Indian general manager Gabe Paul back in 1965. Two decades later baseball remained largely unprepared. Like many other people confronted with the new technology, baseball remained leery of its applications and consequences. No teams used computer technology in any meaningful way before 1983. *Discovery Magazine* reported only a quarter of the teams employed computers in 1987. Baseball people "think they know it all and would like to keep everything in their heads. They wouldn't dream of turning game decisions over to a computer," explained one entrepreneur trying to sell baseball computer systems to reluctant buyers. Most rejected and resented the work of James and other "stat freaks." "People who have spent their lives in baseball tend to distrust the ideas of people who haven't played," observed sabermetrician Gary Gillette.[36]

Newspapers had also failed to recognize the increased demand for statistical information. In 1981, when Bill James and Rotisserie Leagues first burst on the scene, the daily press reported only the most rudimentary elements of baseball information in their weekly summaries: batting average, at bats, runs scored, home runs, hits and runs batted in for hitters; wins, losses, innings pitched, walks, strikeouts, and earned run average for pitchers. Players who did not have the requisite number of at bats or pitching decisions never appeared. Early Rotisserie Leagues turned to *The Sporting News*, the "Bible of Baseball," for more complete statistics for all players. But, as a weekly, *The Sporting News* presented stale, outdated numbers and omitted key information like walks for batters and increasingly popular statistics like on base percentage and slugging average. The original Rotisserie League omitted fielding from its calculations because *"The Sporting News* doesn't publish weekly fielding stats, and without weekly stats you've got no way to compute weekly standings, and without weekly standings you've got nothing to live for."[37]

The new communications revolution, however, provided a solution. On September 15, 1982, Gannett Newspapers launched *USA Today*, the nation's first national daily newspaper. Assembled in Washington, D.C., and then distributed via satellite to printing plants throughout the nation, *USA Today* made an expanded "results-oriented" sports section one of its prime features, "the immediate hook to get people into the paper," according to one editor. The mandate for the sports section, according to in-house historian Peter Prichard, was "to cover every game, every score, and every statistic." *USA Today* offered expanded league standings and box scores, which included up-to-date batting and earned run averages, home runs, runs batted in and stolen base counts, and other pertinent information. A box with details on "how they scored" accompanied each game account. To the delight of Rotisserie Leaguers, *USA Today* published complete up-to-date major league batting and pitching statistics each Wednesday and Thursday. Although the newspaper as a whole received generally unflattering assessments from media critics, the sports section garnered instant raves. "If what matters are results, old-fashioned scores and averages and standings, and more of them than you can get anywhere else, *USA Today* routs its rivals," commented the *Washington Journalism Review*. "And it is just what hardcore sports fans have been craving for years—but not getting."[38]

The *USA Today* sports section became, along with its colorful weather map, its most emulated feature. Local dailies, according to *Sports Illustrated*, "started paying more attention to nuts and bolts," increasing the space allotted to sports and publishing enhanced standings, box scores, and statistical summaries. The "endless columns of stats . . . whetted the public appetite for even more." *USA Today* replaced *The Sporting News* as the primary source for Rotisserie Leagues. The fantasy circuits, claimed *Time* Magazine in 1987, sent *USA Today* circulation soaring each spring.[39]

For those who could not wait until the following morning, the information revolution offered other options. By 1984 Dan Okrent had hooked into a computer service that allowed him to check National League box scores each night on his home computer. The spread of cable television, pioneered by Ted Turner who broadcast Atlanta Braves games as a staple of his innovative national channel, allowed Rotisserie Leaguers to watch a seemingly never-ending flood of nationally televised games and catch nightly scores and details on ESPN, a twenty-four-hour cable sports network. "I once loved baseball as normal men do," wrote fantasy league enthusiast Kevin Cook. Now, "I watch the Cubs on WGN, the Braves on WTBS, the Dodgers on KTTV, and everyone else on [ESPN] SportsCenter, Sports Latenight, and George Michael's Sports Machine."[40] The constant stream of sports results became a precursor for the split screen format, offering an ongoing flow of business and news information that became commonplace in American newspapers and on cable and network television in the 1990s.

Although the early Rotisserie Leagues usually did not rely on computers, by the mid-1980s personal computers were becoming an essential element of fantasy play. In 1985 Ghost League Baseball sold a computer program that instantly calculated Rotisserie standings and a weekly modem service that downloaded current statistics. Other software packages soon followed. "The Rotisserie phenomenon has a lot to do with the development of the personal computer," reported the *Sporting News* in 1989, when fantasy players numbered an estimated half million people. "The computer makes it easier for everyone to get involved."[41]

Fans also became involved on an even more esoteric level, weaving a baseball romanticism out of folklore and nostalgia. Baseball novels proliferated during the 1980s. Major twentieth-century American literary figures like Bernard Malamud, Robert Coover, and Philip Roth had long ago discovered that baseball offered a fertile setting for serious fiction.[42] Their works, most notably Malamud's *The Natural* and Coover's *The Universal Baseball Association*, tended to be foreboding explorations of the limitations of the American dream. The prototypical baseball novel of the 1980s, however, struck a different chord.

The best-selling and most influential baseball novel of the decade, *Shoeless Joe* by W. P. Kinsella, appeared in 1982, roughly the same time that Bill James, Rotisserie Leagues, and Fantasy Camps gained notice. Kinsella's central character, Ray, a baby boomer and former English major, had become a particularly unsuccessful Iowa corn farmer. One day he hears a voice, telling him, "If you build it, he will come." Ray instinctively understands that "it" is a baseball diamond in his cornfield, and "he" is Shoeless Joe Jackson, the disgraced star of the 1919 Chicago Black Sox. In Kinsella's fantasy Ray builds the ball field, conjures up not just Jackson, but the other Black Sox as well, and lures reclusive novelist J. D. Salinger, author of the countercultural prophecy *Catcher in the Rye*, to Iowa, where he discovers America's lost soul. Ray is reunited with his father, a former minor league catcher, who died when Ray was young. *Shoeless Joe* unabashedly paid homage to baseball as the key to a reawakening of the American spirit. "The play reaffirms what I already know," Jackson tells Ray. "That baseball is the most perfect of games, solid true, pure and precious as diamonds. If only life was so simple."[43]

In 1984 film director Barry Levinson and star Robert Redford brought Malamud's *The Natural* to the screen. As a novel, *The Natural* had merged baseball history and the Arthurian legend into a dark, depressing vision of human fallibility. Roy Hobbs, possessor of almost superhuman baseball skills, repeatedly fails to achieve his full potential because of his inability to learn from experience. Like the real Joe Jackson, he succumbs to temptation and accepts money to throw a crucial playoff game. Hollywood's version remained relatively faithful to the original until the grand finale. Amid inspirational music and colorful fireworks, Hobbs, portrayed by the preternaturally handsome, golden-haired Redford, defies the fixers and hits the game-winning home run. He then returns to his midwestern home, reunited with a son he never knew (nor had in the novel), to play catch among waving fields of golden wheat.

The movie version of *The Natural* horrified many critics and viewers. "This may or may not be a good picture, but it . . . certainly isn't my book," Malamud reportedly commented. *Time* magazine critic Richard Shickel lamented that "Malamud's intricate ending is vulgarized . . . [They] transform something dark and open-ended—truly fabulous into something eccentrically sentimental." Malamud's novel, complained Shickel, "was sacrificed on the altar of a happy Hollywood ending." But if the filmmakers had tampered with a literary masterpiece, they had produced a baseball classic. The movie struck a chord among contemporary Americans. Screenwriter Robert Towne explained, "The duties of a screenwriter are not just as a technician to adapt a book. In large part they are to reflect the attitude of his time. Malamud wrote the book following a catastrophic war. . . . From the vantage point of 1984 . . . I'm writing about the ability of man to overcome defeat."

The Natural, as a movie, captured not Malamud's vision, but the sensibilities of 1980s America, risen from the ashes of Vietnam and the uncertainties of the 1960s and 1970s.[44]

Before 1984 baseball films had been considered box office poison. The popular success of *The Natural* opened the floodgates to a stream of baseball cinema, most of it idyllic and romanticized, with uplifting and happy endings. Modern day movie Caseys rarely struck out. Unlike *The Natural*, the most popular of these movies focused around fans, not players. In *Bull Durham*, former minor league player Ron Shelton's bawdy, knowing tribute to small-town baseball, the most memorable character is Annie Savoy, an attractive, intelligent woman who each year selected a player on the team to expose to her special brand of sexual and spiritual enlightenment. "I believe in the Church of Baseball," intones Susan Sarandon as Annie in the movie's memorable opening. "I've tried all the major religions and most of the minor ones. And the only church that feeds the soul, day-in, day-out, is the Church of Baseball."[45] In 1989 *Shoeless Joe* came to the screen as *Field of Dreams*, and Kinsella's hypnotic incantation, "If you build it, he will come," entered the nation's cultural language. Kinsella's message of regeneration through baseball permeated the film. "The one constant through all the years has been baseball," spoke the Salinger character, renamed Terence Mann. "Baseball has marked the time. The field, this game, is part of our past . . . It reminds us of all that once was good, and that could be again."[46]

This type of sentimentality dominated the vast outpouring of baseball writing during the decade, as journalists, academics, and intellectuals offered their thoughts on the game. Poet Donald Hall, echoing themes offered in the movie version of *The Natural* and in *Shoeless Joe*, celebrated baseball in a collection of essays entitled *Fathers Playing Catch with Sons*. Pulitzer Prize–winning newspapermen George Will and David Halberstam wrote best-selling books on the game.[47] Baseball history and literature became the subject of scholarly studies and university courses.

No figure epitomized the romantic elevation of fan and game more than A. Bartlett Giamatti. A scholar of Renaissance literature and lifetime Boston Red Sox rooter, Giamatti had written a lyrical paean to the game entitled "The Green Fields of the Mind" in the *Yale Alumni Magazine* in 1977. "You rely on it to buffer the passage of time, to keep the memory of sunshine and high skies alive," rhapsodized Giamatti. Baseball for Giamatti was "the last place where Americans dream . . . the last great arena, the last green arena, where everybody can learn the lessons of life." When named president of Yale University, he confessed, "All I ever wanted to be was president of the American League."[48] He became instead in 1986 the President of the National League and then, in 1989, the Commissioner of Baseball. Giamatti, the ultimate fan, had achieved the ultimate fan fantasy.

The idealization of baseball in the 1980s might easily be interpreted as a reflection of the era of Ronald Reagan, a reassertion of traditional verities and values in a conservative decade. But remnants of 1960s countercultural thinking ran through much of the fan-based reinvention of baseball. James attributed his dogged independence to his "sixties youth." Much of the rhetoric of "populist" baseball revolved around issues of empowerment. "Where once slouched a slavish fan, dependent on the judgement and money of others, there now stands a Jeffersonian squire with his own team and destiny," wrote Conn Nugent of the Bush League.[49] *Bull Durham's* Annie Savoy embodied the free-spirited, sexually liberated truth seekers of the 1960s, who dabbled in religions seeking fulfillment. *Field of Dreams* transformed Kinsella's incarnation of J. D. Salinger into the fictional Terrence Mann, a former black radical and sixties icon portrayed by James Earl Jones. Disillusioned, Mann had become embittered and dropped from sight. None of these characters, real or fictional, completely surrender their social ideals or spirit of rebellion, but they discover a form of reentry into the American mainstream through the healing power of baseball.

The trend culminated in 1994 when the Public Broadcasting Service (PBS) presented *Baseball: A Film by Ken Burns*. Televised nightly over the course of a week, the eighteen-and-a-half-hour documentary combined magnificent historical baseball footage with the romantic ruminations of celebrity fans about baseball's role in American life. Burns, a baby boomer, veteran of the antiwar movement, and lifelong baseball fan, encapsulated the excessive idealization of the game. Baseball, he argued, "encodes and stores the genetic material of our civilization," offering "the comfort of continuity, the generational connection of belonging to a vast and complicated American family, the powerful sense of home . . . and the great gift of accumulated memory."[50]

The blatant excesses, rhetorical overkill, and obvious self-indulgence of the fan movement of the 1980s invited a critical skewering. For many the quest for vicarious participation epitomized what historian Christopher Lasch called a "culture of narcissism." "What we have here, I'm afraid," complained one sportswriter about Rotisserie Leagues in 1990, "is the worst of the '70s Me Decade (how can I use this thing to validate myself?) and the '80s Greed Decade (how can I cash in without actually doing anything?) creating the baseball fan of the '90s." Rotisserie baseball, protested another critic, "seems like total bourgeois individualism run amuck. It hasn't reinvented the game so much as buried it under the manipulation of stats and the exertion of wills."[51] The obsessive popularity of fantasy baseball posed problems in many workplaces. "In their drive to keep up with the stupefying stream of statistics they need . . . many Rotissereans will make use of the office computer, fax machines, long-distance lines and photocopier," reported *USA Today* in 1993. Some dedicated up to an hour of their workday to their fantasy teams. The Iowa Racing and Gaming Commission suspended its executive secretary for using office facilities and time to manage his club. Even the Rotisserie pioneers seemed appalled by their creation. "Now I know how Dr. Frankenstein must have felt," wrote Steve Wulf in 1989. Dan Okrent agreed. "I'm with the people who say, 'Get a life.' This has just gotten to be nuts," exclaimed Okrent in 1993.[52]

A similar backlash had set in against the new statistics. The game, wrote Roy Blount in 1991, had become "staturated." "Bat, ball and glove have been replaced by computer [and] calculator

. . . or so it seems in this age of statistical overkill," remonstrated George Vass in *Baseball Digest*. Bill James pulled the plug on the *Baseball Abstract* in 1988. In an uncharacteristically churlish farewell, James remarked on "an unchecked explosion" of meaningless numbers, "a Chernobyl of statistics, polluting nearly every discussion." James, who had always encouraged the give-and-take with his readers, wrote, "I get more and more letters that irritate the hell out of me. . . . I am encountering more and more of my readers that I don't even like."[53] James's mission to provide a better breed of baseball statistics and to revamp traditional thinking had been only partially successful. Statistics offered in newspapers and on game broadcasts were now more plentiful and modestly more sophisticated. But the broader messages conveyed by James and his fellow sabermetricians had changed the game minimally. Game strategies remained governed by the traditional wisdom, rather than statistical analysis, and few teams paid any attention to ballpark or other statistical illusions in making personnel decisions.

Indeed, the subconscious, quixotic, often idiosyncratic quest to reclaim and reinvent the game in the 1980s had never been more than a fantasy. Although fans might contend for spiritual dominance, control rested firmly in the hands of the players and owners, who remained embraced in a deadly serious economic struggle. Americans continued to celebrate baseball in the early 1990s. A staggering 70,256,456 fans, an average of almost 31,000 a game, attended major league games in 1993. Baseball seemed on a record pace again in 1994. But on August 12, prodded by intractable owners determined to control salaries, players again went on strike. Unable to reach agreement, the antagonists canceled the World Series, violating a ninety-year-old trust. The strike dragged on into the 1995 season, carrying with it much of the romantic enthusiasm of the preceding decade. Sales of baseball books plummeted from their consistently high prestrike levels. When the labor conflict finally ended, fans returned hesitantly.

Baseball, however, once again demonstrated the resilience and technological adaptability that had carried it through its earlier crises. The Internet offered new ways for fans to follow their teams, both real and fantasy. The democratic vehicles of personal web pages and online discussion lists reinvigorated fan participation. In 1998 Mark McGwire of the St. Louis Cardinals and Sammy Sosa of the Chicago Cubs staged a mesmerizing race to establish a new seasonal home run record, and the resurgent New York Yankees won 125 total games to establish a new standard for excellence. Interest and attendance rose anew as baseball stood poised on the brink of the twenty-first century. Despite the perennial warnings of baseball Cassandras, time has yet to pass baseball by. What remains to be seen is not whether the game will survive, but how Americans in a rapidly changing world will again reinterpret and reinvent their national pastime.

Notes

Chapter 1: The National Game

1. The Currier & Ives print *The National Game* has been reproduced in many histories of baseball. See, for example, John Bowman and Joel Zoss, *Diamonds in the Rough: The Untold History of Baseball* (New York: Macmillan, 1989), 234.
2. Allen Guttmann, *From Ritual to Record: The Nature of Modern Sports* (New York: Columbia University Press, 1978), 100; A. Bartlett Giamatti, "The Green Fields of the Mind," *Yale Alumni Magazine* (November 1977); Michael Novak, *The Joy of Sports: End Zones, Bases, Baskets, Ball* (New York: Basic Books, 1976), 62; Ralph Andreano, *No Joy in Mudville: The Dilemma of Major League Baseball* (Cambridge, Mass.: Shenkman, 1965), 3; Warren Jay Goldstein, *Playing for Keeps: A History of Early Baseball* (Ithaca, N.Y.: Cornell University Press, 1989); Steven M. Gelber, "Their Hands Are All Out Playing: Business and Amateur Baseball, 1845–1917," *Journal of Sport History* 21 (1984), 5–27; Steven M. Gelber, "Working at Playing: The Culture of the Workplace and the Rise of Baseball," *Journal of Social History* 11 (Summer 1983), 3–22.
3. On variations on townball, see George B. Kirsch, *The Creation of American Team Sports: Baseball and Cricket, 1838–1872* (Urbana: University of Illinois Press, 1989), 53–54; and Harold Seymour, *Baseball: The Early Years* (New York: Oxford University Press, 1960), 7.
4. David Quentin Voigt, *American Baseball: From the Gentleman's Sport to the Commissioner System* (University Park: Pennsylvania State University Press, 1983), 4.
5. R. M. Lewis, "Cricket and the Beginnings of Organized Baseball in New York City," *International Journal of the History of Sport* 4 (December 1987), 315; Seymour, 24; Terry R. Furst, "The Image of Professional Baseball: The Sport Press and the Formation of Ideas About Baseball in Nineteenth Century America" (Ph.D. diss., New School for Social Research, 1986), 3; Kirsch, 92; Geoffrey C. Ward and Ken Burns, *Baseball: An Illustrated History* (New York: Knopf, 1994), 6.
6. James M. DiClerico and Barry Pavelec, *The Jersey Game: The History of Modern Baseball from Its Birth to the Big Leagues in the Garden State* (New Brunswick, N.J.: Rutgers University Press, 1991), 25–26; Kirsch, 62–63.
7. Melvin L. Adelman, *A Sporting Time: New York City and the Rise of Modern Athletics, 1820–1870* (Urbana: University of Illinois Press, 1986), 136.
8. Seymour, 35; Adelman, 135.

9. *New York Times*, February 12, 1991; James W. McPherson, *What They Fought for, 1861–65* (New York: Anchor Books, 1995), 30.
10. On the spread of baseball from 1857 to 1860, see Seymour, 26, 29, 40, 43; Bowman and Zoss, 49–52; Kirsch, 70; and Adelman, 132.
11. Seymour, 50; Bowman and Zoss, 366–67.
12. Kirsch, 40–42; Lewis, 317; Seymour, 30; Kirsch, 97; Adelman, 110–14.
13. Kirsch, 97.
14. Guttmann, 95, 97; Bowman and Zoss, 67.
15. Guttmann, 107–8; Novak, 57.
16. David Lamoreaux, "Baseball in the Late Nineteenth Century: The Source of Its Appeal," *Journal of Popular Culture* 11 (Winter 1977), 598; Goldstein, 102; Novak, 57.
17. Gelber, "Working at Playing," 8–10; Goldstein, 162n.
18. Adelman, 293; Novak, 58.
19. Kirsch, 58–62.
20. Adelman, 291.
21. On the debate over the fly rule, see Goldstein, 48–56, and Adelman, 130.
22. Seymour, 30; Chadwick quoted in Goldstein, 49.
23. Adelman, 131, 148.
24. Stephen Freedman, "The Baseball Fad in Chicago, 1865–1870: An Exploration of the Role of Sport in the 19th Century City," *Journal of Sport History* 15 (Summer 1978), 42; DiClerico and Pavelec, 38; Guttmann, 97; Adelman, 156–57; Seymour, 44.
25. Kirsch, 210; Goldstein, 87.
26. Seymour, 42; Henry Chadwick, "Baseball," *Outing* 12 (May 1888), 117.

Chapter 2: The Mortar of Which Baseball Is Held Together
1. *The Echo*, March 20, 1889 (item 128 in the Edwin Chadwick Papers). With thanks to Anthony Brundage.
2. For discussions of Chadwick, see Ralph Andreano, *No Joy in Mudville: The Dilemma of Major League Baseball* (Cambridge, Mass.: Shenkman, 1965), 49–53; Frederick Ivor Campbell, "Via: Henry Chadwick," *Harvard Magazine* 90 (September–October 1987), 60–61; Jacob C. Morse, "In Memory of Henry Chadwick," *Baseball Magazine* 1 (June 1908), 9–11; Mac Sounders, "Henry Chadwick," *Baseball Research Journal* 15 (1986), 84–85; Edwin P. Tanner, "Henry Chadwick," in Allen Johnson and Dumas Malone, eds., *The Dictionary of American Biography*, Volume 2 (New York: Scribners, 1930), 587; Albert G. Spalding, *America's National Game* (Lincoln: University of Nebraska Press, 1992), 339–44; John Thorn and Pete Palmer, *The Hidden Game of Baseball: A Revolutionary Approach to Baseball and Its Statistics* (New York: Doubleday, 1984), 9–19; and Frederick Ivor-Campbell, "Henry Chadwick," in Frederick Ivor-Campbell, Robert L. Tiemann, and Mark Rucker, *Baseball's First Stars* (Cleveland: Society for American Baseball Research), 26–27.
3. Anthony Brundage, *England's "Prussian Minister": Edwin Chadwick and the Pol-

itics of Government Growth, 1832–1854 (University Park: Pennsylvania State University Press, 1988), 4.

4. Ibid.

5. Andreano, 49.

6. Henry Chadwick, *The Game of Baseball: How to Learn It, How to Play It, How to Teach It, with Sketches of Noted Players* (New York: George Munro, 1868), 9.

7. On Chadwick's early career, see Morse, 10, and *Reach Baseball Guide* (1909), 158.

8. Chadwick, *The Game of Baseball*, 10.

9. Biographies of Edwin Chadwick include Brundage, *England's "Prussian Minister"*; S. E. Finer, *The Life and Times of Sir Edwin Chadwick* (London: Methuen, 1952); and R. A. Lewis, *Edwin Chadwick and the Public Health Movement* (London: Longmans, 1952).

10. Biographical portraits of Henry Chadwick, including those in the *Spalding Baseball Guide* that he edited, often mentioned his brother. See also the favorable comments on Edwin Chadwick's call for exercise in the *New York Clipper*, August 4, 1860.

11. The best discussion of the antebellum reform movement is Ronald G. Walters, *American Reformers, 1815–1860* (New York: Hill and Wang, 1978). On sports and reform, see Melvin L. Adelman, *A Sporting Time: New York City and the Rise of Modern Athletics, 1820–1870* (Urbana: University of Illinois Press, 1986).

12. Adelman, 269–86.

13. Chadwick, *The Game of Baseball*, 10.

14. Henry Chadwick, *Hanley's Baseball Book of Reference* (1866), vii.

15. Warren Jay Goldstein, *Playing for Keeps: A History of Early Baseball* (Ithaca, N.Y.: Cornell University Press, 1989), 34.

16. Chadwick, *The Game of Baseball*, 112.

17. *Spalding Baseball Guide* (1889), 54.

18. Spalding, 341.

19. *Spalding Baseball Guide* (1889), 58. See also Goldstein, 139.

20. Ivor-Campbell, "Via: Henry Chadwick," 60.

21. Spalding, 341; John Bowman and Joel Zoss, *Diamonds in the Rough: The Untold History of Baseball* (New York: Macmillan, 1989), 70; Voigt, 67; Harold Seymour, *Baseball: The Early Years* (New York: Oxford University Press, 1960), 69.

22. Patricia Cline Cohen, *A Calculating People: The Spread of Numeracy in Early America* (Chicago: University of Chicago Press, 1982), 225.

23. Ibid., 175, 12.

24. Victor C. Hilts, "Statistics and Social Science," in Ronald N. Giere and Richard S. Westfall, *Foundations of the Scientific Method: The Nineteenth Century* (Bloomington: Indiana University Press, 1973), 211.

25. Cohen, 176, 219.

26. Chadwick, *The Game of Baseball*, 11.

27. George B. Kirsch, *The Creation of American Team Sports: Baseball and Cricket, 1838–1872* (Urbana: University of Illinois Press, 1989), 27; Chadwick, ibid.

28. Chadwick, ibid.

29. Cohen, 225.

30. Chadwick, *The Game of Baseball*, 11–12.
31. Ibid., 10.
32. Ibid., 11; Paul Dickson, *The Joy of Keeping Score* (New York: Walker and Company, 1996), 54.
33. Dickson, 15.
34. Henry Chadwick, ed., *Beadle's Dime Base Ball Player: Comprising the Proceedings of the Annual Baseball Convention* (1861), 58.
35. Dickson, 15; John J. Evers and Hugh S. Fullerton, *Touching Second: The Science of Baseball, the History of the National Game, Its Development Into an Exact Mathematical Sport, Records of Great Plays and Players, Anecdotes and Incidents of Decisive Struggles on the Diamond, Signs and Systems Used by Championship Teams*, 2nd ed. (Chicago: Reilly and Britton Co, 1910), 300; Andreano, 50–51.
36. Branch Rickey and Robert Riger, *The American Diamond: A Documentary of the Game of Baseball* (New York: Simon and Schuster, 1965); Thorn and Palmer, 4; Roger Angell, *The Summer Game* (New York: Viking Press, 1972), 3–5.
37. Thorn and Palmer, 9; Adelman, 124.
38. Thorn and Palmer, 11.
39. For a copy of this box score, see ibid., 13.
40. For a copy of this box score, see *Baseball Magazine* 18 (October 1925).
41. *Spalding Base Ball Guide* (1894), 37.
42. Thorn and Palmer, 11; Adelman, 175; Henry Hecht, "A Box Full of Goodies," *Sports Illustrated* 58 (April 4, 1983), 89.
43. Margo Anderson Conk, *The United States Census and the New Jersey Urban Occupational Structure, 1870–1940* (Ann Arbor: UMI Research Press, 1980), 1, 9–14; John Koren, ed., *The History of Statistics, Their Development and Progress in Many Countries* (New York: B. Franklin, 1970), 244. See also Helen Mary Walker, *Studies in the History of Statistical Method* (New York: Arno Press, 1975), 151–153 and H. Scott Gordon, "Alfred Marshall and the Development of Economics as a Science," in Giere and Westfall, 234–35.
44. Goldstein, 145.
45. Chadwick, 58; Thorn and Palmer, 14; Goldstein, 68–69.
46. Chadwick, *Beadle's Dime Baseball Player* (1864), 59–60.
47. Thorn and Palmer, 11–14; Goldstein, 175–76.
48. Chadwick, *The Game of Baseball*, 68.
49. Thorn and Palmer, 17.
50. Ibid., 28, 14.
51. Chadwick, *The Game of Baseball*, 67.
52. Ibid., 66.
53. *Spalding Base Ball Guide* (1894), 60.
54. *Baseball Magazine* 45 (November 1942); see, for example, Chadwick, *The Game of Baseball*, 112.
55. Thorn and Palmer, 36; Thomas R. Heitz, "Rules and Scoring," in John Thorn and Peter Palmer, ed., *Total Baseball* (New York: Warner Books, 1989), 2244; *Baseball Magazine* 44 (November 1942).
56. *Spalding Official Base Ball Guide* (1878–1883); *DeWitt Base Ball Guide* (1885), 117.
57. *Baseball Magazine* 45 (November 1942).

58. Ibid.

59. Heitz, 2245.

60. *Spalding Baseball Guide* (1889), 21.

61. *The Sporting News* (July 26, 1886).

62. Voigt, 67.

63. Peter Levine, *A. G. Spalding and the Rise of Baseball: The Promise of American Sport* (New York: Oxford University Press, 1985), 53, 62; Voigt, 158, 162; Spalding, *America's National Game*, 289–92; Ivor-Campbell, "Henry Chadwick," 27.

64. Ivor-Campbell, "Henry Chadwick," 27; *Baseball Magazine* 1 (June 1908).

65. Albert Bartlett, *Baseball and Mr. Spalding* (New York: Farrar, Star and Young, 1951), 289; Benjamin Rader, "Introduction," *The National Game* (Lincoln: University of Nebraska Press, 1992), xiii.

66. On Chadwick's final years, see Ivor-Campbell, 27; *Baseball Magazine* 1 (June 1908); *Reach Baseball Guide*, 1909.

67. *Baseball Magazine* 1 (June 1908).

68. Bartlett, 289; Rader, xiii.

69. John Heydler, "How the Batting Records Could Be Made More Accurate," *Baseball Magazine* 22 (January 1919), 140–43; Frank C. Lane, "The Faulty Foundations of Batting Averages," *Baseball Magazine* 42 (January 1929), 347–49.

70. Thorn and Palmer, 22–23.

Chapter 3: Incarnations of Success

1. Connie Mack, "Clean Living and Quick Thinking," *McClure's Magazine* 43 (May 1914), 53; Gustav W. Axelson, *"Commy": The Life Story of Charles A. Comiskey* (Chicago: Reilly & Lee, 1919), 290; William A. Phelon, "The Great American Magnate," *Baseball Magazine* 9 (January 1913), 17–23; Charles C. Alexander, *John McGraw* (New York: Viking, 1988), 7, 3.

2. Frank B. Hutchinson, Jr., "Charles Albert Comiskey—the Man," *Baseball Magazine* 2 (April, 1909), 52–55.

3. Frederick G. Lieb, *Connie Mack, Grand Old Man of Baseball* (New York: G. P. Putnam, 1945), 16–17; Connie Mack, *My 66 Years in the Big Leagues: The Great Story of America's National Game* (Philadelphia: Winston, 1950), 1–10, 21; "Connie Mack as Baseball Manager and Civic Servant," *Literary Digest* 104 (March 1, 1930), 41; Connie Mack, "The Bad Old Days," *Saturday Evening Post* 208 (April 4, 1936), 16–17.

4. Alexander, 9–14, 66.

5. Ed Fitzgerald, "Clark Griffith, the Old Fox," *Sport* 16 (May 1954), 45; Bob Considine and Shirley Povich, "The Old Fox, Baseball's Red-Eyed Radical and Arch-Conservative, Clark Griffith," *Saturday Evening Post* 208 (April 13, 1940), 15.

6. Alexander, 12; Mack, *66 Years*, 16; Hugh S. Fullerton, "Interesting People," *American Magazine* 71 (March 1911), 605; Axelson, 10–11.

7. Hugh C. Weir, "The Real Comiskey," *Baseball Magazine* 7 (February 1914); Axelson, 46.

8. Alexander, 17.

9. Mack, *66 Years*, 17.

10. Benjamin Rader, *Baseball: A History of America's Game* (Urbana: University of

Illinois Press, 1992), 67. On the Irish in baseball, see also Stephen A. Riess, *Touching Base: Progressive Baseball and American Culture in the Progressive Era* (Westport, Conn.: Greenwood Press, 1980), 184–85; and Alexander, 35.

11. David Quentin Voigt, *American Baseball: From the Gentleman's Sport to the Commissioner System* (University Park: Pennsylvania State University Press, 1983), 186; Eugene Converse Murdoch, *Ban Johnson: Czar of Baseball* (Westport, Conn.: Greenwood Press, 1982), 24; Harvey Frommer, *Primitive Baseball: The First Quarter Century of the National Pastime* (New York: Atheneum, 1988), 106.

12. Alexander, 4, 55.

13. Considine and Povich, 98, 127–30.

14. Bob Considine, *"Mr. Mack," Life* 25 (August 9, 1948), 50; Mack, "The Bad Old Days"; Harold Seymour, *Baseball: The Early Years* (New York: Oxford University Press, 1960), 182; Ed Fitzgerald, "The Truth About Connie Mack," *Sport* 10 (July 1948), 63; Lieb, 45.

15. Fitzgerald, "Clark Griffith," 72; "Clark (Calvin) Griffith," *Current Biography Yearbook, 1950* (New York: H. W. Wilson Co., 1950), 198–200.

16. Alexander, 38–39.

17. William G. Fullerton; "Connie Mack and His Athletics," *Harper's Weekly* 59 (September 12, 1914), 259; Axelson, 104, 74; Seymour, 179; Tiemann, SABR, 36.

18. Considine and Povich, 49.

19. *Current Biography Yearbook 1950*; Alexander, 39–40; Bill James, *The Bill James Historical Baseball Abstract* (New York: Villard Books, 1986), 112.

20. Charles C. Alexander, *Our Game: An American Baseball History* (New York: Henry Holt, 1991), 40; Seymour, 61.

21. Axelson, 112.

22. Dean A. Sullivan, ed., *Early Innings: A Documentary History of Baseball 1825–1908* (Lincoln: University of Nebraska Press, 1995), 187; Fitzgerald, "The Truth About Connie Mack," 64.

23. Mack, *66 Years*, 78–79.

24. Axelson, 113.

25. Fitzgerald, "Clark Griffith," 70.

26. Alexander, *John McGraw*, 20–22.

27. Ibid, 44–45.

28. Voigt, 284; Robert Burk, *Never Just a Game: Players, Owners and American Baseball to 1920* (Chapel Hill: The University of North Carolina Press, 1994), 147; Murdoch, 46.

29. Axelson, 128–29.

30. Alexander, 53, 63, 68–70.

31. Fitzgerald, "Clark Griffith," 72.

32. Voigt, 225.

33. On the founding of the American League, see Murdoch, 45–49; Bruce Kuklick, *To Every Thing a Season: Shibe Park and Urban Philadelphia* (Princeton, N.J.: Princeton University Press, 1991), 15–17; and Axelson, 141–42.

34. Francis C. Richter, *Richter's History and Records of Baseball, The American Nation's Chief Sport* (Philadelphia: F. C. Richter, 1914), 282.

35. Weir; William G. Evans, "Comiskey, Prince of Magnates," *Baseball Magazine* 20 (December 1917), 209–13.
36. Murdoch, 46.
37. Lieb, 65.
38. Fitzgerald, "Clark Griffith," 73
39. On the conflicts between McGraw and Johnson, see Alexander, 85–93.
40. Fitzgerald, "Clark Griffith," 74
41. Edward T. Collins, "Connie Mack and His Mackmen," *American Magazine* 77 (June 1914), 13–18; Riess, 161–62.
42. Henry B. Needham, "Connie Mack," *American Magazine* 72 (June 1911), 181–83.
43. Evans, "Comiskey, Prince of Magnates"; Weir; George C. Rice, " 'The Old Roman,' " *Baseball Magazine* 1 (June 1908), 47–50.
44. Rader, 86.
45. On the construction of new stadiums, see Robert F. Bluthhardt, "Fenway Park and the Golden Age of the Baseball Park, 1909–1915," *Journal of Popular Culture* 21 (Summer 1987), 43–52; G. Edward White, *Creating the National Pastime: Baseball Transforms Itself, 1903–1953* (Princeton, N.J.: Princeton University Press, 1996), 10–46; and Kuklick.
46. Axelson, 190–91.
47. Fitzgerald, "Clark Griffith," 74; Phelon.
48. White, 17–23. Kuklick, 15, 17.
49. Axelson, 130; Evans, "Comiskey, Prince of Magnates."
50. Burk, 159, 62; Kuklick, 50.
51. Axelson, 302; Burk, 159; Ring Lardner, *You Know Me Al* (New York: Scribner, 1960).
52. Marc Okkonen, *The Federal League of 1914–1915: Baseball's Third Major League* (Garrett Park, Md.: Society for American Baseball Research, 1989).
53. Considine and Povich, 91.
54. Fitzgerald, "The Truth About Connie Mack," 66.
55. Ibid; Murdoch, 79; Kuklick, 35–36; Mack, *66 Years*, 36.
56. Collins, 13–18.
57. Burk, 206.
58. Evans, "Comiskey, Prince of Magnates."
59. Ibid.; Axelson, 218, 318.
60. Eliot Asinof, *Eight Men Out* (New York: Holt, Rinehart, 1963), xi, 16.
61. James, 111–12.
62. Alexander, *Our Game*, 128–29; Burk, 233–34.
63. Ronald Story, "The Black Sox Scandal," in William Graebner, ed., *True Stories from the American Past* (New York: McGraw-Hill, 1993), 121; William P. Hayes, "Anecdotes of Charles Comiskey," *Baseball Magazine* 48 (January 1932), 345–47.

Chapter 4: New Ways of Knowing

1. Quoted in Warren Susman, *Culture as History* (New York: Pantheon, 1984), 105.
2. H. G. Salsinger, "The Glitter, The Gloss and the Glamor of It All," *Baseball*

Magazine 29 (November 1922), 539–40; Frank C. Lane, "Flashing the World Series to Waiting Millions," *Baseball Magazine* 28 (November 1922), 533–35.
3. Wilmer Thomson, unnamed, undated flyer found at a hamburger stand in Pennsylvania.
4. Quoted in Nick Curran, "How World Series Broadcasts Were Started in 1922," *Baseball Digest* (October 1964), 47–51.
5. Quoted in Curt Smith, *Voices of the Game* (South Bend, Ind: Diamond Communications, 1987), 9.
6. Susman, 111.
7. Walter Lippmann, *Public Opinion* (New York, Harcourt, Brace, 1922), 60–61.
8. Salsinger, 539–40
9. The following discussion is drawn primarily from Norman L. Macht, " 'Watching' the World Series," *American History Illustrated* (September–October 1991), 48–50.
10. Lane, 533–35; Salsinger; Irving E. Sanborn, "Flashing the Series to 50,000,000 People," *Baseball Magazine* 25 (November 1920), 517.
11. For the early history of radio, see Red Barber, *The Broadcasters* (New York: Da Capo Press, 1986), 8; Wayne M. Towers, " 'Gee Whiz!' and 'Aw Nuts!': Radio and Newspaper Coverage of Baseball in the 1920's," unpublished paper presented at the 62nd Annual Meeting of the Association for Education in Journalism, Houston, Texas, 1979; Smith, 6.
12. Smith, 8.
13. For details on the 1922 broadcast, see Towers, 13; Curran, 47; Smith, 9; G. Edward White, *Creating the National Pastime: Baseball Transforms Itself, 1903–1953* (Princeton, N.J.: Princeton University Press, 1996), 208–9; and Charles Fountain, *Sportswriter: The Life and Times of Grantland Rice* (New York: Oxford University Press, 1993), 196.
14. Towers, 13; Graham McNamee, *You're on the Air* (New York and London: Harper & Brothers, 1926), 58–59; White, 209; Smith, 11.
15. Lane, 533–35.
16. McNamee, 52–53.
17. Ibid., 58–59.
18. Barber, 11–12, 15; McNamee, vi.
19. Barber, 25; Gordon H. Fleming, *Murderers' Row* (New York: Morrow, 1985), 373.
20. Raymond F. Yates, "How Radio Magnifies the World Series," *Baseball Magazine* 35 (November 1925), 555–56.
21. McNamee, 184.
22. N. J. Abodaher, "Baseball Via the Ether Waves," *Baseball Magazine* (November 1929), 551–53; White, 211–17; Smith, 12.
23. Abodaher, 551–53; *Sporting News* quoted in White, 214–17.
24. Quoted in White, 216.
25. Quoted in Fleming, 355.
26. Smith, 21–24, 14.
27. Thomson flier.
28. Lane, 533–35; Thomson flier; McNamee, 55.

29. Paul Dickson, *Baseball's Greatest Quotations* (New York: HarperCollins, 1991), 64.
30. Marshall Smelser, *The Life That Ruth Built: A Biography* (New York: Quadrangle Books, 1975), 376; "The New Hero of the Great American Game at Close Range," *Current Opinion* (October 1920), 477–78; *Literary Digest* 73 (October 4, 1922), 58–62.
31. Quoted in Fleming, 86–87.
32. Ken Sobol, *Babe Ruth and the American Dream* (New York: Random House, 1974), 125; Richard Crepeau, *Baseball: America's Diamond Mind, 1919–1941* (Orlando: University Presses of Florida, 1980), 104; Benjamin G. Rader, "Compensatory Sports Heroes: Ruth, Grange and Dempsey," *Journal of Popular Culture* 16 (Spring 1982), 11–22; Susman, 146.
33. Smelser, 560; Roger Kahn, "The Real Babe Ruth," *Baseball Digest* 18 (October 1959), 23.
34. Frank C. Lane, "Why Babe Ruth Has Become a National Idol," *Baseball Magazine* 28 (October 1921), 483–85.
35. James K. Fitzpatrick, *Builders of the American Dream* (New Rochelle, N.Y.: Arlington House, 1977), 263.
36. Gerald Holland, "The Babe Ruth Papers," *Sports Illustrated* 11 (December 21, 1959), 111–17; Crepeau, 94; Fleming, 246.
37. Fleming, 121.
38. Sobol, 23, 141.
39. Silas Bent, *Ballyhoo: The Voice of the Press* (New York: Boni and Liveright, 1927), 190, 196.
40. Kal Wagenheimer, *Babe Ruth: His Life and Legend* (Maplewood, N.J.: Waterfront Press, 1990), 62–64.
41. F. C. Lane, "Baseball Takes the Air," *Baseball Magazine* 59 (June 1936), 293.
42. Laurence S. Ritter and Mark Rucker, *The Babe: A Life in Pictures* (New York: Tickner and Fields, 1988); Bent, 124.
43. Raymond Fielding, *The American Newsreel, 1911–1967* (Norman: University of Oklahoma Press, 1972).
44. Lippmann, 216; Sobol, 121.
45. Robert Creamer, *Babe: The Legend Comes to Life* (New York: Simon and Schuster, 1974), 205; Smelser, 201.
46. Reviews quoted in Fleming, 146–67, 283; Sobol, 19–20.
47. Smith, 8.
48. Grantland Rice, *The Tumult and the Glory* (New York: Barnes, 1954), 112–13.
49. Bent, 122, 133–24.
50. Quoted in Lippmann, 217–28.
51. Creamer, 186; Smelser, 109.
52. Christy Walsh, *Farewell to Heroes* (New York, 1937), 1–2.
53. Sobol, 139; Fleming, 286–87.
54. Walsh, 11–12.
55. Sobol, 122; Smelser, 200; Walsh, 25.
56. Fleming, 286–87.
57. Ibid., 52.

58. Sobol, 168–69, 190–91.
59. Roland Marchand, *Advertising the American Dream: Making Way for Modernity, 1920–1940* (Berkeley: University of California Press, 1986), 96.
60. Sobol, 168–69, 209; Wagenheimer, 86; Ritter and Rucker.
61. Walsh, 2, 14–16; Creamer, 273.
62. Walsh, 25; Sobol, 174–75; Fleming, 52.
63. Wagenheimer, 87; Fleming, 52; Walsh, 43.
64. Creamer, 333.
65. Quoted in White, 214–15.

Chapter 5: Adjusting to the New Order
1. Bill Rabinowitz, "Baseball in the Great Depression," in Peter Levine, ed., *Baseball History* (Westport, Conn.: Meckler, 1989), 49–50.
2. Ibid., 50.
3. G. H. Fleming, *The Dizziest Season: The Gashouse Gang Chases the Pennant* (New York: Morrow, 1984), 19; Rabinowitz, 50.
4. Gerald Holland, "The Great MacPhail," *Sports Illustrated* 11 (August 31, 1958), 58–64.
5. For an excellent discussion of these matters, see G. Edward White, *Creating the National Pastime: Baseball Transforms Itself, 1903–1953* (Princeton, N.J.: Princeton University Press, 1996), Chapters 5 and 7.
6. Rabinowitz, 52–54.
7. *Baseball Magazine* 50 (January 1933).
8. On Mack and the Athletics, see Charles C. Alexander, *Our Game: An American Baseball History* (New York: Henry Holt, 1991), 164; and Bruce Kuklick, *To Every Thing a Season: Shibe Park and Urban Philadelphia* (Princeton, N.J.: Princeton University Press, 1991), 62.
9. Rabinowitz, 52; White, 170; J. G. Taylor Spink, *Judge Landis and 25 Years of Baseball* (New York: Crowell, 1947), 172; Roland Marchand, *Advertising the American Dream: Making Way for Modernity, 1920–1940* (Berkeley: University of California Press, 1986), 305; Fleming, 22.
10. Bill James, *The Bill James Historical Baseball Abstract* (New York: Villard Books, 1986), 170; White, 121; James Vlasich, *A Legend for the Legendary: The Origin of the Baseball Hall of Fame* (Bowling Green, Ohio: Bowling Green State University Popular Press, 1990), 228–29.
11. Robert Rice, "Thoughts on Baseball," *New Yorker* 27 (May 26, 1950).
12. Harold Seymour, *Baseball: The Golden Age* (New York: Oxford University Press, 1971), 413–14; Neil J. Sullivan, *The Minors: The Struggles and the Triumph of Baseball's Poor Relation from 1876 to the Present* (New York: St. Martin's Press, 1990), 97; Robert Gregory, *Diz: Dizzy Dean and Baseball During the Great Depression* (New York: Viking, 1992), 39.
13. Seymour, 414; Paul Dickson, *Baseball's Greatest Quotations* (New York; HarperCollins, 1991), 357.
14. Benjamin Rader, *Baseball: A History of America's Game* (Urbana: University of Illinois Press, 1992), 134; Seymour, 413; Murray Polner, *Branch Rickey, A Biography* (New York: Atheneum, 1982), 81.

15. Rader, 134; Kevin Kerrane, *Dollar Sign on the Muscle: The World of Baseball Scouting* (New York: Simon and Schuster, 1989), 24, 27, 231–32; Gregory, 39.
16. Sullivan, 99–100.
17. Seymour, 417; Rader, 135.
18. Polner, 83; *Baseball Magazine* 44 (January 1930) and 75 (July 1946); David Quentin Voigt, *American Baseball*, Volume 2 (University Park: Pennsylvania State University Press, 1983), 161.
19. Polner, 110, 113.
20. Arthur Mann, *Branch Rickey: American in Action* (Boston: Houghton Mifflin, 1957), 156–57; Seymour, 414.
21. Kerrane, 57; Branch Rickey, *Branch Rickey's Little Blue Book* (New York: Macmillan, 1995), 123.
22. Polner, 103.
23. Kerrane, 176, 143.
24. Don Warfield, *The Roaring Redhead: Larry MacPhail—Baseball's Great Innovator* (South Bend, Ind.: Diamond Communications, Inc., 1987), 3–26.
25. Ibid., 26–27.
26. Ibid., 26–32.
27. Fleming, 223; Warfield, 59.
28. White, 164.
29. Gerald Eskenazi, *The Lip* (New York: Morrow, 1993), 96; Robert L. Taylor, "Borough Defender: MacPhail and the Dodgers," *New Yorker* 18 (July 12, 19, 1941).
30. Mann, 174; Warfield, 31–32.
31. Polner, 106; Arthur Mann, "The Larry MacPhail Story," *Sport* 21 (April, 1956).
32. Roger Kahn, *The Era* (New York: Ticknor & Fields, 1993), 18; Warfield, 48.
33. Warfield, 50–52.
34. Ibid., 52.
35. Ibid., 57–58.
36. Ibid., 58–59; Walter (Red) Barber, "The Night the Lights Came on in Baseball," *Modern Maturity* 26 (October–November 1983), 36.
37. Warfield, 60; Rader, 138.
38. Stanley B. Frank, "That MacPhail!" *Baseball Digest* 4 (April 1945), 7–10; Barber, 36.
39. Warfield, 61.
40. Harold Parrott, *The Lords of Baseball* (New York: Praeger, 1976), 103; Lee MacPhail, *My Nine Innings: An Autobiography of Fifty Years in Baseball.* (Westport, Conn.: Meckler Books, 1989), 4.
41. Leo Durocher, with Ed Linn, *Nice Guys Finish Last* (New York: Simon and Schuster, 1975); Holland, 58–64.
42. Warfield, 72–73; Holland, 58–64;
43. Warfield, 73; Mann, "The Larry MacPhail Story."
44. Warfield, 73; Ray Fitzgerald, "Larry MacPhail Deserves His Niche in the Hall of Fame," *Baseball Digest* 35 (May, 1978).
45. Warfield, 76–77.

46. Warfield, 78; Tommy Holmes, *Dodger Daze and Knights: Enough of a Ball Club's History to Explain Its Reputation* (New York: McKay, 1953), 141; Dickson, 262.
47. White, 182.
48. Mann, "The Larry MacPhail Story."
49. Red Barber, *Rhubarb in the Catbird Seat* (Garden City, N.Y.: Doubleday, 1968), 56–58; Warfield, 90–91.
50. Warfield, 95; Esknazi, 118–119.
51. Taylor, "Borough Defender"; Warfield, 138, 257.
52. Taylor, "Borough Defender."
53. Warfield, 89–90; Polner, 114–15; MacPhail, 23.
54. Warfield, 85–88; Parrott, 125–26.
55. Warfield, 85–88; Parrott, 125–26.
56. Eskenazi, 11; Polner, 119; Taylor, "Borough Defender."
57. Warfield, 265, 88; Parrott, viii, 71, 112, 117; Polner, 114–115.
58. Warfield, 139.
59. Ibid., 144.
60. Eskenazi, 105; Holmes, 176; Parrott, 117; Mann, "The Larry MacPhail Story."
61. Jack McDonald and Charles Dexter, "The Fall of the House of MacPhail," *Saturday Evening Post* 215 (April 17, 1943); Parrott, 141.
62. Parrott, 139.
63. Warfield, 257; Jules Tygiel, *Baseball's Great Experiment: Jackie Robinson and His Legacy* (New York: Oxford University Press, 1983), 50.
64. Tygiel, 51.
65. Warfield, 167; Kahn, 19.
66. Tygiel, 42–46, 57–58.
67. Tygiel, 69.
68. Ibid., 81, 83–85.
69. Ibid., 52; Warfield, 167–68.
70. Warfield, 174–77.
71. Mann, "The Larry MacPhail Story" and Arthur Mann, *Baseball Confidential: Secret History of the War Among Chandler, Durocher, MacPhail, and Rickey* (New York: McKay, 1951).
72. Mann, "The Larry MacPhail Story."
73. Gerald Holland, "The Great MacPhail," *Sports Illustrated* 11 (August 17, 1958), 62–68; Kahn, 139; Warfield, 219–20.
74. Tygiel, 81; Holland, "The Great MacPhail" (August 31, 1958).
75. Dickson, 336; Warfield, 126, 250.

Chapter 6: Unreconciled Strivings
1. On Rube Foster, see Peterson, 103–15; Rogosin, 33; Bruce 31–32; Lanctot, 29; and Jules Tygiel, "Black Ball" in John Thorn, Pete Palmer, Michael Gershman, and David Pietrusza, *Total Baseball*, 5th ed. (New York: Viking, 1991), 435.
2. The literature on black baseball is extraordinarily rich. The pioneering works in this field include Robert Peterson, *Only the Ball Was White: A History of the Legendary Black Players and All-Black Professional Teams* (Englewood Cliffs, N.J.: Prentice-Hall, 1970) and Donn Rogosin, *Invisible Men: Life in Baseball's Negro*

Leagues (New York: Atheneum, 1983). An impressive body of team and community studies has supplemented these overviews. This chapter relies heavily on Richard Bak, *Turkey Stearnes and His Detroit Stars: The Negro Leagues in Detroit, 1919–1933* (Detroit: Wayne State University Press, 1994); Janet Bruce, *The Kansas City Monarchs: Champions of Black Baseball* (Lawrence: University Press of Kansas, 1985); Paul Debono, *The Indianapolis ABCs: History of a Premier Team in the Negro Leagues* (Jefferson, N.C.: McFarland, 1997); Neil Lanctot, *Fair Dealing and Clean Playing: The Hilldale Club and the Development of Black Professional Baseball, 1910–1932* (Jefferson, N.C.: McFarland, 1994); James Overmyer, *Effa Manley and the Newark Eagles* (Metuchen, N.J.: Scarecrow Press, 1993); and Rob Ruck, *Sandlot Seasons: Sport in Black Pittsburgh* (Urbana: University of Illinois Press, 1987). Two photographic histories of black baseball, Bruce Chadwick, *When the Game Was Black and White: The Illustrated History of the Negro Leagues* (New York: Abbeville Press, 1992) and Phil Dixon, with Patrick J. Hannigan, *The Negro Baseball Leagues: A Photographic History* (New York: Amereon House, 1992), were also very helpful as was Jim Reisler, *Black Writers/Black Baseball: An Anthology of Articles from Black Sportswriters Who Covered the Negro Leagues* (Jefferson, N.C.: McFarland, 1994). For those interested in learning more about the stars of black baseball, the oral histories of John Holway and the reference works of James A. Riley are indispensable.

3. W. E. B. DuBois, *Souls of Black Folk* (New York: Vintage Books/Library of America, 1990).
4. Overmyer, 111; Lanctot, 23; Bruce, 44.
5. Bruce, 42, 49.
6. Bak, 135.
7. James H. Bready, *Baseball in Baltimore* (Baltimore: The Johns Hopkins University Press, 1998), 174; Lanctot, 61; Bruce, 45–47.
8. Rogosin, 32–33; Reisler, 49.
9. Debono, 2, 44–48.
10. Lanctot, 23.
11. On the Negro National League, see Debono, 49, 84; Bak, 71.
12. Bruce, 88; Reisler, 60.
13. Lanctot, 66; Bruce, 24, 45; Overmyer, 266.
14. Debono, 101.
15. Overmyer, 15–17, 59, 215.
16. Overmyer, 5, 59–60, 167–68, 174; Bruce, 45; Lanctot, 176.
17. Debono, 74; Steven J. Ross, *Black Diamonds, Blues City* (film); Overmyer, 86;
18. Bak, 183; James Bankes, *The Pittsburgh Crawfords: The Life and Times of Baseball's Most Exciting Team* (Dubuque, Iowa: Wm. C. Brown, 1991).
19. James M. DiClerico and Barry Pavelec, *The Jersey Game: The History of Modern Baseball from Its Birth to the Big Leagues in the Garden State* (New Brunswick N.J.: Rutgers University Press, 1991), 146.
20. Imamu Amiri Baraka, *The Autobiography of LeRoi Jones/Amiri Baraka* (New York: Freundlich Books, 1984), 35.
21. Bak, 126; Bready, 166; Bruce, 42.
22. Baraka, 35; Overmyer, 66.

23. Bankes, 104–5; Ross, *Black Diamonds;* Chadwick, 54; Overmyer, 112; Bruce, 44.
24. Bruce, 3.
25. Debono, 73.
26. Bruce, 44–45.
27. Chadwick, 50; Debono, 180.
28. Overmyer, 34, 64, 97; Reisler, 99–100; Ruck, 157; Bready, 181; Bruce, 47.
29. Bak, 87; Ross, *Black Diamonds;* Overmyer, 63.
30. Overmyer, 63.
31. Brad Snyder, Senior Thesis, Duke University, 1994.
32. Chadwick, 55; Peterson, 113; Ross, *Black Diamonds.*
33. Bruce, 58.
34. Charles E Whitehead, *A Man and His Diamonds: A Story of the Great Andrew (Rube) Foster, the Outstanding Team He Owned and Managed and the Superb League He Founded and Commissioned* (New York: Vantage Press, 1980), 180.
35. Lanctot, 112–20; Overmyer, 107.
36. Lanctot, 40, 62–63.
37. Lanctot, 121; Overmyer, 113–14.
38. Debono, 22, 42; Lanctot, 62; Bruce, 44–45.
39. Overmyer, 166; Reisler, 60, 61.
40. Lanctot, 184; Ross, *Black Diamonds.*
41. Lanctot, 183–84.
42. Reisler, 36–37.
43. Bruce, 29, 51–52; Lanctot, 184; Snyder, 4.
44. Reisler, 61; Dixon and Hannigan, 176.
45. Debono, 20; Lanctot, 20, 23.
46. Lanctot, 60; Overmyer, 104–5; Bready, 167.
47. Lanctot, 37; Bruce 52–53; Bak, 57, 186.
48. Bankes, 25; Bruce, 51.
49. Debono, 66–67.
50. Lanctot, 99.
51. Overmyer, 122.
52. Bready, 175; Snyder, 2–9; Bruce Kuklick, *To Every Thing a Season: Shibe Park and Urban Philadelphia, 1909–1976* (Princeton, N.J.: Princeton University Press, 1991), 146–47.
53. Chadwick, 121.
54. Bruce, 11.
55. Ruck, 116.
56. On Nat Strong, see Lanctot, 29, 62.
57. Lanctot, 29.
58. Overmyer, 269.
59. Lanctot, 73–74.
60. Lanctot, 66.
61. Bruce, 31; Lanctot, 145, 162.
62. Lanctot, 96.

63. Ruck, 221; Bruce, 21–22.
64. Bak, 55–57, 202; Lanctot, 37–38; Peterson 113–14.
65. Dixon, 99; Ruck, 123; Peterson 113.
66. Bruce, 29.
67. Lanctot, 198–200.
68. Bak, 186–87, 192.
69. Lanctot, 200.
70. Overmyer, 10, 272–77; Bankes, 91–92.
71. Rogosin, 104.
72. Bankes, 94.
73. Overmyer, 9–10; Ruck, 149–50.
74. Rogosin, 107.
75. Overmyer, 268–69.
76. Bruce, 90.
77. Overmyer, 135, 139.
78. Overmyer, 134, 138–39.
79. Bruce, 90; Lanctot, 95.
80. Lanctot, 132; Bankes, 115.
81. Overmyer, 113–14, 140.
82. Snyder, 2–24.
83. Overmyer, 204.
84. Dixon, 241–42; Peterson, 59.
85. Dixon, 242; H. B. Webber and Oliver Brown, "Play Ball!" *Crisis* 45 (May, 1938), 137; Bruce, 111.
86. Reisler, 16. 13.
87. Reisler, 80–81.
88. Reisler, 13; Overmyer, 244.
89. Overmyer, 108–9; Debono, 121; Chadwick, 165; Dixon, 252.
90. Overmyer, 235.
91. Bruce, 116.
92. Reisler, 143.
93. Bruce, 116.
94. Geoffrey C. Ward and Ken Burns, *Baseball: An Illustrated History* (New York: Alfred A. Knopf, 1994), 413.

Chapter 7: The Shot Heard 'Round the World

1. George W. Hunt, "Of Many Things," *America* 162 (January 27, 1990); *USA Today*, October 3, 1991; Don DeLillo, *Underworld* (New York: Simon and Schuster, 1997), 59–60.
2. *New York Daily News*, October 4, 1951; *New York Times*, October 4, 1951.
3. For biographical information on Thomson and Branca, see Ron Fimrite, "Side by Side," *Sports Illustrated* 75 (September 16, 1991), 66–77; Bobby Thomson with Lee Heiman and Bill Gutman, *The Giants Win the Pennant, The Giants Win the Pennant* (New York: Zebra Books, 1991); John Drebinger, "Bobby Thomson, Scotland's Gift to Baseball," *Baseball Magazine* 89 (October 1947), 379–81; Ros-

coe McGowen, "Branca, Boy Behemoth of the Brooks," *Baseball Magazine* 89 (October 1947), 365–67; Roger Kahn, "The Day Bobby Hit the Home Run," *Sports Illustrated* 13 (October 10, 1960).

4. Carl Prince, *Brooklyn's Dodgers: The Bums, The Borough, and The Best of Baseball, 1947–1957* (New York: Oxford University Press, 1996), 120–22; Peter Levine, *From Ellis Island to Ebbets Field: Sport and the American Jewish Experience* (New York: Oxford University Press, 1992), 124–25.

5. Peter Gammons, "1950 vs. 1990: A Tale of Two Eras," *Sports Illustrated* 70 (April 16, 1990), 26–32.

6. Harvey Rosenfeld, *The Great Chase: The Dodgers–Giants Pennant Race of 1951* (Jefferson, N.C.: McFarland, 1992), 105.

7. Ibid., 74.

8. Benjamin Rader, *Baseball: A History of America's Game* (Urbana: University of Illinois Press, 1992); Charles C. Alexander, *Our Game: An American Baseball History* (New York: Henry Holt, 1991), 220.

9. On average attendance figures, see Rader, 173.

10. Roger Kahn, *The Era: When the Yankees, New York Giants, and the Brooklyn Dodgers Ruled the World* (New York: Ticknor & Fields, 1993), 286.

11. Russell P. Hodges and Al Hirschberg, *My Giants* (Garden City, N.Y.: Doubleday, 1963), 112; Curt Smith, *Voices of the Game* (South Bend, Ind.: Diamond Communications, 1987), 65.

12. *New York Times*, October 1, 1951.

13. Cecil Powell, "Of Willie Mays, Joe McCarthy, and Bobby Thomson," *Massachusetts Review* 32 (Spring 1991), 106; Smith, 117–27.

14. Thomson, 354–55.

15. Smith, 128.

16. Kahn, *The Era*, 288; Dave Berkman, "Long Before Arledge . . . Sports and TV: the Earliest Years, 1937–1947 as Seen by the Contemporary Press," *Journal of Popular Culture* 22 (Fall 1988), 49–63; Rosenfeld, 253–54.

17. Red Smith, "What It's Like On Color TV," *Baseball Digest* 10 (October 1951), 23–25.

18. Rader, 160; Curt Smith, 136–38; *New York Times*, October 1, 1951.

19. Curt Smith, 138.

20. Ibid., 116–27.

21. Ibid., 112; Jim Harper, "Gordon McLendon: Pioneer Baseball Broadcaster," *Baseball History* 1 (Spring 1986), 42–51.

22. Smith, 127; Harper, 45–46.

23. Dan M. Daniel, "Television Opens Up Fantastic Avenues for Baseball Revenue," *Baseball Magazine* 80 (May 1948); Branch Rickey and Robert Riger, *The American Diamond: A Documentary of The Game of Baseball* (New York: Simon and Schuster, 1965), 194; Kahn, *The Era*, 285.

24. Grantland Rice, "Is Baseball Afraid of Television?" *Sport* 12 (April 1951), 12–13; Dan Daniel, "TV Must Go—Or Baseball Will," *Baseball Magazine* 89 (November 1952), 6–8; William Veeck, Jr., "Don't Let TV Kill Baseball," *Sport* 14 (June, 1953), 10–14.

25. Thomson, 54; Bob Oates, "Thomson's Homer Just a Single in L.A.," *Baseball Digest* 18 (October 1959), 59–61; "The World Series Stare," *Look* (October 1951); Ray Robinson, *Home Run Heard 'Round the World* (New York: HarperCollins, 1991), 16.
26. *Time* (October 15, 1951).
27. *Look* (October 1951).
28. Thomas Kiernan, *The Miracle at Coogan's Bluff* (New York: Crowell, 1975), 61.
29. Irving Rudd and Stan Fischler, *The Sporting Life* (New York: St. Martin's, 1990), 99–102; Ron Briley, "Amity Is the Key to Success: Baseball and the Cold War," *Baseball History* 1 (Fall 1986), 10.
30. *Time* (April 28, 1952); Rosenfeld, 30, 210; Charley Dressen, as told to Stanley Frank, "The Dodgers Won't Blow It Again," *Saturday Evening Post* 224 (September 13, 1952); Powell, 106.
31. *New York Times*, October 4, 1951.
32. Ron A. Smith, "The Paul Robeson–Jackie Robinson Saga and a Political Collision," *Journal of Sport History* 6 (Summer 1979).
33. Jules Tygiel, *Baseball's Great Experiment: Jackie Robinson and His Legacy* (New York: Oxford University Press, 1983), 334–35.
34. Thomson, 182–83.
35. Rosenfeld, 84.
36. Tygiel, 263.
37. Thomson, 179.
38. Gerald Eskenazi, *The Lip* (New York: Morrow, 1993), 249; Hodges, 98; Rosenfeld, 54; Kahn, "The Day Bobby Hit the Home Run"; Tygiel, 305.
39. *New York Post*, October 1, 1951; *New York Times*, October 4, 1951.
40. Thomson, 164–65, 169; Kiernan, 68; Rosenfeld, 184–89.
41. Rosenfeld, 36; Thomson, 254.
42. Gammons, 26–32; Rader, 163.
43. Curt Smith, 133; Harper, 48.
44. Frank Graham, Jr., *A Farewell to Heroes* (New York: Viking, 1981), 231.
45. Thomson, 266, 307.
46. Rudd, 105.

Chapter 8: The Homes of the Braves

1. Howard Cosell, "Great Moments in Sports: Milwaukee Makes the Majors," *Sport* 31 (April 1961), 72.
2. *U. S. News and World Report* (May 18, 1958).
3. *New York Times*, March 19, 1953; David Quentin Voigt, *American Baseball*, Volume 3 (University Park: Pennsylvania State University Press, 1983), 87.
4. Joe King, *The San Francisco Giants* (Englewood Cliffs, N.J.: Prentice-Hall, 1958), 3; Geoffrey C. Ward and Ken Burns, *Baseball: An Illustrated History* (New York: Knopf, 1994), 307.
5. H. D. Robins, *American Baseball Needs Four Major Leagues* (Los Angeles, Calif.: Western Technical Press, 1947).
6. Dyer Braven, "Is the West Coast Ready for Big League Baseball?" *Sport* 17 (May

1947), 11–13; On the Pacific Coast League bid, see Andy McCue, "Open Status Delusions: The PCL Attempt to Resist Major League Baseball," *Nine* 5 (Spring 1997), 288–304.

7. Neil J. Sullivan, *The Dodgers Move West* (New York: Oxford University Press, 1987), 92; McCue, 296; William Marshall, *Baseball's Pivotal Era, 1945–1951* (Lexington: University of Kentucky Press, 1999), 259–62.

8. Voigt, xix.

9. Daniel M. Daniel, "Yankees, Red Sox Take to the Air: Baseball Visions Vast Implications," *Baseball Magazine* (July 1946), 267–69; *The Sporting News* (August 31, 1949); G. Edward White, *Creating the National Pastime: Baseball Transforms Itself, 1903–1953* (Princeton, N.J.: Princeton University Press, 1996), 308.

10. White, 305; Lee Lowenfish, "A Tale of Many Cities: The Westward Expansion of Major League Baseball in the 1950s," *Journal of the West* 71 (July 1978), 73–74.

11. White, 305; James Edward Miller, *The Baseball Business: Pursuing Pennants and Profits in Baltimore* (Chapel Hill: The University of North Carolina Press, 1990), 14.

12. For Veeck's version of these events, see Bill Veeck and Ed Linn, *Veeck as in Wreck* (New York: Simon and Schuster, 1962), 279–90. See also *Life* (March 30, 1953) and Bob Allen, "Unthinkable: Whoever Heard of a Baseball Team Moving to Another City?" *The Diamond* (July 1993), 23.

13. Harold Kaese and Russell G. Lynch, *The Milwaukee Braves* (New York: G. P. Putnam, 1954), 287; Tim Cohane, "None But the Braves," *Look* (August 25, 1953), 87–88.

14. Allen, 23–25; Kaese and Lynch, 288.

15. Allen, 23; Gavin Astor, "Home Are the Braves in Atlanta," *Look* (May 3, 1966), 21–22; Lowenfish, 76.

16. *Life* (March 30, 1953); Gilbert Millstein, "More Brooklyn Than Brooklyn: Milwaukee and Its New Ball Team," *New York Times Magazine* (July 5, 1953), 10, 89; W. C. Heinz, "Baseball Players' Dream Town: Milwaukee and Her Braves," *Cosmopolitan* (May 1954), 90; Cohane, 87, 89; Kaese and Lynch, 289.

17. Heinz, 90; Kaese and Lynch, 292.

18. Al Hirschberg, "Can Milwaukee Keep It Up?" *Sport* 16 (February 1954), 79; Cohane, 87–88; Thomas Meany, *Milwaukee's Miracle Braves* (New York: A. S. Barnes, 1957), xi.

19. Hirschberg, 79; Millstein, 10.

20. Shirley Povich, "Now Milwaukee's Really Become Big League," *Baseball Digest* 14 (July 1955), 29–31.

21. Hirschberg, 89; Millstein, 10.

22. Kaese and Lynch, 283; *Life* (July 6, 1953).

23. Kaese and Lynch, 291; Heinz, 90–93.

24. Millstein, 26; *Life* (July 6, 1953).

25. Heinz, 91.

26. *U. S. News and World Report* (May 18, 1958).

27. Stuart McIver, "Will Baltimore Be Another Milwaukee?" *Sport* 16 (April 1954),

82; James H. Bready, *Baseball in Baltimore* (Baltimore: The Johns Hopkins University Press, 1998), 216; Miller, 69.

28. Miller, 39.

29. John McNulty, "Back in the Big League: Baltimore Orioles," *New Yorker* (May 1, 1954); Miller, 32, 25, 43; Edgar Williams, "The Lowdown on Baltimore," *Baseball Digest* 13 (May 1954), 60.

30. McNulty; Gilbert Millstein, " 'Let's Back Up Them Birds,' " *New York Times Magazine* (May 9, 1954), 34.

31. *Life* (April 26, 1954); Miller, 36; Millstein, "Let's Back . . . ," 34; McNulty.

32. Millstein, "Let's Back . . . ," 17.

33. *U. S. News and World Report* (May 18, 1958).

34. Arthur Mann, "How to Buy A Ball Club for Peanuts," *Saturday Evening Post* 227 (April 9, 1955), 108.

35. *Saturday Evening Post* 226 (June 12, 1954); White, 313.

36. Hall of Fame clipping, February 21, 1969; Gerald Holland, "The A's Find Friends in Cowtown," *Sports Illustrated* 2 (April 25, 1955).

37. Charles C. Euchner, *Playing the Field: Why Sports Teams Move and Cities Fight to Keep Them* (Baltimore: Johns Hopkins University Press, 1993), 17; White, 312.

38. Sullivan, 115–17.

39. Dick Young, "To Hell with the Los Angeles Dodgers," *Sport* 24 (August 1957), 83.

40. Sullivan, 87.

41. *San Francisco Independent*, October 14, 1997; Arnold Hano, "Sudden Success at San Francisco," *Sport* 26 (December 1958), 63.

42. Vincent X. Flaherty, "Miracle Move of the Dodgers—From Flatbush to Fantasia" in J. G. Taylor Spink, ed., *Baseball Register, 1960* (St. Louis, Mo.: Sporting News, 1960), 3–4.

43. Steve Bitker, *The Original San Francisco Giants: The Giants of '58* (Champaign, Ill.: Sports Publishing, 1998), 5–6; Flaherty, 6.

44. Bitker, 6.

45. Young, 83.

46. Bitker, 14; John W. Noble, "What They Say in the Dugouts About: The San Francisco Giants," *Sport* 25 (June 1958), 18, 79; *Sports Illustrated* 8 (June 16, 1958), 15.

47. Sullivan, 159; James Murray, "Coining Gold in the Cellar," *Sports Illustrated* 8 (June 30, 1958), 32.

48. Tim Cohane, "West Coast Produces Baseball's Strangest Story," *Look* (August 19, 1958), 50.

49. Arthur Daley, "Will the Giant-Dodger Gold Rush Pan Out?" *New York Times Magazine* (May 11, 1958), 37; Cohane, "West Coast . . .", 50; Charles C. Alexander, *Our Game: An American Baseball History* (New York: Henry Holt, 1991), 240.

50. Daley, 37; Bitker, 7, 13; Robert W. Creamer, "Smash Hit in San Francisco," *Sports Illustrated* 8 (June 16, 1958), 31–32.

51. On Chavez Ravine, see Cary S. Henderson, "Los Angeles and the Dodger War,

1957–1962," *Southern California Quarterly* 6 (Fall 1980), 261–89; T. S. Hines, "Housing, Baseball, and Creeping Socialism—The Battle of Chavez Ravine, Los Angeles, 1949–1959," *Journal of Urban History* 7 (1982), 123–143; and Sullivan, 83–87.

52. Sullivan, 138, 144–60; Cohane, "West Coast . . . ," 50–53; Henderson, 278.

53. Buzzie Bavasi with John Strege, *Off the Record* (Chicago: Contemporary Books, 1987), 89; Alexander, 243.

54. Sullivan, 161–68.

55. Daley, 39.

56. Henderson, 280–84; Sullivan, 172, 178–81.

57. Sid Ziff, "Incredible Year for the Dodgers," *Baseball Digest* 18 (December 1959), 8–9; Sullivan, 188.

58. Alexander, 243; Bitker, 18.

59. Sullivan, 197, 191.

60. Lowenfish, 74.

61. *New York Times*, November 14, 1958.

62. *New York Times*, July 7, 1968.

63. Clark Nealon, et al., "The Campaign for Major League Baseball in Houston," *Houston Review: History and Culture of the Gulf Coast* (1985), 19, 26–27; Voigt, III–12.

64. Nealon et al., 26.

65. Walter Bingham, "No Feud Like an Old Feud," *Sports Illustrated* 14 (May 1, 1961), 50–51.

66. Nealon, 3, 16; George Kirksey, "Houston—The Next Major League City," *Baseball Digest* 18 (March 1959), 21–27; Danny Peary, *We Played the Game: 65 Players Remember Baseball's Greatest Era, 1947–1964* (New York: Hyperion, 1994) 398.

67. Astor, 22; John Shulian, "National Pastime," *Sports Illustrated* 48 (June 1, 1998), II2.

68. Bill James, *The Bill James Baseball Abstract, 1986* (New York: Ballantine Books, 1986), 39–42.

69. Ibid., 41–42; Hall of Fame clipping, February 21, 1969; Norman L. Macht, "Philadelphia Athletics–Kansas City Athletics–Oakland A's" in Peter Bjarkman, ed., *Encyclopedia of Major League Baseball Team Histories: Volume II, the American League* (Westport, Conn.: Meckler, 1991), 331–32.

70. Huston Horn, "Bravura Battle for the Braves: Milwaukee Braves Fast Becoming the Atlanta Braves," *Sports Illustrated* 21 (November 2, 1964), 32–33; *The Sporting News* (October 30, 1965).

71. Astor, 24; Horn, 32–33;

72. Horn, 32–33; Ron Briley, "Milwaukee and Atlanta, A Tale of Two Cities: Eddie, Hank, and the 'Rover Boys' Head South," *Nine* 6 (Fall 1997), 34; Astor, 22.

73. Briley, 38; Horn, 21–22; *The Sporting News* (August 7, 1965).

74. *The Sporting News* (December 12, 1964).

75. Briley, 35–38;

76. William Leggett, "Atlanta, You Can Have the Rest: Leave Us Eddie Mattress, Our Hero," *Sports Illustrated* 22 (April 26, 1965), 24–25; *The Sporting News* (August 18, 1966).

77. Furman Bisher, *Miracle in Atlanta: The Atlanta Braves Story* (New York and Cleveland: World Publishing Company, 1966); *The Sporting News* (August 18, 1966).
78. Voigt, 113; Macht, 333.
79. Tom Clark, *Champagne and Baloney: A History of Finley's A's* (New York: Harper & Row, 1976), 38–39.
80. Leggett, 24–25; undated Hall of Fame clipping.
81. *The Sporting News* (November 4, 1967).
82. Macht, 334; Clark, 46.
83. Hall of Fame clipping, November 4, 1967.
84. *Sports Illustrated* (January 10, 1977).
85. Alexander, 278; *New York Times*, October 1, 1971.
86. *New York Times*, October 1, 1971; Hall of Fame clipping, February 23, 1971; *The Sporting News* (October 16, 1971).
87. *New York Times*, December 2, 1971, September 23, 1971.
88. *The Sporting News* (October 23, 1971, February 28, 1976); *Atlanta Constitution*, December 5. 1974.

Chapter 9: Populist Baseball
1. Daniel Okrent, "The Year George Foster Wasn't Worth $36," *Inside Sports* (March 31, 1981), 89–90; The Rotisserie League, *Rotisserie League Baseball* (New York: Bantam Books, 1984), 4.
2. Ibid.
3. Ibid.; Steve Wulf, "For the Champion in the Rotisserie League, Joy Is a Yoo Hoo Shampoo," *Sports Illustrated* 60 (May 14, 1984), 8; Debbie Becker, "Fan at Her Best," *Women's Sports and Fitness* (August 1985), 17.
4. Conn Nugent, "How To Own a Baseball Team," *Harvard Magazine* (March–April 1981), 54–56.
5. Jack Friedman, "The Most Peppery Game Since the Hot Stove League," *People*, 21 (April 23, 1984), 40; Michael Walsh, "In New York: Major League Fantasies," *Time* (May 4, 1987), 10–11; Nathan Cobb, "Rotiss: The Greatest Game for Baseball Fans Since Baseball," *Smithsonian* 21 (June 1990), 100–9.
6. Nugent, 54; Marcia F. Coburn, "Men Will Be Boys," *Chicago* 39 (June, 1990), 77–80.
7. Charles C. Alexander, *Our Game: An American Baseball History* (New York: Henry Holt, 1991), 293.
8. For a good discussion, see Bill James, *The Bill James Historical Baseball Abstract* (New York: Villard Books, 1986), 258.
9. Benjamin Rader, *Baseball: A History of America's Game* (Urbana: University of Illinois Press, 1992), 194.
10. Ibid., 201.
11. Okrent, 89–90; Kevin Cook, " 'I Signed Nolan Ryan for $8,' " *Playboy* 35 (May 1988), 126–29; *San Francisco Examiner*, June 30, 1983.
12. M. Demarest, "The Boys of Winter," *Time* (February 7, 1983), 66; Roy Blount, Jr., "We All Had a Ball," *Sports Illustrated* 74 (February 21, 1983), 56–60; Philip Ross, "Days of Heaven," *New York* 46 (February 7, 1983), 17–19.

13. Blount, 60.
14. Demarest, 66–67; Ross, 17; Blount, 56–60.
15. Brian Cahn, " 'The Day I Batted Against the Dodgers,' " *Los Angeles* 29 (March, 1984), 195; Gerard A. Brandemeyer and Luella K. Alexander, " 'I Caught the Dream': The Adult Baseball Camp as Fantasy Leisure," *Journal of Leisure Research* 19 (1986), 28–29; Debra Michals, "Living a Fantasy: Playing Ball with Mantle and Mays," *Business Week* (March 18, 1985), 151–52; Ira J. Dreyfuss, "Physician's Fantasy: Baseball Camp for Grown-Up Kids," *Physician and Sports Medicine* 18 (March 1990), 168–70.
16. Paul McLaughlin, "Play Ball!" *Canadian Business* 61 (July 1988), 54–56; Ellen Karasik, " 'Me, 83 Men, and Baseball,' " *Philadelphia Inquirer Magazine* (March 18, 1990), 29.
17. Cahn, 302; Dreyfuss, 168.
18. Brandemeyer and Alexander, 33; William McNeill, *Dodger Diary* (Woodside, N.Y.: Celtic, 1986).
19. Brandemeyer and Alexander, 26, 31; Blount, 60.
20. Brandemeyer and Alexander, 34–37.
21. John Thorn and Pete Palmer, *The Hidden Game of Baseball: A Revolutionary Approach to Baseball and Its Statistics* (New York: Doubleday, 1984), 46–47.
22. Ibid, 47–48; John Thorn et al., *Total Baseball*, 6 ed. (New York: Total Sports, 1999), 632.
23. Thorn and Palmer, 48.
24. Michael Lenehan, "An Eye on All the Records," *Atlantic Monthly* (September 1983), 58–63, 66; Daniel Okrent, "He Does It by the Numbers," *Sports Illustrated* (May 25, 1981), 45.
25. Bill James, "Confessions of a Stat Freak," *Sport* (September 1979), 1989; Bill James, *The Bill James Baseball Abstract, 1983* (New York: Ballantine Books, 1983), 1; Bill James, *The Bill James Baseball Abstract, 1984* (New York: Ballantine Books, 1984), 3; Bill James, *The Bill James Baseball Abstract, 1988* (New York: Ballantine Books, 1988), 232.
26. James, "Confessions of a Stat Freak," 89; Lenehan, 70; James, *Baseball Abstract, 1988*, 232.
27. James, *Baseball Abstract, 1988*, 231;
28. Okrent, "He Does It by the Numbers," 45, 48; Susan McCarthy, "Looking Backward at Ten" in Bill James, *Baseball Abstract, 1986*, 328–29.
29. James, *Baseball Abstract, 1988*, 231; McCarthy, 329.
30. James, *Baseball Abstract, 1983*, 1; James, *Baseball Abstract, 1988*, 231–32; Okrent, "He Does It by the Numbers," 48.
31. James, *Baseball Abstract, 1984*; James, *Baseball Abstract, 1988*, 23–32; Roger Angell, "Pluck and Luck" in *Late Innings: A Baseball Companion* (New York: Simon and Schuster, 1982), 301; Okrent, "He Does It by the Numbers," 45.
32. Bill James, *The Bill James Baseball Abstract, 1982* (New York: Ballantine Books, 1982), 328–29.
33. Okrent, "He Does It by the Numbers," 42; James, *The Baseball Abstract, 1982*, 9, 132; James, *Baseball Abstract, 1984*, 200.
34. Lenehan, 59; Joe Klein, "The Media Guide," *Sport* 75 (October 1984), 15–16; Sy

Weissman, "The Microchipped Diamond," *Psychology Today* (17 August 1983), 44–51; Bob Cipher, "Square Root, Root, Root for the Home Team: Stalking the Ultimate Baseball Statistic Is Now Serious Business," *Discovery* 8 (October 1987), 87–88, 90–92.

35. R. Zoglin, "Holy R.B.I.—It's Statman!" *People* (June 3, 1991), 93–94; Klein, 16.
36. Thorn and Palmer, 47; Cipher, 90; Weissman, 44–51.
37. The Rotisserie League, 36.
38. Peter S. Prichard, *The Making of McPaper: The Inside Story of USA Today* (New York: St. Martin's, 1989), 1, 187, 327–29, 369; William Taafe, "The Sports Fan's Daily Spread," *Sports Illustrated* 77 (October 6, 1986), 44–48.
39. Taafe, 44–48; *Time* (May 4, 1987).
40. Wulf, 8; Cook, 126–29.
41. *The Sporting News* (April 3, 1989).
42. Bernard Malamud, *The Natural* (New York: Harcourt, Brace, 1952); Robert Coover, *The Universal Baseball Association, Inc., J. Henry Waugh, prop.* (New York: Random House, 1968); Philip Roth, *The Great American Novel* (New York: Holt, Rinehart, 1973).
43. W. P. Kinsella, *Shoeless Joe* (Boston: Houghton Mifflin, 1982).
44. Cited by Darryl Brock, SABR-List, April 13, 1999; Stephen C. Wood, J. David Pincus, and J. Nicholas Den Bonis, "Baseball: The American Mythos in Film, *The Natural*," *Nine: A Journal of Baseball History and Social Policy Perspectives* 4 (Fall, 1995), 149–51.
45. Thorn et al., 2504.
46. Ibid., 604.
47. Donald Hall, *Fathers Playing Catch with Sons* (San Francisco: North Point Press, 1985); George Will, *Men at Work* (New York: HarperPerennial, 1991), 17; David Halberstam, *Summer of '49* (New York: Morrow, 1989).
48. Paul Dickson, *Baseball's Greatest Quotations* (New York: HarperCollins), 155–56.
49. James, *The Baseball Abstract, 1988,* 234; Nugent, 54.
50. Geoffrey C. Ward and Ken Burns, *Baseball: An Illustrated History* (New York: Knopf, 1994), xviii.
51. Steve Rosenbloom and Kelly Garrett, "Why Rotisserie Leagues Are the Best/ Worst Thing That Ever Happened to Baseball Fans," *Sport* 81 (March 1990), 48–49; Coburn, 77–80.
52. *USA Today,* April 6, 1993; *Sports Illustrated,* 73 (September 10, 1990); Steve Wulf, "Rotisserie Revisited," *Sports Illustrated* 71 (August 7, 1989), 78.
53. Roy Blount, Jr., "Staturated," *Sports Illustrated* 74 (April 15, 1991), 133–34; George Vass, "Some of Baseball's Valued Statistics Can Be Deceiving," *Baseball Digest* (June 1987), 41–49; James, *Baseball Abstract, 1988,* 234.

Index

Gary!
Go for it! ... Online.
Be ... Shameless
your friend.
Debbie Allen

Discover the Secrets to Creating Online Wealth from the World's Top Internet Marketing Gurus

Confessions of Shameless Internet Promoters™
By Debbie Allen

Success Showcase Publishing

Here's what people are saying about *Confessions of Shameless Internet Promoters:*

*"If you want to learn how to shamelessly promote your products to serve more customers and make more money then you **must** read Debbie Allen's book, Confessions of Shameless Internet Promoters."*
> —Robert G. Allen, author of *Multiple Streams of Internet Income*,
> www.multiplestreamsofincome.com

"This book is shameless for giving out so many great Internet marketing secrets! Anyone who reads and applies the ideas in this book will have a decided competitive edge over competitors who do not read this book."
> —Dr. Tony Alessandra, author of *The Platinum Rule* and
> *Collaborative Selling*

"I've been a fan of Debbie Allen's books for quite a while now. And her Shameless… series, with all their real-world marketing advice, belong in the desktop of anyone who wants to survive in the world of business. I'm dead serious about this…grab this book now!"
> —Miguel Alvarez, Mexico's #1 Internet guru and CEO of
> www.ThirdSphere.com

"With all the noise and confusion online you'd better have a way to make yourself seen and heard or you might as well reserve some space in the 'dot-bomb' graveyard. With Debbie Allen's newest book you'll have the invaluable insights, ideas, and strategies from people who are actually making it online. That's worth a fortune! Grab it today!"
> —Yanik Silver, author of *33 Days to Online Profits*,
> www.33daystoonlineprofits.com

*"If you do only 10 percent of the **shameless** ideas in Debbie Allen's new book, your Internet income will increase by 110 percent"*
> —Tom Antion, author and Internet marketing guru,
> www.GreatInternetMarketing.com

"*Debbie Allen takes the mystery out of marketing. Now she takes her in-depth, first-hand knowledge to bring together the top talent in online marketing to share their secrets in Confessions of Shameless Internet Promoters. Once again, Debbie makes it easy to get it right and get it now.*"

—Mary Westheimer, founder of BookZone, Inc.,
www.BookZone.com

"*Wow! Talk about fun and fantastic! This amazing new book rocks and socks with ideas, stories, tips, tricks, and other mind-stretching, money-making, and attention-grabbing wisdom! Get this one NOW!*"

—Joe Vitale, #1 Best-Selling Author of *Spiritual Marketing*,
www.mrfire.com

"*Internet marketing is here to stay! Confessions of Shameless Internet Promoters is a 'must read' if you want to take your business to the next level and ensure a passive income.*"

—Patricia Noel Drain, author of *7 Secrets for Building a Business that Has Value*, www.patriciadrain.com

"*I have worked with Debbie Allen on the conference circuit and she always provides a host of wonderful, practical ideas. This is the first practical marketing book for Internet promoters and is full of ideas that you can introduce into your business immediately.*"

—John Stanley, international speaker and author of *Just About Everything a Retail Manager Needs to Know*,
www.jstanley.com.au

"*Debbie Allen's Confessions of Shameless Internet Promoters is marketing dynamite! You **will** make money with this guide. Here are three reasons why: First, Allen is an expert who lives marketing. Second, this book contains money-making gems from internationally recognized Internet marketing gurus—people who actually make money on the Internet. Third, Confessions is jam-packed with hands-on ideas and action steps so you'll highlight every page and race to your computer to begin making more money. A stand-out on today's super-cluttered bookshelf.*"

—Eric Gelb, author of *Book Promotion Made Easy*,
www.PublishingGold.com

Confessions
of
Shameless
Internet Promoters™

Discover the Secrets to Creating Online Wealth from the
World's Top Internet Marketing Gurus

By Debbie Allen

Success Showcase Publishing

Cover design: Jim Weems, Ad Graphics
Phone: 800-358-6196   www.thebookproducer.com

Interior design: The Printed Page, Phoenix, AZ
Phone: 480-460-1707   www.theprintedpage.com

Book Consultant/Editor: Karla Olson, Via Press
Phone: 602-957-1955 or email: Karla@via-press.com

Editor: Joe Liddy, The Printed Page, Phoenix, AZ

Publisher's Cataloging-in-Publication

Allen, Debbie, author

Confessions of Shameless Internet Promoters : Discover the secrets to creating online wealth from the world's top internet marketing gurus

Includes index.

ISBN: 0-9650965-6-4
LCCN: 2002094634

1. Business/Marketing/Internet

About The Author

Debbie Allen, The Shameless Marketing Guru, is an international professional speaker, marketing, and retail expert and author. Debbie addresses over 75 organizations and more than 20,000 people each year in numerous countries around the world, sharing her marketing expertise. Debbie has built and sold six companies including a car rental business, two mini storage facilities, and three retail stores.

Her acute business sense, high energy, and sense of humor is teamed up with her enthusiasm to make her a dynamic presenter. Internationally acclaimed motivational speaker Debbie Allen knows how to touch the minds and hearts of her audiences. She provides practical, easy-to-follow marketing strategies that can help anyone become more successful.

Debbie is the author of three books on business marketing including *Confessions of Shameless Self Promoters*™. Debbie has a unique approach to her marketing books. Her first in the series described the science and strategies of self-promotion. From the early success of this book, Debbie created the highly requested sequel, *Confessions of Shameless Internet Promoters*. Readers of the first *Confessions* were addicted to the easy ways to implement marketing strategies and asked for more.

Debbie is a recipient of The Blue Chip Enterprise Award, sponsored by the National Chamber of Commerce for overcoming business obstacles and achieving fast business growth. She was recently featured in the *Who's Who of Marketing Experts* and has served as president for National Speakers Association, Arizona. Debbie is also the founder of *Self Promotion Month* (October) and *Business Image Improvement Month* (May), both featured in Chase's *International Book of Special Events* and *Celebrate Today*.

Debbie is the editor of two electronic newsletters and has also been featured in numerous publications, including *Entrepreneur, Selling Power, Sales & Marketing Excellence* and *Franchising* magazine. Her *Power Marketing Membership* continues to inspire, educate, and motivate her exclusive inner circle membership to a higher level of success by offering monthly mastermind interviews from the world's top marketing experts.

Debbie is a frequent radio guest expert on dozens of syndicated stations around the U.S. and Canada, and has even survived a live radio interview with shock jock Howard Stern, who enthusiastically promoted her books on the air. And, best of all, she kept her clothes on and her professionalism intact in the process.

Acknowledgments

This exciting book would not exist without the insightful collection of secrets and strategies shared by my successful contributors. My deepest appreciation goes out to each and every one of you. The successful marketing gurus, Internet experts, entrepreneurs, and authors included in this book understand the meaning of sharing their secrets to success with others. Thank you for allowing me to discover your secrets to online success and for permitting me to share them with my readers. Your contributions will continue to inspire, motivate and reward thousands of people as they create wealth from their online marketing efforts.

I would also like to thank my book design, editing, and consulting team for making the process of creating another successful book painless. In addition, I would like to express my appreciation for all my business associates and alliances around the globe who continue to help and support my goals and marketing efforts with every shameless project I create.

Debbie Allen

A truly successful person is one
who understands about giving back.

Introduction

Most people hold themselves back from the success they truly deserve, even when the opportunity is staring them right in the face. One of the biggest opportunities we have today is right at our fingertips. The Internet offers an incredible opportunity to market and promote to the world with a click of a mouse. The Internet has opened up a whole new world to us—a world full of marketing opportunities to create financial freedom and personal wealth without even leaving our homes or offices. Sign me up!

Yet, the lack of online marketing expertise, motivation, and the fear of the unknown still hold most people back from moving forward in the right direction. So, they take no action at all and leave these opportunities sitting at **your** doorstep. You have taken the first step towards learning and implementing those opportunities by purchasing this marketing book.

Don't you deserve to make more money than you are making now? If you answered "yes" you are hungry for new ideas to move you forward in your business NOW. That's what so exciting about the Internet. You can get results in a matter of minutes—not days, weeks, months or years. You don't have to have a huge bank account or be a huge corporation to succeed. Anyone—and any business—can thrive and make it BIG on the Internet today by implementing the strategies shared in this book.

This unique marketing book will make the task of effectively marketing online less daunting with inspiring and easy-to-read short stories of innovation and personal experience. Each chapter of this book is full of extraordinary personal anecdotes. By uncovering these secrets to online success you can begin to implement proven marketing strategies and start to create multiple streams of online income. Be a sponge for the wealth of knowledge you are about to discover. The different viewpoints, personal stories and shared confessions of success will move you into action.

You could read a ton of online marketing books to learn how to do this, but I don't think you have the time to do that. You are too busy marketing! This book offers you an easy read and the best of the best from the world's most successful marketing gurus that have already created wealth online.

Together, their secret confessions offer you endless opportunities, inspiration, a wealth of knowledge and invaluable resources to skyrocket your online marketing efforts. So what are you waiting for?

After reading this book you will know how to:

▼ Send professional, attention-grabbing and charismatic e-mails

▼ Create an effective website and learn how to drive traffic

▼ Get listed at the top of search engines and directories

▼ Take a basic website and turn it into a money making machine

▼ Create more sales and develop multiple streams on income online

▼ Seek out opportunities to build business alliances, referrals and leads

▼ Get tons of free online publicity and create international fame

▼ Easily create successful e-zines and e-books

▼ Create low cost direct mail with an electronic newsletter

▼ Develop powerful headlines and effective copywriting that sells

▼ Promote your expertise with unique marketing strategies

▼ Use the Internet to capture the hearts of prospective customers

▼ Utilize effective online marketing strategies to create wealth

Contents

Chapter One

It Ain't Rocket Science

*The door of opportunity won't open
unless you do some pushing.*
—Anonymous

Shameless Internet Promotion Step 1: Launch Yourself Into Technology

Debbie Allen

After writing my first book, *Confessions of Shameless Self Promoters*, I discovered that my shameless fans wanted much more. They were hooked on the concept of self promotion and the need for many more marketing ideas that would help them achieve shameless success. As my contributing authors confessed their marketing secrets and strategies, it was easy for readers to implement their ideas. Now that the world of Internet marketing has opened many opportunities, it only made sense to make this the next book in the series.

After the fall of "dot coms" in the late 1990s, many felt that the Internet was no longer the answer to their dreams of success. Many others felt that they would have to spend thousands and thousands of dollars to just play the Internet game. And others believed that people could instantly tell the difference between an amateur and a highly successful online marketer. But, all of these myths have been debunked. The Internet is here to stay and the opportunities are endless—for anyone…on any budget.

These are exciting times we live in—online success is there for the taking. You can create an Internet presence that is so strong that visitors will never know whether you are just beginning or already have a highly successful company. Visitors may never know if you are working from a multi-million dollar corporate office with hundreds of employees—or out of your basement, just you and Whiskers the cat.

So if the opportunities are so great, why are people still not taking the Internet plunge? Here are some of the most common reasons. They often:

▼ Fear change and make no effort to take the time needed to learn new marketing concepts

▼ Have closed minds to learning

▼ Lack patience to learn more about the Internet

▼ Believe they are computer-illiterate and fear the unknown

▼ Believe they may make themselves vulnerable to hackers

▼ Mistakenly think that without a huge budget and a fancy website, their online marketing efforts will be a waste of time

▼ Are disappointed that an existing website is not producing results

▼ Think that it's too late to launch an online presence and that competitors have already taken up the market

▼ Must first buy a new computer or invest in another phone line to connect to the Internet

▼ Believe they already spend enough or too much time on the Internet

▼ Adopt a "wait and see" approach—wait until everyone else is online

▼ Claim to have not enough time to read e-mail, much less create an effective website

One or more of these fears may be holding you back from venturing onto the World Wide Web. I had plenty of these fears myself once and used many of these excuses to hold me back from taking action. At that time, when someone asked what kind of computer I had, I repled, "Beige." I was techno-clueless!

But as I began to feel more comfortable with marketing online, I started to implement strategies that I had learned from my marketing guru friends, with almost immediate results. I'm now hooked on the magical marketing power of the Internet. Today, I can't imagine my business without it. Without the Internet as an effective marketing tool, it would have taken me many more years to build a successful company.

If you are just getting started, here are some ideas to help you take the plunge:

▼ Congratulations, you have already taken the first step by purchasing this book

▼ Take a class on how to use the Internet more effectively

▼ Find a consultant and/or a mentor

▼ Just get started—implement now and perfect later

▼ Make it a top priority—your marketing success depends upon it

A World of Opportunities on the World Wide Web
Lee Silber

As a tool, the Internet is here to stay, and that's a good thing. Yes, it will completely change the way we promote ourselves. Sure, that's scary. Anything new is a little unnerving. But if you embrace it and make it part of your promotional plan, you will see results. There has never been a better way to build a buzz about you and what you do.

But the more things change the more they stay the same. It's comforting to know that what hasn't—and won't—change are the basic principles of promotion. All the things you know about marketing still apply when you incorporate Internet marketing. You still must grab their attention, stand out, think creatively, talk in terms of benefits (to them), know your audience, find the most creative (and cheapest) way to reach your target audience, form a plan of attack, and then take consistent action. Simple! Now, just transfer these ideas to the Net.

Where do your customers go on the Internet? Put yourself in their path. Get the word out with online publicity—a website (your online brochure and then some), online newsletters and magazines. Put together and post your portfolio or resume, teach or consult (online), or use the Web to give great customer service. Build a mailing list of e-mail addresses, build a fan base, and stay in constant contact with customers. You do all this using the same methods and message as before, but with a different medium—the World Wide Web.

That said, today's self promoter must be well-versed in the many capabilities the Internet holds. Don't fight it! It is your ticket to stardom—and a very cost-effective avenue! It's ggrrrrreat! For example, take the two freelance writers who made an eight-minute short (film) which they aired on a website for industry professionals. This led to calls from studio executives and to a deal with Fox.

You don't have to wait around for the perfect time to start. Be proactive and jump in. You don't have to drop everything else you are doing. When you can easily find an audience through online research and distribute your creations and marketing materials to a targeted audience (in a personalized way and on a consistent basis) quickly and inexpensively, the

Internet becomes a very sexy and seductive mistress. Keep in mind that even the best online marketing campaign needs to employ basic marketing principles.

The Blair Witch Project Website

One of the best examples of shameless Internet marketing is the success of the film *The Blair Witch Project*—a fake documentary about a legendary witch and the three filmmakers who disappear in the woods making a film about her. It is one of the most profitable movies ever made. What made this the movie so successful? A highly clever marketing campaign that blended traditional marketing with the Web (and a great grass-roots strategy). In addition to putting together an amazing website, it was the guerrilla marketing tactics—missing persons' flyers with the actors' faces on them, comic books featuring Blair Witch lore and T-shirts. All these were used to drive the right people to the website and create incredible "word of mouth" for the film.

It all began when the creators e-mailed a few dozen friends who told two friends, and so on. Many thought the mythology was real and began putting up their own websites. The buzz before the film reached theaters fueled the success of the movie and launched several film careers.

Other filmmakers have used the Internet by submitting trailers, short films and independent feature films to websites that allow exposure. Sure, there isn't money to be made from this but it can lead to bigger and better things. It could be your stepping-stone to sell your product directly to consumers. In many ways it's like going back in time to the days when you could interact with your customers directly. Ever notice that the word customer includes the word "custom" right in it? This is another beautiful thing about the Web. You can customize your marketing materials, products and approach to match the needs and interests of each customer (if you dare).

Get On the "Clue Train"

Ken Arnold

Every shameless self promoter who intends to be in business tomorrow and next year needs to be on the Internet using its vast resources and tools—today.

The Internet has revolutionized the way people and companies market their products and services. It also provides the most immediate form of customer feedback about your company and its products. The Internet's collective content is staggering, running the gamut from the very useful to the totally useless and tasteless.

To get a provocative, but fascinating view of how the Internet has impacted marketing, both from companies' and the customers' perspectives, visit www.cluetrain.com. The main message there—and in the companion book, *The Cluetrain Manifesto*—is that the Internet is an international market bazaar where information and the "truth" can be found in nearly real-time. What you say about your business and how you say it are given meaningful feedback through the Internet community. Shameless self promoters who understand this environment can use this global advertising vehicle more broadly and effectively than was ever possible before. Get on the "clue train" because the Internet is the ultimate medium for self promotion. It's available 24/7, even if you're not, and it's easy to make it work for you.

In fact, every business should be connected to the Internet in some form, if only through e-mail. Having your e-mail address on your business card is as important as your telephone number, but offers greater security and more options for response. On the Internet, e-mail hosts (such as AOL, Yahoo, MSN, Netscape, and many others) provide you very cheap (free to low-cost) electronic "business cards" that can be more easily updated than printed ones and provide a connection to the world at the top of every message you send. In the new Internet world of business, cold e-mails have replaced cold calls as a much more efficient and timesaving way to create new business opportunities. Calls can be saved for other purposes that justify their cost.

But to stay ahead of your competition and to drive your future business success, you need to use the Internet for shameless self promotion, just as you did before the Internet became an international public network, and you need to be savvy about how you do it.

Three Key Elements to Promoting Yourself on the Internet

1. **You need at least some basic Web pages.** You can host this information on your own computer—if it is connected to the Internet— or use someone else's Internet-connected computer. It's easier to pay a hosting service to do it.

2. **You need to offer something that people care about**—expertise, products, resources, important information and announcements, links to other sources, entertainment, etc.—that drives them to your Internet presence, and just as importantly, keeps them coming back. Your Web presence should contain current, accurate, core information about you, your business, products, services, and contact data. Spend most of your time creating the content of your Web presence, rather than on gaudy graphics and silly gimmicks. People rarely come back for fluff.

3. **People need to be able to find you.** This element is the most important message for anyone who creates a Web presence. With Internet marketing, the concept of 'build it and they will come' does not apply. You have to use the Internet to guide your customers to you. To do that, you need to understand a few basic principles of Internet searching and promotion.

Three Ways People Can Find You on the Internet

1. **Send them an e-mail,** and your e-mail address is already posted there in the "From" field, "Reply" field, or perhaps in a signature at the end of your message. Include your e-mail address on your business cards and every other piece of paper and marketing collateral you create.

2. **Create a Web presence.** Your Web pages should contain key elements of standard Web page information that help others on the Internet find you—a title and some descriptive keywords that summarize you and your business (like a Table of Contents). It also helps tremendously if your website gets linked to others. Shameless self promoters always look for ways to advertise themselves, and Web links are often

free ways to open new doors. Contributors to this book will have links from its website to any of their own information they choose to promote. Include your Web page address on every piece of marketing collateral you create. Find every conceivable opportunity to pass this information along to your friends, customers, colleagues and strangers.

3. **Participate in online forums** such as newsgroups, bulletin boards, or chat rooms. The main value to these, if they are reputable and archived, is that you can become recognized, and better yet, recognized as an expert about something. That something probably relates to your business or interests, and that's probably what you want to promote. Find every conceivable opportunity to drop your name, e-mail address, and Web address into every discussion you enter.

Helping others find your business on the Internet is critical to promoting your products and services. From big corporations and government agencies to startups and mom-and-pop shops, the Internet has impacted practically every business segment. Those who use it to promote themselves will win the lion's share of new business. We can see the power of Internet Marketing in an example from the industrial sector.

Internet Marketing in the Battery Industry

No more than three to four years ago, when many major corporations and smaller businesses had already joined the Web community, most of the world's major battery manufacturers were not on the Internet. Sales and marketing efforts were handled in the traditional way: cold calling, trade shows, contacts made by battery reps in the field and through sales offices, and "word-of-mouth." Now, all of them have websites, and the industry has found that over half of their new business is coming from the Internet, and the numbers are increasing each month! E-commerce websites, specialized websites that allow most of the elements of a business transaction to be carried out online, have provided many of these major suppliers a cost-effective way to do business online with their existing customers and their new ones.

In the midst of all of this, there has been an upsurge of small to medium-sized battery manufacturers in Asia, particularly in China, Taiwan, and Korea. These new companies rely heavily on the Internet, especially through cold e-mails and referrals to their websites. Most of their customers reach them through the Internet. Search for batteries on the Web when you need them and find the contacts there, practically anywhere in the world. This major turnaround in the way business is done has opened the door for a wider range of manufacturers that could not have survived locally just a few years ago. Now, they can compete side-by-side with the major players, and are consequently pressuring pricing downward on those who once dominated the industry. Thanks to the Internet, they are also growing rapidly due to increased business volumes. Retailers in the battery industry also have converted to the Internet marketing channel. As a result, their new customers might come from down the street or across the ocean. Many of these retailers might not even have a storefront. Good luck to those businesses that have not yet jumped on the "clue train."

So, we see significant growth in business for the battery industry because the Internet has allowed smaller players to enter the market and compete successfully. Advertising costs are lower through this medium, and it has also led to a subsequent downturn in other, more costly advertising/promotional activities such as attending trade shows, and simply having armies of sales reps beat the bushes for business. More focus is put on customer service staff and field engineers. The Internet revolution in the battery industry has increased the number of manufacturers in the market, but consolidated the number of factory reps and distributors that once clung to the large manufacturers. Customers get more choice, better prices, and better service.

What does this mean to you, the shameless self promoter? Go revolutionize *your* industry on the Internet!

The Big Secret to Online Success I Almost Learned When I was Eight Years Old
Yanik Silver

When I was eight years old, my best friend Jamie and I loved to read comic books. (I think I still have my collection somewhere in my parents' garage.) One day we decided we would get rich by drawing our own comic books with characters like 'Big Nose Fred', 'Meteor Mouse', 'Benjamin Bunny' and a whole slew of others.

We named our company 'Silver Dragon Publishing'—his last name as you probably guessed was Dragon—and we were going to make a fortune selling our comic books for a quarter each! We got hard to work drawing and writing our comic books. When we were done we set-up shop on Jamie's front lawn using his mom's card table, and waited for the money to pour in.

And we waited…and waited…and waited!

Silver Dragon Publishing was only in business for one day before our little eight-year old dreams were shattered since we only ended up selling two copies of our comic book—one to his parents and one to mine.

So what's the big secret I almost discovered? Simple. It didn't cost us a quarter to create those comic books and if we had sold a couple thousand copies we could have made some big-time money.

So let's fast-forward to today. I'm doing essentially the same thing—only now I am successful at it. I create information products (electronic books, online courses, membership websites, audios, etc.) that people buy online and do you want to know the best part?

Since everything is delivered over the Internet my cost is—get this—zero, nada, zilch. It's almost 100 percent pure profit! I love that part! Pretty good, right?

Well, I'm convinced I can shamelessly show you how to do the same. I bet you heard that the only people making any real money online are those sleazy porn websites and people peddling "get rich quick on the Internet" information. Well that's not me. I've taken a simple website and turned it into a massive six-figure income for myself. But that was just the beginning because I've taken that expertise and successfully launched five other profitable websites.

Back in January 2000, my friends were rolling on the floor laughing when I told them I was going to build a profitable website. And they had every right to be amused, since I had absolutely no website design skills, zero HTML (Hyper Text Markup Language) or coding knowledge—in fact, not much computer "know-how" whatsoever (still don't). But that didn't stop me from going ahead with my simple website, and the flood of orders hasn't stopped.

So what does that have to do with you? Lots actually! Because I want to confess exactly how I started from scratch to give you the motivation to achieve your own online success.

Of course the money is great, but there's actually a much bigger benefit to having an Internet business that runs itself almost completely on autopilot—and that is the freedom! I have built an automatic website that spins off more money than when I was busting my hump working 50-plus hours per week. Now I have the time to do pretty much whatever I want to. I have time to have fun. I go rollerblading, work out at the gym, sleep in late or work on new moneymaking projects. It's my choice.

Now, I'm not trying to brag or boast shamelessly. I simply want to make the point and prove to you that I've actually done "it." Everything you've heard about the Internet could be true for you. Imagine waking up every morning and finding orders waiting for you in your e-mail box. As you were sleeping, customers from all over the world were giving you money. And you don't have to do anything because your computer takes the order, processes the credit cards, delivers the product and then deposits money in your bank account—you don't even lift a finger. It's like having your own perfect money-making machine working tirelessly for you day and night.

The Perfect Web Business

- ▼ You have no competition. Everything you sell is copyright protected so your product can't be knocked off.

- ▼ You have incredibly huge profit margins. People aren't paying for bits and bytes, they are paying you for the value of the information you provide. With a digitally delivered or "downloadable" product your profit margin is nearly 100 percent. (Compare that to any giant online retailer who can only compete on price and eke out a slim, single-digit profit margin.)

- ▼ You can work from anywhere you wish. It doesn't matter if you're playing beach volleyball in Aruba or skiing in the Rockies. You can run your website from anywhere you can find an Internet connection.

- ▼ You can set up your business so it works on complete autopilot (that's how my website works right now).

▼ You need no employees. I have absolutely zero employees and I couldn't be happier not to deal with all those headaches and hassles.

▼ You have incredibly low start-up costs. You don't need a factory or even a store front because you can run your business in any spare space a computer fits.

▼ You get paid over and over again for work you do one time. Once you create your digital product you can keep selling over and over again. The work is done one time and you profit repeatedly from it.

Those are some pretty powerful advantages, right? Your online opportunities await you. I don't believe there is a better opportunity right now to create success with your online marketing. I turned a profit after the first few weeks and now it just keeps growing and growing. You can do it too!

> *Take the first step in faith. You don't have to see the whole staircase, just take the first step.*
> —Martin Luther King, Jr.

"Nah, it can't just be that the plug's out. That would be too simple and inexpensive."

Chapter Two

The Art of Hypnotic E-Mails

They always say that time changes things,
but you actually have to change them yourself.
—Andy Warhol

Shameless Internet Promotion Step 2: Seek Out Opportunities Via E-Mail

Debbie Allen

While writing this book, I contacted dozens of Internet marketing experts from around the world. During just one hour I had written to and received replies via e-mail from all over the United States, Canada, Mexico, the United Kingdom and Australia. That's five countries around the globe in just **one** hour. That powerful access to the world is now available to all of us at lightning speed.

In my first book of this series, *Confessions of Shameless Self Promoters,* I mentioned briefly that I had a client in Australia who was searching for another speaker with expertise in the retail industry and who lived in Australia. Now I will fill you in on the whole amazing story.

Since I live in Arizona, USA, I did not know a soul in Australia, much less a great speaker in the same niche market and the same topic of expertise my client was looking for. But, following my motto to "Never Throw Business Away," I set out to find my Australian client a dynamic expert who lived in her country.

First I did a search on Yahoo Australia. Since my website comes up very high on the search engines and directories when typing in the keywords *retail speaker*, I was surprised that another speaker appeared first on the list. His name was John Stanley. I thought: "Who is this John Stanley and why am I not coming up first on the search engines under *retail speaker*?" I clicked onto his website and viewed it in great detail. I discovered that I had some tough competition on the other side of the world. Not only was John an expert in retail, he was the perfect fit for my client. So I sent him an e-mail with the client's contact information. Now you may be thinking "why would you send your client to your competition?"

Five Big Reasons Why

1. **My client would have found this speaker on her own anyway** by doing a search on the Internet or by contacting a speakers bureau. So why not be the hero and help the client out at the same time.

2. **Servicing my clients is first and foremost on my list of priorities.** I take ordinary service and turn it into extraordinary results. This is easy to do, just stop *selling* and start *servicing* and you reap amazing results.

3. **My clients are pleasantly surprised that I would not only refer them to a competitor, but that I would take the time to personally introduce them.** My referrals are often sent in the form of an e-mail (first choice because it is quick, easy and effective), a personalized letter or one-on-one in person.

4. **Business will come back to you many times over when using this method effectively.** I have personally experienced this for years in the many different businesses I have owned. Most people are afraid of, and therefore avoid their competition. This builds a wall around you and a competitor who happens to have the same core customer base as you do. Don't fight 'em—join 'em! Build alliances with competitors and send them business. They will most likely turn around and help you back. It is a win-win for everyone involved!

   Note: If after sending numerous referrals to my competition with no reciprocating action, I simply stop sending the referrals and find another expert competitor who is willing to trade referrals fairly.

5. **We like to do business with people we like,** and we like people who treat us fairly and honestly and who truly care about making personal connections and offering supportive service. That's just good business!

And Now, the Rest of the Story . . .

When I sent my new-found competitor, John Stanley, my client's contact information, I didn't know if I would hear back. And I did not know that he would want to reach out instantly and help me back. At the time I was just helping a client in need. But, John replied to my e-mail within 24 hours. John thanked me for the referral and mentioned that in two weeks he would be in Arizona, just 20 minutes from my home. He said he would

15

give me a call when he arrived. Now what are the chances of this happening with someone from the other side of the world who I just met via the Internet? A couple of weeks went by and the phone call came. John was in town and wanted me to stop by where he was presenting to meet and "chat up a bit."

We "chatted up a bit" all right—two hours of non-stop chatting later we had discovered more and more ways to refer each other. During our conversation, John told me he had to confess to something that he could not tell me via e-mail or by phone. "Just two days before I got your e-mail, I did a search on Yahoo and found Debbie Allen. I thought 'Who is this Debbie Allen and why am I not coming up first on the search engines under *retail speaker*?' So I went onto your website and discovered your expertise. I thought this lady is some tough competition on the other side of the world. Then I printed out a couple pages from your website. Those pages were sitting on my desk when I got your e-mail!"

Wow! It gives you chills, doesn't it? The chances for this type of opportunity to happen to you are endless now with the World Wide Web. If that is not enough to convince you to do more marketing via e-mail and passing on referrals to your competitors, let me share with you what happened with those referral leads.

John and I have shared many contacts and created business opportunities in many countries including the United States, Australia, New Zealand, Canada, Singapore, the United Kingdom and South Africa. We have even presented together on the same platform in England and were dubbed the "The Ginger Rogers and Fred Astaire of The Speaking Business". In addition, John has become one of my most successful distributors and resellers of my books in his part of the world. Read John Stanley's contribution in Chapter Three.

Don't Ever Throw Business Away Again!

Seek out, connect and refer your clients to another expert if you can't take the business for some reason. Become the resource for referrals and connections—the Internet Rolodex. When passing business along make sure that you keep yourself in the referral loop. Send an e-mail introduction to your client with a copy to the person you are referring so that they can see how the contact was made. Pass on all the contact information for the referral. Then wait for it to come back around to you with tons of personalized referrals and increased business.

The Art of Networking Online
Merle

Yes, that's right I said "art." Learning to network online is an art form in itself. If you learn the ropes and do it correctly, you'll get the word out on your Net business and "win friends and influence people" all at the same time.

Don't get me wrong—it's not easy, and it will involve donating some of your time and energy to help others. You'll be contributing your knowledge and experience, which in the long run will make you "shine" and come out looking like an expert in your field.

Four Internet Tools

There are four main tools you'll need to incorporate into your daily life in order to become an "online networking warrior."

1. **E-Mail:** E-mail is an important part of your life as an online entrepreneur. You should be answering all of your e-mail within 24 to 48 hours to show you're actually reading it and taking care of business. Nothing will turn people off faster then your not responding to their e-mails in a timely fashion. Stay on top of it. No matter what the requests are take the time to answer each and everyone even if it's just to say "thank you."

2. **E-Zines:** You should be subscribed to as many e-zines as possible that cater to your field of expertise. By doing so you'll be keeping "your ear to the ground," and will always be aware of any new trends or competitors in your field. I subscribe to hundreds. Do they take time to read? Yes. Is it time well spent? Absolutely. Many times I hear about new products/services before anyone else in my field, which gives me a competitive edge. Find e-zines that are right for you and start subscribing to them today. You'll find many at:

www.DirectoryOfEzines.com	www.EzineDirectory.com
www.Marketing-Seek.com	www.EzineUniverse.com
www.Ezine-Dir.com/	www.EzineLocater.com

Another way of utilizing e-mail is to reach out and touch someone. No, I'm not talking about sending Spam here. Maybe you've just read a great article online, why not drop the author a note telling him or her how much you enjoyed it. It's always nice to receive a friendly e-mail with a sincere compliment. Who knows, that one e-mail could turn that person into an alliance down the road who may be willing to do you a favor. They may even visit your website through your e-mail signature and eventually become a client. Never miss an opportunity to "make friends" online and increase your networking circle.

Another tactic I often use comes into play when I see an article or a mention of a website where I know the site owner. I'll send him or her the link with a short note stating "Hey, did you know you're mentioned here?" You'd be surprised at the number of people who didn't know their article was being run or that their website was being discussed and they really will appreciate the "heads up" from you. Again, never miss an opportunity to do something nice and get your name out there.

3. **Discussion Lists:** This is another important area in your networking efforts. You should know where the best two-way discussions are taking place and subscribe to a few. With discussion lists you'll be rubbing elbows with the "Internet Elite." Not only can you learn a lot by actually contributing to these lists your comments will be posted live to thousands of eyeballs. Make sure you use a good signature line when posting.

This tactic will drive the curious to your site and again, maybe a potential customer later on. Be ready to give sincere help and show you know your stuff. By doing so, you'll be establishing yourself as an expert in your field. You may even obtain some level of "Internet Notoriety" for yourself and you'll meet and make friends with many other experts along the way.

Make sure you spend time reading the posts and visiting any websites that may further your own Internet business. I honestly believe what you put out comes back to you threefold. So, if you help someone, eventually it will come back to you. When you help someone else you're also helping yourself. Again, join lists related to your field. Some of my favorites can be found at Adventive's site. www.adventive.com/join.html

4. **Message Boards:** If you've been working the Web for any length of time you know what a message board (a.k.a. forum) is, and where the best ones can be found. Again, make it a habit to post to a few every day with a good signature line. You'd be amazed at the number of powerful people you can meet through a board. Make sure you share information, resources, and answer others' questions when you can.

Before long you'll be known as a helpful reliable resource who knows what they're talking about. If you do a search you'll find thousands of boards on which to post. It's up to you to decide which ones are worth your time.

Some of my personal favorites are:

http://www.ablake.net/forum/
http://www.williecrawford.com/cgi-bin/index.cgi

You'll find a nice list here:

http://www.entrepreneur-web.com/index_1.shtml

As you can see networking online means getting involved and getting your name out there every chance you get. Don't be afraid to participate. By utilizing these three networking tools it won't be long before others turn to you for advice and guidance, and who knows, you too may wind up becoming one of the "Internet Elite."

Avoid Being a Slave to E-Mail Marketing
Thomas Murrell

How many times have you sent an e-mail and later regretted it?

In the e-marketing seminars that I present around the world, I ask that question of participants, and 95 percent of people say they have. Communicating and marketing your business by e-mail has a number of benefits, but to really harness the power of it, you need to start by understanding its limitations.

Seven Myths about E-Marketing

1. **Myth: E-mail will give you more time.** E-mail is a great time-waster. Some companies estimate that e-mail occupies up to one workday per week. It is more time consuming than we think, particularly when responding to personal and junk e-mail.

2. **Myth: E-mail will make your job easier.** A recent survey has found that dealing with e-mail is as stressful as dealing with performance reviews, new technology and meetings. So e-mail definitely won't make your job easier.

3. **Myth: E-mail will deliver a paperless office.** Producers of office paper report that the office paper market has grown five-fold since 1983, mainly due to e-mail. People believe printed information to be more believable than information on a screen. Therefore most people print-off most e-mails they receive, especially the important ones.

4. **Myth: E-mail will improve the quality of your communication.** A survey has found that 35 percent of people who have sent e-mails have sent an e-mail they have later regretted, and 56 percent of people in the survey said they had problems with receivers misinterpreting the information in their e-mails.

5. **Myth: E-mail will make you more efficient.** A survey showed that 20 percent of employers report that their employees spend more time on personal e-mails than on business correspondence, and a study of 200 British executives, found that businesses may be wasting up to 50 million dollars a year on information black holes. People also lose a lot of time looking for information—the study found that 65 percent of people spend 15 minutes a day looking for documents and 36 percent said they had prepared documents that already existed.

6. **Myth: E-mail will be a way to improve your writing skills.** We're actually going the other way; sentences have become brief, they are written in a hurry and people try to rush through the deluge as quickly as possible. Sure it is informal, it is casual, and it is a different style, but e-mails these days are riddled with misspelling, typos, and just generally people have a common lack of attention to detail. If you are marketing yourself and your business, how does it reflect on you if your e-mails are full of typos?

7. **Myth: E-mail will improve your business relationships.** Sure it's taking over from telephone and face-to-face communication, but it is faceless. E-mail is one-way communication because you don't see the person and you cannot have the richness of communication that you can have with face-to-face communication. There is a certain feeling of anonymity with sending information by e-mail.

Online Marketing Trends

Despite these limitations, many successful companies are now using e-mail as a cost-effective marketing tactic. Having online communication skills is vital in today's dynamic business environment. Without these, you are lagging behind your competitors. Here are five reasons why online communication is fast becoming a necessity:

1. **Uptake:** The Internet has the fastest adoption rate of any medium.

2. **Adoption:** It took less than five years to get 50 million people connected to the Internet. This compares with 38 years for the same number of people to be connected to radio, while television reached 50 million people in 13 years.

3. **Usage:** 65 percent of Internet users use the Internet daily. E-mail is online communications' most popular application. 90 percent of organizations use e-mail for global communications.

4. **Changing Media Habits:** Adult users of the Internet report that their use of television, magazines, etc., declined as a direct result of using the Internet.

5. **Growth:** Four trillion e-mails were sent in 1999, while that number jumped to seven trillion by 2002. Fast and furious growth continues.

But how do you maximize the power of e-mail? How do you write powerful and persuasive e-mails? And what are some of the myths and traps of using e-mail marketing? Again, before you can take advantage of e-mail marketing you need to understand how it is different.

What Makes E-Marketing Different?

E-marketing differs greatly from traditional forms of communication. It is of paramount importance not to just replace one with the other, because the benefits of traditional forms of communication and e-mail are maximized when used in conjunction. Sending a client's account through the mail and then using e-mail to confirm that they have received it is a fine way to go. Meeting with a new client for the first time to discuss marketing strategies is perhaps best done in person.

There are fundamental differences between online communication and face-to-face communication, and it is critical to understand when and under what circumstances each should be used. If you're dealing with a sensitive issue where personal relationships are important, you should communicate face-to-face. This type of communication involves human interaction, and you will be able to observe body language, mannerisms, and facial expressions and obtain a general "feel" for the person. You will get the two-way interaction and the richness of the exchange, all of which you will be unable to experience with online communication.

However, this process can be time consuming, especially for the high-powered executive with little time to spare. If it's quick, information-based communication that you want, or if you want to communicate to a wide range of people immediately, e-mail is the way to go.

Marketing on a Shoestring

One of the great things about using e-mail as a marketing strategy for your business is the fact that it is so cheap. It is a very cost-effective way of getting your marketing message to literally thousands of people with the click of a button.

Permission Marketing

The challenge for marketers is to persuade consumers to volunteer attention—to "raise their hands and to agree to learn more about a company and its products" according to Seth Godin, permission marketing expert. "Permission marketing turns strangers into friends and friends into loyal customers," he says. "It's not just about entertainment—it's about education." Permission marketing is anticipated, personal and relevant. Godin argues permission marketing lets you turn a person who may not care less about your message into someone who is willing to pay more attention to you when your message arrives in an expected and appreciated way.

Permission marketing is a marketer's dream and is currently one of the fastest growing areas of marketing.

There are some important things to remember with e-mail. Keep in mind that time is valuable. It is a common courtesy to get permission before sending an e-mail. Do not e-mail unrelated advertising. Do not bombard them with too much information.

Five Ways to Improve Your E-Mail Writing Skills

1. Use short words instead of long ones.
2. Prefer a familiar word to a fancy word.
3. Be specific—don't go on and on.
4. Use an active instead of a passive voice.
5. Review, check and evaluate before hitting the send button.

The CLEAR Principles

C. Communicate ideas to a reader
L. Lasting records are easy to keep by printing a hard copy
E. Easily convey information by highlighting key text before you hit reply
A. Arrange points logically
R. Reinforce your message and communicate in a precise way

In this world of ever-improving technology, it is important to realize that, along with the many benefits the modern information age has produced, there are also some unfortunate side-effects. Many organizations have unrealistic expectations of what technology will be able to do for them.

Ten Tips for Highly Effective E-Communication

1. Don't forget the people factor—avoid relying on technology entirely
2. Have a plan and set strategic goals
3. Aim for a clear, direct transmission of your message
4. Keep it brief and to the point
5. Use relevant information of interest to your target market
6. Check for accuracy
7. Offer benefits
8. Communicate on a regular basis
9. Take a break—don't be a slave to your e-mail
10. Evaluate and review your e-mail marketing strategy on a regular basis

Your Signature Is You Online

Jeanette S. Cates, Ph.D

At some time in your life you practiced your signature. It may have been in third grade, right after you learned to write in cursive. It may have been in junior high when you were preparing for the annual yearbook autograph party. Or it may have been when you prepared to sign your first check. You recognized that your signature says a lot about you. It represents you to the world when all others can see is your name.

An electronic signature serves the same purpose. Your signature is the file that you append at the end of your e-mail messages. It tells people about you and makes it easy to contact you in other ways. It's an electronic advertisement for you and your business. Yet many people fail to append this signature, leaving the recipients clueless on how to contact the sender.

Before going further, let's talk about what a signature file is **not**. It is not the same as a digital signature. A digital signature is a legal "stamp" equivalent to your written signature in authority and binding agreements. It is encoded into your message or document. A digital signature must be applied and paid for through a specific authorizing agent. As opposed to a digital signature, the signature file we are discussing is a text file that you create and modify as needed. It is stored on your hard drive and carries no formal authority.

What a Good Signature File Should Include

▼ **Your full name.** Often you want to sign your e-mail more casually with just your first name or no name at all. The signature file should have your full name so that others know how to address you. If appropriate, include your company name and job title as well.

▼ **Your e-mail address.** The recipient may want to print your message for later reference. If so, having your e-mail address close to your name makes it easier to get back to you.

▼ **Your "snail mail" address.** Occasionally a response needs to be greater or more formal than an e-mail message. Make it easy for others to send you documents and other materials. This also saves you having to type this information each time you request that something be sent to you. Include the street address and your city, state, and zip.

▼ **Your telephone number.** Although e-mail proponents prefer using the asynchronous mode, sometimes a phone call is the easiest, fastest means to an end.

▼ **Your website.** I'm often asked how to advertise a website. Including it in your signature file is one of the most effective ways. Each time you send e-mail, it's advertising your website. When you contribute to online discussion groups, everyone reading that message reads about your website. Your signature file is quietly advertising for you.

▼ **A slogan, tag line, or favorite quote.** This is optional, but may make you stand out. Include your tag line particularly if your company name does not convey the type of business you are in. Keep it short so that it doesn't add substantially to the message.

What You Need to Know About Signature Files

▼ Typically the signature file is a separate file stored on your hard drive. Many e-mail programs let you create the file in the program. If your program does not provide this option, create your signature file as a text file and store it in the same directory as your e-mail program.

▼ Generally, you check a box in your e-mail program to include your signature file in your messages. If you can, set the preferences to automatically include the signature file.

▼ Because the signature file is a text file, you cannot use tabs and other formatting. Use the spacebar for creating the layout.

▼ I prefer a "flat and wide" layout, rather than successive lines of information. This keeps the overall length of the message short, which requires less scrolling. It does demand more creativity on your part to be sure everything is visible and neat. Keep in mind that many e-mail windows are narrow, so restrict the width to 80 characters. Keep your file to six lines or less.

▼ Test your file. Send yourself a message with the signature file appended. Get feedback from your friends. Keep revising your file until it reflects "you." (Remember practicing your signature in third grade? This is the same thing.)

Don't take a chance on someone not being able to contact you. Your image and your business depend on it. Remember, your *signature* is *you*!

> *Small opportunities are often*
> *the beginning of great enterprises.*
> —Demosthenes

Chapter Three

Build an Effective Website Step-by-Step

> *There is no security on this earth—*
> *there is only opportunity.*
> —General Douglas MacArthur

Shameless Internet Promotion Step 3: Create a Highly Effective Website

Debbie Allen

I frequently present to audiences of business owners and managers from small- to mid-size companies and I ask a couple of questions about their websites.

How many of you have a website?

Most people raise their hands high and with pride. Clearly, more and more companies of all sizes are creating websites and beginning to get serious about the Internet. Notice I say *beginning* to get serious about the Internet.

How many of you have a highly effective website?

The number of hands raised is considerably lower and those who respond don't raise their hands quite as high. They're clearly not confident about the effectiveness of their websites.

I can relate. Back in 1997, when my website first went up, I was *so excited.* Now the entire world could find me just by typing www.DebbieAllen.com. It didn't matter that I was not getting any business from it—*I was online!*

I thought all I needed to do to find fame and fortune on the Internet was to build a website. I thought I could use my traditional marketing background and expertise to direct existing and prospective customers to my website. I was very busy running two companies at the time and spent what spare time I had sending out e-mail messages directing people to my ineffective website.

It was like having a crumb when I wanted a big slice of pie! The only way I was going to get that slice of pie and create my own Internet dream was to learn more about Internet marketing. Internet marketing is different from the traditional marketing I had known. My Webmaster had created a nice-looking website but did not have the marketing expertise to make it highly effective. I needed to learn how to create a website that would promote my expertise nationally and internationally, build sales and profits and create online wealth. I needed to learn it from the top Internet marketing gurus and I needed to learn it fast.

One of the best choices I made was to take Tom Antion's *Online Marketing Butt Camp—How To Make Money Sitting On Your Butt.* I learned so much from Tom's camp (I'm now a two-time graduate) and hit the ground running. To learn more about Tom's Butt Camps view his website at www.Antion.com and check out his submission to this book in Chapter Six.

I instantly made my website more visible to search engines and directories by adding "keywords" to my title bar and other areas of my home page—a simple trick I learned from Tom.

After adding my new-found knowledge and support along with a fresh new look and personality to my website, it began to stir emotions in my visitors. They reacted by sending me tons of business. This dramatic change came almost overnight. That's why I'm so excited about shameless Internet marketing—this stuff really works!

It still amazes me how using well-thought-out text and graphics can build a sense of trust and communicate your expertise online. The Internet opens opportunities for anyone to do business anywhere in the world. It also opens endless opportunities for any size business to achieve incredible wealth and success.

I made it easier for people to get in touch with me. I added a new look and a new logo. I introduced features to give my customers a sense of who I am. I used photos to convey my personality and included testimonials to build trust. I added a pop up to help close the sale and capture more information about visitors to my website. I took a basic website that showed I was a "newbie" and created a dynamic website that proved I was the successful expert that viewers would trust, hire and buy from.

Do you want a website that will promote your expertise nationally and internationally, build your sales and profits, and create online wealth for you? If so, it's time for you to learn how to build an effective website that will incorporate the specific Internet marketing savvy you will need to enhance your traditional marketing expertise.

You can't count on other people to do all the work for you…unless you have *tons of money* to throw into your online marketing. If that's the case I don't think you would be reading this book—so keep reading learning and most of all *implementing*.

KISS—The Key to Success
John Stanley

In the early 1990s, our clients kept asking, "When are you going to get e-mail? We want to communicate with you by e-mail!" We always want to keep our customers happy so in the early nineties we became e-mail enabled. And what a blessing it was to our business. No more frustrations with trying to reach a client in a time zone 12 hours away.

No sooner had we become e-mail efficient and confident than our clients started asking us to post information on our website (which we did not yet have). So we took up the next challenge—deciding what we wanted our website to achieve—for our customers and for us.

We believe in the KISS principle: Keep It Simple Sells. We use this principle with our clients and our marketing, and we adopted the same philosophy when we approached the Internet.

The first step we took was to look at other websites. We found that the websites we liked were always easy to navigate. Our website had to be easy to navigate, too. We saw so many websites what were designed to be impressive instead of convenient to users. We researched what was happening in the marketplace. Audrey Langford's research (Business Marketing Tape, March 2000) helped us considerably in planning how we would develop our website.

Using large graphics and Flash animations may impress, but we wanted our home page to be useful. Large graphics and Flash animations slows the download. Consider these findings from Langford's research:

  ▼ 50 percent of people click off if a download is 70+ kilobytes or more
  ▼ 30 percent click off if a download is 40 to 70 kilobytes
  ▼ 6 percent click off if a download is less than 35 kilobytes

What does this mean? Consumers don't care about pretty pictures, but they do care about how quickly they can get to the information they seek. Use less kilobytes and consumers don't have to sit around and wait—because they won't!

We also realized that we needed to see our website as a marketing tool. In marketing, you need to have a great headline, be customer—not "me"—focused, and provide clear and precise benefits to the customer. We found that many websites were too "me" focused, so much so that it was difficult to find the company's e-mail address. Instead we followed this rule: Try to eliminate the mental effort visitors must expend locating the information they require from your website.

Another major issue for us is easy and intuitive navigation. If users have trouble finding their way around, they will give up and, in just one click, be gone. We make it easy for our visitors to get back quickly to where they started to ensure they feel comfortable navigating our website.

People feel comfortable in familiar territory. For that reason we change our website only a little at a time, never more than one third at once.

In the electronic age, our customers expect an answer immediately. Our office policy is that everyone must respond to absolutely, positively every enquiry or order within 24 hours.

Has this KISS principle worked for us? We get enquiries from around the world, and our website is our most effective marketing tool. Like all businesses, we aim to constantly improve what we are doing, including our website.

The Key KISS Points

▼ The website should not be your total marketing strategy, but part of an integrated marketing strategy. Don't think it will solve all your marketing problems.

▼ We promote our Web page whenever and wherever we can. When I'm a conference speaker, it's on delegate workbooks, at the end of my PowerPoint presentation, on business cards, flyers, and all correspondence.

▼ We place a sticker inside the products that we sell that directs purchasers to our website. We want to turn every one-time shopper into a lifetime customer, and our website is one part of building that relationship.

▼ Don't be misled by developers who may try to sell you on the idea that appearance is everything. It's not! Functionality and speed of access are more valuable.

▼ If you do decide to have an all-singing, all-dancing, wiz-bang website, then give the user the option of going down the "flash" route, or skipping the "flash" route and going direct to information.

▼ Provide information for your customer and keep the information relevant and regularly updated.

Put yourself in your customers' shoes. Think about the problems, stresses, or issues they may have, and analyze how your website might help solve some of their issues.

▼ It is surprising how many businesses do not have a logical domain name. What would your customer type in the address line as the logical address for your company? We have seen addresses that seem to bear little resemblance to the company name. Again, KISS.

▼ Don't store customer information on your Web server. Protect your customers' privacy by protecting their personal details.

▼ Above all else, strive always to give your customers what they need and you will create lifelong friends from your global customers.

Your Internet Presence Is a Distribution Center
Karen Post

Your website may be a stand-alone location or complement other brick-and-mortar locations. In either situation, following these guidelines will significantly aid in acquiring and keeping market share.

Make a Name for Yourself
A memorable name is worth a million dollars. Customers are inundated with marketing messages everyday. Their attention span is shrinking.

Effective names are easy to say and remember. Relevance to your offering is a plus!

Decide the Role Your Website Will Play

Your website strategy should support your business model's goal. Create a plan early on and stick to it.

Make a Great First Impression

First impressions can make or break your business opportunities—especially in the online world. You have a split second to get the viewer's attention. Your website must get their attention fast and must be professional and powerful enough to keep them on your website.

Test Your Website

Mainstream users are limited to 56k; test how fast your website downloads on an average connection. Test your website on all platforms and all browsers.

Design Your Website to Be Like a Department Store

Make your website visitor-friendly. Weave your unique brand through every element and every page. Use graphics to add the excitement of effective visual merchandising.

Provide Content that Is Rich and Valuable

Regularly ask your customers what they want. Pay attention to your customers' needs, concerns, and frequently asked questions. This information is invaluable; it will help you create the content and value that will enable you to provide a highly effective website.

Summarize Whenever Possible

This goes back to the KISS method mentioned in John Stanley's contribution above. Give your viewers the option to scan over the information briefly or click to another area of your website that offers more detailed information. Use concise headlines to guide your visitors through your website. Offer your viewers options by cross-promoting your content with relevant links throughout your website. Don't over-inform your customers but eliminate as much work as possible for them.

Create a Brand Experience

The language of your content should paint pictures in your viewers' minds. You can also add special effects, but they must be strategic. Integrate a multi-media mix only if it supports your brand message. Keep your brand message in everything you do, including partnering with and linking to other websites. Make sure that everything you do complements your website and your brand image.

Build Excitement with Online Promotion

Promote visits to your website by offering better pricing, free gifts, or exclusive offerings that are only available online. Extend the experience and build customer loyalty by inserting a special offer in the purchase package that can be used on their next online or brick-and-mortar purchase. You can also use special events to drive traffic to your website. Give away items that will enable viewers to experience your brand and will encourage them to do business with your company.

Reward Customers

Create a win-win for everyone by offering a reward, gift, or contest entry to your customers for taking the time to answer surveys. In return you will receive valuable information about them as well as suggestions for how to improve your website and your interaction with your customers.

A 12-Step Guide to Starting a Website

Aaron Turpen

Here are 12 steps you should follow before, during, and after your website project. This is by no means a complete account, as I will try to be as industry-nonspecific as possible. Using these steps in your planning process will help ensure your success online.

1. **Ask Why.** Before you do anything, you'd better know why you need to be online. Are you planning a full e-commerce endeavor or just an online advertising brochure? The answer will determine the scope of your project, so consider the questions carefully. If you change your mind later, you'll have to begin the whole planning process again. Be informed and know what you plan to do.

2. **Outline.** Now that you know why you're going online, you should start with a general outline and begin brainstorming with your partners and affiliates. Set down a rough estimate of the number of pages the website will have, decide on the basic style you would like, and list every idea you have for the website—outlandish or ordinary.

3. **Create a Rough Draft.** Take the list you created in Step 2 and refine it. Mark each item as being **necessary, valuable,** or a **perk.** If you don't know how an item qualifies, it is not necessary and therefore is one of the other two. Only items that you **must have** for the website to exist should be listed as necessary. Items such as *logo, brochure content, contact info,* etc. are considered necessary. Items such as *e-mail form, graphical interface,* and *product catalog* are valuable. *Flash animation, automated link-through-systems,* and *really cool graphics* are perks.

    Create three new lists, one for each category. On a sticky note, write your proposed budget for this endeavor and paste it on the *necessary* list. Now you have the basics and are ready to begin contacting designers.

4. **Begin Shopping.** If you have a small budget, if your list of necessary items is small, and if you don't see anything on your list that appears complicated or unusual for a website, then just about any good and reputable designer will suffice. In this case, you should shop by price and service instead of portfolio and pizzazz.

    If, however, you have a large budget, a complex list of tasks to accomplish, and you need experience over price, then you are better off looking for a large firm of designers who specialize in your type of website or market.

    In either case, you should ask up front (on the phone or in your first meeting) if the designer will supply a rough website map and/or set of mockup designs for your proposed website. Usually a designer is more than happy to excite you with nifty pictures of your website-to-be. You need this, as this will give you an idea of where the designer wants to go with your website. If it is not where you want to be, clarify your expectations now before you write a single check for the designer's service.

    The sticky note with your budget figure will restrain you from going overboard. Know what you can afford and what you really need. It's easy to go crazy with all of the nifty options and cool widgets, but ask yourself if they're necessary. If something is a worthwhile addition, make a note of it. You may use it later during the website's long-term development.

5. **Choose a Domain Name.** Choosing a domain name for your online presence is as important a step as selecting a name for your business. A lot of thought should be given to your choice of domain. A good place to start is www.yourbusiness.com.

   Start a list of the domain names you think would be appropriate. Once you have six or eight of them, show them to your spouse, your friends, or anyone else who can give you a fresh perspective. Narrow the list down to two or three names. Mark them: 1—most wanted, 2—wanted, and 3—least wanted.

   Go online and find a good registrar. You should not pay more than $15 (U.S.) per year for the registration of a .com, .net or .org name. If a service charges more than this, go somewhere else. I recommend www.IsThisDomainTaken.com.

   Check to see if the domain you wish to have is available. However, don't register it yet. Type in your desired domain address, and then search for suggestive alternatives—sometimes something you hadn't considered will pop up that may be even better.

   Now register your domain. I suggest registering for a year to get started. If the domain name is working for you the same time next year, then go for a longer period. No use spending more than you have to right away!

6. **Create an Initial Design.** Unless your website is very simple it will have to be built in stages. Check the navigability, the color scheme, the general look and feel, its ability to sell product or get customers interested, etc.

   Be sure to spend a lot of time with your designer to discuss these attributes and your likes and dislikes. Print the pages of the website and then write or sketch on them to show changes to graphics, text, and whatever else. Write up a detailed list of the changes you'd like to see made and present it to your designer. Your designer should not be resentful of this, so don't worry about stepping on toes. Your input only makes the designer's job easier!

Every website, no matter how small, has at least three design stages: mockup, rough draft, and the final version. Changes may be made at each stage—even the final one! Don't let a designer fool you into thinking that you only get to make changes so many times. Until you are happy, the website is not done—no matter what they say!

On the flip side of the coin, however, don't be nit-picky or wishy-washy. Know what you want and point it out the first time. Don't change your mind halfway through and force the designer to scrap the whole thing. If the designer is smart, he or she will refund your deposit (minus a fee for time spent) and bid you farewell. Designers know that an indecisive client will never be happy and will end up costing them money. As a professional, a designer has better things to do with his or her time.

During this process, you should evaluate your soon to be launched website from the customer's point of view. What will your customers expect when they first type in that URL (Uniform Resource Locator or website address) or click on that link? Will they want to come back? Will they be disappointed? Your website needs a "draw" or a reason for being. Interesting content, prizes or coupons, and other items are good "draws." Content is best—a tutorial perhaps, or a continually changing tour of your factory—as it gives customers a reason to tell their friends about your website, stay interested, and come back to double-check information they have seen.

7. **Begin Marketing.** The marketing of your website should begin as soon as you know when it will be complete. Your marketing should begin in earnest when a finish date is set in concrete. Change all of your printed materials, business cards, letterhead, phone listings, etc. to include your new website address. Having your company's new online presence (www.yourcompany.com) listed is as important as having your telephone number listed. Consider giveaways or other interest-grabbers (freebies are always popular) and use them as tools to launch your website. Promise a lottery, prizes, coupons, or anything else that can only be had by visiting the website and entering the contest or printing the coupon. Whatever this "getter" is, make sure it is good enough to generate interest. Once your viewers are on the website, they should have a reason to stay.

8. **Decide Who's Hosting.** Now that your website is nearly complete, you'd better find a place to put it! Your choice of Web host is very important to the long-term success of your website. Verify several things before you hand over any money for this service:

▼ Is the host reliable?

▼ Will this host be around next year…the year after?

▼ How much are they charging?

▼ What are the limitations of their service (bandwidth, e-mail accounts, etc.)?

▼ Will this host be flexible enough to keep up with the increasing demand of your website as it grows?

▼ Does the host offer several plans that can be easily upgraded to facilitate growth?

▼ How quickly do they respond for customer service via e-mail or the telephone?

All of these questions are very important. Before I began hosting my own websites, I would first answer questions one through four about each provider and then narrow the list down to one provider using only questions five through seven. Finding a flexible host who also offers great customer service is difficult. Generally, if you send an e-mail to your final prospects, the one who answers first is your best bet. The one who takes longer than 24 hours to respond (including weekends!) should be removed from your list. At this point, you should have no more than one or two prospects. If you have more than one, the final question to ask is "Who has the best facility, best hardware, and offers the best technical support?"

Check the Web host's website or ask them via e-mail to describe their facility, how many connections their server has to the outside world, and where the hosting company is located. If you are in the United States and your prospective host is offshore, consider whether you want to take this risk. Remember, each country will have different laws that may not protect you from data theft or other potential problems. As a rule, two outside connections for a server or rack is the bare minimum. The more the merrier! What kind of machine would they be hosting you on? Check the library or another source of up-to-date magazines and find out what the newest technologies are. Chances are you can take the names of the hardware—RAQ 4 for instance—and guess that a RAQ 3 was the last generation of that machine. The newer the better! The technical support should be equivalent to the server and the facility: more is better!

9. **Launch Your Website.** Now that your website is complete and you have a host and domain name, you're ready to launch! If all of this happens earlier than you expected or earlier than the announced date (which it should if all is well), then **do not** launch your website before the announced time. If you do it too early, you may give the impression that you are over-eager and desperate. Worse, people may believe that you pad all of your estimated dates too heavily and will have less trust in you. Keep in mind, though, that one day early is a far cry from a month early. A day will not hurt but a month could kill! Stick to your plan and don't jump ahead of yourself. Use the extra time to keep publicizing your upcoming website. When the time comes, fire away!

10. **Maintain.** Once your website is open to the world, you will begin to deal with the day-to-day chores of owning a website. Keeping your website up-to-date and well maintained requires time and effort. Eventually it will become a regular routine and only the details will be different each time. It may sound mundane, but if done right, you will never lose interest in your website. You may need to contract a professional (generally the developer who created your website to begin with) to do your technical updates. On the other hand, you may wish to make these updates yourself and learn a little about how a website is built from the inside out. Most likely, you will hire a professional—it's the smart way to go!

Contracts can vary in scope and price. Find the one that fits your needs and use it. Always take full advantage of what you're being given in a contract. If it's a by-the-hour list (say four hours per month), then utilize all of that time. Have your marketing department (or whoever fills this role) create new and interesting website content. Include updated information, tutorials, new features, and other enhancements. Keep the website's focus at the forefront of your ideas, but continue to update and change things.

If you create a website and leave it the way it is, changing it yearly or less, your visitor count will begin to drop, as people get wise to your lack of maintenance. You change your other marketing regularly to keep them fresh, right? You must do that with your website too. The advantage here is that a website is generally cheaper than other forms of mass-media advertising, so changes can take place a lot more often.

11. **Freshen with New Looks.** In general, a website should be completely revamped to receive an entirely new look or design at least once a year. This helps to keep the content fresh and forces your users to take notice once more. Marking the anniversary of your website with plenty of hype can be an added bonus. Several months before you wish to change, consult with your original designer or maintenance provider. Get a tentative quote on the time frame and cost of these changes.

12. **Reach for Success!** By the time you're ready for a fresh new look, you should have an idea of how successful your website has become. You should also have projections of how successful it will be if it keeps to its current path. Like most businesses, a website should start out small and become larger and larger as time passes. It should also become more and more popular.

After the first year, begin to make more long-term goals and at minimum a yearly prospectus for your website. Goals reaching out as far as three years are not outlandish, but make sure they're flexible enough (and are reviewed for relevancy) that they can be altered to meet new challenges or changing viewpoint. Your yearly prospectus should match your first year's goals in scope. If your goal is to have a certain number of visitors per week six months from now, then your prospectus should show how this is going to happen—and whether, realistically, it can happen. Above all, keep your focus! Know where you want to be, why you want to be there, and how it's going to happen. Your website and your business should share common threads throughout—including their goals. Stay on track and you'll have nothing but success!

The Seven Most Critical Website Design Elements

Lenny Laskowski

When designing a website for your business, it is critical to incorporate the elements that will allow search engines and directories to not only find you, but to help you reach a higher ranking. Here are the seven most critical elements that must be addressed:

1. Develop a Website Theme
2. Create a Separate Page for Each Product or Service
3. Use Keyword Phrases for Each Web Page
4. Include Text-based Links
5. Avoid Frames
6. Avoid Flash
7. Establish a Linking Strategy

Before discussing these elements, let me first define some technical terms.

Alt Text Tag: This is a special type of html tag which is placed within the HTML code and is associated with graphics (photos, diagrams, etc.). A visitor using an Internet browser that is slow because of the quantity of graphics on your website may elect to "turn off" the graphics on their browser to speed things up. In doing so, all the graphics do not appear. If you have alt text tags behind each of these pictures, they will see these instead of the graphics. Since search engines **only** see text, these are effective ways of adding information behind graphics on your website.

Cookie: If you have a Web browser on your computer, you also have a cookie file. As you view a Web page, HTML code—the language of the Web—directs the browser on your computer to write a cookie in your cookie file, recording whatever data the server specifies. Subsequently, the Web server can read your browser's cookie file. Each website creates a separate file and can read only its own cookies; in other words, they can't read a cookie created by another website.

Websites use cookies for several reasons. One is to gather targeted or personalized content, as in the example above. A cookie could also record the links or advertisements that you click on and add that information to a profile of your interests located in your cookie file. Cookies can remember your member ID and password so that you don't have to retype them every time you visit a membership website. Or a cookie can serve as a shopping cart for an electronic commerce website so that your browser remembers the items you wanted to purchase, even if you leave the website and return later. The point is to make the website more appealing to you, so you do come back again.

Dynamic Page:
Dynamic pages allow you to display dynamic content on a Web page. This can be visitor specific information unique to each visitor. For example, it may say "Welcome Lenny Laskowski" as I visited the page.

Flash:
Flash, a Macromedia plug-in, is the standard for interactive vector graphics and animation for the Web. Web designers use Flash to create beautiful, resizable, and extremely compact navigation interfaces, technical illustrations, long-form animations, and other dazzling website effects.

Frames:
Some websites use a framed design. This is a design where the table of contents sits in its own frame, usually on the left side of a Web page. As one clicks on a specific link within the table of contents frame, the information frame on the right changes. The individual pages are "framed" within a separate window.

Keywords:
Many of us use certain words to find information when searching on the Internet. These words are commonly referred to as keywords.

Meta Tags:
These are optional HTML code lines that can be added to the HTML code of your website and are read by some search engines in order to identify the subject matter or content of the website.

Ranking:
When we search for information using our favorite search engine, we get a listing of Web pages and websites based on the specific keywords or keyword phrases we used. The listing of these pages is referred to as the ranking.

Web Page: This is a single page of information. Many individuals and businesses are represented on the Internet through a single Web page.

Website: Most businesses, mine included, have more than one page. In fact, my website has several hundred Web pages. A website contains several Web pages. If a business' presence only has **one** Web page, this is sometimes referred to as a website; however a website usually has more than one page.

The Seven Critical Elements

Now let's look at the seven most critical elements that will allow search engines and directories to not only find you, but to help you reach a higher ranking.

1. **Develop a Website Theme.** Your website should have a theme based on your keyword phrases. Your keyword phrases are those phrases your potential clients will use when performing searches using their favorite search engine. These phrases must be incorporated in various parts of your website. For example, my website focuses on presentation skills and public speaking; therefore some keyword phrases I would use for my website would include:

   ▼ presentation skills
   ▼ presentation skills seminars
   ▼ public speaking seminars
   ▼ public speaking skills

   If your business provides information about your legal practice and you exclusively work with divorce cases, you might use the following keywords for you website:

   ▼ legal services
   ▼ divorce lawyer
   ▼ marriages

   Once you have decided on your list of keyword phrases it is important to incorporate these phrases within the text of your website. Each Web page may have its own set of unique keyword phrases. If your entire website focuses on one area, you can use the same keyword phrases for each of your Web pages, but generally each page will provide some slightly unique information and you may want to consider creating keyword phrases for each page. If your website and business is involved in several unique areas it is critical that you have unique keyword phrases for each of your Web pages.

2. **Create a Separate Web Page for Each Product or Service.** If your business provides a variety of different products or services, I recommend that you create a separate Web page (or website) for each of these services. You can link these Web pages and websites to each other to show that you offer other things, but keeping them separate will allow you optimize the individual website pages for the additional elements I will describe below.

3. **Use Keyword Phrases for Each Web Page.** It is important that keyword phrases are properly positioned within the HTML code of your website (or title bar). Here are the main considerations about using keyword phrases.

    ▼ It is critical that these elements are provided as **text** and not as graphics. Search engines can only read text. **They cannot read graphics.**

    ▼ Your keyword phrases should be located in your title statements, your meta tags, and your alt text tags (the actual visible text on the page and the name of your website links). Note that some search engines and directories **do not** look for all of these, but you need to include them for the search engines that do.

    Examples of the two most important meta tags are provided below—these are usually placed immediately after the title tag.

    <META name= "description" content= "a description of your page">

    Depending on the search engine, this will be displayed along with the title of your page in an index. 'Content' could be a word, a sentence or even a paragraph to describe your page. Keep this reasonably short, concise and to the point.

    <META name= "keywords" content= "a, list, of, keywords">

    Choose whatever keywords you think are appropriate, separated by commas. Remember to include synonyms, Americanisms and so on. For example, if you had a page on cars, you might want to include keywords such as car, cars, vehicles, automobiles.

▼ The number of times your keyword phrase appears on each page is important.

▼ The acceptable percentage of keywords in relation to your entire text should be between 3 percent and 10 percent for most search engines. Note that if your website provides only graphical text, a search engine cannot and will not see **any** text. Search engines only see straight text.

▼ You need to think about the actual text you provide on your website. The first 25 words on your website are most critical, but so are the last 25 words and the middle 25 words. Including your keyword phrases at various locations within each of your pages will pay off in higher rankings. Therefore, you should locate your keyword phrases near the top, middle, and the bottom of your websites.

4. **Include Text-based Links.** Your website should contain "text-based" links. Search engines cannot follow graphical-based links. If you do have graphical-based links, you should also include text-based links somewhere on the page.

5. **Avoid Frames.** They create all kinds of problems for search engines. Search engines find it difficult to navigate your website if it contains frames. While there are some options, such as the NOFRAMES option, most websites that rank higher do not contain frames. A framed website, which is converted to a non-framed website, will usually see a higher listing quickly after the frames are removed.

6. **Avoid Flash or Dynamic Pages.** There is a trend with many websites today to add all kinds of fancy flash movies and changing dynamic pages. While this may appeal to some visitors, search engines do not like them and you ruin your chances of search engines ranking your website well, since most search engines cannot deal with Java script and other special website design elements. If you have dynamic pages (pages that change or come back customized based on the cookies you set), these will also not list well. *In fact, some search engines will not list any dynamic pages.*

7. **Establish a Linking Strategy.** Many search engines determine the importance and relevancy of a website based on the number of "relative" links it contains. Exchange links with business associates who are pursuing the same types of customers you need and want. Establishing

links with related websites and (even competitor's websites) can help increase traffic to your website and improve search engine rankings, some search engines look at this and determine the importance of a website based on the number of links it has added to the website.

Make It Personal

Natalie Buske Thomas

I started off thinking that my website should be so professional that it almost looked generic template—sort of an online resume. However, later I found that it was convenient to use pages of my business website to display family photos and stories. It was far easier for my computer-challenged relatives to click on my website link than for me to explain how to download pictures.

I soon added a newsletter that promised updates on my business and personal lives. The subscriber list grew over time, and hits to my website **always** increase after I send a new issue of "Natalie's News." I also began to receive feedback from fans of my newsletter and my website. Many of these people had purchased and read every book I have written! My "fans" also know me very well, approaching me as if I am a personal friend, obviously because virtually my whole life is online.

Clearly, sharing both my professional and personal lives with people was working. What an easy marketing strategy—just being myself! Soon I began to have fun with this and added a scrapbook-style series of pages. Some pages describe my career path and others are about my personal and/or family life. All pages include photographs and stories.

My latest addition is "StorkCam," capturing the progress of my pregnancy with Web cam photos. This has been a huge success! I hear from visitors who tune in to see how big my belly has grown! People are even making guesses about baby's gender, weight, and date of birth.

As always, when hits to my website go up so do sales for that month, which is the whole point to online marketing. However, it is amazing how many friends I have made by sharing my life online. I've heard from old friends too—people who found my website online and popped in to see what I'm up to. Making it personal has been a successful Web marketing style for me and I sure am having fun doing it.

Even More Shameless Internet Marketing Tips

▼ Add more pages and fill up that Webspace! Make creative business-related pages, pages about the history of your business, hobby pages, regional pages—more, more, more. Over time, your website will develop into a mammoth website all about you and your business.

For example, I live in Minnesota and some of my pages are regional in nature. I have a recipe for chicken wild rice soup—you gotta know how to make that if you hope to be a Minnesotan. I have photos of various fun spots in Minnesota, photos and journal pages of fishing trips in Minnesota, pictures of Minnesota book signings and other business-related events, and even a page with a story and photos of my meeting with Minnesota Governor Jesse Ventura. As a result, some of my visitors find my website after running a search for Minnesota, Governor Ventura, Cannon Falls, etc. Anything that makes my website more searchable is good news!

▼ View traffic reports to tell you more about the number of people visiting your website. If you have a good website tracker, you'll learn how visitors are reaching your website. Sometimes this information will surprise you. There have been times when I have been amazed to learn about websites and other resources that have given publicity to my website. I have also discovered that one of my books was favorably reviewed on various book-related websites. I wouldn't have learned of these reviews if it had not been for my sleuthing with the website tracker. The free online trackers involve a simple copy and paste of a block of code into your Web page.

▼ Networking is very important, even on the Internet. We need colleagues and contacts to succeed. As a work-at-home mom of two—with a third baby on the way—I rely almost solely on the computer to grow my business. I am very enthusiastic about Web marketing because 90 percent of my now marketing is via the Internet.

Finding the Time for Online Success

Tony Alessandra

I'm sure everything you have read so far in this book sounds great, but I bet you are also wondering, "How do I find time to create my own winning website?" The answer is: Hire the experts and learn to delegate! The ability to delegate will be necessary as you grow your own online business. Delegation is an art and a learned skill that sets leaders apart from followers. That's because many people find it difficult to give up control. But if you don't give up some control, you will never find the time to start creating and developing an effective "service and sell" website.

The following key points will help you master the art of delegation when setting up your website:

▼ **Find the right Webmaster for the project**

Don't assign the project to just any warm body. That's fine if any outcome is acceptable. If you want the job done right, however, you must find the right person for the job.

▼ **Delegate authority and accountability**

The worst thing you can do is delegate a task and then tie a person's hands. If you have picked the right person, you must then give them authority so the job can be done without your supervision. In addition, you should make the person accountable for the quality of the work performed.

▼ **Make the task perfectly clear**

Carefully explain the nature of the project to the person to whom you are giving responsibility. This may be done verbally or in writing, depending on the complexity of the task. The newer and more complex the task, the more questions your Webmaster will have. Answer all questions promptly and thoroughly.

▼ **Agree on a deadline**

When your Webmaster fully understands your expectations, both of you are in a position to determine a mutually acceptable deadline.

▼ **Review and coach**

There is a learning curve associated with any new activity. During this time, you should periodically review your Webmaster's progress and offer additional information about your business to keep the project moving along productively.

*The moment you commit and quit holding back,
all sorts of unforeseen incidents, meetings and material
assistance will rise up to help you. The simple act
of commitment is a powerful magnet for help.*

—Napoleon Hill

Chapter Four

Develop a Website that Sizzles and Sells

*Everybody has to try just a little bit harder,
do just a little bit better, think just a little deeper,
work just a little longer.*
—Mary Lou Retton

Shameless Internet Promotion Step 4: Create a Content Rich Website that Sells

Debbie Allen

Content is king on the Internet. Forget the flash, bells and whistles—what website visitors want is content. Companies that are serious about using the Internet as a marketing and/or customer service tool, have realized that content must meet their visitors' needs. And they recognize that it must be delivered in easily digestible, bite-size nuggets.

People come to your website voluntarily or read your e-mail messages because they are looking for value and they believe you can provide it. Your challenge is to sell the value of your products and services and ask your visitors to take action to receive that value.

Unfortunately, many websites take a passive approach to e-commerce—the customer must choose to seek out interaction and the steps required to complete a purchase are often time consuming and complicated. An effective e-commerce website—one that sizzles and sells—promotes customer interaction, sells benefits, and makes it easy for the visitor to take action.

The key to successful e-commerce is *selling*. The common misuse of e-commerce for online shopping is no shock; many confuse exchanging funds for products or services with selling. Selling is persuading someone to act in a new or different manner than they usually would. Selling happens all the time and usually involves no exchange of funds.

If your visitors come to your website and leave having simply read your information no one wins. Success is not found until you persuade your website visitors to *take action* and contact you, buy your product, sign up for your newsletter or visit your brick and mortar location. It you don't *sell* them on *interacting* with you—they simply won't!

Five Ways to Get Your Visitors to Respond

1. **Make it easy and get to the point.** Study after study shows that Internet surfers don't read on the Web. They simply scan over text, hoping to pick out what they need. Therefore, you must state the facts clearly and briefly.

2. **Don't be self-serving.** Many websites overwhelm visitors with too much hype and played-out marketing fluff. What visitors want are the facts—just the facts, unsweetened and unadulterated, in an informal tone.

3. **Survey your customers.** By surveying your customers you will uncover their most important needs and discover why they came to visit your website in the first place. Armed with this information, you can push those hot buttons and align your copy for maximum impact. This will help you to create effective copy and attention grabbing headlines that connect them to your website like a magnet.

4. **Stress the benefits.** Discover what is most important to your customers and feature it in benefits, benefits, and more benefits! Tell visitors why they should do business with you instead of your competition. Stress the benefits of doing business with you as the only and best possible solution to their problems, needs and/or concerns?

5. **Make it easy for all forms of communication to take place.** Since many viewers print out Web pages to read at another time—it is crucial to post your contact information on every page of your website. Make sure to post **all** of your contact information. People communicate differently so provide your street address, telephone and fax numbers, as well as your e-mail and website addresses. Do the same for **every** e-mail you send. It amazes me how many people still send e-mails without a detailed signature line full of contact information and a branded business image. It is very frustrating for visitors to have to search for information or send another e-mail to get the contact information they need.

Home, Home on the Web
Mary Westheimer

Just having a website is not enough. You have to build it in such a way that the people you want to come there will indeed come, and then will do what you want them to do. This means that it is critical to know who your audiences are and what you want them to do. If you're selling items for children, do you want parents and grandparents to come? They are, after all, the ones with the wallets! Or, do you also want kids to visit? Once you have identified your audience, you know how to talk to them; you know what they know and don't know, and what they expect to see. Moreover, if you have a clear sense of what you want them to do, you will be able to guide them accordingly. Focus on bringing together your audience and goals to keep your "eyes on the prize."

That leads me to my second big tip: Help steer your visitors through your website to facilitate achievement of your goals. Failing to tell visitors what to do—a next action—is one of the biggest mistakes website owners and designers make. If your homepage copy doesn't have a clickable link to take visitors to an interior page, such as an order page, you are leaving them to their own devices, and they might do anything, including just leave your website altogether. Including "calls for action" that lead people appropriately is a subtle but important part of successful website copy.

One of the best places to put a call to action is what Jaclyn Easton, author of *Striking It Rich.com*, a book that profiled 23 successful Internet entrepreneurs, calls "the most valuable real estate on the Web." Think about how great it would be if you could reach visitors at the very moment they are feeling great about themselves *and* actually have a bit of free time? Well, you can.

Anytime visitors have filled out an interactive form of any kind and pushed the "submit" button, there is a brief moment of satisfaction and availability, which is exactly the same time that the website delivers what is known as a "confirmation page." Now, you can simply have that page say "Thank you for your order" or something similar, but this moment is actually an excellent time to recommend a next action. You might want to encourage visitors to sign up for your e-zine (electronic magazine), go to a part of your website they may not have yet been to, or even visit a strategic partner. Your website host or programmer can help you place your text, images, etc. on that valuable piece of property.

That's not your only opportunity for good location, by the way. Indeed, "location, location, location" is as true online as off. When designing your website, you also want to make sure that you use your homepage effectively. Don't squander it on huge, slow-loading graphics (which really only "run-off" potential customers who have yet to understand the value of what you're offering them!), but rather make it work for you by getting as many keywords as possible on it for the search engines.

You also want to have as much key material as possible on that page "above the fold." Now we all know that computer screens don't fold in two. That expression hails from the world of newspapering, which quickly learned that stories that were presented in the top section of the front page—above the fold—get the most attention. Accordingly, anything that appears in the first screen of a Web page, and particularly a homepage, will get the most response. Tim Carter, the syndicated home repair columnist, learned just that with his very successful website, www.askthebuilder.com. When he moved his e-zine signup form to the top half of his homepage, his subscriptions increased nearly 300 percent!

In and Out and About

There are many ways to market online outside of a website. Any marketing done online can also pay rich benefits offline. All of these promotions raise awareness of products and services, getting the multiple impressions any business needs to succeed. Online marketing can even pay off without a website, although in these days of instant gratification, doing so without having someplace to send potential customers who are ready to buy can make your job harder.

That didn't stop Betsy Lampe of Rainbow Books of Florida, however. Rainbow Books had published more than 50 nonfiction titles during 20 years of business when the company took on a mystery title. Determined not to invest much more than "sweat equity" in the project, Lampe did all of her marketing online, with the exception of one $350 ad in an industry publication. Using various online resources and her own marketing knowledge, she was able to sell out her entire initial press run of the book before publication.

For the complete story, read *Marketing Online Is No Mystery* at www.bookzonepro.com/insights/articles/article-73.html.

But, just how do you market online and stay within the bounds of "Netiquette"? Certain approaches, such as sending unsolicited, commercial e-mail (also known as spam) and posting messages that simply say, "Hire me" or "Buy my product" can backfire, angering potential customers and causing headaches with service providers. Fortunately, as Betsy Lampe and many others have proven, there are productive ways to market online. In fact, the Net is uniquely suited to online marketing because users actually organize themselves into neat groups that are relatively easy to find and approach.

One of the biggest surprises in BookZone's *Survey of Publishing Websites* was the reported effectiveness of approaching members of online interest groups: those publishing professionals who used newsgroups and mail lists to market online were the happiest with their website traffic.

Newsgroups are online clubs that are not on the Web, but actually reside on another part of the Internet known as the Usenet. Participants go to the newsgroups, where previous postings remain while new messages are added.

Mail lists (which are sometimes called "listserves" because of a popular software program used to run them) use e-mail to create similar groups, with everyone who is interested in a particular subject sending an e-mail message to a certain address. Then everyone who has subscribed that way receives every message that is sent to the mail list.

Newsgroup postings are effective because the messages remain online for a long time, sometimes forever. That means posting such messages will make your information available longer. In contrast, mail list messages disappear after they are deleted from an inbox (unless the mail list owner archives them on a website), but the fact that they come directly to participants increases the possibility they'll actually get read. And because people subscribe to the mail lists—which they wouldn't do unless they were interested initially!—they are more likely to open them.

Here's how to use both newsgroups and mail lists effectively:

- ▼ Find newsgroups by visiting Google at www.groups.google.com. You'll find mail lists at groups.yahoo.com, www.topica.com, www.ezinecentral.com, and www.listfish.com

▼ Spend a little time pinpointing those groups that best serve your goals and then visit them regularly—at least once or twice a week. "Regulars" are usually treated with more respect.

▼ Get a bead on the culture of the group before getting involved. Some are more appropriate than others. You can do this by what is called "lurking," or just reading messages before posting your own. If the group has a FAQ, or list of Frequently Asked Questions, be sure to read it. This will reveal the culture and acccepted behavior in the group. You may also learn whether or not you can use signatures, mention products, etc.

▼ Communicate rather than sell. Participating in these online clubs is very much like promoting your business on a talk show. Simply hyping your offerings turns off the audience and the host, potentially harming rather than helping you. The most effective posts will likely be responses to questions or contributions of information.

The Right Tool for the Right Job

If you aren't supposed to sell on mail lists and newsgroups, how do people know about your products and services? While nearly every company has a website now, only one in five even knows about what I call "the Net's secret weapon" and one of its most powerful marketing devices, the lowly "signature."

A signature is a small text message that automatically attaches to the end of your e-mail and newsgroup postings, allowing you to add information about your company, services and products. This addendum helps spread the word about your offerings without actually selling. You can mention a special sale, promote a client, or boast about your benefits, even if your message itself doesn't even mention your business.

Just let your signature tell readers who you are and what you can do for them. I use signatures just this way on publishing mail lists, letting members know who I am while "showing them my stuff." After joining one list recently, within days I picked up a new client who knew about us but was finally prompted to act when he saw my post on an entirely unrelated subject.

You can tout your company's services in your signature, and have different signatures for different audiences (for instance, one for friends, one for customers, and another for vendors). Does it work? I change our signature daily to promote our publishers and have found that a signature campaign can increase sales as much as 75 percent.

Here's an example of one of our signatures:

+
BOOKZONE: website development, hosting & promotion for
3,500 publishing professionals: http://www.bookzone.com/
800-536-6162 480-481-9737 mwestheimer@bookzone.com
TODAY'S BZ HOTSPOT: Demos Medical Publishing—Patient &
professional publications at http://www.demosmedpub.com/
+

Keep your signature small—rule of thumb is that a signature shouldn't exceed six lines—and focus on benefits and urgency in the brief description. Also always use the full URL (Uniform Resource Locator, or website address) including the http://. That makes the address "hot" in most e-mail programs, letting curious readers automatically click through to see the website. And don't forget some actual contact information, such as your phone number and e-mail address!

Other Places, Other Names

Newsgroups and mail lists aren't the only places where people with similar interests gather, though. Many websites have interactive forums where visitors can exchange ideas, share their thoughts and learn more about specific subjects.

Another, newer hybrid way to communicate online that is become extremely popular is the Web log, or blog. A blog is perhaps more closely related to an e-zine than interactive venues like mail lists, newsgroups and Web forums in that it is basically a one-way communication. Blogs use the Web as their platform, but unlike a standard website, blogs are more conversational and more personal. This helps create a stronger bond, according to Anne Holland of MarketingSherpa.com Although Holland gets several messages each day in response to her weekly e-zines, she receives 20 e-mails a day in response to her blog. She credits her blog's informality for making a personal connection between company and customer, thereby increasing by "ten times" the likelihood they'll order. To learn more about this fascinating use of the Web, read an article about blogs at www.clickz.com/em_mkt/b2b_em_mkt/article.php/870481.

Tying It All Together

Remember what I said about people on the Net organizing themselves into neat little groups? Well, another place they congregate according to subject matter is on websites. That's right, you can find them—rather, they can find you!—on other websites that serve them using a technique that's been around since the beginning of the Web in 1993.

Back when we started BookZone, there were no search engines. Today, there are thousands, but back then, people leaped from website to website with simple connections called reciprocal links ("we'll give you one if you give us one"). You still often see links pages on websites, because they're an easy way to provide content…and can be a great marketing tool.

For instance, BookZone's own Literary Leaps at www.literaryleaps.com offers free links to owners of publishing-related websites. Visitors can add their own links in five different categories. When our Leapmaster accepts them for our listings with a single click of a mouse (this approach avoids inappropriate links), the other website owner automatically gets an e-mail with all the code they need to put a link to our website. Not only has this approach helped us create thousands of links to our website—thereby improving our ranking in search engines that assess "link popularity," or how many websites are linked to a particular destination—but we also find that Literary Leaps consistently is in the top five of referring websites to BookZone.com, right up there with Google and Yahoo!

There's another type of linking, too, which is more like public relations. It's sometimes called content linking because it's all about giving other websites content—which they often want and need—with a paragraph at the bottom that links back to your website or to a place where they can buy your product or service or whatever it is you're trying to achieve.

Linking is a little more time consuming than some kinds of marketing, but it creates recurring traffic from qualified locations. Often we see a customer get one link that then sends their traffic skyrocketing.

One Hand Washing the Other, Washing the Other, Washing …

As marketers learn more about what happens online, they are able to better leverage their knowledge. One thing the most successful marketers have already learned is the importance of cross-pollinating all of their marketing channels.

The Internet is not an isolated avenue, but rather a part of a larger whole. Larry Bram of Teaching Strategies, Inc., is a firm believer in cross-pollination—and in the lessons of other disciplines. "The people who are making money were direct marketers to begin with," he observes. "Almost 100 percent of our products are sold through direct marketing, so it was not a big leap for us." Key, he says, is integrating distribution. "If you have a website, are you going to cut off your 800 line? You make it as easy as possible to order from you." Teaching Strategies leverages the direct contact by making sure new customers get into the company's other marketing channels. "Hopefully they register for the e-mail newsletter, but they definitely get the regular catalog and all the other direct contact, too," says Bram. Under his leadership, the company's original website (now one of four) was to pay for itself in 18-24 months. "We did it in nine," Bram reports.

Bram, and other smart marketers, cross-pollinate all of their marketing. You'll find their website address and e-mail address everywhere: on their stationery, business cards, and fax cover sheets; in their print advertising and news releases, and in their TV and radio presentations. You never know how people are going to be most comfortable contacting you, so give them every possible way to do so. In fact, the Web has become the initial contact point of choice for so many people because going to a website enables them to get information anonymously. Although it deprives you of future repeated contacts, it does save time spent with "looky-loos."

If you have not been marketing online for a while, you may be feeling a bit overwhelmed right about now. But, please don't get overwhelmed and stop your progress. It's easy to look at all the things you can do and feel you'll never get it all done. Instead, break down your tasks and establish a reasonable plan. You may be able to visit two newsgroups, participate on a mail list and request three links a week. Then, as you progress, reassess your plan and adjust it to something achievable. Take it step-by-step and before you know it, you'll have your own online success stories.

What Your Website Needs to Create More Sales

Lenny Laskowski

Now that you have read about the key elements to make your website more visible to the search engines and directories, you should understand the elements your website needs to make it sizzle and sell. Here are some important issues to consider if you want your website to sizzle and make the sale:

Navigation

> ▼ Can your potential client easily navigate your website?
>
> ▼ Can they easily find their way back to the home page?

Provide navigation options (buttons and/or text links) on **each** of your web pages. This will allow your potential client to move easily around your website and find the information they are looking for.

Information They Want and Need

> ▼ What does your client need to know about you and your business?
>
> ▼ What information do your clients typically ask for when they call you on the telephone?

Make sure your website provides the information your existing and potential customers are actually looking for. Most people will ask for the same information over and over again. By posting the information that is most requested, you will be offering potential clients a way to get the information they want without waiting to talk to you. At the same time, make sure your website includes information they **need**.

Useful Information

> ▼ Do you establish credibility with your website visitors by including expert articles, feature stories, or free audio or video demonstrations, etc.?

Be sure to include some useful **free**—truly **free**—information on your website that potential clients can read such as articles, ask the expert questions and answers, etc. Feature your expertise by adding client lists, testimonials, published articles, and special products or services.

Your Contact Information

▼ Do you make it easy for people to get a hold of you?

▼ Does your website provide contact information on each page?

Provide your name, photograph, address, telephone number, fax number, e-mail address, and even website address. By doing this you are saying that you are a legitimate business and willing to allow people to actually contact you. Many businesses only provide an e-mail address and do not even include a name, phone number, or snail mail address. I personally do not trust businesses that do this on their websites.

Their Contact Information

▼ Do you ask visitors for their contact information?

▼ Do you require detailed and specific information be provided?

Most people don't usually take the time to e-mail you their contact information. It's too much work. I provide a few online forms that visitors to my website can easily fill out then automatically send this information to me by e-mail. Do not **require** too much specific information. Many people are turned off by this requirement. Allow them to provide as much information about themselves as they are willing. If you don't ask for it they will usually not provide it. Besides the typical name, address and phone number, I also ask for their Web address, fax numbers, and even provide a comment field where they can provide any additional information they feel is necessary.

A Reason to Come Back

▼ Do you provide a reason for visitors to return to your website again and again?

▼ Do your customers understand the added value you have to offer from your website?

Many times your visitor may only visit your website once. Most sales are **not** made on the first try. Make sure your information is current and up to date. Do not leave on your website "upcoming events" that occurred last month or even last year. Visitors, as well as search engines, will know your website is not updated frequently and will never return.

Incentives

▼ Do you provide incentives for people to give you information?

▼ Do you reward your customers with free gifts?

Offer drawings and provide various offers for people who fill your guest book or even participate in your discussion board. Reward them for providing information. I have given away free copies of my books and videotape programs and even a free telephone consultation as rewards.

Does Your Website Pass the "Who Cares" Test?

Jeff Rubin

I'll get right to the point: 40 percent of my income as a newsletter publisher comes from companies that found me on the World Wide Web. Yes, that's 40 percent! My business has doubled in the last three years. In fact, as I write this I have eight customers outside my local area, including five in states throughout the United States other than my home state of California.

How have I done this? One word: **Value.**

In more than two decades of helping companies, non-profit organizations, and sole proprietors to communicate with their customers, prospects, and employees, I can tell you with much certainty that the only thing that matters in marketing is **value.** That's because all successful marketing must appeal to a customer's sense of need. This is especially true if you're selling a service, rather than a product.

Aside from developing personal relationships that will, in the long term, result in an endless stream of referrals, the Web is the best and fastest way to get your message to the masses. It's an incredibly efficient marketing tool; if you don't have a website you're not only missing what might be a once-in-a-business opportunity, but you're lagging behind your competitors.

The Web is also one of the most abused and misused marketing showplaces. Tragically (and it is tragic, because a bad website is not only a missed marketing opportunity, but can sabotage a business), the Web is strewn with websites that contain nothing but garbage. Unadulterated crap! Page after page promoting services, items for sale and information about the company. Blaring banners and intrusive images screaming "buy this" in your face.

Websites that draw my rapt attention must pass the "Who cares?" test:

- ▼ "Last year you did $1.5 million in business." Who cares?
- ▼ "You got your doctorate from Harvard in six months." Who cares?
- ▼ "You will beat any published price by 10 percent." Who cares?

Who cares? Not me. I'm looking for the person who has the solution to my problem. I don't care who your customers are, where you were educated, and how much cheaper you are than your competition. I want to know if you can help me. That's your **value,** and your website must convince me you have it. If it doesn't pass my "Who Cares?" test, I move on.

While the Web presents an exciting marketing opportunity, it also presents some formidable obstacles to conventional, face-to-face customer contact. These include:

- ▼ Distance
- ▼ Hesitation about developing trust
- ▼ Reluctance to do business with vendors a customer might never meet.

How do you overcome these obstacles when your prospective customer can't look into your eyes? How can your website pass the "Who Cares?" test? Try **value!** For example, my website includes:

- ▼ 25 reasons why your company needs a newsletter
- ▼ Tips for spotting a bad newsletter—pitfalls and effective solutions
- ▼ Characteristics of effective marketing and employee newsletters
- ▼ Components needed to produce a quality newsletter
- ▼ Newsletter design and writing tips
- ▼ Every article from the print version of my company newsletter

My website reinforces my **value** by giving away a lot of my knowledge. I encourage my prospective customers to try publishing their own newsletters; then they'll realize the **value** in having me do it for them. Usually, though, by the time they reach my website, they already know this.

There's not a single word about cost. I don't want customers who are looking for a "deal." I want customers who appreciate my **value** and are willing to pay a fair price for it. And they do! **How do you find your value?** Here are two suggestions:

▼ **Ask your customers.** I asked my customers this question: "I'm trying to find out why my customers do business with me, and I need your help. If you were to recommend me to one of your business friends, what would you say about me and the way I do business?"

The results were astonishing. I learned about services I perform for my customers (like bugging them to meet their deadlines) that I had no idea they thought were valuable. These have become some of my key marketing and selling points. I also created 16 additional pages on my new website; one devoted to each customer who replied, with an image of their newsletter and their response. My customers are helping me sell my value!

▼ Split a piece of paper in two columns and answer these questions: "What makes me special?" and "Why should anyone do business with me?" You'll end up with a list of services and personal characteristics that make you unique. How do these benefit your prospective customers? They're your **value!**

The design of your website counts, too. As an example, let me tell you of a conversation I had in August 2001, as I was preparing to update mine.

My first website, in 1995, was primitive by today's standards, but the information it contained was solid. It has been revised a few times, each time adding more value, not glitz.

As we prepared to put up the latest incarnation, my Web designer told me my website had a dated look; many of the newer websites featured spiffy graphics, reverse type, and lots of other high-tech-looking bells and whistles. They looked bolder and had a sharper edge to them.

So I thought, that's great! Without changing my website a great deal, it was once again different from my competition. It would stand out from other websites in my industry. Other than two classy, animated graphics on the home page, my website is gimmick-free. No flashing lights or buttons or banners, nothing that screams my services to the viewer. It's contemporary again, just like art deco furniture.

Don't make your website an ad. Make it a resource for information, a repository of your knowledge, a place where people come for answers. Once they're on your website, show them what you know. Educate and inform them, and they'll flock back like geese migrating south for the winter.

65

Make your website a place of **value**. Who cares? You had better, because your prospective customers do!

Bring Your Visitors Back Clamoring for More!
Judy Cullins

Once your website is up, you must maintain it. Maintenance means changes, and each time you make a change, you may make a mistake. I'm really grateful when people point out glitches on my website, and I check it carefully each week. I check to make sure that all my links work properly, that my instructions are complete and easy to follow, and that the passion I have for what I do comes across in my copy.

If your visitors get a link that doesn't work, or see incomplete instructions, or read dull copy, they will leave your website immediately, and not bookmark it. Before you invite folks to see your masterpiece you need to check and correct all parts of your website, and especially the home page.

Test Your Headlines

You have four seconds to get your visitor's attention. Test your title or the opening sentence of your copy. This one item alone can make a huge difference in the number of responses you receive. Instead of wasting words "welcoming" the visitor, put a benefit with a link to either a benefit story or sales letter about your product or the product itself.

When I changed the copy on my original home page to read "Quadruple your Web Sales in Just Four Months" and added a "click here" link to my sales copy, my Web sales increased tenfold in only four months. People learned about my e-books and tele-classes on *Write Your e-Book* or *Other Short Book—Fast!* In 2002, after being online eight months, Web sales are consistently over $3,000 each month.

Test Your Offers

If your headline doesn't say benefits, the game is over. People perceive more value when you add an incentive to buy. Give them a bonus free report or a list of tips with the order. It takes little time and effort to create, but it increases sales by as much as 30 times.

Each month, I motivate my visitors with "Discounts of the Month" available as a navigation bar on home page. In each discount I include testimonials and benefits, and perhaps a bundling of several books or tele-classes for a deep discount—often half price. If your headline doesn't say benefits, the game is over. People perceive more value when you add an incentive to buy. Give them a bonus free report or a list of tips with the order. It takes little time and effort to create, but it increases sales by as much as 30 times.

Testimonials

Testimonials lend credibility to your website. When people see that other well-known leaders like your products or services, they are more likely to buy. It's relatively easy to get these too. Here are a few testimonials that worked:

> "Save yourself from headaches, disappointments, and money down the drain. Read *Write Your e-Book or Other Short Book— Fast!* before you write another word. The author puts you on the fastest track to publishing success."

> "Wow! My sales letter worked! Thank you, thank you, thank you for presenting your three-session Tele-class *Create Your Homepage With Marketing Pizzazz.* You helped me focus on who my target market really is——a major accomplishment. Knowing the difference between benefits and features helped me produce a sales letter that got me a sale the next day I put it up on my website."

> "In just one coaching session I learned how to strengthen my article's language, got a perfect acronym for my coaching business, learned the difference between benefits and features, got a new bio/benefits statement to use for networking, and most of all the "bigger picture" to see a series of products and services to sell—definitely worth her fees."

Benefit Statements

Test your copy by e-mailing several groups in your address book with several choices. Call it a survey. Ask them, which benefits make their heart skip a beat…enough to take out their credit card and buy. Emphasize different benefits. Try out different headlines, phrases, power words or metaphors. Appeal to emotions and to different senses. Remember most people are visual and kinesthetic.

Test Your Price

A price that is too low is as bad as a price too high. Too low a price devalues your product or service. Potential clients or buyers may think, "If it's that cheap, it must not be good." If your service is invaluable, be sure to charge what you're worth. Always start your prices high. You can offer a deep discount later.

Test Your Copy

Change testimonials or pictures every so often. Redo your opening page and closing page. Instead of "Subscribe to my e-zine," put a short testimonial from a famous person in your field right before the "click here" to subscribe. Always give your visitors a reason to buy.

Make your copy "you" oriented. Use bullets to make your Web pages easier to read. Keep your paragraphs short, around one to four sentences. Short paragraphs are more effective in sustaining attention.

Check also for passive sentence construction. Why? Because you slow your reader down with passives—they want clear, concise, and compelling information. You can use your spelling and grammar checking tools to analyze your writing and get a percentage of passive sentences. If your sentences are more than three to four percent passive, you need a professional coach to check your copy.

Test Your Website Layout

Know where people are entering your website and exiting. Many companies can provide this service. If potential buyers keep leaving at a particular page before they go to the products and ordering page, your words deceive, and some changes are in order. You can track:

- ▼ Where your traffic is coming from
- ▼ What pages visitors like
- ▼ What page the majority of visitors enter and exit
- ▼ How long are visitors are there, and even
- ▼ Which visitors signed up for your electronic newsletter.

Test Your Order Process

Ask friends and associates to run through different parts of your website. Show your appreciation by paying them for their efforts with free product or service. Tell them you have a thick skin, and that you appreciate their honesty. One would-be customer couldn't finish the order for one of my tele-classes. It took a lot of effort to get that mistake rectified. I know a famous e-book author from whom I tried and tried to buy a book. I even e-mailed him about it. He said he didn't take e-mail orders and sent me back to where the problem was.

It's much better to have all links work, so your customers will have an easy ordering experience. Also, be sure to offer your customers several ways to order. Not all people like to order on the Web.

Know that your job of testing never ends. It's what we call maintenance. *Eighty percent of life is maintenance!* Just experimenting with these tests will bring more sales. Keep testing to know what your potential buyers really want.

A Unique and Interesting Website Is a Marketing Hook

Julia L. Wilkinson

I have stumbled upon a great, unique Internet marketing concept that I'd like to share with you so that you can also use it for your own marketing purposes.

Since my book, *My Life at AOL*, is a memoir about my career working in the Internet industry, marketing the book online seemed natural. After both e-publishing and print publishing my book, I searched for ways to get the word out about it, since most of the onus of marketing a book falls on the author—unless you're already a top seller like Stephen King or Danielle Steel.

After trolling around the Web to see what came up under various searches for "AOL," I came across several websites that displayed collections of AOL compact disks. That's right! People actually save and collect those disks that you probably threw into the trash! There are actually thousands of them, all with different designs.

It occurred to me that I had a very large stash of trinkets, t-shirts, disks, and other items that I had received as an employee of AOL. I realized I could display them on a website and create a stand-alone curiosity that would draw people in—for free! I had a virtual museum, if you will, that I could leverage to market my book. If people were looking at AOL disks online, they must already have an affinity for computers and/or collectibles…that, or they had an extraordinarily large amount of time to kill!

So in essence, I could create a hook to draw in a ready-made target-marketed audience to buy my book!

I got to work right away. Even though my knowledge of HTML (Hyper Text Markup Language) was very basic, I was never one to be daunted by such challenges. Moreover, learning HTML is not difficult at all. I created a very basic website using the very simple tools offered by Yahoo's GeoCities (which are free as long as you don't exceed a certain amount of disk space). Within a day, I had a simple "AOL Disk and Memorabilia Museum."

I didn't waste time with bells and whistles on my website; personally, I think simple, clean designs that are clearly labeled and not too graphic-intensive are the most effective—think Martha Stewart's magazine, with plenty of white space. Too many Web designers load up their website with pre-entry graphics, animation, and loud colors, which do more to hinder than help their cause. And let's not forget that simpler websites are much easier to design and create!

Finally, my most shameless trick: I put a "glamour-shot" of myself on the website, sporting a stylish AOL black leather jacket! Hey, if you can't look good on your own website, where can you? The whimsical picture sets the light tone for the website. It says, "Let's have a bit of fun here and enjoy looking at all this crazy stuff." Who said collecting made sense? If it brings joy into people's lives, isn't that important enough?

Get Similar Websites to Share Links and Pass Each Other Traffic

The website plodded along steadily the first few weeks, as I doggedly scanned my items, tweaked the image sizes, and added them to the website. As the number of items became substantial enough to start publicizing the website, I sent e-mails to the people who were running similar websites. It turns out that there are several AOL disk museums out there!

Should you worry that people with similar websites won't want to help you because you have a competitive website? Not at all!

Most people running such websites are happy to share links and pass traffic back and forth…and besides, each website is unique in its own way. It's not unlike how you often see three fast food restaurants on the same corner, each getting more business than they would if they were alone, because the clustering draws so many more people.

So my advice to you is: think of what you can offer, that is related to the general subject matter of your book, in order to create an engaging, free online experience for people. You will have a powerful tool to attract a ready-made, target market to your website to buy your book or other product!

Put that Website Address Everywhere!

Include the website address in all your correspondence and in your regular e-mail signature.

I sell various items on eBay including an e-book I wrote. When I ship the items out, I include a flyer for *My Life at AOL*, with a picture of the cover of the book, copies of my five-star "reader ratings" from Amazon.com, and a quote from a piece about the book in *The Washington Post*. I also have a flyer for my e-book called *What Sells for What on eBay*.

I'll never forget what I heard mystery author and former *Washington Post* food critic Phyllis Richman say about her books…that they each had to find an audience, one reader at a time. Well, I thought, there's Phyllis Richman, a well-known big-name newspaper reporter-turned successful mystery writer and she's struggling with the same marketing strategies as the rest of us.

That's what you're doing when you create a compelling website that's topical to your product's subject matter…you're drawing in prospective viewers, in the hope that your materials and teasers will turn them into buyers…one viewer at a time.

> *Once I decide to do something,*
> *I can't have people telling me I can't.*
> *If there is a roadblock, you jump over it,*
> *walk around it, crawl under it.*
> —Kitty Kelley

"Guess what happened when I started accepting credit cards on my website?!"

Chapter Five

From Website Basics to Mega Profits

Money will come to you when you're doing the right thing.
—Michael Philips

Shameless Internet Promotion Step 5: Implement Online Marketing Secrets to Drive Traffic to Your Website

Debbie Allen

You have now learned how to create a website or improve the one you already have. Yet that's just the beginning. Don't stop there! The real work is just beginning. You are not in the business of selling your products or services off your website. You are in the business of *marketing* your website. The better the job you do of marketing it, the more profitable it will be—period! On the Internet, success is all about marketing!

One of the challenges with the Internet is that the customer's interaction with a website is limited to reading text and viewing graphics. The customer is not dealing with an individual or a personality. Because of this, it's difficult to create a sense of trust and build the loyalty of prospective customers.

However, with some effective and innovative marketing you can create a charismatic personality, professional image and strong online reputation for your business. And many of the marketing strategies in this book won't even cost you a dime!

Too many online businesses fail miserably after they create an online presence because they simply walk away. They count on people to simply stumble across their website, and then they wonder why no one visits. They complain that the Internet doesn't work for them. They gripe that they have no time to improve the website and so on. Yet, they do nothing to market the website to even their existing customers much less to prospective customers. Those websites sit there all alone, not a visitor in sight.

Have you ever seen a website where a traffic counter shows a very low count? This drives me crazy! Here's what the website is screaming at the viewer: "We are a very small company"; "We created an ineffective website to save money"; "We work out of the garage to save on rent"; "We are so lonely no one ever comes to visit—please stay!"

Build a website and they won't come! Build an effective marketing plan and they will! And they will come in BIG numbers. I used to have one of those lonely websites! But after using just a few of the marketing strategies I learned from my shameless Internet marketing friends, my website soon found fame, fortune and tons of new online business. It will never be lonely again.

Show Me the Money
Chris Bloor

WARNING! The following information can change your life—if you know what to do with it!

After surveying several thousand consumers over a period of five years to find out why businesses lost customers, the experts discovered that:

  1 percent of the customers had died
  3 percent had moved out of the area
  5 percent had been "influenced" away
  9 percent had found "better service" elsewhere
  14 percent had experienced "unresolved conflicts" with the company.

That adds up to 32 percent! Now, look at this and tremble…

  68 percent of customers leave because of "perceived indifference"

That means they:

  ▼ Don't give you any precious referrals
  ▼ Quit buying your "stuff"—and make your competitors rich!

So we take one simple extra step to blow these statistics away—and it is something you can use to immediately blast your online marketing efforts through the roof! While everyone else is busy giving away **free** bonuses online, you can take the concept a step further and whenever people order from your website give them **free** offline bonuses as well! This will make your bonus stand out from your competitors and bond your customers' loyalty to you.

Here's how it works:

▼ Every time someone places an order with you, whether online or off, send them something as a bonus that blows them away and "superglues" their loyalty to you. For example, when someone places an order from our website for Better Marketing Cards we send bonus extras like audiotapes, manuals or "insider" reports.

▼ The customer opens the package when it arrives to find much more than they ordered. Everyone loves getting a free bonus, especially when they least expect it.

The concept of giving things away to create customer loyalty is something many of today's Internet gurus seem to have forgotten. No matter how much money people have—no matter how much they love your latest wiz-bang product—everyone gets a special buzz when they receive something in the mail that they can see, open and feel!

We are so serious about this concept that we have invested tens of thousands of dollars into various reprint rights to some of the best information products available anywhere. We not only sell them both online and off, but we also give them away each time someone purchases a certain amount of product from us.

Does it really work? Yes, it does. So if you really want to grow your business and increase sales both online and off:

▼ Exceed your customers' expectations.

▼ Stay in regular contact with your customers.

▼ Keep in contact with them at least eight times a year.

▼ Over-deliver. Use the power of special surprise bonuses to knock their socks off!

From Ho-Hum to Destination

Eric Gelb and Joe Gelb

Yes, you can absolutely earn mega-profits on the Web. The key is to transform your website into a destination stop that drives your business. If your website is merely an address that people stumble upon while they crawl through the search engines, you're probably getting hits but not visits. And more important you aren't ringing up many sales. Passersby are likely to move quickly to the next website in search of the information and products they seek.

After two years of online losses, three Web hosts and four designers, we conducted a study of what works on the Web. My dad and I combined our 5-plus years of book publishing and 70-plus years of marketing and selling experience and discovered the keys to success on the Web. Here's how you can capitalize on today's technology and catapult yourself and your business into mega-profit status.

Transform Your Website into a Destination Stop

Think of your favorite store in a shopping mall. You might stop at a number of stores en route but your goal is to reach that favorite store—the destination stop. A destination stop entices visitors to come back, time and time again, and spend relatively long periods of time and large amounts of money.

To create a destination stop and to position yourself as a recognized expert and leader in your chosen field, you must offer an array of unique and valuable materials. These materials must be both important to your customers and cover your subject matter in a way that positions you as the expert in your field. When your customers cannot obtain your unique information anywhere else, in essence, you are transforming your website into a destination stop. And this will help you build your business.

Provide Unique How-To Content for Your Website

Develop unique material based on your topic, business, field and expertise. You must have a specific perspective and competitive advantage in your field. You bring your own outlook, background, experience, and point-of-view to your work. Use this as the foundation for your unique offering. Provide information first in a way that demonstrates your expertise on your subject matter and second explains and expounds. The goal is to create "how-to" material that is valuable to your customers and content that helps your customers build their businesses, make money and/or save time.

Explain and discuss your products and services, but emphasize providing information and value rather than selling. Use the soft sell so that your customers become more comfortable with you and gain confidence in your products and services. At the bottom of each piece of content, include your bio along with your website address, links to selected website pages, and the name of a relevant product offering (include a link). The key is to draw people to you and your business and encourage them to make a purchase. Potential consumers will return to your website again and again when they can obtain your unique and invaluable information only at your website. This increases the likelihood that they will purchase, again and again.

Give Away Some Content for Free to People Who Visit Your Website

Offer a reasonable chunk of your material at no charge, free, to entice your customers to make a purchase. At the same time, offer most of the items for sale at your website. Even if you sell services, you can expand your business by selling written material on your website. When we say free, we mean absolutely free—no strings or gimmicks attached. Freebies are a terrific inducement to bring traffic to your website and get people involved with you and your business. Create content that promotes one of your products or services at a time and leads the reader to make a purchase.

For example, we developed a special e-report—*Merchandising Secrets.* This report explains how you can make more money selling products and services at events and public speaking engagements. This five-page "how-to" is loaded with common sense strategies and tactics that are designed to help readers make more money. The strategy behind this report is to establish a rapport and credibility with our customers. Specifically, this report is designed to promote Eric's book, *Book Promotion Made Easy: Event Planning, Presentation Skills & Product Marketing.* Below the title, a brief paragraph mentions that the report is based on Eric's book. The bottom of the report features Eric's brief bio that emphasizes his marketing and selling credentials and the title of his book. In addition, the website is listed along with ordering information. Many people have placed orders through this promotion. A copy of this downloadable report is free for shameless fans and can be obtained by visiting www.PublishingGold.com or www.SmallBusinessAdvice.com

We featured this offer in another author's electronic newsletter to test the results. Over 4 percent of the subscribers requested our e-report and over 10 percent of that group placed orders directly with us. That's a fantastic conversion rate, much higher than the typical 2 to 3 percent response rates in direct mail, and that's just one e-newsletter. The promotion cost us nothing, and those sales were all at full retail. We can continue to promote to these new customers with the use of our shopping cart auto-responder targeted directly to this group.

Distribute Your Free Content Widely

Put forth great and continuous effort to seek out and encourage other marketing experts, publications and websites in your field to promote your free material and offer it to their readers and customers. When your material benefits that other group, it's a win for the publication and organization to offer your material to its members. Send press releases liberally to leading magazines, websites, electronic newsletters, smaller publications and media companies in your field. Encourage them to offer your material as a benefit to their readers and members. Editors and publishers constantly seek fresh and valuable content. In particular, those with tight budgets love free content. Trade associations like to add new benefits to their membership kits. This insatiable demand offers you the opportunity to capture valuable publicity, cultivate a following and bring traffic to your website. And, of course, your business will profit.

Below are some websites that offer opportunities to distribute your free content.

▼ www.ideamarketers.com
Idea Marketers is a media-matching service, where you can post your articles for free to be featured on the website. Writers, publishers, Web masters and electronic newsletter editors come to this website to find valuable content. They then request permission to publish your article including your bio/contact information on their website for free.

▼ www.freesticky.com

Free Sticky is a source of free and low cost content that anyone can use to increase the appeal, usefulness, traffic and eventually the stickiness of their website. Changing content is the driving force behind return visits to a website.

▼ www.ezinearticles.com

E-zine Articles' directory connects publishers with your articles. When you add your article to the directory, the publishers will be able to access it from an auto-responder or from your website for free.

More ideas on where to post your content information for free:

▼ Contact websites that are related to your field and send them a query that offers your content for posting on their website.

▼ Query publications in your field and offer them the opportunity to feature your free content as a benefit to their readers.

▼ Develop relationships with the key opinion-molders in your field and become a source of information for their work.

Case Study: Promoting Articles on Your Expertise

Joe Gelb wrote and published 14 articles on personal finance for Strong Mutual Funds' www.strong.com. Strong provides valuable information for free to people who visit the website. Joe's articles include material on setting financial goals, budgeting and completing a mutual fund application. Since these topics are timeless compared to articles that explain current tax rules and recommend specific mutual funds, their longevity should exceed the more time-sensitive material. This means greater publicity and exposure! Each article features Joe's byline that lists two of his book titles and the website address. We have piggybacked off of Strong's traffic, expanded our reach and built our customer base. This exposure has boosted our book sales, consulting and speaking engagement fees. But remember, continuous and constant shameless promotion is always the name of the game.

Add New Features and Benefits to Your Website on a Regular Basis

New material creates excitement, just as a retail store's new display entices visitors to return again and again. Think of your favorite magazine where you eagerly wait for each issue to arrive in your mailbox to see this month's features. Post free content on your website now, even if you have only a few pages of text to offer. When we posted our first set of free content, we had completed only about 25 pages of text. Based on customer feedback and product sales, we continue to develop new content at least once every month. The content may be a brief article, an editorial, a how-to story, an explanation of a business calculation or an FYI about your business. Work at making the content fresh, valuable and relevant to your customers. Make your customers feel that they always get good value when they visit your website.

Create a Free Electronic Newsletter

Today, there's a continuing and growing trend towards specialization and targeted, valuable information. People want to hear from experts. At the same time, there is a lot of clutter—loads of publications that cover the same ground. And most people lack the time to read lengthy material. So the key as a content provider and publisher is to develop truly useful and unique information. Create an electronic newsletter or e-zine around you, your business and your field. As a publisher, you choose the content you want to disseminate to your customer base.

Divide your e-zine into sections, provide value first and promote your business second. Report current news within your industry, discuss strategies and tactics, describe your products and include a calendar of events. Issue your e-zine religiously on the same date(s), preferably twice a month. Distribution is relatively straightforward when you use an e-mail management program and your e-mail database list. Keep each issue short (no more than five to six pages in total). Keep each topic short and make sure to invite people to subscribe by visiting your website and simply entering their e-mail address. [Learn more about e-zines and how to create an effective one in Chapter Nine.]

Create a Free E-Course

This is another powerful way to connect with your customers and establish credibility. By using your knowledge and expertise in your field, you can demonstrate your leadership by creating a multi-segment course. Once again, you can benefit your customers. For example, Small Business Advisors offers a free seven-day mini e-course on building your business. Topics range from developing a business plan to obtaining financing to boosting sales—all presented in such a way as to help the reader make money, and yet realize they could make even more money by hiring us to help them. Provide a lot of free information, but don't present so much material that your customer no longer needs to buy your products and services. Post information about your services and products along with other related websites, your bio, and all other contact information.

Excluding the advertisements, each of our lessons runs approximately three to four pages long and links to our website. If your course is longer, you might consider distributing each lesson every other day by auto-responder.

To learn more about auto-responders and how to use them, view these websites:

www.sendfree.com
www.getresponse.com
www.myreply.com

Make sure your auto-responder does not send other people's advertisements along with your material. Many, so called, free auto-responders make money by selling advertisements or memberships. Members can use the auto-responder to distribute their material, including e-books, but the auto-responder attaches someone else's advertisement to your material. This dilutes your message and is likely to irritate your customers. You may want to consider an auto-responder such as www.aweber.com that charges a monthly fee but does not place ads.

Our auto-responder is embedded in our shopping cart program. This feature enables us to increase the power of our marketing efforts by controlling our content and sending sequential offers to our customers depending on what materials they request and which offers they respond to. People can enroll while you sleep and the spillover orders can be fantastic.

Create an Interactive Analytical Tool that Your Customers Can Use Again and Again

We created a break-even calculator that helps business people analyze projects and how many units they have to sell before they recover their investment. People can visit our website and use this handy tool to analyze a project. Another one of our websites features a compound interest calculator to help you determine how much you need to save to reach your retirement goals. *Larry Chase's Web Digest for Marketers* at www.wdfm.com is another great example for the use of this analytical tool. This website features a media-buying calculator that helps you determine how much you spend per eyeball on advertising programs. Why should you use this interactive marketing tool on your website? Again, you're using your website to build a rapport with your customer base and drive sales.

Feature a Daily Pop-Up or Useful Fact

Create a succinct, one-sentence daily idea or tip designed specifically for your audience. Your server changes the tip every day. At the bottom of your slogan, list your website and you'll gain invaluable publicity. The key is to sign up a number of relevant and related websites who'll feature your daily tip. In the works, we have a daily Small Business Tip. Each tip is a one-liner. Topics range from marketing to business development to finance to taxes to organizing your business to growing your business. This type of broad and continuous publicity can significantly help you expand your business online.

The Payoff

When you develop your website into a destination stop, you build credibility in your space and develop a strong rapport with your customers. Then your customers are likely to buy from you again and again. With technology, you can program your website to shamelessly promote yourself 24/7 and capture the mega-profits you deserve.

How to Find Your Exact Buyer on the Web

Dan Seidman

My website of Sales Horror Stories exploded onto the Web in 1999 and in a short time garnished acclaim from over 200 sources. The most notable article came from *Sales & Marketing Management* magazine. The editor claimed that my website, SalesAutopsy.com, was fast becoming a "cult hit" among salespeople. That "cult hit" phrase is now used in all of my marketing literature.

As entrepreneurs and salespeople from around the world have confessed their most embarrassing sales moments at the website, their collected stories have evolved into a wildly successful book, *The Death of 20th Century Selling: 50 Hilarious Sales Blunders and How You Can Profit From Them*. The book's success is directly related to the relationships I developed with those 200 editorial reviewers and writers. In the next quarter, I have commitments from over two dozen print publications to review or use excerpts from the book. Why is this important to you? Because I found out how to hunt down my exact target market and I plan to share that simple marketing strategy with you.

Three Steps to Selling on the Internet

Marketing experts like Jay Conrad Levinson, Joe Sugarman and Jay Abraham agree on one thing: The jumping off place for marketing yourself or your product or service is to identify your exact potential buyer. On the Internet, it's fairly easy to locate watering holes where people interested in your topic gather to drink of the knowledge, experience and wisdom of their peers. Here are three strategic steps to take in your journey to sell on the Internet:

1. **Set up a free e-mail account at hotmail.com or yahoo.com.** I prefer Yahoo because it gives more space to use.

2. **Sign up for all the e-zines that fit your business or consumer's market, using this new account.** This keeps your existing e-mail account from becoming cluttered. You'll find where to discover these newsletters at the websites listed at the end of this article. You must subscribe to every newsletter that is offered by your competitors.

3. **Read through these e-zines each week to find out which ones are quality newsletters, who is writing articles for them, who is advertising in them, and how many subscribers are receiving the e-zine.** If the newsletter doesn't tell how many subscribe, request advertising information and you'll receive that number immediately.

Now that you found them, what are some possible ways to get them to "discover" you—then buy your product or service? Here are four strategies:

Contact the Best E-Zines

Ask if the publisher or editor would review your website or service. If you are making money from visitors and can convince the publisher to split revenues with you from the traffic he or she sends your way, be prepared to create a special page for readers to visit. Another option is to use software that monitors traffic. An inexpensive and highly effective tool is the Ultimate Ad Tracker, located at www.ultimateadtracker.com

Submit Your Own Articles, Gaining Exposure Directly

Observe closely what other writers contribute to the e-zines you are monitoring. Another great way to leverage writers who are already contributing to these e-zines is to e-mail them and comment on their articles. Be sure to mention that their writing caught your eye because your expertise is in that business area and you respect their insights. These are also good potential strategic alliances. Visit these writers' websites. Just begin to invest a little time communicating with others in your marketplace and you'll find a herd of buyers.

Keep a Log of Advertisers

You will find numerous advertisers who spend money on e-zines in your target market. Obviously, they have money to spend on you—assuming you can put out a quality e-zine and product yourself. You already have an idea what they pay since you requested advertising information from each of the quality e-zines, right? If you haven't done that yet, start gathering ad information immediately.

Discover Who Is Linking to the Websites Where These Quality E-Zines Are Located

You can do this by doing a reverse search in the www.altavista search engine. Here's what you do: go to AltaVista and type in the search box: link: www.ezinewebsite.com. This will reveal who links to that website. Most search engines have this reverse search capability. Now you've found other web businesses that have interest and expertise in your niche. Subscribe to their e-zines, too.

And don't forget to stop from time to time to simply sip from the wisdom of others in your industry. You just might be someone else's buyer, too! Here are some of the top websites to find e-zines on your topic or expertise:

- ▼ www.e-zinez.com
  This search engine website is exclusive for e-zine publication

- ▼ www.meer.net/~johnl/e-zine-list/submit.html
  John Labovitz e-zine list

- ▼ www.dominis.com/zines/
  The ultimate electronic magazine database

- ▼ www.lifestylepub.com
  The directory of e-zines from Lifestyles Publishing

- ▼ www.ezinesearch.com
  E-zine Search website

- ▼ www.oblivion.net/zineworld
  E-zine World website

- ▼ www.liszt.com/
  The List

Target your market on the Internet and you will sell tons more! Happy Hunting!

Don't Believe Everything You Hear

Shel Horowitz

Want to succeed on the Internet? Here's some of the "expert advice" I've heard over the years:

- ▼ Spend hours and hours creating doorway pages for specific search engines

- ▼ Submit to thousands of Free for All (FFA) pages to build up your links count

- ▼ Keep your website tightly focused on just one area and have everything move toward the sale

- ▼ Create a thorough business plan and go out for venture capital or even a stock offering

- ▼ Base your revenue models on affiliate programs and/or banner ads

- ▼ Promote your website by buying ads of your own

- ▼ Trick the search engines with hidden keywords or other sleazy techniques

- ▼ Use a fancy and flashy design

▼ Hire an expensive designer who can keep you updated constantly in order to 'keep up with the Joneses'

▼ Chunk all the content into itty-bitty parcels of one to two screens, and include plenty of graphics

▼ Use serial auto-responders to keep in front of your prospects

▼ Spend a lot of money on pay-per-click search engines

Guess what? I don't do ANY of these things! And yet I currently average over 122,000 page views per month at my main website. I have well over 12,000 subscribers to my newsletters. I generate significant revenue online through both product and service sales, and I have made myself a household name among a lot of online communities. People are always saying things like "I feel like I've known you for years" or "You seem to be everywhere, how do you do it?"

Since setting up www.frugalfun.com in 1996, I've never bothered to get involved with the various fads of Internet promotion. A lot of the "expert advice" I listed above is worse than useless now. Tricking the search engines will get you tossed out of their databases. FFA page links are now discredited (search engine algorithms check for relevancy), and they'll bring you a ton of unwanted junk e-mail. The luster has long since worn off banners and affiliate links.

Here is what I do to make my website successful:

Make Your Site Multifaceted

Frugalfun.com is extremely multifaceted. There are about 500 articles up right now, covering a myriad of interests: marketing, business, travel, entertainment, politics and, of course, saving money. Individual articles range from a few paragraphs on up to 20 or more pages (I assume most readers will print out the longer ones, and I don't put obstacles in their way). Of course, there are a number of pages dedicated to my books, which are all about saving money on fun and on marketing.

Limit the Graphics

I have four on the entire website: three book covers and my photograph on the "people behind this website" page. One of my other websites has no graphics at all.

Grow Organically with a Long-Term Strategy

What about a business plan? Well, when I first put up my website, I knew I wanted it to support sales of my books and of my marketing copywriting and consulting services, so the first 40 pages went up with that goal. I got into online magazine publishing a couple of months later, when I had a press pass to review a play and despite my best efforts, couldn't find a newspaper or magazine that wanted the review. Then I had a brainstorm: "Shel," I said to myself, "you have 20 megabytes to play with on the Web and you're using less than a megabyte; start your own magazine!"

Not exactly a well-thought-out strategy, but it led to the first of four magazines on the website, which account for most of the overall content and many, many hits. The magazines and other parts of the website continue to evolve on the basis of what people submit and what I choose to print, rather than as the result of any big plan. In fact, I went totally off in a new direction following the September 11th attacks: I put up a page of peace resources and added a "sustainability" section to my business magazine. To put it another way, my website grows organically, and not according to an outline.

When I realize the website's functionality can be improved, then and only then, do I work up a redesign. For instance, a year into the website, when I put up the first redesign, I added a navigation bar and signup forms for the tip sheets, two enhancements that significantly improved the website. When I realized that the search engines were returning my nav bar instead of the first sentences of the articles, I added a summary at the top of every page, where the search engines would pick up relevant text instead of the nav bar.

Of course, since my website costs almost nothing, I don't need investors. An intern who taught herself, and me, the rudiments of HTML did my first design; when I needed to update, I bartered with a web designer; she redid my website, and I wrote a few brochures for her. I had the website running for over three years before I spent a nickel on website design! I did spend $200 on my third design, and about the same on the coding for my order form. But averaging over more than five years, I've spent less than $100 per year on website design, and to this day, zero on content. With that kind of investment, the payback happens pretty quickly. In fact, I've even gotten paid to run workshops on "the zero-cost website!"

Instead of a real business plan, I have a solid long-term strategy: I offer a lot of value to my visitors in the form of free content and promote through techniques that have lasting impact, rather than the latest fads.

Although most of my traffic comes from the search engines, I don't make myself crazy keeping up with the latest search engine optimization fads. In fact, I spend essentially no time ensuring great listings. I get the listings because my website delivers the content people want.

A lot of the search engine traffic I get is looking for very specific information: on places featured in my travel magazine (*Global Travel Review*), artists featured in my arts magazine (*Global Arts Review*), marketing and management concepts featured in my business magazine (*Down to Business*), or money-saving tips such as frugal Halloween costumes (the sort of thing they can find in the back issues of my newsletters or on my frugal resources page).

Those who don't come from the search engines typically come from one of several sources: exchange ads with other newsletters and e-zine publishers, my constant posts to various discussion lists, my own articles (on my own and others' websites, in e-zines, printed magazines and books), links from websites that have given us an award, offline promotion including dozens of radio and print interviews, speeches, business cards, and my own books, and on and on and on.

Are there any rules I do follow? Yes, actually:

▼ NEVER spam

▼ Capture visitor addresses—but only through true opt-in

▼ Let the visitor find content through the tool that works best for that person

These are all crucial, but again, I do them in my own way. Instead of spamming, I participate actively in discussion groups. It takes time, but many visitors come to my website because they were impressed by one of my posts. They already like me, and are predisposed to do business with me. Often, in a post, I give a reason to visit the website, because it provides information that answers a question someone posted, for instance. And unlike spamming, this strategy is effective.

I do believe that website owners should give visitors a way to keep in touch, and my solution is to publish three monthly e-zines. With millions of web pages out there, even if visitors bookmark your website, they may never make it back. Yet so many websites put barriers in their visitors' paths; they request all sorts of personal information! I keep it simple. If you want to subscribe to one of my e-mail newsletters, I need an e-mail address. That's it. The subscription form doesn't ask for any other information, just the address where they want to receive and which newsletter(s). Yes, I'm missing out on the opportunity to create targeted marketing based on their answers to a survey, but I don't have to worry about people getting frustrated in the middle of a long form, or worrying about how the information will be used. As a result, I enjoy a large number of subscribers, and every month, they all see my information, complete with reasons to visit the website again, and reasons to do business with me.

The only other form on my website is the order form for my books. Of course, that form requires full name and contact information, but I don't use the information for any other purpose, just to ship the products or answer any questions I have about the order.

As for making my website easy to navigate, readers can find their way around through the usual navigation bar (on the right, so the search engines index the page contents instead of the nav bar!), a drop-down menu with more choices, a search box at the top of the home page, internal and external links—and even a custom "404 page" that offers a few alternate destinations if anything comes back "page not found."

The Internet experts will continue to tell you new and different things to do, to replace the things they told you three months earlier that no longer work. I will continue ignoring most of their advice, and I expect my little Web empire to continue growing by using timeless methods, and to continue producing an excellent return on my investment of a little bit of time and almost no money. That's my confession and I'm sticking to it!

Seven Decisions Customers Make Before Doing Business with You

Lenny Laskowski

How many of you have a website that "looks" great, but does not generate any real business? Unfortunately, too many business owners admit to having a website that has not produced any qualified leads or actual business for them. This may be because their website does not satisfy seven key decisions a visitor will make before doing business with you.

I use my website to successfully market my speaking services and now receive between 90,000 and 140,000 visitors each month. It is, therefore, critical that my website is properly designed to attract highly qualified potential customers.

It is said that over 86 percent of people today use search engines to find information on the Internet. This is especially true of your potential customers. Most of them will also use search engines to find you—or will they? Here are seven decisions your website visitors will make before they actually decide to contact you:

1. **Which search engine or directory will I use?** The first decision your potential customers will make is which search tool (search engine or directory) they will use to find information on the Internet. Most people have their favorite search engines and if your website is not listed with the major search engines your customers will not be able to find it easily.

    Search engines don't actually search the Internet. They search their own databases and your website needs to be "properly" listed in these databases. Make sure your website is designed to be search engine friendly before submitting it to each of these search engines and directories.

2. **What keyword phrase will I use?** The next decision your potential customers will make is what search word or keyword phrase they will use. Most people today are smarter about how to do effective search engine searches and use keyword phrases to look for information. Your challenge is to determine what keyword phrases they will use. Ask yourself, "Is my website optimized so it can be found when the right keyword phrase is used?" Websites have even paid to be listed in

the top search engines and still don't get visitors because they have not been optimized.

Your potential customers will probably not find you if your website is not optimized so that it is listed in the top 30 positions or in the first three pages of the search engine or directory. Statistics and recent studies have shown that those websites listed in the top 30 positions receive over 96 percent of the Web traffic. Those listed in the top ten positions (wouldn't we all love to be listed here), receive 78 percent more traffic than those websites listed in positions 11 to 30.

3. **Which website listing will I select from the search engine or directory?** A search engine listing usually has three main parts—the bolded title, a brief description (usually less than 200 characters or 25 words) and the actual Web address. This information is usually obtained directly from your website and is displayed as an "all text" listing. The text for these listings is obtained from the specific HTML (hypertext mark up language) design elements of each website. If your website does not contain these critical design elements, it will not be properly listed and will not even be on the search engine radar screen. This is critical since your potential customers will select the listing they will click on based on the text description of the website.

These first three decisions are made primarily on search engine listing criteria. If your website is not listed in these top search engine positions, you will not satisfy the first three decisions your potential customers make.

4. **Does the website make a positive initial impression?** Assuming visitors actually decide to click on the search engine link to your website, the next decision will be about their initial impression of your website. If your website does not satisfy their initial impression, they will not proceed any further. For your visitors to proceed any further you must satisfy their initial interests on the actual page they're looking at.

5. **Can I easily explore the website?** Now that you've satisfied your potential customers' first four decisions, does your website encourage your visitors to explore your website? Your visitors need to be able to easily find the information they are looking for (sometime what they are actually looking for is FREE information only). Do you provide tools for your visitors to easily navigate your website? If not, they probably will not come back again.

6. **Can I easily reach the website owner?** You have worked very hard to attract visitors to your website. However, getting visitors, even tons of visitors, does not guarantee that these visitors will do any business with you. I don't care if you have a million visitors each month. The number of visitors does not matter. It's the number of visitors who are willing to do business with you that counts. Now that you got them this far (Decisions 1 through 5), you need to make it easy for them to reach you. It always amazes me many websites stop short here and fail.

   Ask yourself how many times you've visited a website only to find little or no information on how to reach the organization—no phone number, no address, no e-mail, etc. Or the website provides no vehicle for you to provide your information for them to contact you? Make it easy for visitors to contact you and provide them choices on how they can contact you. My website visitors can contact me by telephone, e-mail, and fax or by completing one of my many guest books or information request forms. At this point, your visitors still may have questions and be willing to call you, e-mail you or take the additional time to fill out one of the online forms.

   Does your website provide these options to your visitors? If not, how else will you know they have been to your website and, more importantly, how else do you expect them to reach you? Your visitor will not spend a ton of time trying to figure out how to contact you. Make it easy for them to do so.

7. **Will I contact this company for more information?** At this point, a customer has to decide whether or not to contact you for more information. In many of my cases, my visitors have already decided to hire me or do business with me. To me, a website visitor who contacts me is a more highly qualified "potential" than one who was referred to me. I say potential because the sale is not complete yet. Don't get me wrong, referrals are the best type of potential customers, but your website may have not answered all the customer's questions yet.

   Once a website visitor (or word-of-mouth) visitor has contacted you, it is now up to you to close the deal. How effectively you do this will depend on the actual sales process you have in place. Here are a few little things I think are very important:

▼ How quickly do you get back to them?

Do they have to wait days or even weeks for you to get back to them? If they do, you will lose the sale. I get a lot of business because I always return phone calls and e-mails within hours, not days.

▼ How often do you check your e-mail?

Some people do not check their e-mail often enough. If you do not check frequently (I check at least three times each day due to the volume of e-mail I receive), you may not know of a golden opportunity someone is offering to you, but they need to know that day!

▼ How effective are you at answering their questions?

▼ Do you have all the answers they are looking for?

One other question: Does your website provide any sales closing techniques? Add information and tools to your website to help your visitor make the "buy" decision without further interaction with a salesperson at your company. This leads to…

8. **Will I do business with you?**

The Secret to Getting People to Your Website
Dan Janal

The secret is Publicity!

People are more likely to buy things from you if they hear about your business through a newspaper where you get the endorsement of a credible, unbiased source. Online tools such as search engines are useful in sending targeted prospects to your website, but they don't bestow the credibility you need to make the sale! Only newspapers, magazines, TV and radio can do that!

So, how do you get publicity? Here are two ways:

▼ Hire a PR firm and pay them about $2,500 a month to cold call reporters and try to convince them to write about you. This is like trying to find the proverbial needle in a haystack—the one reporter out of a hundred who is actually interested in what you have to say. Many people do this—and spend a lot of money.

▼ Use a service like ProfNet, which is used by large corporations, to find out what stories reporters are researching—and what sources they need to quote. This process turns PR upside down: reporters want to hear from you if you have the information they need to write their story! Imagine how quick and easy it would be to get PR if you knew which reporters wanted to talk to you!

Unfortunately for writers, speakers and entrepreneurs, ProfNet costs about $2,000 a year. But even if you could afford this fee, ProfNet doesn't sell the service to writers, speakers and entrepreneurs or individuals who want to promote themselves to the media!

When I realized this, I negotiated an exclusive license to resell their content to this select group of experts. How's that for the entrepreneurial spirit!

The service is called PR Leads. We make sure our subscribers get every possible lead by interviewing them thoroughly. When a reporter posts a query that matches our customer's needs, we send them the query, complete with contact information. The customer contacts the reporter directly with the simple instructions we provide.

If all works well, you'll find yourself quoted in *USA TODAY*—as several of our customers have—or other top-tier publications and trade journals like *Entrepreneur, Redbook, The Philadelphia Inquirer, Christian Science Monitor* and many others. Even if you aren't quoted on the spot, you might have earned a spot in a reporter's Rolodex for use in future stories! At the very least, you are being introduced to reporters who are ready, willing and able to be approached by experts!

But enough about the service, here are several tips you can use right away to go get publicity whether or not you use PR Leads:

▼ Place your contact information—phone and e-mail—on your website and press releases. If reporters don't know who to call, they won't call. This happens more times than you could imagine.

▼ If reporters contact you, respond immediately. They are on deadline and will quote the first person who calls back.

▼ Place information article for reporters on your website. Establish yourself as an expert—and let them know you are ready, willing and able to be a resource for them.

▼ Create a page on your website that lists articles in which you have been quoted or profiled—no matter how modest the publication. This builds credibility for other reporters to call you.

▼ Press releases aren't just for reporters. Send press releases to customers, prospects, vendors, investors and relatives. They want to know what's going on with you or your company. Post press releases on your website.

Good luck in building your online business with the power of the press!

If at first you don't succeed, try, try, again. Then quit.
There's no use being a damn fool about it.
—W.C. Fields

Chapter Six

Promoting Your Needle in the Internet Haystack

*Ideas won't keep; something must
be done about them.*
—Alfred North Whitehead

Shameless Internet Promotion Step 6: Build Repeat Traffic and Create Dramatic Results

Debbie Allen

I find it surprising how many companies seem to view their websites as a necessary cost of doing business and not as an opportunity to attract an audience and gain new customers. The two biggest online marketing challenges companies face are:

▼ Getting their websites discovered and then
▼ Keeping visitors on their websites for longer than a millisecond.

Getting Discovered

How do you get discovered? You can market and promote your website yourself by driving your existing customers there, but you need many more potential customers to find you as well. The best way to do this is optimize your website in order to get listed higher on search engines.

Most businesses still don't take advantage of search engine optimization, but few things on the Internet can be as beneficial. A recent Forrester Research report showed that 80 percent of Internet users employ search engines to find solutions and resources. A properly executed search engine optimization campaign can drive numerous, highly targeted visitors to your website every day. Without a high search engine ranking, you will only get visitors who find your website address through word of mouth, traditional advertising or other limited means.

Although your existing offline marketing is not enough to attract prospective customers it is still an extremely important way to cross-promote your website. Too many companies are still using the same old marketing materials that they used before they had a website. By doing this, they are missing out on a great opportunity to build traffic. Make sure that *all* of your existing marketing materials promote your online presence. Your website address should be prominent in your print advertising, business cards, letterhead, fax cover letter, brochure, e-mails, etc.

Another way to promote your website offline is to mention your website address in your telephone message. Adding my website address to my telephone message created instant results! It states:

> *"Sorry we are not here to take your call right now, but in the meantime we would like to invite you to visit our extensive website at www.DebbieAllen.com. From there you can find Debbie's current speaking schedule, view her presentation topics, sign up for her free online newsletters, download a free chapter of her books and use articles in the press room free of charge for your publication."*

This simple, free and highly effective marketing strategy can drive a great deal of qualified prospects to your website and also help you to pre-sell that prospect. Often, by the time I get the opportunity to return the call, the caller has already visited my website and decided to do business with me, promote my expertise and/or purchase products online. I love it!

Are You Being Outrageous Enough?

Joe Vitale

One confession I made in my e-book *Unspoken Marketing Secrets* was that people want to believe a wild claim even if it is only slightly believable. Some of my readers thought I was going overboard but I wasn't. People will believe just about anything, and the sooner you accept that, the sooner you can profit from it.

Want proof? Let me march in just a little of the colorful evidence.

1. In 1749, two noble Englishmen wanted to prove that people would pay to see the absurd. They ran an ad that said a man would appear on stage then jump into a common wine bottle. Once inside, he would sing. Did people respond to the ad? Yes! The public stormed the theater at the appointed time, while hundreds more stood outside. When nothing happened, they rioted, trashed the theater, carried debris into the street and burned it all. They were really mad.

2. In the mid-1800s, P.T. Barnum displayed a mermaid at his museum. How did the public respond? His ticket sales tripled. Yes, tripled! It didn't matter that the "mermaid" was an obvious manufacture, a

weird blend of monkey and fish. People wanted to see it and decide for themselves what it was. Get that: They wanted to see it.

3. When a circus in the mid-1950s said they had a unicorn on display, 50 percent more people came to see the show. Yes, 50 percent more sales. How can you argue with a 50 percent increase in business? Were the people stupid? No, they were curious.

4. When a network television show in the 1980s aired an "alien autopsy," ratings increased. Surely people didn't think they were about to see a real alien! Or did they? Maybe they just hoped to see one.

5. Today I live outside of a small Texas Hill Country town called Wimberley. In 2001, my girlfriend and I saw this screaming headline on a local newspaper: "UFO Lands in Wimberley!" Did we think a UFO really landed near us? No. Did we pick up the newspaper? Yes! In fact, we grabbed extra copies to give to family and friends. We also agreed that if we were going to advertise in any newspaper, it would be that one. What did the headlines on the other newspapers that day say? I have no recollection because I didn't care.

People are fascinated by the outrageous. They want to believe in aliens, ghosts, mermaids and more. They want to watch a man sing from inside a wine bottle and see a pony with a horn on its head. Who can blame them, really? Which would you rather see: A pony or a unicorn? A wine bottle or a man inside it singing? A fish or a mermaid? Another boring show on TV or the world's first alien autopsy?

Most people in business simply aren't outrageous enough! This doesn't mean you should mislead your customers, but you can certainly entertain them with something unbelievable—but possible. This is even easier, and more important, on the Internet. It's easier because anyone can do it. It's more important because without a reason to hold people to your site, they'll click and go. How have I used this principle to shamelessly promote myself and/or my clients on the Internet? Well, let's see.

In 1995 I circulated a joke about my just released book, *CyberWriting*. The funny was based on David Letterman's "Top 10" lists. This one was "The Top 10 Reasons to Read *CyberWriting*." The reasons were all written by *Tonight Show with Jay Leno* comedy writer Paul Seaburn.

People loved the humor and forwarded the joke to friends. It inadvertently promoted my book, pushing it up the Amazon.com sales chart. It seemed outrageous to make fun of my own book—but it was a shameless covert act to increase sales. It worked, too! Check out this fun list if you are curious enough at www.mrfire.com/articles/0001.html.

I advised one client, executive level coach Paul Lemberg, to create a wild idea: an Organization for Unreasonable Thinking, or OUT. He got national publicity! The whole outrageous idea was to bring attention to Paul and his new book, *Faster than the Speed of Change.* A national training magazine, among others, picked up the story and Lemberg was flooded with applications to join OUT. See the outrageous news release that shamelessly plugged him at www.lemberg.com/release010207.html.

I recently helped my girlfriend promote her new pet lover's business by urging her to create a unique image of a pet that tied to patriotism. That image was distributed across the Internet and brought attention to her new website that she otherwise would not get. She thought it was shameless to promote her website by tying it to national pride. But, I pointed out that she and I *sincerely* believe in our country, as well as her service, so it wasn't so *shameless* after all. If you are curious enough, you can see the photo she created and distributed online at www.mrfire.com/photogallery/snickers.jpg.

For my latest book, *Spiritual Marketing*, I gave away the e-book version. Some thought that move was outrageous. It was actually shamelessly successful marketing. I knew that people would tell their friends about the book. I also knew that it would increase sales of the printed book.

My hunch was right! People passed the e-book to friends. The result made the printed book climb the Amazon.com sales chart, ending up being the #1 best-seller there on June 4 and June 5, 2002. You can read the entire e-book at: www.mrfire.com/spirit/index.html (And yes, letting you read the e-book is yet another shameless promotion on my part. Notice how much publicity I'm getting?)

Finally, I invented an entirely new way of making money online by being outrageous and shamelessly promoting the idea. I wanted a BMW Z3 (luxury sports car or new age hot-rod). I also wanted to pay cash for the dream car. So I decided to teach an online e-class entirely by e-mail. I then decided that I would ask for 15 students, and divide up the cost of the car between them.

In short, I asked 15 students to pay $1,500 each for a five-week **e-mail only** e-class. I shamelessly promoted the e-class to my own e-list, which at that time was only 800 names. The result? I raised $22,500 in one week. And yes, my car is sitting in the driveway right now. You can see the whole shameless story at: www.mrfire.com/articles/0047.html

So the real questions are these:

▼ *Are you being outrageous enough for your customers and clients?*

▼ *Are you taking full advantage of the "anything's possible" potential of the Internet?*

▼ *Are you being shameless enough in your own promotions?*

If you aren't, you're probably disappointing everyone. Think about it!

I have to go right now—we have a neighborhood UFO watch and it's my turn to hold the flashlight.

Harnessing the Power of the Internet
Thomas Murrell

Marketing has become the catchword of the new millennium, but how many people truly understand what marketing is? Many businesses and organizations perceive marketing as promotions and advertising. They think being good at marketing is producing a glossy brochure and having an ad on the local radio or television.

But marketing is much more than slick promotions and expensive pamphlets. It is a process with a clear strategy. It is structuring every aspect of your business to include a marketing function.

Truly successful companies are now doing this by building brands and customer loyalty around their names and symbols. It is the brand and well executed marketing strategies that are the assets of new companies in this information age. In today's highly dynamic global business environment, truly successful leaders know how to harness both marketing concepts and the power of the media.

In terms of marketing, the Internet has developed into an integral tool for communication between businesses and clients, an instrument for selling and promotion and a powerful medium that has the potential to reach everyone with a computer and connection to the Internet. As such it should be seen as a burgeoning opportunity to market your business, your branding statements and your products and services while maintaining close communication with your customers.

A Strategic Internet Marketing Plan

There are many persuasive reasons for developing and implementing a strategic Internet marketing plan. It is an excellent, cost effective way of conveying information and detail to both prospective and established customers. It is an effective way to achieve both short and long-term promotional objectives and capture information, build customer loyalty and implement permission marketing strategies. Seth Godin in his book *Permission Marketing: Turning Strangers into Friends and Friends into Customers* (1999, Simon & Schuster) defines permission marketing as powerful advertising that is anticipated, personal and relevant.

Three Golden Rules of Web Marketing

The three golden rules for effective Web marketing are accessibility, dissemination, and interactivity.

1. **Accessibility** relates to ensuring that you are visible on the Internet by creating links from other websites and search engines, and it has some useful advantages such as:

    ▼ Reducing the distance in the value chain between suppliers and customers

    ▼ Increasing the size of the market and, as a result, increasing the size of profits through greater sales, and

    ▼ Increasing the service experience through information availability.

2. **Dissemination** refers to the content you distribute via your website, depending on your message and who your target audience is. The advantages of information dissemination are that, while promoting your products and services, you are also reaffirming your corporate image and branding statement. Dissemination also lowers communication costs such as printing, distribution and customer service staff. Other advantages are that it increases the quality and richness of the information

available as you can deliver text, graphics, audio and video to your customer.

3. **Interactivity** relates to the ability of both you and your customer to interact with each other and the information available. There are several advantages to providing interactivity on your website. The first is the ability to test products or services by allowing customers to download free samples. This approach increases profits through online sales, and interactivity also allows you to capture information on prospects and customers.

Three Objectives to Ensure Effective Marketing

1. **Promote your corporate image** and build product awareness. If you have a well-developed brand, customers will identify with your website.

2. **Enhance customer service.** A well-constructed website will always have a link that enables customers to provide feedback or suggestions about your service and products. It should also provide potential customers with the ability to contact your business if they need to ask questions or gain clarification on any matter.

3. **Provide an opportunity for online transactions.** This objective is essential as once you have an existing or potential customer logged on to your website, it is the perfect opportunity to sell your product or service online without the need for a sales staff. Your product or service will almost sell itself with the right marketing strategies.

In short your website must **PEP—Promote, Enhance and Provide.**

Permission Marketing

Another important aspect of Web marketing is the growing importance and effectiveness of permission marketing. Permission marketing is one of the hottest topics in marketing circles at the moment. It's the dream of all marketers to establish the kind of close relationship with customers where they welcome marketing messages and ask to buy a product or service. The Internet and e-mail has made permission marketing a powerful tool to build and grow your business. We've had great success with this strategy!

Must Do Tips to Drive More Traffic to Your Website

- ▼ **Do** ask permission to communicate with your leads, prospects, customers, clients or advocates online.

- ▼ **Do** have a system in place to collect data, manage your database and send out information.

- ▼ **Do** write in a style that has impact on the reader. Write shorter sentences and provide information in bite-sized chunks.

- ▼ **Do** communicate frequently.

- ▼ **Do** know your strengths and build on them, know your weaknesses and improve on them.

- ▼ **Do** be consistent with your brand, message and products/services benefits.

- ▼ **Do** add value to existing services on your website—offer something for nothing.

- ▼ **Do** initiate and maintain a relationship with your target market.

- ▼ **Do** evaluate and review on a regular basis.

Must Don't Tips to Keep People Away from Your Website

- ▼ **Don't** spam or send people e-mail without their permission. For example, **never** subscribe people to your newsletter without asking!

- ▼ **Don't** ever sell your database to third parties. Never, ever compromise your integrity!

- ▼ **Don't** send out poorly written or unfocussed messages.

- ▼ **Don't** try to be all things to all people.

Online Results in the Booklet Business

Paulette Ensign

In 1991, I was broke and desperate! I needed to breathe some new life—any life—into my speaking and consulting business as a professional organizer. I began by creating a booklet as a marketing tool. This creation became my *biggest and best* marketing idea ever! To my surprise, not only did I create a great marketing tool, I spurred an entire new business along the way. And best of all, I did it without spending a penny on advertising, PR, a staff or fancy marketing materials.

Since then, I have sold over 500,000 copies of my informational tips booklet, *110 Ideas for Organizing Your Business Life*. This simple booklet earned me a quarter of a million dollars and got me invited to speak in countries around the world. And it didn't stop there, *110 Ideas for Organizing Your Business Life* has even been printed in three languages.

The Internet Is Creating a Magical Turning Point

In 1994, I signed up for Internet access solely for the purpose of marketing my business. Little did I know the doors I would open. Being online was like being a kid in a candy store—roaming around the forums, reading the postings, and chatting with people online. I saw opportunities to market everywhere I looked!

By the third day online, I exchanged e-mails with a man in Milan, Italy, who had a marketing company. I read his post in a forum. I asked who his client base was. When he said small businesses and vendors to small businesses, I told him I had something he might find useful. I asked his permission to send him a sample of my tips booklet.

Eighteen months later, he wired me several thousand dollars for the sale of the Italian version of my booklet. To this day, we have communicated solely by mail, e-mail, fax, and electronic funds transfer. I have no idea what the Italian version says, although my former hairdresser said it's a great translation. What I do know is that the deal was a good one. Since then, the booklet has been translated into two other languages—and all from my online contacts.

My story has captured the attention of audiences in several online forums and decision makers for conference bookings. Everyone is always looking for an interesting success story—especially one that is easy and that really works!

My results have come from using a buffet of basic online formats, most of which I used before I ever had a website of my own.

Here is my recipe for online marketing success:

Sprinkle Lots of E-Mail Around

- ▼ Submit articles and queries to online and hard copy publications
- ▼ Send promotional information to media and prospects
- ▼ Answer questions from prospects and clients
- ▼ Respond to promotional opportunities like being in this author's book
- ▼ Process orders directly

Toss in Some Great Seminars

- ▼ In real time
- ▼ Post read-only lessons in forums
- ▼ Deliver e-mail-based seminars
- ▼ Participate in others' seminars

Cook Up a Great Website

- ▼ My own website—providing information, facilitating discussion, and generating product sales
- ▼ Link to others promotionally
- ▼ Write articles and send them out along with your online newsletter

Spice Up Your Marketing with Listservs and Discussion Boards

- ▼ My own discussion board is a way to bring traffic to my website and build business
- ▼ Initiate postings on other people's boards
- ▼ Respond as an expert or as a helpful contributor

One of the best ways to get involved in discussion boards is to post questions seeking advice about all kinds of additional opportunities. *Does anyone know who, how, where, what…?* Questions like this bring many new connections, one after the other. In some cases, they also bring new ideas you may not have considered. Asking for information or suggestions is one of the best-accepted forms of marketing yourself online. It's a more benign way of publicizing yourself than a blatant sales approach, and is one very acceptable way to be a Shameless Internet Promoter.

Yet, I did not become *shameless* overnight. It took a while for me to wrap my brain around the idea of putting a free discussion board onto my website. I was concerned about giving away lots of information that I charge for as a consultant and in the home study kits. Colleagues of mine assured me that creating such a board would, in fact, increase my sales not diminish them. They were right!

Having your own discussion board is an excellent way to get people to your website. Promote your discussion board everywhere—in publicity, at public speaking engagements, while talking to a prospective client on the phone, sending an e-mail or networking face to face. A **free discussion board** even keeps your website changing through the efforts of the community that is drawn to your board. When promoting your free discussion board, invite viewers to take some time and look around the rest of the website while they are there. And, if they just cannot help themselves and absolutely must pull out their credit card, that urge can be well-satisfied by visiting the products page on the same website. Framing that invitation in humor goes a long way to making the point effectively.

A frequent question that comes up on my free discussion board relates to the sometimes-perplexing issue of making large-quantity booklet sales. Visitors to my board often share their own experiences of opening doors and closing sales. I jump in and reinforce my visitors contributions by mentioning how that person's story was so effective that it earned its rightful place right among the many useful and unique anecdotes contained in the *How to Promote Your Business with Booklets* home study kit manual—something I just know the reader wouldn't want to live another day of their life without owning

Reading the postings in the forums, listservs, discussion board, and anywhere else is like mining for gold. Responding to other posts allows for a soft sell of your products and services, while being helpful and providing solutions to their concerns at the same time. Make reference to your publications and/or services in such posts. That often generates at least an inquiry, if not a direct sale. Many discussion boards operate on software that has a place for a link to your website at the bottom of your post. That is a great place to put an invitation to your discussion board.

Posting onto boards paired with having your articles published in e-zines—with your resource contact information included—gives the kind of broad exposure that prompts people to say, "I keep seeing your name everywhere I look! And that is how you get known online!"

We Shameless Internet Promoters like that...a lot!

More than ever, a combination of online and offline promotion makes for the necessary frequency to create the marketplace presence you want.

It Doesn't Take a Lot of Techie Stuff

Low-tech vehicles like Tele-classes can be promoted online, administered online and delivered on the phone, worldwide from your own office. Tele-classes are an inexpensive, non-intimidating way to deliver workshops, worldwide, as both a revenue stream and a marketing tool. Promoting the Tele-classes online crosses over the technology border, using the best of both online and offline capabilities. I have made direct sales, worldwide contacts, and been featured in several books because of people who have attended one of my free Tele-classes.

I view my technological capability, savvy, understanding, and certainly equipment at the mid-to-lower end of the scale. In spite of this, I still manage to receive huge successes with my online marketing, and you can too.

Consider this: I have never taken a business course, I am not very technology savvy and I created my original booklet copy on a primitive computer. Everyday my online marketing brings me new possibilities and opportunities. My website is still and always will be evolving, piece by piece, and remains a very simple design that is easy to navigate.

Much More to Come

My latest addition has been an e-booklet catalog that sells other people's booklets electronically as fully automated downloads. This happened after I heard some other Shameless Internet Promoters, with whom I shared the podium at a three-day Internet marketing super conference, talking about how much money they made through downloadable sales on their websites. It dawned on me that the same thing could be done while serving my booklet authors' interests in helping them market their booklets.

Once the e-booklet catalog was in place (now with over 100 different titles available for sale), other product developers approached me to do joint ventures with the content from my website and their formats. It is early in the development of screen savers, online courses and other products that will be based on the contents of many of the e-booklets featured in the catalog.

The possibilities are endless when you discover how to shamelessly promote through the wonderful mechanism of the Internet.

HOT Online Marketing to an Overlooked Consumer
Gary Onks

As online marketers we are always looking for the **hot market**. We want to be where the action is. We want to sell to anyone who is buying and we want to do it right now! A hot market is made up of people who have money and will spend it today. A hot market is one where people will buy what you have to sell. If you have the greatest widget in the world but people won't buy it because they are afraid of buying online, you will end up with a warehouse full of widgets. In a hot market, people will buy wherever, whenever and whatever you are selling.

A hot market is one that will keep growing. As marketers, we work very hard to test our ideas and prove our theories. We do this so that when we find the right formula we can roll it out to the masses. To succeed, there have to be masses to roll it out to. The best definition of failure is to get an increasing share of a shrinking market. In a hot market, the market potential is growing.

Once you clearly define your market, make sure it's a hot one. Then you can confidently build marketing strategies that will ensure your long-term success.

The Hot Market Today

Recent studies show that 92 percent of seniors and aging boomers shop online and 78 percent make online purchases. They are 30 percent more likely to buy online than any other surfers and 74 percent of this market use the Internet to find health information. Few companies are focusing on seniors and aging boomers or even know how to market to them. You can beat your competition to this vast, lucrative and profitable consumer group. So, "Get 'em while they're hot!"

Still wondering if this market is worth your time and attention? Here are a few more facts:

Size: Strength in numbers—growing to 81 million adults

Power: Controlling 79 percent of all financial assets in the United States alone

Worth: Spending two trillion dollars on goods/services annually in the United States alone

Income: Offering disposable income 26 percent higher than other groups

Growth: Growing faster—every seven seconds this market gets larger

Those facts should convince you that this is the consumer market to focus on. Translation—lots more discretionary funds than any other group of customers around. This all adds up to customers who are almost recession-proof with more money for wants. So, let's get ready to explore ways to attract and keep seniors and aging boomers online at your website.

This recession-proof market buys everything that any other customer buys, and then some. The only real difference between these consumers and others is that they have had more birthdays. They are truly the "Millennium Marketplace." Companies that notice and then proceed to pay very special attention to them will not only comfortably ride out any recession, but will reap a marketing bonanza of absolutely astounding proportions. You can "Gain Market Share, If You Show Them You Care."

Show the Consumer that You Care

The pursuit of happiness does not change as one gets older; in fact, if anything, the older we get, the more we desire happiness. Aging makes us acutely aware of how short our time on Earth is and as we grow older each enjoyable moment becomes sweeter. Seniors and aging boomers yearn for the things they never had before, and have a sense of urgency in their pursuit of happiness.

This market's primary focus is to squeeze the most happiness possible from the time they have remaining in this life. If you can help them to achieve this desire, you can reach all your sales goals, and achieve your own happiness as well. People will spend their last penny to feel good. The single most important way this market wants to feel good is to feel secure. To be effective in making them feel secure, you must always address them in a caring fashion. You must understand them.

To successfully do this, you have to go back in time to their *formative years*—to when they were just children. The reason for this is that, according to psychological experts, we have developed our dominant personalities, habits and traits by the time we have reached the age of 14. Linking your marketing to these earlier times will score well with seniors and aging boomers.

Most of these *times gone by* are outside the comprehension of the people who are now creating ads and marketing materials, because they are too young to know of them. Therein lies the problem. No "memory connecting points" are being offered to bridge the generation gap between your company and this market.

Memory Connecting Points

What are memory connecting points? They are things that link you to your past. One of mine is the smell of dill. My grandmother, Meemaw, canned vegetables from the garden every summer. She used lots of different spices and dill was the primary one she used for pickling. All I know for sure is that to this day the smell of dill takes me right back to her kitchen. In an instant, I'm a kid again with warm "at home" feelings from that one aroma—precious memories.

Inside each senior and aging boomer is a "kid" full of memories who still wants the same things all kids want: safety, security, attention and to have a little fun. This market may be older in their bodies, but they are not at all old in their spirits. They are still "young at heart."

Translating Memory Connecting Points into Marketing Strategy

Think about it yourself. What reminds you of childhood? It may have been something "corny" then, but it's warm, wonderful and friendly now. Those long-gone words, phrases, slogans, television images and personalities, songs, smells and sounds are wonderful. Heck, I still have a crush on Annette Funicello of the *Mickey Mouse Club.* Hearing a train whistle makes most people remember happy childhood days. Do you remember such things?

Building Trust

The next big challenge is to build their trust in your company. Trust is extremely important—a "must"—for this market segment. To seniors and aging boomers their word is still their bond. Until they "feel" they can trust you, they will not buy from you—at any price. That feeling of trust is more important to seniors than all the nice features your product or service may offer. Without sincerity, your marketing efforts towards this market will be in vain.

Honesty sells not just in this market, but in all market segments. Numerous studies have shown that lack of trust is the number one reason people don't buy. But there are others. Here are three factors and criteria that this market considers in all buying decisions (in order of importance):

1. Safety—Low risk to me and my money
2. Independence—Keeps me free in my life choices
3. Security—Maintains peace of mind and lifestyle

These are the "meat and potatoes" factors that represent the really "big picture" in their daily lives. To be successful in selling your products and services to this market, these critical "decision triggers" must be fully satisfied, or else it's **no sale.** All other elements of the buying process are just window dressing.

The Internet Is an Ideal Medium

On the Internet, everyone is equal and age is not a factor. The wrinkles and gray hair are not visible on-line. The Internet offers independence, safety, security and anonymity, and seniors love it!

Design Tips to Attract Seniors and Aging Boomers

- ▼ Make your website easy to use and user-friendly
- ▼ Create fast-loading pages
- ▼ Develop a professional look and feel that inspires trust and rapport
- ▼ Add larger fonts and lots of white space—12 to14 point type size
- ▼ Times New Roman and Arial fonts are best
- ▼ Create easy/intuitive hyperlinks and navigation
- ▼ Add easy-to-find contact information
- ▼ Develop super-easy checkout functions
- ▼ Add pictures of real people in your company—a must—seniors link a business to a face.
- ▼ Avoid novelty images and fancy graphics—text is preferred
- ▼ Avoid patterned backgrounds—plain colors are best
- ▼ Present information in a clear, easy-to-understand and familiar way
- ▼ Use a guest book format for subscribing to information and updates

Marketing Tips to Attract Seniors and Aging Boomers

- ▼ Offer an ironclad money back guarantee and/or lifetime warranty
- ▼ Tout your experience, expertise and credibility with testimonials and professional endorsements
- ▼ Accentuate high quality workmanship and services
- ▼ Promote lasting value versus the basic cost
- ▼ Make it very easy and hassle free to return merchandise
- ▼ Emphasize service after the sale (very important to this group)
- ▼ Add a toll-free number for customer orders, service and support
- ▼ Answer the telephone "live" instead of using voice-mail
- ▼ Offer written information about your products and services
- ▼ Publicize community involvement (this scores very high marks)

▼ Ask for their business

▼ Tell them you want to be a "personal" representative

▼ Always be personable and treat them like respected family members

▼ Use easy-to-understand, customer-focused words—do not use slang, acronyms or business lingo

▼ Create a consumer checklist showing all the pros, cons and cost comparisons of your product, versus that of your competitors. Adding long copy is fine; these folks love to read in great detail

▼ Focus marketing on the positive benefits and experiences of aging (e.g. time to enjoy grandchildren, freedom to travel and the financial benefits offered by senior discounts)

This dynamic consumer group dominates the marketplace and will for decades to come. So beat out your competition today by making strong connections and repeat business with this market.

The Secret to Successful Membership Websites

Tom Antion

If you have material on a hot topic, you can start a membership website that will bring you recurring income. With the right Internet services you can automate the entire process.

Membership websites typically have password protection to "supposedly" restrict access to actual members. They also use recurring billing companies to relieve the website owner of the duty of processing each member's credit card each month.

The reason I say "supposedly" in the above paragraph is because a member could give his/her password and user ID to someone else. Unless the website owners have taken the extra precaution of using the services of a password security website like www.pennywize.com, they will suffer some losses because of this kind of thievery.

To fully automate the credit card processing when members are charged monthly or weekly, a recurring billing company like www.netbilling.com is needed. A company like this will take the initial membership, charge the new member's credit card, keep track of the member's chosen user ID and pass code, and charge the member's charge card at regular intervals. In addition, the company will help the members retrieve their pass codes automatically when they forget them…and they will.

A membership website is quite different to operate than a straightforward "shopping cart sales" website. Situations will arise where the website owner may want to give a complimentary membership or offer a free 30-day trial membership, etc. Each situation may require a visit to the recurring billing company's virtual terminal to override the normal settings.

Promoting a membership website is more of a challenge than it would be for a typical free website or free electronic publication. There is so much free stuff on the Internet that it's important to do a good job of promoting the value of your material. That can be done with good advertising copywriting, good online and offline promotion along with reputation building by means of speaking, media appearances and authorship.

Also, the information had better be *really good* because the members can close their wallet any time they feel that the value they get from your website is less than the money they are paying. I didn't even attempt a membership website until I already had a big following that could be reached via e-mail. This cuts out all my marketing costs to reach them.

A nice addition to a membership website is a discussion board or chat room. These website additions can be used by members only, or you could use them to attract prospective members by providing them limited access to the "members only" portion of the website. I bought a very nice discussion board from www.vbulletin.com. You can participate for free and post your Internet marketing questions and comments at www.greatinternetmarketing.com/forums/

Getting and keeping good content should not be that much of a challenge especially if you are an expert in your field. In my opinion, you should welcome the opportunity to include content from other experts you believe in. It makes the production of the website much easier for you and you still reap the benefits of the monthly payments and any advertising revenue the website produces.

If you have extremely high priced back end products like speeches, consulting, public seminars, etc., you may want to limit your use of outside content providers so that you don't distract your members from using you for these advanced services.

116

My membership website was profitable the first day it was announced. The design was simple and it didn't take long to create. The hardest part was getting a feel for the recurring billing system and the operation of the virtual terminal provided by the company to handle setup, security and customized functions.

Before you jump in to create a membership website check out all the individual entities **before** you begin. The recurring billing company may only work on certain types of servers and may only be compatible with certain merchant companies.

Since hosting companies are a dime a dozen you may want to make your decision on where to host after you pick your recurring billing company and merchant account.

The best part about membership websites is the fact that you can create recurring income. Each member you retain adds up to a lot of money during the life of his or her membership!

> *When we lose the right to be different,*
> *we lose the privilege to be free.*
> —Charles Evans Hughes

Chapter Seven

No-Cost Ways to Drive Traffic to Your Website

From birth to age 18, a girl needs good parents,
from 18 to 35 she needs good looks,
from 35 to 55 she needs a good personality,
and from 55 on she needs CASH.
—Vaudevillian, Sophie Tucker

Shameless Internet Promotion Step 7:
Act on Opportunities for Free Online Promotion

Debbie Allen

Many of the businesses I consult with tell me they don't have the time or the money to market their website effectively. Yet, they consistently tie up thousands of marketing dollars in traditional twentieth century marketing that is completely ineffective. This drives me crazy!

Many of these companies—small and big—are still doing things the same old way and fight any attempt to bring their marketing efforts into the twenty-first century. Take Montgomery Ward for example. This company was in business over 128 years and what was it known for? You might say that they were known for their catalog. Well, who cares! It was no surprise that they closed their doors forever when the retail marketplace changed around them.

This is the twenty-first century! Times have changed and so have consumers. We live in the information age. Not only must you stand out in the consumer's mind, but you must adjust your expensive and ineffective traditional marketing efforts before it is too late. Quit wasting marketing dollars and losing customers!

How would you like to spend less money on print advertising by directing customers to your website? I'm not saying to stop your traditional advertising—I just want you to *adjust* it.

Let's take Yellow Pages for example. If you had a highly effective website you could easily cut down the size of your Yellow Pages ad by posting your website address as the largest text in your advertisement. Today, most people are online and if they want to know more about your company from your advertisement, they will simply pick up the phone, drive to your location and/or visit your website to learn more. From your website you can offer so much more information for a very low cost and even interact with your prospective customers. Since I can't even remember the last time I opened a Yellow Pages book, I predict that this type of traditional advertising will be non-existent in the near future.

Direct mail is another highly effective way to connect with your existing customers. In fact, I am a big fan of direct mail postcards. I send out my mailers like clockwork with mailing dates carved in stone. I sprinkle my database with these mailers six times a year.

But, I also am a big advocate for direct mail without stamps—e-mail marketing. In fact, my online marketing efforts are already winning out over my postcard mailings because people read their e-mails and can easily reply. With a postcard you never know if it got read before they threw it in their circular file. With e-mail you can personalize each message just by adding the person's first name. By noting this change, I have already adjusted my direct mail marketing efforts. I have kicked into high gear with my online marketing efforts because of the amazing results. And the best part of direct mail without stamps is that it is so cheap. Cheap and effective—my favorite words to describe marketing that works!

How to Get Free Publicity in Thousands of E-Zines

Dr. Jeffrey Lant

Got a product, service, opportunity, charitable cause or great idea you want to promote, but you don't have a lot of money? Listen up. I'm going to show you *exactly what you need to do to get your message in thousands of publications without it costing you one red cent*. Got your attention? Then, let's go for it!

This promotional miracle is the online newsletter, popularly called e-zine (short for e-mail magazine). Nobody knows just how many of them there are, but if you reckoned in the high tens of thousands you'd probably be about right. What's more, collectively these e-zines have millions and millions of subscribers—the people you need to get to and motivate to buy whatever you're selling. So, how do you get your message to them without spending a cent? Here are the seven steps that will help:

Seven Steps to Get Your Message Out

1. **Find E-Zines.** The first thing you've got to do is find the e-zines. Go to any major search engine like Yahoo.com and enter the words "e-zine directories" in the locator box at the top of the page.

   Within seconds you'll get a list of e-zine directories and related resources, collectively listing tens of thousands of e-zines and hundreds of related resources, including tons of specialized promotional resources. Oh, mama!

2. **Hit E-Zines again and again.** Which makes more sense: Hitting an e-zine once with just one promotional attack, or hitting them again and again with lots of different promotional gambits over time? Put like this, it's obvious, isn't it? The question is:

   Where are you going to store all the e-zine information you need so you can best use it repeatedly?

   To get started, you will need the following software:

   ▼ LISTSERV®
   LISTSERV® is e-mail list management software that enables you to send any given message to everyone on any given e-mail list at the touch of a button. E-Zines use LISTSERV® to publish their editions and reach their subscribers.

   If you already have LISTSERV®, you have **one** list. You can e-mail to that list whenever you want, but you cannot differentiate who gets what message. Everyone on that lists gets the same message.

   ▼ Sales Manager®
   Sales Manager® enables you to create unlimited e-mail lists and to e-mail these lists either individually whenever you want to or create up to 25 specific letters **per list** which the software will automatically send out (and personalize) within any given 90-day period.

   With Sales Manager® you can use e-mail in a more targeted way. You can have a list of specialized health publications, specialized marketing publications, general interest consumer publications, etc. and you can e-mail to each list separately whenever you want to. This enables you to use precise target marketing for whatever you're promoting.

Note: there are more advantages to using the Sales Manager than the space here allows. We'll be glad to help all readers implement this superb technology. Just mailto:drjlant@worldprofit.com with "Sales Manager Details" in subject, along with your name, address, and phone.

3. **Compile your "all important" lists.** Once you've decided how you want to store the e-zine data, it's time to find the e-zines that suit your product or service. Again, go to any search engine or directory and enter the words "e-zine directories." You'll see an incredible cornucopia of promotional possibilities. Now dig in.

    Select a directory and call it up. The best directories are divided into sensible categories and subcategories. Select the category that best reflects what you're selling and the audience you want to reach. Now click on each entry.

    You'll find information on:

    - ▼ The name of the publication
    - ▼ A description of the target audience
    - ▼ A description of the purpose of the e-zine
    - ▼ The editor's name and e-mail address
    - ▼ The website address/URL so you can see the website
    - ▼ How to submit your contribution, etc.

    Enter the e-zine addresses you find either into your LISTSERV® and/or relevant Sales Manager® lists.

    This is an ongoing project. Don't kill yourself doing it. Select 10 to 20 per day. The key here is consistency. Add some to your list every single day. If you do this for just a week you'll have up to 150 publications on your list to deal with. That's incredible!

4. **Create your first article submission.** The best way in the world to get publicity is to seem like you're not seeking it. In other words, provide an article packed with useful information that ends with complete details about how to purchase whatever you're selling.

    Let's talk about the article first. E-Zines have limited space, so your article has to be proportionately short and punchy. Articles should be one to two pages at best, unless the individual publication specifies longer; you can always ask to see a sample copy. A three-page e-zine article is pushing it!

The best kinds of articles are "how to", e.g.: *Seven things you can do right now to lose 15 pounds in the next 60 days!* Articles should be short, punchy, fact-filled, and offer real value to the reader. They should also have a line length of not more than 60 characters so they fit neatly into the e-zine's format.

Each article should end with a "Resource Box"—an area that includes your name and specific information about how to buy what you're selling, how to subscribe to your e-zine, or how to visit your website, etc.

5. **Write a few more articles.** Before you approach any e-zines, write three to five articles. Start Saturday morning and you'll have most, if not all, of them finished by Monday! Think in terms of a promotional campaign, not just random, one-shot approaches to e-zines.

6. **Draft your cover letter to the e-zine editor.** It's time now to draft your letter to the e-zine editor or publisher, the person who will make the decision about whether to run your article and with whom you'll be working on this and future submissions. This letter needs to be good!

Here's an example of a letter you might send by e-mail to editorial prospects:

> Hi, I'm submitting for your consideration my article entitled *Exactly what you need to do to get FREE publicity in thousands of online e-zines!* As you see, it addresses a popular subject, which your readers are sure to want to know more about. This article is ready to publish and has a line length of 60 characters or under for your easy use. My credentials are listed at the end of the article.
>
> In addition to this article, I also have the following articles available for your immediate publication:
>
> ▼ Five things you can do right now to get immediate free publicity for whatever you're selling
>
> ▼ How to write a "how to" article in less than an hour that generates thousands of dollars worth of free publicity.
>
> If you would like any of the articles, please mailto: drjlant@worldprofit.com. Now here's my immediate submission. (Post your article here).

124

7. **Resend your submission.** Wait about 72 hours and then resend your original submission with "Standing by. Hoping to hear from you today!" at the top. If you still don't hear from the editor, try this again. If the editor still doesn't answer, don't fret. The editor's name is in your LISTSERV® and/or relevant Sales Manager® lists and he or she will be hearing from you over and over again as you persist with your publicity campaign!

If you use these techniques faithfully you will get heaps of free publicity in dozens, even hundreds, of e-zines worldwide. In relatively short order you will become a recognized as the kind of person people want in their publications because your well-known name and the value of your well-considered information will improve the worth of **their** e-zine. As such, other editors will seek you out and ask for the privilege of reprinting your articles and publishing everything you write.

In short, when you follow the steps in this handy dandy report you will launch yourself on a lifetime of incredible free publicity, with all the advantages that derive therefrom, without even having to buy a postage stamp!

Sell Your Product or Service While You Sleep
Judy Cullins

Have you wasted valuable time and money on promotion that doesn't work?

Have your announcements and releases been ignored?

Have you been too quiet about getting the word out about how your product or service will help solve people's problems?

You have put passion and creativity into your business; now it's time to put passion and creativity into promoting it! Since no one really cares as much about your products as you do, you must take the time to learn this new, effective way to sell them. Know that the World Wide Web audience wants and needs your information, your expertise, your "how-to" tips, and your experience or entertainment.

If you are willing to take four to five actions each day to promote your products, you will have successful sales.

Seven Simple Steps to Promoting Yourself Online

1. **Take personal responsibility for online promotion.** Online promotion is great if you are totally bashful or reluctant to "sell." You don't have to talk to anyone in person. You promote straight from your home or office. Now, that's convenience! Learn the basics from tele-classes and seminars, from the Internet, and from professional networking organizations.

2. **Develop internet savvy.** When you don't take this step, you will hang back, and stay stuck in fear. Action spurs you on. Take a free community college course, or visit your library for help. In just three hours, I learned about search engines, and other basics. If, like me, you are passionate to succeed, then hire a coach or virtual assistant from a local high school or tech school. Jump in, get yourself an e-mail address and try surfing the Internet. You won't need a website right away, but if you want to be a market leader, you eventually should have one.

3. **Visit the top websites in your field.** Without them, your product won't get much exposure. Websites are always looking for new material (your articles) to entice their visitors to come back, again and again. Notice their signals: "New material added daily." In turn, they will put your "signature," which includes the product name or service and the Web address, where it can be purchased. It doesn't have to be your website. With just one short article posted in an e-zine, one client of mine received eight e-mails asking for more information. These responses give the creator another chance at a sale and to be known as the market expert. Many product folks also have a professional service to offer. So when the person contacts them, they can mention these other services.

4. **Run a search on the top search engines to find the top ten websites in your field.** Visit the top ten websites to see their layout and whether or not they have a regular e-zine that needs tips, excerpts, or stories. If a site puts new articles up regularly, your information has a chance to bring you increased product sales. Here's a great shortcut: Instead of searching for "product marketing" or something that is very targeted, use the keyword "business" (without the quotations). Type the word "business" in the blank "search for" box and press the "Enter" key. This search will return several million websites that are about business.

Now for the fun part: Replace the keyword "business" with two words: "submit article" and then click on the box just below the "Search for" box and click where it says: "Search within these results." This sub-search will generate a list of pages that allow you to submit business articles. You will be able to target business people who offer products and services and get a much bigger piece of the pie.

5. **Write a note to the webmaster submitting the titles of your articles or stories**. You may want to send an article along as a sample of your writing. It may be a tip about how your service benefits or it solves a problem for the website's visitors. Think benefits when you submit. What can your material do for their site—their visitors? Before you send anything out, after several peer edits, have it professionally edited.

6. **Place your articles on as many websites as possible.** Now, you can be in control of your promotion, with far less effort, and get the respect, support and sales you deserve.

7. **Organize your research.** Start a file called "Websites to link with." If you don't keep track of your promotion contacts, you will not be able to follow up. Professional people always follow-up! They develop relationships with the people they want to do business with.

Start a communication sheet for these people either on your computer or in a physical file. For instance, for publishing sites, list the contact person (Web Master or content person), their e-mail and website address. Include your note to them. Keep track of what you offer, what they like, and what they take. Date your communications. Not everyone will respond but, with persistence, many will! At the end of your note, ask that they include a link back to either your site or other sites where your products and services are offered.

If, like me, you're not a technical person, hire a person who can do the research for you. Remember, people who visit top websites are looking for information and entertainment. They will appreciate your articles and may even pass them on to friends and associates. Many will go to your site or other sites to check out your products—even buy them. Websites want your information. It seems like a marriage made in cyber-heaven.

How to Generate a Million Visitors, a Brand Name, and a Six-Figure Annual Online Income for Free

Terry Dean

It was a cold weekend in December 1997. Christmas was fast approaching and I decided my e-zine subscribers deserved a free Christmas surprise. So I spent three days scanning through my notes and writing the e-book, *101 High Profit Businesses You Can Start Online with Little or No Money.*

It was a short book that most people could probably devour it in one sitting, but it wasn't the length that mattered. What mattered was how it opened people's eyes to the many different options and tremendous possibilities of online marketing.

The results from my **free** e-book offer were amazing! Of the 7,000 subscribers we had at the time, 1,500 downloaded the e-book within the next seven days. Some people downloaded it, learned from it and moved on. But I never expected what happened next. By the middle of January, I had received nearly 500 e-mails from people asking if they could give away the e-book from their websites. Of course I said yes, knowing this would put me in contact with more potential customers.

To this day, I still receive at least five requests a day to distribute my e-book from other people's websites. Although the e-book has been available for two years, it is still marketing my website and my other products and services. This amazing free gift has become one of my best marketing tools. It has resulted in orders from new customers who come to my site everyday—and I don't even have to advertise. These new customers read the free e-book on someone else's website and link to my site to order.

A Beautiful Traffic Virus Is Born

What is a traffic virus? Unlike a computer virus, which can destroy your software and damage your business, a traffic virus isn't harmful at all— except to your competition. In reality, a traffic virus isn't a virus at all. It's just termed a virus because it has a few of the same features.

A computer virus is passed automatically from computer to computer without any effort from the creator. A file, disk or e-mail attachment sent from an infected computer can also carry that virus to any computer receiving that file, disk or e-mail attachment. Many recent viruses have been programmed to be automatically forwarded to any of your e-mail contacts. They automatically spread themselves and you may not even know about it!

A traffic virus has this same feature built into it. It will spread itself around the Internet automatically without your even being involved. But, unlike a computer virus, the key aspect to a traffic virus is that it helps the users, and this causes them to send it to their friends.

For example, one type of traffic virus is a website postcard system. Many websites have installed a free postcard system so their users can send postcards to friends and family. They pick a picture, choose an audio presentation, write a short note, and then e-mail it to their friends.

The key to the viral system (another term for a traffic virus) is that friends and family must come to your website to pick up their card. Your website gets automatic traffic without your active involvement.

Then—we hope—these visitors will send postcards to their friends and family. This never-ending cycle will continually bring new visitors to your site where they will learn about your products and services. The viral marketing system becomes an automatic traffic generator.

People are always asking why they need to start their own viral marketing strategy—it's simple. A traffic virus means you may never lose money advertising again! That's right. Having your own traffic virus could mean that every ad you place from now on can be a winner! That is a pretty strong statement—but it's true!

I was surprised myself at just how powerful a traffic virus can be when I first put mine in place. Every ad I placed instantly became a winner—even when I lost money!

Here's How It Works

Let's say you place an e-zine ad, which costs you $200. You make $20 for every item you sell. You sell nine of them through the ad so you bring in $180. You have now lost $20 on your ad. Most people would call it a failure.

I use a different system, which reduces my advertising risk. Instead of advertising directly for a product, I advertise to bring in e-mail leads. My goal is to get people to give me their e-mail address so I can follow-up with them. By using auto-responders that automatically follow-up, I have the ability to set up a completely automated follow-up system for the product. Three, seven, or even 30 e-mail follow-up messages can be used to generate sales for my product instead of only having one shot to sell my visitors from a website. I have 30 tries to sell them. Who do you think will make more sales?

My system actually goes one step further. I always try to use an element of viral marketing in the promotional aspect of the offer. My favorite technique is the traffic virus e-book offer. In exchange for prospects giving me their e-mail address, I will give them a highly informative free e-book, which they are allowed to pass around and give to their friends.

Not only will the book teach them, but also they can use it to produce more traffic and sales at their website. They win by getting a very valuable book for free. I win because my traffic virus gets started. I still get to follow-up by e-mail to sell them my products and services—so I am still bringing in immediate profits from my advertising.

Let's say I place the above ad for $200 and only bring in $180. I lose $20 today, but this is only the beginning of the traffic the ad will generate for me. All of those people who visited my site—who may or may not have purchased my product are now passing around my free e-book and sending more visitors my way. More sales are made next month, and the month after, and the month after. It is a never-ending process of sales being made.

The $20 I lost originally from the ad will be replaced hundreds of times through new visitors I never have to work or pay for. Every single ad I place becomes a launch point for another aspect of my traffic virus.

Having a Traffic Virus Reduces Your Advertising Risk

Look at this way. If you are paying for your advertising, then every time you place an ad you are risking your money. Your ad may or may not produce a profit. You could make $1,000 from your $200 ad or you may lose $100.

If you have a traffic virus in place, then your ad can continue to work for you years into the future and it reduces your advertising risk. Even when you lose money, you still win in the long run.

What if you only use free advertising methods? This system still reduces your risk. Free advertising costs you time and, like money, time is limited. You may spend your time placing free ads and produce $100 in profits. If those ads took you 10 hours to place, then you only earned $10 an hour for your time.

Ten dollars an hour wouldn't be very good time investment for your business. If you had a traffic virus in place, other people would then start advertising for you by taking and handing out your traffic-generating machine to others. You may have only earned $10 an hour while working on your free advertising, but your traffic virus then goes to work for you 24 hours a day 7 days a week. You generate traffic forever for the 10 hours you spent advertising this week. Wouldn't it be better to profit today—and build a residual income for the future at the same time?

Make Your Free Offer Great

The Internet is continually changing and growing. As each new change takes place, a marketing method either dies out or takes a step to the next level. Viral marketing changes too. So, if you plan to jump on my viral e-book concept, *understand the importance of giving a good product away.* All the e-books I've given away were perceived as having *strong value—* that's why this concept works for me. Make sure your product is worth the electrons it is printed on!

Another way to step up your viral marketing is to sell your e-book instead of giving it away. Sell it with a very special bonus attached. This type of offer would get a much higher readership rate. People who pay for an e-book are much more likely to read it and use it than those who download it for free. This creates more qualified leads for your business. In fact, it can produce thousands of pre-qualified leads composed of people who are willing to buy other products and services you have for sale.

Magnify you marketing by giving away the resale rights for free with the purchase of your e-book. This will drive sales through the roof. Sell to one customer and you may have hundreds of others buying from them—all the while generating backend leads for other products and services to your site.

A Five-Step System for Creating Your Own Traffic Virus

1. **Make it short and easy to use and offer valuable tips.** The right length for an e-book is much shorter than for a traditional book—in most cases this is somewhere between 30 and 80 pages. Get to the point quickly. Cut unnecessary communication. Provide links to websites. That's what people are looking for in an e-book.

   Come up with a series of tips about anything related to the product you're marketing. Example: *47 Ways to Improve your Home, 37 Ways to Generate Traffic Online, 101 Ways to Romance Your Wife,* etc. Don't try to come up with 77 tips in a day or a weekend. Give yourself a good month to come up with ideas for your series on this. The longer you give yourself to do this, the more tips you'll be able to come up with.

   Keep a notebook handy for all of the tip ideas as they come to you. If you come up with a good tip or idea and wait till later to write it down, you will likely forget. You'll find that most of your best ideas will come while you're going about your daily life and not while you're working.

   When you get finished coming up with your tips, write a paragraph or two explaining each one in more detail. A simple explanation is all you need.

   Now create a short introduction for the e-book and give your readers a reason to contact you by e-mail. Promise a specific freebie such as an extra report or anything you may offer in your business to get people to send you their e-mail addresses.

2. **Create a killer title.** One of the most powerful sales tools for any e-book is the title. A poor title or a title that doesn't immediately tell your customers the benefits they'll receive will not work.

   Here is my secret formula for coming up with a great title:

   ▼ Write down the number of tips you have
   ▼ Choose the next phrase
   ▼ Add in the benefit produced for your customers

   Examples: *74 Secrets to Training Your Puppy; 79 Free Tips on Writing Web Copy; 92 Ways to Improve Your Lawn*

3. **Package it as a .pdf file.** Acrobat® is the free reader provided by Adobe and it is the standard for online publishing. You can purchase the stand-alone program to create these types of documents for a little over $200, or you can try out their online system for free at http://cpdf.adobe.com. This site allows you to create up to five Acrobat e-book documents for free. All you have to do is create your e-book in any word processing document, upload it to their online system and the automatic system will create the document.

   Note: E-books can be created in other formats, but none of them are as versatile or as easy to use as Adobe Acrobat®.

4. **Create sales copy and price your e-book.** Now create sales copy for your website. Now price your e-book at $9.95, $17, or $27 depending on just how valuable the tips are. You'll sell a large number of copies at these prices—especially if you're including resale rights to it for free.

5. **Place E-Zine ads.** The quickest way to get results with your e-book is to place e-zine ads. Write a short, five or six line ad and then purchase sponsorships in several e-zines. You can usually pick up ads for anywhere from $50 to $500 (depending on the size of the audience). This will expose your new product to thousands of potential customers. Here are a couple of directories you can use to purchase e-zine ads: www.tope-zineads.com and www.lifestylepub.com.

Remember, your goal is not to earn a big profit. You may earn some cash, but that's not your primary goal. Your goal is to generate leads for any other product or service you may be selling. If you can break even or earn a small profit selling your e-book, then you are successful. Just by having it out there will begin to build your reputation, brand your business, and create pre-qualified customers.

If you think you can't handle all the extra work your e-book marketing will create you should understand this. I am one of the most recognized small business Internet consultants, speakers and publisher of weekly electronic newsletter (over 85,000 subscribers), yet I do this all without employees. And you can too!

The best way to predict the future is to invent it.
—Alan Kay

Chapter Eight

Linking Up

Attitudes are contagious.
Do you want people around you to catch yours?
—Bob Moawad

Shameless Internet Promotion Step 8:
Co-Market and Create Greater Visibility with Link Exchanges

Debbie Allen

Would you like some great *free* exposure for your website plus tons of third party endorsements…just for the asking! Well, it's easy. By sharing links with other websites, your exposure can be magnified in an instant. I find it funny when people ask me if they can link to my website. Well, let me think about it…*free exposure* and a *free advertisement.* Yes, yes, oh did I say YES! Are you kidding? This shameless one will take all the promotion she can get—that's just good marketing.

Shameless Plug

By the way, if you are enjoying this book and you feel compelled to pass on the contact information to all your online viewers to enjoy as well, go right ahead. You have permission to link to www.ConfessionsofShameless.com.

Link Up or Lose Out!

Linking up creates a win-win situation for everyone. Your business associate links will:

▼ Promote yourself and your website by distributing your URL in locations where potential customers can find you with a click of a mouse.

▼ Get your website listed higher on search engines and directories—the more links you have the higher your ranking will be.

▼ Create increased traffic to your website and will even help to build your expertise online.

▼ Help to build strong online alliances.

136

▼ Offer your visitors a valuable resource guide. You allow your visitors to find more information from other companies that relate to your business in some way.

Links work beautifully when they support your website and your visitors. Just make sure that if you send your visitors out of your website they can easily come back with the next click of the mouse. Links that send away visitors who cannot return to your website are called **dead links**. Everyday, I see websites link to another website and throw their visitors away with these deadly links. Remember my motto—**"Never throw business away!"**

The Buzz on Being a Shameless NetShaker

Larry James

So, what's the buzz on being a shameless NetShaker? Can you keep a secret? To sum it up in one word: **collaboration**. It is one of the most important keys to shamelessly successful promotion on the Internet. Some call it **connectivity**; others call it **networking**. Whatever you call it, having a community of support to assist you in your promotion efforts must be a top priority.

Collaboration (connectivity or networking) is using your creative talents to help others achieve their goals as you cultivate a network of people who are strategically positioned to support you in your goals…expecting nothing in return!

It's the "expecting nothing in return" that stops most people. I suggest that we are all in this to help others and ourselves…in that order. What you put out to the universe always comes back to you.

Disappointment may follow if you expect a return from the person or website to whom you have contributed. Collaboration is about building supportive personal and business relationships; it's consistently connecting with new people and making new friends, sharing ideas and having lots of fun in the process.

Collaboration Is Key

Having a clear understanding of the definition of collaboration is a prerequisite for Internet success. Never fear the competition. Fear of the competition nails your feet to the floor. Everyone is moving and shaking the Internet except you. Fear is an energy drain. It thwarts your creative imagination. Your worry keeps you from moving forward.

Whatever you are doing to shamelessly promote yourself on the Internet is either moving you closer to your goals or further away. There is no middle ground. Know this and there is no competition…only insecure people who fear losing something or someone to another website. And they usually do.

Create Links

Studies of the Internet have shown that the majority of people find other relevant sites by clicking on "links" to other interesting sites. While search engines do bring hits to your site, keeping them updated can cost you time and money. Getting "linked" or linking to other related websites through your collaborative efforts is an opportunity for your site to be discovered and a much more reliable way to ensure steady traffic to your site.

It's also a lesson in the economics of collaboration. It doesn't cost you a cent…only the time and energy you are willing to put forth in making the right connections. This is something you can do. You will only need the services of your Webmaster to post the links to your site unless you learn to make these simple changes on your own website.

First-time hits to www.CelebrateLove.com more than quadrupled within two weeks of posting, not one, but several links pages and making those pages more visible on our site.

To most of the major search engines, the more links coming "into" and going "out of" your site make your site appear more valuable when someone is searching for your product or service. Having links to your website is essential to getting a good listing in most of the major search engines.

The innovative trend of trading links will multiply hits to your site. Reciprocal links with similar sites are free, and provide long-term traffic. The biggest problem with great information is that people aren't willing to share it. NetShakers trade links! Trading links is about sharing information.

There are two more benefits to exchanging links. One is the immediate increase in traffic to your website from referral partners. The second benefit is the ongoing funnel of new, pre-qualified prospects it brings to your doorstep. Our philosophy is that if a person comes to our doorstep and chooses not to stay, we would rather share other quality relationship sites than have them drift off into cyberspace with no direction. We know that they appreciate this opportunity. The fact is that the more links we post to other relationship sites, the more hits we receive on our site. We shamelessly and consistently contact other quality website owners with an invitation to link to our site provided that they have a reciprocal links page.

If we really like the site we will first add their link to our site, then send a personal e-mail to the site owner telling them something we like about their site so they will know we have visited their site and are not just randomly sending the e-mail to everyone. Personalize this e-mail with the site owner's name if you can.

We then list several benefits of linking to our site and ask for a reciprocal link. Include HTML code in your e-mail so all they have to do is cut and paste the link to one of their Web pages or refer them to a special page on your site that explains your reciprocal links trade plan. This page should include text link examples, a photo image, small banners, "cut and paste" HTML code and detailed link instructions to make it as easy as possible for them to link to you.

Webmasters know the value of having the appropriate keywords written into the HTML code of each page on their websites. In the "link invitation" e-mail we send, we also tell them that we will add their name and website into the keywords on the page on our site where their link appears.

There are two advantages to doing this. First, it gives them additional exposure to the top-ten search engines we submit to, and second, it will often result in Web surfers finding our site while looking for them. If there is no response and we feel the site is good, we will keep it linked anyway. We also check the keywords of other similar sites that may fit on our links criteria for keywords that might help us move up in the search engine rankings.

Content—Lots of It

Most sites will respond favorably provided you have a site with content that their visitors may find interesting. So, there's another "shameless clue." Add content—lots of it. This is another key ingredient to being a NetShaker and an Internet success.

Unfortunately, a lot of websites that we might consider as being good link candidates are only about their service or product and have little or no content. As a result, we do not consider them for our information rich site. Content is king. Content is what our viewers expect from our site and we will not compromise just to add more links.

When it is right we provide lots of links—in prominent places—on each page to encourage our visitors to move between the related areas without getting lost. If you can achieve this, your visitors will have the maximum opportunity to eventually gather the information that came to see. You can also use these internal links to cross sell. If, for example, you have posted an information page about dogs be sure to include several links to the best selling dog books, toys and other products your viewers may be interested in.

Watch Out for Broken Links

Broken links and malfunctioning site features cost you page impressions, customers and respect. Broken links are bad for your business. They drive customers away! Internet users rate broken links as the second-biggest problem online, right behind slow-loading pages. (Source: A Web usability study by the Georgia Institute of Technology.)

Maintaining the integrity of your site is critical to building a captive audience of repeat visitors. If your site does not function correctly, you are likely to lose the visitors you have worked so hard to attract.

It takes constant work to keep your site in the best working order. No matter what you do, errors will creep into your Web pages. Finding broken links can be time-consuming, tedious task. Be your own "link police" or at least wise enough to hire an outside Internet company to automatically give you a weekly report of "link rot," or broken links.

I cannot stress the importance of collaboration and the use of effective reciprocal linking strategies with similar sites enough. They are the hidden power of the Internet. It should be one of the first rules of building your presence. So give some very serious thought to the economics of collaboration.

When we work together to support one another, everyone benefits!

The Inside Secrets to Our Business Network Success

Jeremy Allen and Dr. Ivan Misner

In 1985, a shamelessly organized networking effort got a huge boost. In sunny Southern California, a new business networking group, called BNI (Business Network International) began meeting weekly in hopes they would increase each other's business by referring business to one other.

Together they agreed that they would allow only one person per profession to attend the networking meetings on a regular basis and that they would adopt the age-old Golden Rule—figuring that if they gave business to each other, the members would do likewise and reciprocate with more referrals.

The idea worked and it worked well! Little did each of the members know the tremendous impact their efforts would have on the future of business and professional networking.

Seventeen years later that one group of business professionals has spawned over 2,200 additional groups that meet weekly as a part of BNI. Each of these groups, called chapters, has an average of 20 members, totaling over 44,000 active members worldwide. Spanning more than 12 countries, five different languages and numerous cultural differences, BNI is recognized as the world's leading business and professional networking organization.

Each year, members of BNI shamelessly generate hundreds of millions of dollars of new business for one another, further supporting the fact that networking is "…mandatory for making it," as bestselling author and networking expert Susan RoAne wrote about in Chapter Seven of *Confessions of Shameless Self Promoters*, by Debbie Allen.

Enter, the Internet

When BNI was first formed in 1985, business professionals were networking together by way of toting around business card-files and old-style rolodexes, which look *nothing* like the helpful PDA devices we have today. And the Internet was an infant, barely in existence. Technology for BNI consisted of a fax machine, a copier and an old, old style word-processor. In fact, BNI didn't even register their first website until 1994.

From the beginning, we kept our website and its material relevant to our mission—to help our members increase their referral business. In this way, we made sure that our website contained material our members would find useful, informative and educational.

We didn't set out to sell the world our product or service, nor did we set out to sell memberships in our organization online. Instead, we worked on creating a credible extension of our organization's name, further adding value and building recognition and loyalty online with our members.

Since the early days of our first website, www.BNI.com has undergone many transformations—too numerous to count. Through those changes we discovered the best strategies to help us promote it effectively.

Seven Shameless and Successful Strategies

1. **Register and keep domain names.** Since our humble Web-based beginnings in 1994, we have continued to register and keep our domain names renewed yearly and when a new domain extension comes available, like .biz or .info, we are quick to register BNI for those domains as well.

    In fact, www.BNI.com was originally taken and registered to another business. So we registered our second choice, which was www.BNINET.com and then registered BNI for the other major domains, like .net and .org. While registering these BNI domains, we looked to see who owned the existing bni.com address and made a note of the expiration date on our founder's calendar.

    We waited patiently and months later, www.BNI.com indeed expired (it seems the previous owner simply had not renewed the domain) and thus, the domain name we wanted was available to purchase—so we grabbed it quickly. Today, we have over twelve different names registered to BNI, including most of the new extensions such as .ws and .info as well as most national extensions such as: .ca, .au and .uk. All of these addresses are forwarded to point to our main site address on the Web.

    Ever since those early days of working to acquire our domain names, we have closely monitored and maintained our Web presence, in order to avoid others marketing on the Internet with our name; and that strategy has worked well for us.

2. **Create credibility.** When you look at our site today, you'll find that our focus is still the same as it was when we launched our first site over eight years ago—to help our members increase their referral business.

   Sure, we've added a host of great interactive features, photos, more information, an e-newsletter and the ability to purchase our books, tapes and marketing materials online, but our overriding focus has always been to maintain and establish credibility so that our site is a valuable extension of the way we do business—with high standards and strong ethics and with our members always first on our mind.

3. **Fill a need.** Our site is a strategic extension of our business and not just a business in itself. Whenever possible, we look to and think about our thousands of members worldwide (who are our customers) when we are considering adding or removing features from our site.

   Nearly every change we make to the website is done with our members in mind. We are very aware of and want to fill the real and relevant needs of our members. We have come to accept the fact that we can't meet every specific need requested, so we look for the common needs voiced by our members.

   Although basic advice, it's worth mentioning a second time. A website, just like any business, must fill a genuine consumer need. The stories of expensive websites going bankrupt and disappearing are everywhere. No matter how great the idea, *the website must fulfill a genuine consumer need.* Those websites that have disappeared missed out on this very important and crucial business strategy.

4. **Add useful and interactive resources.** There are thousands of fantastic-looking websites on the Internet that are visited only once. What a shame! They look great, feel great but are lacking in depth. For BNI, our successful "depth" comes from our useful, interactive resources.

   Our members are primarily business owners and sales and marketing professionals from a variety of professions. They all share a common goal; they want to increase their business and profits and believe that networking for warm referrals are one of the best ways to accomplish that goal.

   To help our members increase their referral skills and become "masters of networking" we have created several online, interactive resources full of useful information, articles and forms.

For the officers who run each chapter, we created a password-protected area that may be accessed from the website. In this 'Leadership Team Only' section, we took many of our useful and most requested paper documents and converted them to a downloadable .pdf format. This .pdf format makes these documents conveniently available to our leadership team, as the cliché goes, "24 hours a day, 7 days a week." It's amazing how much time and money we save every year by providing our documents to our customers online.

When we first introduced this new feature a few years ago, our members found it so helpful that we have created two more password-protected, resource-rich sections. We discovered that members love to have an interactive section that only they can access by password, and it's a value-added feature we will keep for years to come.

5. **Touch them differently every time.** Our site receives hundreds of thousands of visits each year. While many thousands of these visitors are first timers who are looking for membership information, the majority of the visits are repeat visits from members. Because so many of our members visit the site regularly, we focus on creating content that touches them differently every time.

   On our home page, we display headlines of stories and facts that are important to our worldwide membership. When a new chapter of BNI opened in Singapore, we shamelessly created a headline and photo to place on our home page.

   When we have new stories and headlines to display, we place them at the top and push the older headlines towards the bottom. After a while, we remove and retire the oldest headlines to make room for newer ones. This allows our homepage to be fresh and different for our visitors each time they visit our site.

   We also make sure to update our online material often. When we publish a new document, form or article, we are careful to update it online as we make changes in the paper world. If our members point out a misspelling, we correct both the paper document and the online digital document.

6. **Anchor them.** New, flashy designs are great and new content is critical to bringing visitors back to your site, again and again. But you must

strive to keep your site fresh by focusing on creating content that touches visitors differently every time.

However, understand that your visitors have a strong need to come back to a website that is familiar and friendly to them. You can solve this challenge by placing a standard link bar on the left of *every* page that will take your viewers to familiar places on the website. The familiar link bar will help returning visitors feel comfortable with your site and will "anchor" them with each visit.

7. **Go from paper to digital.** Going from paper to digital is an interesting process. Although the process is mildly technical to explain, it's really useful and important information for any shameless Internet promoter, so read on.

In most cases, there are two preferred methods we use when publishing useful information to our website. We either convert our paper documents to HTML (Hyper Text Markup Language) or to the Adobe Acrobat® .pdf format.

HTML is what nearly every Web page is written in. Anyone who can surf the Web can see an HTML created Web page, so HTML is usually the preferred method for creating a site. Our free online e-newsletter is created in HTML, with a special added feature that allows our readers to print the e-newsletter out to a printer. In most cases, HTML is the preferred way we go from paper to digital.

Sometimes we want to create a secure document that our members can download, save to their computer and print out later. In that case, we use Adobe Acrobat® to convert our paper documents to .pdf documents. This allows us to easily convert paper documents into digital documents that we place in our password-protected sections that our members can use, but not make changes to the information.

As a special note, we are very careful when we choose to convert a document to .pdf format. We are very aware of the fact that .pdf documents require a special program to be on the visitor's computer in order to see and work with .pdf documents. Although this program, Adobe Acrobat® is readily available and free to everyone, some Web surfers do not have a copy.

Thus, to avoid confusion and the potential of losing our visitors because they might become frustrated by needing additional programs like Acrobat®, we only place .pdf documents in our secure section. This allows us to make sure that those members who have passwords to our useful, interactive resources also know that they will need an additional, yet free, program to view this material made available to them.

There you have it. You have all of our strategies and secrets to shameless Internet promotion. As we mentioned earlier, www.bni.com has undergone many, many transformations since the early days of our first website in 1994. We believe that our website will continue to change in the coming years as we listen to and respond to our members' needs. Wishing you the best of success as you apply some or all of these principles as you shamelessly promote yourself and your business online!

> *Life's most persistent and urgent question is:*
> *What are you doing for others?*
> —Martin Luther King, Jr.

Chapter Nine

Using Your Expertise to Build World Wide Fame Overnight

Your dreams are not meant to put you to sleep,
but to alert and arouse you to your immense possibilities.
—David Phillips

Shameless Internet Promotion Step 9: Build Your Online Fame and Become an Internet Star

Debbie Allen

When you're the best at what you do you've got to get the word out to your existing and potential customers. Your existing customers want to know they're dealing with the best and that you're dedicated to a mission of continuous improvement. Potential customers also want to work with the best—they're just not aware of your expertise or how you can help them to get better. The World Wide Web is a great tool to build your worldwide fame. So, how exactly do you build your fame online and become an Internet star. Here are some ways that you can start to build your online fame today.

How Good Are You?

The first step to becoming an Internet star is to identify and define your areas of expertise. Ask yourself:

▼ How do you stand out from your competitors?

▼ What is unique about your products or services?

▼ In what ways do you customize your products or services to offer the best possible solutions to your customers needs?

▼ How do you WOW your customers?

▼ What do your customers say you do better than anyone else?

Express Yourself

Some of the most successful online marketers are just good copywriters. They know how to use well-written words to build trust with their customers, connect with their emotions and needs and then get them to respond.

Write a Dynamic Biography

List your expertise shamelessly—don't hold back. *Tell viewers why you and your company are the experts.* Most people hold back from shamelessly promoting themselves and their expertise—but you must tell people how and why they need to trust your expertise. List everything you have done to build your business success.

Here are some questions to get you thinking about what to add to your bio.

- ▼ Have you ever won an award or even been nominated for an award? (It does not matter if it was ten years ago—there is no time limit on promotion and your expertise.)

- ▼ Have you overcome business obstacles and turned around your business or consulted with someone who has?

- ▼ Are you listed in a Who's Who of Experts?

- ▼ Do you belong to numerous community organizations?

- ▼ Have you served on boards of a non-profit company, or supported and served your community?

Get the idea? List it **all** in a well-written format.

Get Lots of Endorsements

A third party endorsement is a statement or recommendation about your products and/or services from your customers and business associates. Third party endorsements are powerful! They are a key element in boosting the effectiveness of your website, your sales letters, and your ads. Third party endorsements work especially well when the person who is considered a specialist or an authority on your area of expertise passes on that endorsement to you.

How do you get lots of endorsements? *You just have to ask!* Yes, it really works. When writing my book, *Confessions of Shameless Self Promoters,* not only did I want to find the top marketing experts—*I wanted to get big name endorsements.* By asking my friends and associates to help me track them down and get my foot in the door—I achieved results. *Just by asking!*

The book received shamelessly supportive endorsements from such famous people as Jay Conrad Levinson (author of *Guerilla Marketing*), Joe Girard

(World's Greatest Salesman), Mark Victor Hansen (author/creator of *Chicken Soup For The Soul*) and Stuart Anderson (Founder of Stuart Anderson Restaurants).

Fact: Television and radio ads have been using third party endorsements for years. And have they been successful! When was the last time you gave a recommendation (good or bad) about a movie, restaurant, or any type of product or service you recently bought? See my point? Third party endorsements and honest testimonials will definitely take your business farther than you have ever dreamed!

Build an Online Pressroom

Showcase your expertise by continually sharing your knowledge with your visitors. Give away your expertise by giving away articles from your site. Create a pressroom that includes every article you have ever written and post a short bio at the end of each article.

It amazes me how much publicity I get from my online pressroom. It makes it easy for editors to select from articles they need and promotes my expertise at the same time. All for *free*! This type of exposure beats paid advertising hands down. Editors also contact me for personalized interviews and ask me to write extended articles for a fee. Still they publish my expertise and drive more traffic to my website.

The pressroom also is a valuable resource for anyone visiting my site. Often people who have attended my presentations spend up to two hours on my site reading my articles. This builds confidence in my *expertise*, encourages visitors to return time and time again and generates online sales. You don't just want to hear "You've got mail." You want to hear, "Cha ching—you have orders!"

Create a Photo Gallery

Never leave home without your digital camera. A photo gallery is a great way to personalize your site and enhance your reputation at the same time. Post photos of yourself receiving an award, or add smiling photos of you with some your satisfied customers. Feature pictures of yourself with famous people or with other experts in your field. Get creative with your photo gallery and don't be afraid to have fun with it. Humor is often underused in advertising, promotion and marketing.

Ask the Expert

An "Ask the Expert" column is another great way for your viewers to interact with you and use your expertise to become an Internet star. You will also learn a lot about your customers and how to adjust your business practices to build more sales and profits.

You're already the expert—it's time you became an Internet star!

YOU are Worth a Fortune Online!

Jeanette S. Cates, Ph.D.

You are an expert. You have a lot of information to share—even more than you recognize! This concept will help you to develop a strategy that will work for you and your target audience. But how do you package that information and expertise for the Web? How do you provide enough information to attract visitors to your website, without *giving away the store*? And how do you make money from the content you want to sell?

Only you know what is best for your clients. You know whether or not they will respond to online banners or shy away from pages that have blinking banners. You know whether they want quick tips, books, or written reports. You know their problems and the way to provide solutions for them. In short, *you're the expert!* You provide your expertise in the form of information and information is structure. The three most common forms of information available online and offline are: *Tips, Groups of Tips and Articles.*

Tips

The smallest piece of information that you typically create is a tip. You do it all the time! People ask for suggestions or a quick how-to and you rattle it off. You're not even aware of how many tips you give in a week's time. So I'm going to raise your consciousness.

First, list three areas where you are an expert. These may be in the professional realm or in the personal realm. Are you a parent? Do you have a hobby?

Next, choose one of these areas of expertise and write five tips on it. Your tips don't have to be grammatically correct—they just need to be on paper! (It's okay to write tips in more than one of those areas).

Now here's the key. Next week write five more tips—then five more the week after. Make it a habit to write tips. I carry a small notebook with me so that each time I answer a question or think of an idea, I write a tip for it. You will be amazed at how quickly tips multiply!

As you work with information, you will find that one of the basic tenets is to repurpose and reformat information. Let's look at how that idea works with tips in an online environment.

Ask the Expert and Frequently Asked Questions

One of the most effective ways to show your expertise on your website is to have an "Ask the Expert" column. For example, view my online at www.techtamers.com/free_resources/ask_expert/index.htm. To get started with an "Ask the Expert" column, think of questions that your customers would ask. People always have questions—you hear them every day in your business. When you make a sales or service call or give a presentation, you should know the top ten questions your customers ask. With those questions in mind, formulate your answers and create a separate page and form for viewers to ask additional questions.

You can keep your "Ask the Expert" column interactive by changing the questions and answers weekly. Then move previous questions to your FAQ/Frequently Asked Questions section on your website. Repeat this process each week (or month or whatever period you've chosen) changing the question and answer and moving the current one to your FAQ.

Frequently Asked Questions are an accumulation of questions you receive—either live or via your website. Most FAQ documents list the questions at the top of the page and then post both the Q&A further down on the Web page. The questions at the top of your page will serve as a Table of Contents. When you accumulate a lot of questions, you can split them into categories to make it easier for your visitors to navigate.

FAQs may be used for visitor questions, as we've discussed. But they are also helpful when selling a product or service online. For example, people may have questions about the online ordering process—How safe is it? How do I know my credit card is safe? When will I get the item? Put FAQ in your sales area and link it to your product pages.

Another good place for FAQ is in the customer service area. People may have questions about a product or service they have already received. Providing the answers online will significantly reduce the number of telephone phone calls you need to answer and cut the costs associated with answering these calls. Increasingly, people are going to the website first, before calling a business with their questions. Where can you use FAQs on your website now?

As you receive a question, formulate your answer and e-mail it directly to the person who posed the question. Explain that you'll also post the question on your website. People like to get an answer quickly, but they also like to know they've helped you and other visitors to your website.

Groups of Tips

In Chapter Six you read about how to create tip booklets from Paulette Ensign. This is a great way to promote your business and offer a free gift to you customers. Best of all you can take your print booklet and also offer it online viewing for sale or as a give away. An electronic version of your booklet can be a product that you sell from your website individually. Or you can bundle several booklets to create a "special" offer. The advantage of an e-version is that it can be downloaded immediately after purchase, so your customer may be more inclined to purchase the booklet—especially if they need the information *now*!

As a way to build your visibility online, consider offering free copies of your tips booklets or shorter collections of tips to newsletter editors. They often are looking for filler content and in exchange for a link to your website, and will be glad to publish your tips. If you offer these free copies, be sure to get their contact information in exchange for the tips!

Tips booklets are a wonderful source of income and publicity. But there are several other ways you can use a group of tips.

- ▼ Provide a tip of the day (or week!) e-mail subscription. Many people are more likely to read a short tip than an entire e-mail newsletter.

- ▼ Provide your tip of the day (or week) as a pop-up window on your website—this may be an automatic pop-up or one that the visitor chooses to click-on.

▼ Send weekly tips postcards via traditional mail. This will draw attention to your business and to your website, particularly if you tell readers they can get more tips at your website!

Articles

Articles are a great way to build credibility and show off your expertise online. They are also probably the single fastest way to build traffic to your website. There are several tricks to developing an effective article strategy:

Who is your audience?
Yes, you've heard that question before. But look at it again.

What problems can you solve for your audience?
Some of the universal problems are time, money and energy. What others can you think of? When you think of your target market what specific questions do they have? What complaints do you hear repeatedly?

Take some time to brainstorm three articles that your target audience needs. It's okay to use articles you've already written or considered. Great! Now you're ready to write. Write! Many people panic at this point. Let's look at two approaches to writing articles.

Keep it Simple and Informal

When you write articles for online publication, they don't necessarily have to be the academic work we had in school. Online articles tend to be more informal. Use short paragraphs and lots of bullet points. While the spelling and grammar should be correct, you can get by with language that is more relaxed than if you were writing for a printed publication.

Have a Conversation with Your Readers

Consider that you're having a conversation with your readers. Literally talk your article onto paper. You can do this by talking out loud to yourself as you type. Or you could talk into a tape recorder and have someone (yourself?) transcribe it. You could also record a conversation with a friend and then transcribe it. Or you could record a presentation you make, and then transcribe the content. There are plenty of ways to get the article onto paper.

Prepare your article for distribution and provide a one to three sentence bio paragraph. Last but not least, include a permission to reprint statement. I use a short one such as:

Permission to reprint is granted as long as the bio paragraph above remains intact. Please contact the Webmaster or expert on this website and let them know where the article will be published. A copy of the online publication or print version mailed to our office is greatly appreciated.

This reprint statement makes it easy and conscience-free for others to reprint your article. Many website and newsletter editors in a moment of panic can grab your article and include it in their publication. Often they'll forget to tell you they printed it. But you'll know when you start getting traffic from that publication.

Distributing Your Article

Just writing the article is not enough. You have to get it out into the world. Here are 7 ways to effectively distribute your article:

1. Post the article on your website. On the page with the article, include a catchy page title, appropriate keywords and a good description in the meta tags.

2. Register your article in the search engines and directories.

3. Include a reference to the new article in your e-mail newsletter.

4. Set up a page on your website for *free articles*. Put the links to all of your free articles on this one page. Register this page on the search engines, including the words free and articles.

5. Include your free article page in your signature file, especially when you e-mail writers, editors, other website owners, and the media.

6. Find at least five other websites that serve your target audience. E-mail the article or a description of the article with a link to the article at your website to the editors of these sites. Be sure to offer to let them include it as a newsletter article or as an article on their website.

7. Register at www.ezinearticles.com. Once you're a contributor you can send in the titles and short descriptions of the articles you have available. These are sent out to all of their subscribers weekly in their e-zine. Those interested in your topic and your articles, will ask for them. Ask the people who request your article or who agree to post or print your article if they would like to be notified when you publish more articles. Then set up a separate e-mail list for them so that it's easy to contact them.

Build Credibility with an E-Mail Course

Consider offering an online course via e-mail. Basically a course is just a series of articles on a specific topic. Your course will consist of several lessons, delivered at pre-set intervals. You'll compose the lessons once so that you're ready to deliver them to anyone who signs up for the course. Now won't that be a bear to administer, you ask? Not if you use one of the online services that is designed to do this. In using one of the e-mail engines, for example, you have up to seven lessons for your "course." Your first lesson is set to go out immediately after your new "student" sends an e-mail to the course address (you set this address!). Then each lesson goes out automatically on the day you prescribe. It may be daily for the first three days, then every three days thereafter. Or it may be weekly. This is an automatic e-mail series, also known as a sequential auto-responder.

Regardless of the interval, you enter each lesson as you want it to appear to the enrollees. Since you don't know when someone will sign up, the system tracks each enrollee individually so that they receive their e-mails on schedule, regardless of when other people sign up. It's like having a private secretary to track all of the enrollments and mail outs!

You can opt to receive a notification each time someone signs up to take the course (fun at first, but overwhelming in the long run). At any time you can log into your control panel and see who is enrolled in your course, which e-mail they have received and when they last heard from you.

Why would you want to offer an e-mail course? Maybe you have a complex subject on which you need to educate prospects. Why not create a course with a small commercial in each lesson? Maybe you delivered a great seminar and you now want to keep in touch with audience members. Why not create a series of reminder e-mails to be sent at regular intervals? Or maybe you want to offer an online course, but you're not sure how well it will go over. Why not pilot some of the content with an e-mail course to test the market?

Remember that if you offer a weekly course over seven weeks, you'll want to keep the course active for several months. Coincidentally, you generally get a discount when you pay for several months in advance with one of the e-mail engines. So why not just add an e-mail course to your online strategy on an ongoing basis? You won't be sorry. You'll probably find yourself back starting a *new* course shortly!

Now that you understand the basics of an e-mail course, how could *you* use it? List at least three topics that would be good for an e-mail course. Now take one of those topics and list the subject lines you'll use for the six e-mails.

If you begin to think in terms of "repurpose and reformat," you'll begin to see the possibilities for marketing your business and your expertise with information shamelessly online. A tip is never just a tip—instead, it is part of a tips booklet, part of an article, part of an online course. An article is never just an article—it's a potential e-mail lesson, a group of tips, and an ongoing advertisement for you. When you look at it that way—You Are Worth A Fortune Online.

How to Write and Market Profitable Special Reports

Joan Stewart

My friends who are (or like to think they are) Internet marketers often brag about how much free information visitors can find at their websites. Some of them offer hundreds of articles, columns they write for newspapers and magazines, and a plethora of information that can be downright overwhelming.

I tell them they're crazy. Sure, offer free information. But why give away the store when they can repackage most of it into profitable special reports, like I do, and create a nice revenue stream?

Special reports are my most profitable product. I started writing them two years ago when I reluctantly admitted that I needed to publish my first book, but I had no time to just sit down and write it. Writing it chapter by chapter, then selling each chapter as a special report from my website as soon as it was written seemed to be the answer.

I learned quickly that no other product is as easy and inexpensive to produce as a special report. It requires nothing more than a computer and a printer. There's no fancy packaging—virtually no investment up front. No damaged merchandise that will be returned. In some cases, no shipping costs.

A special report is a multi-page report packed with valuable how-to information that buyers can begin using immediately. Each of my reports is five pages, single-spaced, delivered electronically, and focused on a very specific problem.

For example, I'm a media relations speaker and consultant, so my special reports focus on media and publicity topics. I provide specific step-by-step directions on how to solve a particular problem. Some of my reports include: *How to Write Compelling Letters to the Editor, How to Create Media Kits on a Shoestring,* and *How to Pitch Story Ideas to Reporters over the Telephone.* The secret to special reports is to pick a very narrow topic and offer a glut of how-to information. In other words, go an inch wide and a mile deep.

So far, I've written 37 special reports. This year alone, I estimate I've generated about $20,000 in revenue just from the reports. And I've concluded that I'd be crazy to repackage them into a book, which I could sell for probably no more than $25. What I did do, however, was take some of the information from the reports, combine it with new information on a variety of other topics, and co-author my first e-book with Internet marketing guru Tom Antion (another online marketing expert featured in this book). The book sells for $97. We made $5,000 profit from the book in the first two months. And you can do this too with your expertise! Why such a high price for an e-book? Because the customer is willing to pay it to get the information instantly. And when you update the copy, you can offer the update for free.

Where to Start

Start by identifying your audience's number one problem. That should be the topic of your first special report. Remember to keep the topic as narrow as possible.

Research your topic using the Internet and the library. In many cases, you can find exactly what you need on your computer, in the comfort of your home or office.

Check your bookshelf and your file cabinet. If it is a topic you're already familiar with, chances are you have a variety of books and file folders stuffed with information on the topic. This is a great starting point that's often overlooked. If you publish an e-zine or a print newsletter, go through your back issues and recycle appropriate content.

Choose a Format

This isn't the Great American Novel, so you don't need great prose. It's a "how-to" piece, so you need lots of solid tips. My special reports are written in a variety of formats. My first report called *Damage Control: How to Keep the Media from Making a Mess of Your Story* simply lists a problem, and then explains how to solve it. I've written special reports in question-and-answer format, too.

Example: My *Special Report #15: Publicity Tips for Schools, Colleges and Universities* simply includes 15 tips numbered one through 15 and accompanied by sub-heads, with detailed information on each.

Most special reports, however, are written in a simple format, like this one, in which you write instructions the same way you would explain them to someone verbally. Open with an introduction, and then follow with blocks of information on your topic, separated by sub-heads.

Close with a resource box at the end that offers other related products that can help the reader. I frequently mention my media relations workshops and other special reports that relate to the topic. You can offer information on audio tapes, books, videos, workbooks and other items you sell.

Example: Sometimes I also offer other valuable resources that I have come to rely on for that particular topic, even if they aren't my own products. This builds credibility and shows readers I am truly interested in helping them with their problem.

Tips for Writing Your Special Report

▼ Use dozens of solid "how-to" tips.

▼ Use short sentences and paragraphs. Avoid big blocks of gray, which are a turnoff and difficult to read.

▼ Use sub-heads.

▼ Use lists and bulleted items.

▼ At the end, invite readers to contact you if they have questions. Few of my customers do. But it's comforting for readers to know they can zip me an e-mail if they have a simple question about one of my reports. One of your customers may want to buy more products in quantity or subscribe to your free e-zine. Allow people to communicate with you in different ways.

▼ Write directly to the reader. Use the word "you."

▼ Consider customizing the cover page of each special report. The title could say something like *Special Report #3: How to Make Cold Calls* for Sally Smith.

▼ Note, if you hire a freelance writer, there is no need to include the writer's name on the report. It can be ghost-written under your name.

Other Things to Consider

▼ Set up a shopping cart on your website so that customers receive your reports by auto-responder. If you don't accept credit cards at your website, start now, or lose what could be thousands of dollars in sales.

▼ Update your special reports at least once every two years. If you mention a website in your report, for example, check two years later to make sure it's still a live website. Double-check all phone numbers and other information. Also, cross-promote your reports whenever possible.

▼ Don't worry about the cover. Just be sure all your contact information is at the top of the first page. Customers do not expect fancy graphics and a document that looks attractive. All they want is solid information.

▼ Place a copyright notice at the top and the phrase "Reproduction strictly prohibited." Remove that phrase when sending a special report to the media.

How to Price Your Special Reports

Most special reports are priced from $5 to $10. I sell mine for $7 each. You can also offer them in groups of three at a discount rate. I offer all 43 special reports in a "Value Pack" for $207 and let customers save $94 if they buy the entire package.

If you are offering hard-copy reports, consider selling them for at least double what customers would pay for the electronic version. You have to cover the cost of the paper, envelope, the postage stamp, plus the trouble it takes to print and mail the report. I discontinued offering hard copies because they are too much trouble. Not one person has complained.

If you publish an e-zine, promote the special reports heavily. In my e-zine, I often choose topics that will tie in nicely to the special reports I have for sale. I then write a small promotional piece with three or four solid tips and create a link to the shopping cart at my website.

How to Market Your Special Reports

- ▼ Sell them from the back of the room during public speaking engagements.

- ▼ Sell them at your website and be sure to tell customers the subtopics they include. Each report for sale at my website includes a "You will learn:" section, with five or six bulleted items on specific things people will learn if they buy the report. Visit www.publicityhound.com/reports.html to see how I did it.

- ▼ Send a shorter version of your special report to the media, and mention at the end of the article, in the identifier paragraph, that you have special reports on similar topics at your website.

- ▼ Excerpt a few tips from each report at your website to give people a flavor of what they will be getting.

- ▼ Send them free to clients as a way of thanking them for doing business with you.

- ▼ Offer excerpts or a shorter version of your report to publishers of print and online newsletters. Don't forget the valuable identifier paragraph at the end that tells people who you are, what you do, how they can find you, and a link to your website. Ask editors how many words they want, and then write to fit.

- ▼ Tuck them inside your media kit or business portfolio.

- ▼ Give away your special report, or give customers two or three reports of their choice for free, as an incentive to buy one of your more expensive products. Consider bundling special reports by topic and offering them at a discount price. For example, six special reports on how to make a sales call that normally sell for $7 each can be offered for $35. Bundle special reports with other products such as books and audio tapes, and sell them as a package.

▼ Keep a database of every customer who buys your report and ask them if it's alright to contact them later when you write more reports they might want to know about. Send postcards or an e-mail to them as soon as you have written a new one.

Now get going. You already have lots of ideas in your head. Start writing and then start profiting.

Shamelessly Promoting Two Names into Stardom
Miguel Alvarez

What I'm about to confess to you is something that my wife and I swore to keep in absolute secrecy—but Debbie Allen sure knows how to twist some arms in a friendly but irresistible way. (The proof is that this is her third book!)

This strategy alone helped me launch both of our names into Internet stardom and raise our website sales by an almost incredible 2,300 percent. Here are the shameless details of how I did it.

The first thing I did was write a very deep and insightful report that showed readers how to create mini-websites—one- or two-page websites—that sell like crazy. On it, I analyzed and dissected a very notable formula that some of the best Web marketing experts have been using to build websites that sell and sell and then sell some more. I know exactly how to do it because I've been using that same formula myself to earn a very nice income from all my different websites.

After I finished writing the report I just knew it would be a hit! I had managed to create a winning product that people would be willing to pay good money for. Inside the report I included plenty of links to my websites and to the websites of some of the top-rated Web marketing experts (via their affiliate programs). I also talked about a brand new Web hosting service that I had launched only two weeks before.

This report was also guaranteed to position me as a successful author on the "Internet Marketing Arena"—a good perk. So if things went as planned, the report would create several avenues to make money in addition to sales of the report itself.

I was about to launch the website and e-mail my list one morning, but I decided to check my e-mail first. The first message was a very interesting article that pointed out how a good package for your product could easily increase the perceived value and boost sales. It made me think.

The report already had a great package but I knew that I could increase its value by taking a different approach. This made me think of another question. What if, instead of increasing the perceived value of the report, I increased my own perceived value and positioned myself as a "guru"? Being the author of the report would make people consider me as an expert, but since I was talking about how "marketing gurus" promoted their websites, including my name on that list would make people relate me to them and position *me* as one of the top marketers—and not only as an author.

After arriving at that decision, I had to make quite a few changes to the special report. One of the most important changes would be the name of the author. After all I could not be depicted as the author *and* showcased as a guru at the same time.

So instead of including my name as the author, I talked to my wife—Alpha del Bosque—and asked her if she would like to appear as the author of the report. I explained that her name (and her online business) would benefit from all the recognition of being an author gives. She was a bit hesitant at first, but she accepted the idea.

And here comes the second part of the strategy…

Making the changes to the special report gave me time to analyze and think about how to spread the word for this product faster than it had ever been done before. I figured that I would set three different prices for the product:

1. The first price would be set low and the buyer would get the report "as is" and would be able to sell the report for the same price…this is very attractive, because with just two sales the buyer can make a profit.

2. The second price would be a mid-level one and, in addition to the report itself, the buyer would also get the rights to modify the links that go to my websites and enable the buyer to include his affiliate ID on each of them. This option is even more attractive because the buyer's resale customers would visit my websites and very likely buy from them—thus generating an affiliate commission aside from the initial profit that was generated from the sale.

3. The third price would be higher and would include the complete rights to the report. The final user would be able to change the links *and* include his or her own advertisements and banners on the report.

So, all pricing options included the basic "resell rights," but the higher the price, the more attractive the offer sounded to the customer—and the more profitable it would be for him or her to make the investment.

The Result

I generated over $7,000 in direct sales of the report in the first week. But the real profits started flowing three weeks after that when everyone else started selling the report to their customer lists. We saw no direct profits from those sales, but we did see a 2,300 percent improvement in the sales from my other websites. To view the website of that special report check out www.killerminisites.com

Shameless self-promotion? Yes. But it worked like a charm and the report brought in a very nice income for us. There were some other nice benefits, like getting tons of e-mails inviting me to participate in all sorts of joint ventures, and having people ask me (and my wife) to write a few paragraphs on their e-books, etc.

The next time you need to increase the perceived value of your name, find a way to make others do the promoting for you…and help them make some money in the process. People will thank you for it, and you'll become an Internet star!

Over Exposure in Mass Media Is a Myth

Barry Urquhart

Over exposure on the Internet is an impossibility! Yet, some self-promoters would reasonably be deemed shameful in their poor use of the Internet.

Currently, the most important and the most complex issue for business and marketers to address and to redress is the difficulty of being included on shopping lists. The World Wide Web, when properly employed, can be an effective channel initiator and integrator of an ongoing communications strategy.

Self-promotion and self-generated publicity are the stepping-stones to a higher order of success. However, sporadic publicity is insufficient to penetrate a seemingly impregnable wall that envelopes most contemporary prospective clients and customers. Most people are exposed daily to an estimated 3,400 advertising, marketing, merchandising and promotional messages that stimulate among individuals the process of selective perception. As a result, that which is considered irrelevant is not dismissed; it simply never registers.

No Customer Loyalty

The emerging reality is that customers or clients do not feel loyalty to you. Instead they feel that at any time you and your business is relevant to them. Existing customers and clients are not motivated to be disloyal. Rather, they act out of self-interest and are attracted to and rewarded by that which is of relevance and of personal benefit.

Consequently, shameless self-promoters on the Internet need also determine and monitor those things which will ensure the self-promoter communicates benefits, advantages and aspirations for those with whom they wish to deal.

Purist marketers often wish to divorce themselves from the ranks of shameless self-promoters. Sadly, they fail to recognize and respect the two foundations of marketing, which are communication and opportunism. The more one communicates, the more opportunities are created. And the Internet is, or should be, everyone's window on or to the global village.

A few words of caution—the world and prospective customers do not need more communication and more self-promotional activities. It is estimated that the World Wide Web presently abounds with 16 billion pages. The pressing issue is why will anyone chose the pages of a self-promoter over those of the other 16 billion.

Moreover, an overwhelming majority of adults in advanced western societies read very little. Even fewer comprehend the messages and fewer again retain or take action on the communication.

Implicit in this message is the need to determine and promote that which one wants to be famous for. Few people in any community, city, state, nation or the world at large enjoy celebrity. Seldom is it that a hushed reverence descends upon a restaurant, concert hall or public mall with the arrival of an individual. The exalted exceptions include General Colin Powell, David Letterman, Michael Jordan and possibly Australia's own "Crocodile Dundee" Paul Hogan. Each has celebrity.

To effectively promote yourself on the Internet, as in all marketing, you must determine the one or two ways you can establish and sustain the status of fame (if not celebrity). For instance, I have written the two largest selling books on quality customer service in Australia. At every opportunity in life, in the mail, on the telephone or over the Internet I mention and promote that reality. Why? Because no one else can!

Self-promoters need to pinpoint what they can declare about themselves, their business, products and services that no one else can claim. Their total commitment and focus on those limited elements will enhance the effectiveness of their self-promotion. Brevity on the Internet is a virtue. We make extensive use of "postcard" communications there. Receivers understand the messages will be concise, with a little levity and require a resultant action. We need to get to the point quickly.

In the absence of celebrity, self-promoters have 15 minutes in which to stimulate interest, generate business and establish a positive, mutually rewarding and sustaining relationship. As Andy Warhol observed we all have 15 minutes of fame.

Respect Your Logo

It is shameful that so many self-promoters under-utilize and arguably even abuse their use of the Internet. No self-respecting self-promoter would tolerate a newspaper, radio station, television channel or magazine producing an advertisement that did not feature their logo, image or photographs. Would you allow someone in your organization to mail correspondence that was not printed on company stationery? Why then do some self-promoters tolerate that on the Internet?

This may be a sobering reality check but it does immediately reveal an overwhelming majority of e-mails transmitted throughout the world. Amazingly they do not feature the logo or signature of the organization. You must respect and utilize your image, on the Internet and in all media.

The Internet must be accepted and exploited as a complementary channel to all other mass media. The "click" must be supported by the "brick." Reflect upon some of the fundamental lessons of the "dot.com meltdown," when countless Internet-based businesses collapsed and disappeared.

It is folly to believe that a single medium can be effective in advertising, marketing, and merchandising, and in promotions, sales, service and client retention. Therein lies the reason why so much of the money, time and resources that is dedicated to advertising is wasted. Don't be too ambitious. Study, analyze and understand the nature of the Internet. Then utilize it to its best capacity.

Have Fun

Recent research concluded that 87 percent of adult consumers contend that they did not believe nor directly respond to advertising. So why take yourself so seriously. Introduce a little levity into your communications and connect with customers personally.

Effective self-promoters on the Internet have fun, limit the text of their communication and respect the importance of the two foundations of the marketing discipline—communication and opportunism. I confess that our promotion on the Internet has been effective in generating more than half of our annual speaking engagements from overseas, being in Europe, North America, Asia and Southern Africa. Over exposure—it's just a myth!

> *Whenever you are to do a thing,*
> *though it can never be known but to yourself,*
> *ask yourself how you would act were all the world*
> *looking at you, and act accordingly.*
> —Thomas Jefferson

Chapter Ten

The "E" in E-Books and E-Zines Stands for Exposure

Perseverance is a great element of success,
if you only knock long enough
and loud enough at the gate,
you are sure to wake up somebody.
—Henry Wadsworth Longfellow

Shameless Internet Promotion Step 10: Promote Your Business with E-Zines and E-Books

Debbie Allen

You have been hearing about e-zines and e-books throughout this book. Now my contributors will confess their secrets to creating highly effective "E"s—everything you always wanted to know about e-zines and then some.

Publishing an e-zine is one of the easiest and most important steps you can take when it comes to promoting your website. An opt-in list of people who want to hear from you on a regular basis is priceless. In addition, the actual process of writing your own e-zine and connecting with people is an inspiring experience in itself. It's a way of building a genuine sense of community around your website and opening the lines of communication with your customers.

According to a report from *E-Marketer*, more than one billion e-mail messages are sent daily in the United States alone. Eighty percent of the messages are responded to within 48 hours (some within minutes), while response to direct mail often takes six to eight weeks. An *AWE-Marketer* survey found that people were nearly twice as likely to respond to e-mail as regular mail. The average cost per e-mail message in the United States is less than one cent; compared to $1 to $3 for tele-marketing and 75 cents or more for direct mail.

Benefits of Electronic Marketing

▼ Speed of market and customer base
▼ No cost or low cost
▼ Low risk
▼ Wide distribution
▼ Minimal skill required

Creating an E-Zine or Electronic Newsletter

▼ Develop a newsletter by copying format and text.

▼ Learn more details on creating an e-zine view www.e-zinez.com.

▼ Cut and paste your message.

▼ Add hyperlinks to direct customers to your website.

▼ Test by sending to friends before sending it to your online customer base.

▼ Send to your customer base BCC (blind carbon copy—lists only one e-mail address on the e-mail) with the use of an e-mail list manger. An affordable service that offers to store your e-mail lists, offers multiple list capability and forwards your timed message is www.mindsharedesign.com.

▼ Experiment, and have fun with it—you are now an online publisher!

If you consider your regular mailing list as **golden**, then you should consider your e-mail list as **platinum**.

E-Zines: The Ultimate Self-Promotion Tool
Alexandria K. Brown

Three years ago when I founded my business as a marketing writer and consultant, I was delighted. I could work at home and on my own schedule. But along with that independence came the realization that I was going to have to work a lot harder to keep myself on everyone's radar screens. Sorry, no sitting around all day eating bon-bons and waiting for my toll-free number to ring! If I had done that I would never have created my online fame as "The E-Zine Queen."

I needed a cheap and easy way to stay in touch with past associates, current clients, prospects...just about everyone! And I wanted them to realize I really knew my stuff about writing compelling copy for websites, ads, brochures, etc. I wanted them to see me as an "expert" and to encourage them to hire me and refer me to other possible clients.

One of my specialties was developing print newsletters for clients, so it seemed natural to publish my own. But the cost for design, printing, and postage would have run my new little biz into the ground. My best bet was to publish an e-mail newsletter, or "e-zine." As a result, *AKB MarCom Tips* was born!

I first sent out an announcement to **everyone** I knew inviting them to subscribe. I was ecstatic to receive 50 responses, a huge number to a rookie entrepreneur. "Imagine," I thought, "all these people want to hear **my** tips!"

I pretty much let my list grow on its own from people visiting my website or current subscribers passing on my e-zine to others. I had no idea about all the ways to promote my e-zine until I began researching for an article I was writing. Thanks to the promotional methods I've learned and implemented, my subscriber count is now in the thousands. And you can do this too, quickly and easily.

The Birth of a Book … and a Brand

During my research, I downloaded many e-books on the subject of e-zines, but none of them covered the entire publishing process from planning content to writing to setting up a list service to gaining subscribers and promoting an e-zine. Many of them were full of hype, trying to convince people they could make a million dollars from e-zine advertising. My situation was different: I already had a successful business that I wanted to promote using an e-zine. There were no e-books geared specifically for the small business owner. Here was *my* chance to capture this niche and write my own manual!

I began furiously researching and writing. You know when you're onto something good when you go into that "zone"—nothing else matters but what you're working on. I couldn't even sleep because my head was swimming with ideas. I'd jump up in the middle of the night to record some great revelation, driving my husband nuts in the process.

As the book neared completion, I realized this was really its own animal and did not deserve to be lumped in with the information on my corporate site. I wanted my website to remain targeted toward my higher-end writing and consulting work. I didn't want corporate prospects visiting my site and being distracted by my $49 "E-Zine Queen" package when they were considering me to write a $20,000 brochure.

My book definitely deserved a site of its own. So, one night (another two a.m. revelation) the name "E-Zine Queen" popped in my head. I raced to my computer and purchased "www.ezinequeen.com", and—voila—a brand (and my self-ordained title) was born!

I hired a designer to develop an "E-Zine Queen" logo and a gorgeous site. Now, you don't necessarily need such luxuries to market yourself online, but it helps. (Anyway I'm a Leo, and we just have to do everything with style.)

Marketing Yourself, Your Products and Your Services

To increase the awareness of your products and or services, you may want to share your expertise with prospective buyers through your own e-zine. For example, I began a new e-zine called *Tips from the E-Zine Queen*. It covers how to write, publish, and promote a dynamic e-zine that builds customer relationships and increases sales. Since this e-zine covered the same topics as my book and report, the subscribers I'd attract would be ideal prospects.

Five Reasons Why You Should Publish an E-Zine

1. An e-zine is the perfect way to **stay in touch** with your clients and prospects. Unless you continually follow up with clients and prospects, they'll soon forget about you. An e-zine achieves the goal of keeping you on their "radar screens." And here's the best part— they've all asked to receive this regular communication from you!

   Most folks won't buy from you the first time they visit your site. If they don't make an effort to bookmark your site and come back later, you've likely lost them forever. Goodbye prospect. But if your site invites them to sign up for your e-zine, you guarantee you'll have many more chances to prove your worth.

   Getting your name and ideas in front of prospects weekly or biweekly makes them much more likely to think of **you**—not the person who called them last week.

2. An e-zine allows you to **effortlessly spread the word about you and your business.** If you write a decent e-zine, your readers will be very likely to pass it on to friends and colleagues. Remember that old shampoo commercial that went, "And I told two friends, and she told two

friends, and so on, and so on...."? That principle—clients passing on the word about your product or service—is called "viral marketing."

Most publishers begin with only a few dozen subscribers, mostly clients and associates. But after several months they can end up with thousands of readers, thanks to viral marketing mixed with a lot of promotional legwork. (Psst...My manual and report tell you exactly how to do this!)

3. An e-zine is **a credible and subtle way to promote your services or products.** Instead of simply saying how great you are, an e-zine lets you *show* how great you are by sharing your expertise through tips or case studies. (As my old journalism professor said, "Show me, don't just tell me!") You're avoiding simple bragging and instead are offering useful information that demonstrates your knowledge. Bravo!

4. Publishing an e-zine **positions you as an expert in your field.** By showcasing your knowledge and skills, you're likely to attract more clients. And by sharing what you know well, you're saying, "Hey, I know my stuff! I'm an expert! You should listen to me."

   Don't be scared of the word "expert." You don't have to know everything in the world about your topic to call yourself an expert. You just need to know a lot more than most people. If you make a living doing what you do, you're likely an expert in your own right. If you're still uncomfortable with that term, try on the word "resource." Okay, feel better?

5. **An e-zine is cheap and easy to publish**—especially compared with a print newsletter. If you were to produce and mail a snazzy-looking printed newsletter, you could easily spend thousands of dollars each year. But an e-zine is essentially **free** to put together and publish—it just takes a bit of your time.

   And you can make it as long or short as you'd like. (Some of the best e-zines I receive feature only one tip per issue and are less than one computer screen long.) For best results, keep it simple!

Other Ways to Market Yourself

Write new articles on a regular basis. Submit them to dozens of announcement lists and websites. Make sure to include your contact information and a link to your site.

Host monthly or weekly tele-classes (workshops delivered over the phone—similar to a conference call). You can charge a fee (usually around $20 for a one-hour class) or offer them free to promote your business to prospective customers.

Add some creativity to your marketing. For example, I had new, funky business cards printed just to promote my E-Zine Queen site, and to give to any small business owners I met in person or sent a note to. The card invites them to visit my site and sign up for my free e-zine! (That's often what really gets them to visit the site.)

Stay true to your brand. Everything I do promotes my E-Zine Queen brand. Make sure all your communications are consistent. If I only said I was the E-Zine Queen once in a while, it wouldn't be nearly as effective as using that as my e-mail signature, in all my ads, and in all my articles.

My Most Important Advice

If your e-zine only talks about how great you are, you won't attract new subscribers (or clients, for that matter). Constant news that's only about you, you, you gets boring and turns off readers.

Instead, focus on providing information that will be useful and educational to your readers. This will make them love you! If you're a Web designer, how about giving tips on designing a good website? If you're a PR pro, tell us how to get some free publicity! Accountant? Give tax pointers for small businesses. Get it?

Besides, there's plenty of room to plug yourself at the end of each issue. Give a paragraph or two about your business and the benefits you offer your clients and customers.

Take the time to plan a quality publication from the start, and you'll reap amazing results!

What Is Your Purpose in Sending an Electronic Newsletter?

Thomas Murrell

In the business world, e-newsletters are fast replacing traditional newsletters. Just as traditional newsletters have promotional goals, so too should e-newsletters. And, as with traditional newsletters, you will need to think about and answer some questions before you launch your e-newsletter:

- ▼ Who is your target audience?
- ▼ How frequently will you communicate with them?
- ▼ How popular and how widely read will your e-newsletter/e-zine be?
- ▼ What is the perceived value of the e-communication activity?
- ▼ What is your planned budget?
- ▼ How much will you charge for the e-newsletter/e-zine?
- ▼ How will you charge for the e-newsletter/e-zine?

Your e-newsletter should have specific features as well as some advantages over your competitors' newsletters. Take into account how you will measure the success of your e-newsletter and always keep in mind how you can increase its usefulness and relevance.

Tips for Electronic Newsletters

How can you write an e-newsletter that will help build your business? The first thing to do is have a facility to capture the e-mail addresses of people who visit your website.

Make sure you write for scanners, because people who read e-mail and e-newsletters are scanning; they're reading light and not ink on a page. They blink less and are unable to adjust the text size, so you've got to write for people who are going to scan a computer screen, rather than touch, feel and hold a printed document.

Write short—at least 50 percent less than printed newsletters, and each article should be about two page-downs at most. Maximum length for sentences should be 15 to 20 words; a paragraph should contain no more than five sentences; and the length of each article should be a maximum of four paragraphs.

Write friendly. Use a conversational tone, let your personality show through and make it personal.

Use bite-sized chunks as well as bullet points, numbers and lists rather than lengthy and complex sentences. Lists are easy to scan and help the reader absorb each item once at a time.

Limit each article to a single concept and add resources or links back to your site for more complex, detailed information. Remember the Mohammed Ali principle—accurate and frequent rather than wild and infrequent.

Focus on easy distribution. Encourage people to forward your e-newsletters and remember the privacy issue. Never write anything you don't want the whole world to see, including your competition.

Strive for low cost. It really only costs your time to write e-newsletters, and it's certainly one of the most successful and economical marketing tools you can have.

Newsworthiness and relevance are crucial. You've really got to make it newsworthy, because unlike other direct mail information, newsletters enjoy the same status as newspapers and other media. Respect that privilege, and be sure your e-newsletters are accurate and newsworthy. Enjoy the marketing advantage while maintaining your integrity with your readers.

Free Publicity Using E-Zine Articles
Yanik Silver

Remember the movie *Field of Dreams*? "If you build it—they will come." Wrong! If you build your website, nobody's going to come. Your mom might come to check it out, but that's it! That's why you need to focus your efforts on promotion and marketing. I'm going to give a few of my most powerful promotion methods. (And the best part is most of these don't cost much to start producing results.)

I generate thousands of dollars in free advertising every month with my e-zine–and you can too! At last count, I heard there were approximately 100,000 e-zines. I now have over one million people reading my articles online all over the world. Best of all, I get better results and free publicity by posting e-zine articles instead of placing expensive ads. And my e-zine even promotes me as the expert and authority on my subject. Sounds pretty good, right? Let me show you how you can do this too.

Content Is King

There's tons of e-zines out there with a need for content and I'm one of the guys who meet this need by creating content. I establish a *quid pro quo* relationship where I place a resource box at the end of each of my articles. It's like a five- or six-line ad that gives my pitch and a link to my website.

Here's my e-zine article formula in a nutshell:

1. **Create a list of editors who are interested in your articles.** Several free e-zine directories are available to help you collect information about e-zine editors. Howerver, you usually get what you pay for. I suggest the *Directory of E-Zines* by Ruth Townsend (www.lifestylespub.com/wow/). One of my favorite parts of this database is the field that indicates whether or not the editor accepts articles. You can search for all e-zines in your area of interest as well as all those who are interested in receiving articles. The database has all kinds of topics from A to Z—you'll most likely find listings for your topic or area of expertise as well.

2. **Create a powerful article on your subject.** Now you will need to write your article. Your article only needs to be about 500 to 700 words. Creating the article is pretty easy. Simply take an excerpt out of one of your products, write about your business strategies or share tips and secrets on your areas of expertise. Then add a compelling title.

   For example: *The Ten Secrets to* ____ or *The Seven Mistakes Most* ____ *Make and How to Avoid Them.* Include a paragraph introduction, a paragraph about each secret or mistake and then a closing paragraph and you're all done. Trust me, 500 words is not difficult to come up with.

3. **Develop a powerful resource box to promote your product.** Finish up the article with a killer resource box. Your resource box should contain your bio and killer ad all wrapped into one. Usually, you can get away with five to six lines of promotional material here. When your article gets published, your resource box is what people read to find out more about you. You need a compelling one that makes them want to click over to visit your website! (Or whatever action you want.)

Here's an example: Hot on the heels of Yanik Silver's first Internet project (www.instantsalesletters.com) comes the new "Instant Internet Profits" course. Yanik spills the beans and reveals his simple blueprint for online success. Check it out at www.instantinternetprofits.com.

4. **Submit articles to all these e-zine editors.** And watch the sales roll in!

Easy Steps to Creating a Highly Successful E-Zine
Merle

It seems as if everyone and his dog is publishing an e-zine these days. And from what I've seen, the dog's may be better than most. Why are there are so many e-zines out there? Despite what you just read above, do you need to publish one?

The answer is simple: If you sell goods and/or services online you need to establish a way for your visitors to opt in or ask to subscribe to your website.

By offering visitors to your website an opportunity to sign up for your e-zine, you get a chance to extend your communication with them, establish a "relationship," and convert them into customers. If you don't already have an e-zine or electronic newsletter here's how to get started.

1. **Decide on a title for your e-zine.** Incorporate your business name into the title or choose something related to its theme. For example, if your company's name is "Bob's Automotive" you may choose something like *Bob's Automotive Press.*

    Speaking of themes, your e-zine's theme needs to relate to your website. If your website is a pet supply store then your e-zine might be on animal care or training. If your website sells your services as an online marketing consultant, your e-zine might center on teaching people how to market and promote their own websites.

2. **Decide where your e-zine will live.** This is often referred to as list management and your best bet is to outsource it or check with your Web host to see if they supply this service as part of your account. Don't think for a minute you can manage an e-zine with just your e-mail program. A list can grow to a substantial size and you need to think about this from the start.

If you're trying to save money, I'd highly recommend you sign up with one of the many free list host services that are available. They work great, and make it easy for people to subscribe and unsubscribe at will. The only trade-off is the advertising they will place at the very top of your e-zine for the privilege of your free account. Remember, they are hosting your list for free so they've got to get something in return, too.

Here are some list hosts you may want to try:

▼ **Yahoo Groups: http://groups.yahoo.com**

This is my personal favorite and the one I use to manage all three of my e-zines. The service works great and is free in exchange for a banner ad they place at the top of each issue. (The ad can be removed for a nominal fee.) Make sure you set your list up as "moderated." This keeps outsiders from posting to your list, which is something you'd only want if you were setting it up for two-way discussion.

▼ **Cool List: http://www.coollist.com**

This is another free mailing service similar in functionality to Yahoo Groups.

▼ **Topica: http://www.Topica.com**

Another online leader when it comes to list hosting, it is free to set up. Easy step by step instructions and they have excellent customer service.

▼ **Group Mail Software: http://www.Infacta.com/**

If you are daring enough to want to download some free software to manage your list, you won't find anything better than Group Mail. It's an excellent tool for handling and mailing to large groups of people. You can also download some free handy plug-ins that will increase its versatility.

3. **Get subscribers.** Make sure you add a subscriber sign up box on every page of your website to encourage sign ups. Some people add a pop up box to promote sign ups—be aware that many people find this approach to be annoying. If you do decide to go the pop up route, create one that only pops up when the visitor exits your website.

4. **Decide how often you will publish.** Shoot for two to four weeks. If you go longer than one month between issues, your subscribers will forget who you are; if you publish weekly it may be overkill. Whatever you do, pick a publishing schedule and stick with it. *Consistency* is the key! If you say your e-zine will be published on the 7th and 23rd, then you need to get your e-zine out on those promised dates.

5. **Format your e-zine.** The issue of whether to adopt an all text or an HTML format for your e-zine sparks much debate. At this time, most e-zine publishers stick with text, and I strongly recommend you follow suit. Many people are still using e-mail clients that cannot read HTML messages—others prefer the speed, ease and security of receiving their e-zines in text format. It is safer to use the format that is compatible with the largest number of users.

But there are other readers who appreciate the design quality and visual appeal of an HTML newsletter. How can you please both sides? You can always publish a text version and include a link to an HTML version online. This is what I do and it seems to make the majority of my subscribers happy. This approach does call for twice the amount of work since you'll have to make two versions of your e-zine, but in my opinion it's well worth the extra effort.

What is an all-text e-zine? Basically, it's just an e-mail with some special formatting applied to make sure it's readable by everyone, no matter what e-mail client they may be using. You'll want to stick to a fixed width font like Courier or Monaco, and you'll need a plain text editor like Notepad or Textpad. One drawback with Notepad is that it has no built-in spell-checker, so I'd advise you to download Textpad or a similar product. Many free text editors can be found at www.Download.com.

You'll need to set up a template for your e-zine so its look will be consistent, issue after issue. This should include your e-zine name, date, and issue number at the very top, followed by a table of contents. If you're not sure on how it should look, you can obtain some free e-zine templates by sending an e-mail to: template1@e-zinez.com.

At the very end of your newsletter template you'll want to include a paragraph on how to subscribe and unsubscribe, and provide copyright and advertising information. It's vital that you include unsubscribe information in each and every issue. Don't hold people "hostage" by making it next to impossible to get off your list. This is unprofessional and won't be appreciated, and you could get into real trouble with the spam cop.

When typing your text you need to keep your line length at 65 characters per line and hit a hard return at the end of each and every line. This is imperative. If you allow the words to wrap automatically, the e-zine your readers receive may have lines chopped off in mid-sentence and will look terrible. By using the hard return you'll ensure that your newsletter will be readable and attractive in the majority of e-mail clients. Never type your e-zine in all caps as this is equivalent to screaming at your readers.

6. **Create content.** I highly recommend you write at least one original article a month for your newsletter. Write more if you can. It's Okay to include work by others on an occasional basis or for filler, but your e-zine will carry more weight if you take the time to write your own material. When you do need outside content, here are some excellent sources:

> www.EzineArticles.com
> www.IdeaMarketers.com
> www.Certificate.net
> www.Family-Content.com

You can also download this free e-book: *400 Articles You Can Use in Your E-zine* from http://www.web-source.net/web/Free_Ebooks/Writing_Publishing/

Another idea for getting original articles to reprint in your e-zine is to go to e-groups and subscribe to article announcement lists like:

> www.website101.com/freecontent.html or
> www.web-source.net/articlesub.htm

They will supply you with a steady stream of new articles that you can publish on a daily basis.

As you can see, there are many online sources that exist solely for the purpose of helping e-zine publishers succeed. With the massive amount of information available to you, there's really no reason to not start your own e-zine. So come on—what are you waiting for? Your Internet fame awaits!

7. **Build your e-zine subscriber base.** Now that you have a terrific looking e-zine with interesting content, where do you find subscribers? I was hoping you'd ask. In order to grow your subscriber base you'll need to promote your e-zine every chance you get. To get more subscribers you may want to add a free sample copy by auto-responder. To set up a free auto-responder check out www.getresponse.com.

The next step is to get your e-zine listed in as many online newsletter directories as possible. Do your homework by browsing the search engines for directories where you can add your listing for free. This is an important step as many people look to these directories when looking for newsletters to subscribe to. Some of them are:

> www.Lifestylespub.com/mcp/
> www.E-zinedirectory.com/
> www.Webscoutlists.com/signup.epl
> www.Ezineadsource.com/
> www.Zineconnection.com/
> www.Ezine-Universe.com
> www.EzineLocater.com/
> www.EzinesPlus.com/

Remember many of these online directories will allow you to post your ad rates as well. This is a double bonus which allows you to pick up advertisers as well as new subscribers.

Announcement lists are also good for promoting your e-zine. Search at http://groups.yahoo.com for lists that exist for the sole purpose of announcing new lists. You'll also want to participate in online discussion boards with a good signature line that mentions your e-zine. You'll find some great boards to post to at www.DiscussMarketing.com.

Other great ways to grow your subscriber base include swapping ads with other publishers and writing articles to submit to other publishers for possible publication in their e-zines. Again, a strong signature line is imperative. Try some of these websites for swaps:

> www.BizPromo.com/EzineTrades.htm
> www.Ezine-Swap.com

Free Software to keep track of your swaps:
> www.nowsell.com/pages/ad-tracker.html

Other e-zine Publishers you can swap ads with:
www.alacarim.com/adex/

Free Directory of e-zines and other helpful resources for today's e-zine publisher:
www.FreeZineWeb.com/

The *Handbook of E-zine Publishing:*
www.e-zinez.com/

EP Digest offers many helpful resources:
www.EpDigest.com

After writing your own articles syndicate them:
www.linkcounter.com/go.php?linkid=184827

Then submit your articles to:
http://groups.yahoo.com/group/article_announce

If you don't mind paying for opt-in subscribers you can pay a small fee for them at World Wide Lists:
www.linkcounter.com/go.php?linkid=184828

Or try Marty Foley's List Builder Service Lead Factory at
www.linkcounter.com/go.php?linkid=184830

I've used both of these services extensively and they're truly remarkable for growing your list quickly. These are opt-in list builders who will sell you opt-in subscribers, not Spam techniques. Here's the difference. When you purchase opt-in subscribers these are people who have willingly signed up to receive your e-zine. If you buy a list from a broker, this is Spam and not the way to build a list. By purchasing subscribers from a reputable list provider you can be assured they have requested a subscription.

8. **Sell ad space.** Once you reach a minimum of 1,000 subscribers you'll be able to start selling text ads. Don't include too many ads in your newsletter or you'll lose subscribers before you get started. It's really a balancing act—good content with a few ads mixed in. If your e-zine is just a billboard of ads your subscribers will reach for that unsubscribe button in a hurry.

If you can, it's a smart move to collect demographic information from the beginning. This will give you an idea as to the types of people who subscribe to your e-zine and will be helpful to ad buyers who will want to know what "target market" your e-zine hits. Set up a short form asking for basic information—age, sex, and occupation and ask new subscribers to fill it in when they subscribe. You'll be amazed at how easy it is to gather this type of information.

A few websites that will help you to sell your available space:

> www.Ezines-Ads.com
> www.Opt-Influence.com (must have 5,000 subscribers)
> www.EzineAdAuction.com (must have 1,000 subscribers)
> www.EzineAdAuction.com

Don't let this incredible marketing tool pass you by. Follow my steps and those of the other shameless contributors to this chapter you'll be well on your way to publishing an e-zine that will pay you back in more ways than you can imagine—and that's an online marketing tool fact.

What are you waiting for? Get busy!

The Power of E-Zine Marketing

Ilise Benun

My world was turned upside down when I was fired from my job, a small travel company that booked African safaris. I thought to myself, "How could anyone possibly fire me?" I was angry at first and definitely determined to never work for anyone again! What was I going to do now? After the dust settled, I began to brainstorm for a new career. Ah ha! A professional organizer—everyone I knew was unorganized, and I soon discovered that many of them wanted my help and would pay me for it.

As I dug through piles of paperwork with my clients, it amazed me so much of it was important material that never got attended to—stuff that could actually make or break their business. Much of it was marketing-oriented—including requests from prospects who wanted to know more about their business. But, because they didn't have a standard package ready to go, they had to reinvent the wheel every time, which wasted time and kept the important task of growing the business on the back burner.

I started to help my clients put together their marketing packages, and what I learned inspired me to write. I published a two-sided newsletter which began as a promotional tool for my consulting services and quickly turned into a subscription publication that went out to 2,000 people and paid for itself. At the same time, I started giving workshops to teach people the marketing and organizational skills I'd been writing about.

I also began writing magazine articles on self-promotion for *HOW* magazine, a publication for graphic designers. This group seemed to get my message about the importance of marketing. I knew that *HOW* had a publishing division and I was patiently waiting for them to ask me to write a book. I approached one of my contacts, who happened to be the president of the company, and asked if I could write a book for them. He said "yes."

He put me in touch with one of the acquisition editors who told me they were looking for a book about marketing online. Although I knew very little about the Internet at the time, I said "yes," and started to delve into my topic by interviewing people and surfing the Web. From the research for the book, I had so many ideas to pass along that I created *Quick Online Marketing Tips*, and started sending it out to everyone I knew. It wasn't long before my e-mail list had grown to a few thousand…and counting.

In addition to networking and my efforts to be a resource to everyone I come into contact with, my e-mail newsletter is my best, easiest and least expensive marketing tool. It gets my name out to a lot of the right people on a regular basis and they pass my information along to others. It actually generates work—recently, several consulting clients and a lucrative writing project have come as a direct result of my newsletter.

Recently, I ran into the man who fired me from the safari company and after some initial awkwardness, it occurred to me that I should thank him for doing me the best favor of my life. So I did.

The Secret to Developing a Revolutionary, Money-Making Marketing Idea

Bob Kish

Iced tea with soy milk was the fuel I used to develop a unique e-mail marketing strategy. This concept opened up a world of advertising opportunities for all those with their own e-mail newsletter. E-Zines are the advertising method of choice for many of today's Internet marketers.

The key is to capture the visitor's e-mail address via a giveaway or free report and then e-mail them on a regular basis. Once you develop a database of those interested in receiving information from you, you help them grow their business by providing information and links to resources that you have found valuable.

As you help them, you can also help yourself by sharing information on programs or products that have helped you. Many of these products have affiliate programs that will put money in your pocket when others sign up or join via your affiliate link.

If you are looking to get started for free there are several sites that will help you set up your own newsletter.

> www.yahoogroups.com
> www.topica.com
> www.notifylist.com
> www.smartgroups.com

Developing a large enough e-mail list to see significant profit takes time, as does swapping ads. You can also pay to place your ads in various e-zines but this can be costly and time-consuming as well.

Solve a Problem

As with many new ideas that take hold, my idea for a revolutionary way to advertise in e-zines was generated by asking a simple question, "How can I solve a certain problem?"

In this case, the problem was that of overcoming the expense of advertising in e-zines along with the time spent hunting up other newsletter publishers with a similar subscriber focus and subscriber count. The interesting thing here is that people get so used to doing things in a certain way that most times they don't even realize there is a problem.

That leaves the playing field wide open for you to come in and solve a whole host of problems that others are either too busy to address or don't know exist.

Idea Generation

How do you set about creating a new idea that you think might be effective, successful, or profitable? What I like to do is hang out in coffee shops, sip my favorite iced tea with soy milk combination and stare out the window. While many passers-by might simply think I'm in a coma, for at least some of the time the wheels are actually spinning.

I use two different methods to come up with new ideas. One is to start with a blank sheet of paper and then just jot ideas down as they pop into my head. The second is to list a variety of things from marketing techniques to sales strategies to whatever and then to draw lines from one item to another and see what I can do with the combinations.

In order to come up with a new idea I think you have to strike a delicate balance. First, you need to have a storehouse of information related to the topic you're brainstorming about. You can build up your own storehouse by reading everything you can in that specific field. When it comes to actually creating the idea, you have to empty your mind of preconceived ideas about what can work and what is acceptable. Then let your mind start creating connections with all your stored information, sit back, sip your beverage of choice, and see what ideas pop up.

In the case of my unique e-mail marketing strategy, ezineADventure, a connection with e-zine advertising and multi-level marketing jumped out at me. That immediately spawned a host of ideas on how to develop a program that would benefit e-zine publishers by not limiting them to simple subscriber for subscriber ad swaps or cost them money to advertise.

The program that I developed, ezineADventure, involves multiple tiers and allows any e-zine publisher to join for free. The only requirement is that each participant must run four ads a month in their e-zine. When an e-zine publisher recruits or sponsors another e-zine publisher into the program that new publisher is required to run the sponsoring publisher's ad. In fact, three of the four ads are those of the new recruit's upline sponsors; the fourth ad is an ezineADventure system ad.

In effect, Bill, an e-zine owner just starting out who might only have a couple of hundred subscribers, could recruit Ted, another e-zine owner with 50,000 subscribers. Overnight, Ted would be required to run Bill's ad in his e-zine—every month. And, every e-zine publisher recruited by Ted would also run Bill's ad.

When I designed the program I made sure that one of the four ads that each new participant is required to run would be my ad. And, in the name of *Shameless Internet Promotion*, I make sure that my name is included in the ad. If my ad is touting a certain program, I use my name along with the name of one of my websites to promote myself and the program at the same time. For instance, if I was promoting product XYZ, one of my ad lines would be: "XYZ listed as an Affiliate Winner by Bob Kish."

Here, with one line, I advertise the product, my website and my name— shameless exposure but certainly not indecent. And, to further promote myself I include a picture of yours truly on my website. This is another good branding technique that builds trust with your visitors.

Let Auto-Responders Do the Work for You

In any ad you can also include a "mail-to" link to an auto-responder message that you have developed regarding a specific product you are selling. You can set up an unlimited number of messages that can be automatically delivered to your prospect at predetermined intervals.

It has been said that it takes up to seven contacts to sell a person. With that in mind, why not set up a sequence of ten messages to sell a particular product. You set it up once and the auto-responder makes the recurring contacts.

There are now dozens of free auto-responders out there that you can use; just type in "free auto responder" into any search engine. Many also include personalization features so that when someone gets your e-mail it automatically has their name in it. I use www.getresponse.com for one of my lists.

A Little Laughter Goes a Long Way

E-Zine advertising has been called one of the best advertising methods that you can use. If you are looking for a method to get the word out about your product then you should consider advertising in e-zines. A little known but effective niche in e-zine advertising is to *advertise in joke e-zines*. Why joke e-zines? Very simple—they get forwarded more than any other— especially if the joke or jokes are good ones. So, you pay for an ad that goes out to 10,000, but the ad may get forwarded on and on and be seen by a much wider audience.

In fact, I liked the advertising power of forwarding jokes so much that I purchased the domain name www.ForwardJokes.com and plan on using it for some viral marketing.

One thing with e-zine advertising in joke e-zines is that you want to make sure that the jokes aren't too risqué, or that the product or program you advertise doesn't conflict with the joke told. Otherwise, the joke is on you!

Don't Be Afraid to Have Fun

Many people go online to get away from the stress of the everyday work world. If you can combine a money-making idea with something you love to do and are passionate about, then you'll have some fun while you provide others with quality information and a little bit of joy. And you'll generate some cash as well!

You can also turn a hobby into an e-zine. This is a great way to stay in touch with others who share a similar interest. If your list gets big enough you can begin to profit from something you enjoy—the dream of many trapped in a "nine to five" work routine!

When I first got onto the Internet, I set up a cheesy little site, www.thelotterylover.com. I figured a free shot at the Power Ball lottery every draw would entice folks to sign up for my newsletter—and they did.

At the Lottery Lover site I was known as Captain Bob and in the spirit of *Shameless Internet Promotion* had a picture of me in a Star Trek uniform on the main page.

Cheesy? Yes—but effective and profitable! Continuing on with my shameless efforts, I entered a "Lotto Beefcake" contest held at another site, www.Dave'sFreeTexasLotto.com. Because I encouraged those on my list to vote for me, I walked away with the $100 prize. Now, that isn't a lot of money but that was just one little promotion that basically took no work other than e-mailing a small list to help me out. Imagine what you can do if you develop a *Big List* of folks who want your particular information?

Walk Your Talk
Yanik Silver

I've found that one of the biggest challenges for would-be "infopreneurs" is how to create online products when they don't have the expertise to do so on their own. I want to share with you a case study to illustrate how to take an e-commerce idea from conception to actualization.

It's easy for people to simply talk about Internet marketing and about selling information online, but it's a whole different ballgame when you can learn from people who "walk their talk."

Here's how I created a winning information product called *Get Fit While You Sit* even though I had no expertise in the fitness arena. Check out my website at www.getfitwhileyousit.com.

The Idea

I saw an article on CNN.com about how Internet traffic has increased by something like 300 percent over the last few years. Since I'd been doing some talk radio interviews, it occurred to me that this might be a great topic to generate radio publicity. I asked my personal trainer, Jeff Ball, if he could create an exercise program for people who were stuck in traffic.

After thinking about and researching the idea he said it couldn't be done. I then asked Jeff, "What about a fitness program that could be done anytime and almost anywhere?" Of course he didn't think he could do that either, but he said he'd look into it. At my next workout session he told me that it might be possible. I came up with the name *Get Fit While You Sit* and we were off.

The Format

The next step was to decide on the format. I thought about creating an online video but then decided to go with a simple e-book because it was easier to create.

During the next few weeks Jeff went to work developing the exercise program and writing the e-book while I focused on the marketing side of things.

Ten Steps to Internet Success

Here are the 10 steps we took to make it a success.

1. **We registered the domain name.**

2. **We wrote the sales letter.** I wrote the sales letter first then gave it to Jeff to make sure he covered this information in his writings. (This was a very important way to do this.)

3. **We created a website header and the e-book graphics.** We hired a consultant to do this work and it really helped me to visualize how the website would look.

4. **We added bonuses.** In most cases, bonuses really help increase product sales. We decided an e-book of healthy recipes would be a great bonus. I went to www.elance.com and posted this listing: "We will need a healthy recipe booklet, including pictures if possible. We need low-sodium, heart healthy recipes." We received over 26 bids in response. For $200 we created a terrific e-book complete with pictures of all the recipes.

5. **We completed the manuscript.** Jeff finished writing and my wife Missy edited it.

6. **We conducted the photo shoot.** We used a vacant office and the reception area at our gym. I learned a valuable lesson: **use the lowest resolution when taking digital photos for an e-book.** The first batch of photos took up 6 mb of memory; the files were huge. We had to re-shoot everything at a lower resolution to make it work. We then ran the photos through a shareware JPEG optimizer program to reduce the photo sizes even more. (I found this program at download.com.)

7. We combined the edited e-book with the photos and then created a .pdf file using Adobe Acrobat® (the full version).

8. **We set up payment, tracking and administrative processes.** We signed up with Clickbank.com to accept payments, got our web statistics program (web-stat.com), and set-up our download page for product fulfillment.

9. **We created an exit popup window to capture exiting traffic and send visitors a free report using www.getresponse.com.**

10. **We created a series of affiliate tools for our affiliate sign-up page.**

We were now ready to go.

Since my existing e-mail list didn't have much to do with fitness we had to start our promotional efforts from the ground up. I bought keyword traffic from www.Overture.com and advertised in several fitness-related e-zines. Then I contacted possible joint-venture partners I found while doing research into the topic.

I hope this helps inspire you to get your own information product together. Just remember, it's not as hard as you think, especially when you've got a good plan to follow.

Getting What You Want from an E-Book
Rick Butts

My two favorite things about getting music, software, and information from the Internet are:

1. That I can get what I want without a sales person bugging me to death, and

2. That I can get these things instantly—without shipping charges

The e-book is the perfect product vehicle for both of my hot buttons.

I am not alone. A recent study by Anderson Consulting concluded that by 2003 e-books will account for more than ten percent of all retail book purchases in the United States alone. Imagine this—one out of ten of all the books sold in all the bookstores could be an e-book. The e-book has moved from being a cool idea to become a real and viable force in the next wave of publishing.

What does this mean to you, oh shameless one, and your quest for cheap and easy self-promotion? If you are smart, and have useful information that solves someone's problem, then it could be the Holy Grail!

The extremely low cost of development, production, and delivery of an e-book means anyone with even the most basic computer can do it all. There is no real reason that you can't start now and have an e-book in 30 days unless you are completely lazy. Creating the primary book is simply a matter of typing the information into your word processor. Conversion into a format that can be read across platforms, like Adobe Acrobat, (my favorite because of minimum customer hassles and the "reader" is distributed free at www.adobe.com,) is a matter of clicking on a button.

You don't even need a website to sell the book, because once the file is created, it can easily be sent as an e-mail attachment. You could run a quick ad in someone else's e-zine or newsletter and take orders and ship via e-mail. Now don't laugh; many people are doing this very thing.

Now that you have the basic idea, here are some tips I'm using to get tons of self-promotion, and more importantly, cash sales, from the e-book.

Create Your E-Book With the Purpose of Getting Self-Promotion

Fill the book up with hyperlinks back to your website, or the websites of affiliates who will pay you when you send customers to them. Add plenty of "bounceback offers" such as: how to subscribe to your e-zine, your 800 number, special discounts on your full line of products, or anything else you want to let folks know about. You can easily use positioning statements inside your book to show readers how you've helped others, and how you can help them with your products and services.

Give Your E-Book Away For Free!

That's right. Give it away! Remember, you created this beauty with all of your fabulous PR skill, and it costs less than a single business card! The key goal of all Internet marketing and cyber self-promotion is to expand your e-mail list! Give it away to capture e-mail addresses for your e-zine or newsletter. Give it away to people who hear you speak or promote your business. In turn, they will have to give you their e-mail address to get it. Have other people give it away as a bonus to their customers. This way you get them into your **maybe pond** where they can get to know and trust you and buy something you are selling that solves their problems.

Sell Your E-Book!

Sell your e-book from your website with a shopping cart and real time credit card processing and you will create a 24/7 money-making machine! Few things in life are as cool as opening my e-mail in the morning and counting the notices of how many people bought e-books from me, downloaded them electronically, and deposited money into my merchant account while I was sleeping soundly!

You can also sell your e-book on someone else's website, let them keep half the money and the profits you make are entirely yours. No inventory costs, no returns, no shipping, no handling and best of all…no waiting! This is the exact model of web stores like www.EBookSource.com.

Worried that someone might "loan" your e-book to a friend who didn't pay for it? Don't be! When your customers share your information—and they will if it is good—this *viral marketing* effect will drive more customers to your website. The payoff will be even greater.

Face it; the odds of writing a book that makes it through the eye of the needle called *big time publishing*, then has the good fortune of selling well enough for you to get the kind of shameless self-promotion that will do you any good, are microscopic.

Create Something People Want

For example, an associate, Larry Johnson wanted to promote his website www.CustomerServiceVideos.com with a free e-book. He noticed that National Customer Service Week was a few months away. Larry simply contacted several of his customers and searched the Web to find out how different organizations were celebrating the week, documented these ideas, commented on the effectiveness of the ideas, and had himself an e-book! He uses this very original product as a bonus for buying his video series, and customers really love it!

Did I mention that his book is loaded up with shameless self-promotion that really works?

You can't hit a home run unless you step up to the plate.
—Kathy Seligman

Chapter Eleven

I'll Take It: The Science of Internet Selling

> *Aim for success, not perfection.*
> *Never give up your right to be wrong,*
> *because then you lose the ability to learn*
> *new things and move forward with your life.*
> —Dr. David M. Burns

Shameless Internet Promotion Step 11: Develop Online Marketing that Makes the Sale

Debbie Allen

Customers buy out of emotion—not logic. Most consumers would like you to believe that they sit down and logically compare a product's features and make logical decisions. But they don't! They make emotional decisions and create a logical argument to justify their buying decision. Think about it—doesn't everyone want to own a house they can't afford, drive the car they can't afford and so on? So, often people justify their emotional need to get what we want by adjusting their logical thinking.

The Infomercial Approach

Have you ever noticed how TV infomercials are basically selling three things—how to be healthier, wealthier and sexier. They're selling an image of a more beautiful and confident you, with a better lifestyle and an improved personal image.

Famous speaker and author, Anthony Robbins, has a dynamic infomercial that sells just that—a lifestyle. He shows people how to build their dream lifestyle by featuring examples of successful people who have turned their lives around and achieved mega success as a result of listening to his tapes and reading his books. As you watch you see people who are already living the lifestyle you may be dreaming about. TV infomercials work because they create an emotional response in the viewer's mind. The viewer makes an emotional decision to pick up the phone and place an order because they are ready to change their lives at that very moment.

Anthony Robbins is not selling tapes and books—he's selling dreams. Dreams of a happier, healthier, wealthier and more successful lifestyle. His infomercials have been extremely successful because viewers buy—they buy because they want these same results for themselves.

Infomercials don't sell products—*they sell the results that those products can create*. Even when there is only a sliver of truth—people still want to believe that this product will change their lives for the better and they convince themselves to give it a try. After all there is a money back guarantee—"What do I have to lose?"

I've said that to myself time and time again—especially when I've had insomnia and a foggy mind at two in the morning. I've been hooked on the emotion numerous times, picked up the phone and pulled out my credit card. The only person I know who has me beat to this is my dad—I think he has an infomercial warehouse. Most of the things he has ordered have never even been used and never returned. But he does enjoy talking about them and showing them off to family and friends. And we love hearing about them too! Maybe my great entrepreneurial dad will own the first ever infomercial museum someday.

Steal Ideas that Work

How can you create the same emotions in your prospective customer's mind, build that same type of trust and get them to buy from you online? Remember, *you're not selling products and services—you're selling results*. Keep this in mind as you write your sales text. If your prospective buyer had a remote control, how would you change your sales pitch? Get rid of what is not working, keep it simple and make your benefits so irresistible that they can't *logically* refuse.

Why Are They Lying to You?
Grady Smith

Yes, you're being lied to. Everywhere you turn someone's pushing down your throat the belief that the secret to earning big money online is to drive tons of traffic to your website. **I'm here to tell you the truth!**

Even though traffic is a huge component of online success, the real "secret" is converting more of your visitors into buyers. You do this by crafting yourself the best "grab them by the throat" sales letter and proposition, and by making it downright impossible for the majority to refuse.

Just look at these facts, and you be the judge.

Imagine you're driving 300 visitors a day to your website, and sell to one in a hundred of your prospects. Sure, you can begin a massive promotion and drive 900 visitors to your website, making nine sales a day. Or, you can polish up your sales letter, turn one in three into buyers and make nine sales without increasing your traffic.

Just think of the money you'll save, and make, on polishing your sales presentation. Now that you know the importance, how do you put it to work? There are a couple of options.

You can hire someone to do the writing. Find a copywriter who shows you samples and writes in a style that you want on your website. Or, you can do it yourself. Here are some suggestions to apply to everything you write:

▼ **Start with a headline.** Right up front give your product's strongest benefit. Make a promise in your headline, and then explain how the promise and benefits work to the customer's advantage in the body of your sales letter.

▼ **Tell a story.** Give a little of yourself in your sales presentation. Let the reader know you, your hopes and dreams. Share the disappointments you encountered along the way, and divulge how you overcame them. Nothing endears a reader and turns them into a customer quicker than knowing who they're handing their money to.

▼ **Sell your product hard.** Grab your product's best benefits and assemble them into easy to skim, exciting mini bulleted headlines. I've often bough products online after reading the first three benefits and seeing one I need.

▼ **Close your sales letter with the disadvantages of not accepting your offer.** Explain how their quality of life will improve with your materials, and then explain the tremendous risk they take at not owning your product.

▼ **Give the reader something to think about.** Present them with questions that keep them interested and make them think. "Are you ready to take your business to the next level?"; "Are you willing to invest in your financial future?"; "Can you really afford to walk away from this offer?"

▼ **Sell your product with confidence.** Assume that anyone with any sense is going to buy your product. Use phrases like "With your order today." These are assumptive phrases. Everyone wants to act like they know what's going on, and some will even feel wrong not having the product because your sales letter presents it like there's no other option for them.

▼ **Have someone who knows nothing about your product read your sales letter.** What questions does the letter leave unanswered? Would they buy? Why, or why not?

▼ **Write your sales letter from a customer's perspective.** Put yourself in their shoes as you compose it and really feel what someone visiting your website is feeling.

▼ **Place strong calls to action and offer additional bonuses for ordering now.** You'll see this on every infomercial you watch. Bonuses worth ten times the cost and large flashing letters that scream order now! A call to action instructs to act now, and it works! Plus, if the potential customer doesn't order at that instant, chances are slim they'll make the purchase later.

▼ **Give multiple ordering opportunities.** Make it easy to pay by placing links in multiple places. Use bold print to make them stand out. Create a mini headline for your order link that makes it hard to resist clicking it.

▼ **Use the word "because" in your sales letter.** Believe me, your sales will go through the roof when you can give a person the reason why he or she should buy. Instead of saying, "You need this product," turn it into "You need this product because it will dramatically change your life."

▼ **Appeal to the reader's dream.** Center in on what your readers hope to accomplish by visiting your website, and tell them how you're going to give it to them. If your classified ad was for an offer to make money online, then you know these people have dreams of working in their underwear. Address that dream, and you've made yourself a customer.

▼ **Use "action" words in your copy.** Adjectives liven up a sales letter and keep the reader interested. If you can get potential customers to read your entire letter, you have a good chance of getting them to purchase your product.

▼ **Walk them through the ordering process.** Lead your customer through each step and tell them what you want to do. "Start your online success today by placing your order now and begin applying the same secrets I use to make thousands online!"

▼ **Write your letter in a conversational tone.** Imagine your prospect is sitting down across the table from you. Speak like you would to a friend. Don't try to impress with words. Instead, strive for clarity.

▼ **Include a hard-hitting P.S.** Most people will read your headline, then skim down to the bottom of your sales letter. Hit them hard with another great headline type P.S. that explains the benefits received and the risk of not accepting your offer. If your P.S. works, the reader will backtrack and usually read your sales letter word for word.

▼ **And finally, offer a strong satisfaction guarantee,** and you've got a sales letter that grabs the reader by the throat and doesn't let go until they input their credit card information.

Of course, this is a basic list of your sales letter's goals. There are plenty of resources and articles online that will teach you the complete story on banging out a sales letter that works. Explore and learn. Never give up the pursuit of making a sales letter that puts money in your pocket. It's the best time and money investment you'll ever make for your business.

Quadruple Your Online Sales in Three Months or Less

Judy Cullins

I am a non-techie book coach who has been in business for 20 years, but only online for the past two years. I had only been selling e-books and special reports for three months when I contributed to this book. Yet, in just three months I manifested amazing online profits. My first month's sales were only $75 but by the third month my sales had already grown 10 times that and still growing.

How Did this Happen?

Certainly I'm not an overnight success. I had a huge learning curve. I kicked and screamed when business friends said, "Judy, you have to have an e-mail account." My Webmaster friend said, "Judy, you have to have a website." That was two years ago, and now people already refer to me as the *E-Book Queen*.

As you've read in this book, creating an e-zine or electronic newsletter is one of the best ways to let people know who you are and what services you can provide. Be open to new ideas. Ask people who have greater knowledge and expertise than you for their advice. You'll find they'll be more willing to help.

My assistant (a techie-computer person) and I work as a team—I write and create, and he offers technical support to get the word out to millions of Internet savvy people who want to buy online. We spend two hours a day, three days a week on these online projects.

I've discovered that marketing is everything and that online marketing is so much easier, faster, and more profitable than offline marketing. Online marketing is convenient! You don't have to travel; you don't have to talk to large groups or sell products at the back of the room. And like me, you can sell many more products online each month than through traditional publishing and promotion methods.

Online costs are low: no printing bills, no wrapping, no postage, no trucking, no inventory, and no sales tax. Another benefit? Your customers will be happy because they get immediate delivery of their books to their e-mail address.

The Biggest Benefit

This endless virtual marketing machine is out there for everyone. You can learn how to take advantage of this opportunity to boost your online sales beyond your wildest imagination by taking a tele-class, learning from a qualified teacher or author, or by getting individual coaching. What are you waiting for?

Providing Digital Format Is Sensible and Cost Effective

Stephen Renfrow

Information that is provided in digital format can be viewed on or downloaded from the Internet easily and inexpensively. Even better, it can be done without assistance from you. You can literally set up an automated system where your products are sold, processed, and delivered online—24 hours a day, seven days a week, 365 days a year.

If you are offering a product online, you have many choices for delivery: In order of priority they are:

1. You can offer downloadable products
2. You can mail out products yourself
3. You can have someone else drop-ship for you.
4. You can have a fulfillment company take care of the shipping.

If you plan to ship, I would highly recommend using a fulfillment company unless you enjoy being overwhelmed with orders—not always a bad problem to have. Research your fulfillment company before you decide on one. Too many of them have bad reputations because of poor service and mistakes in order fulfillment. If you use a fulfillment company, keep a close eye on their service performance metrics.

If you offer a downloadable product for sale, and you don't have a merchant account, ClickBank (www.clickbank.com) may be the ultimate easy solution. We use them because they handle the credit card processing. You provide the real time fulfillment, the product download, and your own sales monitoring program. Then, you receive a check for all of your orders every two weeks. For all of this, they charge a $49.95 setup fee and $1 + 7.5 percent per order. I am now using them for several of my products, because everything becomes worry-free and work-free after they are set up and running with your product.

Another effective resource is eTapestry (www.eTapestry.com). Their new software is making business more affordable and accessible. By using an Application Service Provider model, they are hosting the actual application on their server, allowing for the convenience of low maintenance and easy upgrades. This is an ideal solution for organizations that have limited budgets, limited staff or expertise with technology, or need to give access to a wide variety of locations.

One of the unique features of eTapestry is the ability to fully integrate its functionality into an existing organization's website. Simple links allow the user a specified and secured access to groups or individuals like board members, volunteers, donors, and staff. The website can become a true communication source for those who play a big part in your organization's success.

How to Ensure Excellent Customer Service Online
Dan Harrison

It takes a great deal of effort to gain a customer, but it can take just one slip up to lose one! You will need fully prepared systems and procedures and well-trained employees to create the quality customer service needed to support your online sales.

Many online sellers think they can merely hire employees, give them a short training course, let them go just before they need to ship out product, and hope for the best when it comes to customer service. What they don't realize is that the training process to properly handle all customer service possibilities takes a few months (not weeks). With improperly trained people, mistakes will happen and customer service will suffer.

Loyal, long-time customers can be quickly turned off if their problems or complaints are not handled properly. Customers don't care that the employee is seasonal, or a temporary hire, or a college student home for a holiday vacation—they just want their transactions handled properly.

The Art of Properly Handled Returns

You must face facts! You are going to get returned products or "returns"— and returns must be thought of as a way to gain customer loyalty. Many online retailers view returns as "the enemy" when in reality they are just another aspect of completing the transaction—whether it be online or in a traditional "bricks and mortar" store.

Just because the customer wants to return something does not mean they hate you or your business. In fact, nine times out of ten they are not trying to rip you off, or "take money out of your pocket." A properly handled return procedure can be a great selling tool by actually showing the customer how good your company can be—even in a return-type scenario.

Customers will become repeat customers as long as they feel comfortable with the return procedure of a particular business. Look at *Craftsman Tools™* and *Sears™*. Many people will only buy *Craftsman Tools™* because they know their return policy is *great*. *Sears™* makes it easy to make a product return or replacement. That is why they have built such strong brand loyalty over years and years.

It's important for every business, big or small, to carefully analyze their entire customer service structure and look at it from the *customer's* point of view. From initial interest, to the actual purchase, to the fulfillment and then to the inevitable return, the customer must walk away feeling happy, comfortable and confident about their decision to use an online retailer. This will ensure strong customer loyalty and repeat business in the future.

Five Steps to Avoiding "Shopping Cart" Abandonment

A great deal of study and research is being conducted about the psychology of "shopping cart" abandonment on the Internet. The jury is still out as to exactly why folks do what they do when in the theater of the shopping cart.

1. **Have a great, easy-to-use shopping cart program.** Go buy something on amazon.com and drugstore.com. Then go to your own website and buy one of your own products online. Compare those experiences because that is the yardstick that you are being measured against (either consciously or unconsciously) by the consumer. How does your online shopping experience measure up?

2. **Secure your shopping cart and checkout area.** Customers still look for that little gold key at the bottom of their browser window. If you are not secure, you will probably lose a lot of sales.

3. **Create an easy to use check out process.** Don't make your checkout cumbersome and don't require too much information from the customer up front. If you do the customer is not likely to complete the transaction. If it is too difficult, a customer will simply click away from your website and try someone else's!

4. **Make it fast.** If you have a painfully slow server, you are going to get a lot of abandoned orders. People like *fast*—they hate *slow*. Make sure that your back end technology is capable of handling the amount of orders you require to be profitable.

5. **Post everything upfront.** People don't like surprises, so post your delivery times, shipping charges, return policies and terms upfront in the checkout process, preferably on one of the first pages. If you are upfront with the customer about your policies they will be more comfortable buying from you and you will get less abandoned orders. For instance, people hate to think that they are getting free shipping—only to find out on the last screen of the cart that shipping is very expensive. This will make customers abandon their shopping carts in droves.

Avoiding Customer Complaints

Unlike many online retailers, we list our telephone number on our website. This comes with mixed blessings.

On one hand, I know we get a lot more orders because a great many online consumers like the comfort of seeing a telephone number. Many people shop online, but then prefer to call in their order. This helps if they have product questions and also eases concerns about online credit card security.

On the other hand, we get a lot of "where's my order" calls. Consumers have now developed an expectation of "immediacy" from the Internet. Many people think that they can place their order at three a.m., and then call the company at ten a.m. wanting to know the status of their order and why they don't have it yet! "When is it coming? When is it coming? It isn't here yet! Why? Why? Why?" This, as you can imagine, really sucks!

After dealing with these problems for a few years, we developed a Call Center policy of not giving order status information on the telephone. It was taking up too much telephone and agent time and, more often than not, was causing "bad blood" with the customer—even before they received their order. So we established an online Order Status Request. To view it, go to http://www.poolandspa.com/page818.htm.

This has practically changed the lives of all our Call Center Agents. When a customer requests the status of their order from our website, this form is e-mailed directly to our shipping department and to an expeditor whose job it is just to track down orders. He gets the status (good or bad) and e-mails it back to the customer within 24 hours. This has worked out great. It takes the pressure off the phone agents, reduces "bitchy customer calls," and allows potentially hostile situations to be defused by the time he customer gets a response. Compartmentalizing these customer service functions greatly improved employee morale which in turn enhanced the overall experience the customer gets from a transaction with our company.

Little Known Secrets to Using Popup Pages
David McKenzie

Many companies run their own electronic newsletters, often producing them either once a week, or once or twice a month. By the way, if you don't already run an electronic newsletter, you should! The only challenge is the struggle to increase subscriber numbers. I know, because this was a constant struggle for me too.

You probably are very familiar with **popup pages**. For those who aren't, they are separate pages that pop up usually when you either enter or exit a website. I was reluctant to use popups in the past for fear of the backlash that might result. I understand that many people hate them. In fact some people hate them so much they have installed software on their computer to prevent popups popping up!

So I struggled on, gaining many new subscribers each month and building my e-zine. But it just didn't seem that I was gaining as many subscribers as I should have.

I had read how some people were huge supporters of popups. They stated they increased their subscriber numbers and/or sales dramatically. So I thought, "Oh heck, I'll give these popups a shot—I can always take them off if they don't work or if they upset my viewers."

Wow!! What happened next was a huge surprise. I set up a simple popup on my home page for subscribers to subscribe to my free twice-monthly newsletter for affiliates. The first month my subscriber uptake increased 366 percent. The second month my subscriber uptake increased a whopping 600 percent!

All because I put a very simple popup on my home page! And it only pops up when people leave my website. But guess what else happened. Since I put up the popup page I have not received one single complaint. Not one. This doesn't mean I am going to put dozens of popups all over my website—on the contrary. From my research, people generally do not seem to mind one simple popup page about a quarter to a third the size of a normal page. It's when the popups get out of control that people get angry.

You have probably seen those pages where another three full pages popup immediately behind the website you entered. These types of websites will annoy just about anybody. But one simple popup page off the homepage getting subscribers to subscribe to a newsletter has worked like "magic" for me.

Get High Praise Testimonials for Your Product—FAST!
Grady Smith

If you've spent any time browsing through online sales pages, you'll be familiar with the use of testimonials. How do online marketers get people to scream such high praises for their product?

I'm about to let you in on the secret. But first, I want you to understand why testimonials are one of the most powerful sales generating tools you can apply to your marketing efforts.

When you visit a website that sells something, your defenses are automatically on high alert. You're downright skeptical, and don't believe a single word that the sales letter is telling you. Then, out of the darkness, comes the sweet refreshing voice of someone who's actually bought the product. You read how, just like you, they were skeptical at first, but now they've got the product in their hands, and can tell you from their own experience that it's everything and more that they've been looking for.

The words in the sales letter begin to weigh with truth, and, as you read a few more testimonials, you become convinced that everything you've just read is the complete and undeniable truth.

Isn't that the true job of a sales letter? To convince the reader that you are telling them the truth, and that any claim you make is one they can believe.

Now that you know how a testimonial works, and why it's imperative to have them on your sales page, I want to show you a few methods that can assure you have great testimonials for your own product.

Offer Free Product in Exchange for Testimonials

One technique to get instant testimonials is to offer your material for free. Yes, I know, you didn't create your fantastic product to just give it away. But this is a practice that will make you more money by just giving away a few copies of your product. So, whom do you give it to?

I recommend setting up a temporary website where people can download your material for free. Explain in your sales letter that the one reason they're getting this material for nothing is that they're expected to give a testimonial in four days.

After you have your trial website up, start to notify people of your offer. To get some testimonials that really pack a punch, contact e-zine editors and Webmasters in the same field as your materials. Send them a sales letter with your offer, and direct them to your website for their free download.

Your best testimonials will come from those respected in your field. By targeting Webmasters and e-zine editors, you're getting words of acclaim from some of the best. And you'll want to tag on the author's website address below their comment to let readers know that the remark did in fact come from an expert.

Offer your promotion to as many editors as you want. Some won't respond to your deal at all. Others will, but you'll never get a comment from them. And you may need to consider that some of the editors won't like your material, and while they might write you a comment, it wouldn't be one you'd consider using on your website.

Although you're giving your materials away for free, a great testimonial will sell ten times better than no testimonial at all. It really is a small handout when you consider how much the right comment from a respected authority will increase your sales. Just work on creating a quality product, get some free copies of it in the hands of respected authorities, and the chore of getting money-making testimonials will take care of itself.

Ask Your Friends for Testimonials

Another method of getting testimonials is to ask your friends. Let them read your materials, and write a comment on what they think. Encourage them to be honest. Don't try to coax them into writing something that they don't feel. You want a real quote that potential customers can relate to.

Write Your Own Testimonials

Writing your own testimonials? You've got to be kidding! Isn't that illegal?

I know what you're thinking. You're picturing some guy banging out praises for his product, then pulling names out of thin air to tag onto them. But you've got it half wrong. While I have written some of my own testimonials, the names below them are actual people who agree with what the testimonial has to say.

Confused? Let me tell you what I mean. When customers purchase my product, they have a chance to look through it and make a decision about it.

About a week after their purchase, I send them a letter asking for a testimonial. However, this letter is unlike any testimonial you've ever seen! My letter offers a selection of about five testimonial comments—each reflecting a different opinion. I ask my customers to choose the comment that best sums up their review of my product.

Each testimonial focuses on a different positive characteristic of my product. For instance, one might say it has helped them make good money. Another might say they were skeptical at first, but came to realize after their purchase how great the product is. A third testimonial might comment on how thorough the product is and how it answered all their needs. I would also have two or three other testimonials designed to put to rest different fears or concerns that many deter potential customer from making a purchase.

At the bottom of the letter, I ask if I can use the customer's name on my website—along with the testimonial they chose. In my experience, most customers will give you permission to use their names. If they like your product, they usually have no problem lending their name to a testimonial that mirrors their thoughts. In fact, they probably would have said it themselves, only they didn't feel competent to do so or didn't want to take the time to express their thoughts.

You still may wonder if this approach is too shameless for you. I don't believe so. I feel that if someone doesn't agree with the testimonials I've written, they're not going to let me use their name. Writing my own testimonials simply lets people express their feelings without the labor of writing them.

Here are a few other tips you'll need to write your own testimonials:

▼ Write your first five to seven testimonials, and then send them out to one customer. Wait for a reply. If that customer decides to tag his or her name to one of them, replace that comment with a new testimonial and send it to your next customer. Keep track of the testimonial comments you've used, and replace them as you go.

▼ Give customers the opportunity to enhance the testimonial. Let them change words or phrases. Allow them to add or delete sentences. In a sense, let them really make it their own.

This is a powerful method of securing testimonials for a new product. Almost half the testimonials on my web page were acquired this way. As I get new unsolicited testimonials that are really powerful, I swap out the older ones. If you do the same you have a powerful tool that reassures potential customers and turns them into buyers.

> *One of the reasons people stop learning is that*
> *they become less and less willing to risk failure.*
> —John W. Gardner

Chapter Twelve
Internet with a Heart

Passion persuades.
—Anita Roddick, Founder of The Body Shop

Shameless Internet Promotion Step 12: Show Your Customers that You Care

Debbie Allen

Using the power of the Internet we can now touch lives and support others anywhere and everywhere around the world. You just never know when the power of your words may be supporting someone in need or making a positive change in someone's life forever. I have devoted this special chapter to this book to share with you some of these heartwarming stories and support that has helped so many others online.

One special way that you can show others how much you care is to offer to share your stories of inspiration, faith, discovery and support. My signature story about my grandmother often moves my audiences to tears as it touches their hearts and inspires their dreams towards positive change. I want to share it with you now.

Water Works

When my grandmother, Bernadette Dault, was 85 years old she was not the healthy, active person she once was. Her failing health, high blood pressure and pain left her dependent on a walker or cane to get around. She could hardly open her fingers because of the pain her arthritis had caused and she was bent over from her shoulders. Pain pills and lots of sleep helped her cope with day-to-day life. It became frustrating to her when doctors told her that there was nothing they could do to help, since there is no cure for arthritis. At that point in her life she felt weak and depressed.

She decided to try another doctor for one last hope. This doctor suggested that she try water therapy. "Oh, No!" were the first words out of her mouth. "I never go into the water! I'm deathly afraid of water." With her great sense of humor she added, "The closest that I ever came to water was a walk on the beach and even that made me nervous."

Not only was she afraid of water, she was also afraid of exercise because she was in so much pain. But, because water therapy was her last hope for feeling pain free and having her back on her feet she reluctantly decided to give it a try.

As she sat on the steps of the pool the first day she was shaky and afraid to go in. Her therapist coaxed her to walk across the pool with the help of her walker. She did it!

Each day became a little easier and she started to build her confidence and stamina. "I knew that I couldn't give up and was determined to keep going no matter how hard it seemed at the time. I just knew that I didn't want to feel sick and in pain any longer and I wasn't willing to give up on life just yet."

As she improved she no longer needed the help of the physical therapist and joined a local health club. Her first water aerobics instructor was a fit 90-year-old man retired from the military. He inspired her to continue and get even better.

She came a long way since her first days in the water, and believed that *Water Works*. After less than a year she was free of pain and began to live a very active lifestyle again without the use of a walker or a cane. In fact, her last few years of life were some of her happiest and most fulfilling.

My grandmother Bernadette lived to be 92 years young. And amazingly, just three short weeks before she passed away she was actually teaching water aerobics at the retirement community were she lived.

My grandmother's zest for life, enthusiasm, sense of humor and strong determination touched everyone she met. She was an inspiration to me and to so many others whose lives she touched over the years.

Giving Is the Greatest Way to Receive

Rick Beneteau

I was flattered when Debbie asked me to contribute to her new book, but I faced a dilemma. I consider myself a promoter, but not quite a *shameless* promoter. Yet, as we began to communicate back and forth online, Debbie had the great idea of adding a "heartfelt" chapter to her book. This was something I felt more comfortable contributing to. So as fate seems to have it, I was made aware of my confession that could inspire her readers.

We'll Be Victorious

After the September 11 terrorist attacks, D Laurance and I were inspired to write and produce a song of tribute. In fact, if you are near your computer, you may want to download the song at www.interniche.net/victorious.htm before you continue reading, as I believe you will get a lot more from this story if you do.

On the morning of September 11, 2001, I received a phone call from my eldest daughter who screamed "Daddy, put on CNN, I think World War III has started!" I stared in utter disbelief at replay after replay of the second airliner melting into the mammoth 110-story structure, that famous symbol of free enterprise. I could only imagine the sheer terror of those thousands of innocent victims. My heart sank as each tower collapsed.

I never thought that I (or my children and now grandchildren) would live to see the day when such evil and horror would hit so close to home. The devastation I witnessed went far beyond the loss of thousands of innocent lives and the destruction of monumental buildings. The innocence of the entire free world was forever changed and life for all of us will never be the same.

Like you I'm sure, I spent the next several days fluctuating between states of anger and sadness. But more than that, I felt totally helpless, just sitting there fixated on CNN, wanting so much to do **something** to help. But what could one simple home-based Internet entrepreneur do in light of such a tremendous tragedy? It was while discussing this with D Laurance, my dear friend and former partner in music, that the answer came.

D reminded me of the theme song we were asked to contribute to a huge charity event to benefit an AIDS organization some ten years ago. We wrote "We'll Be Victorious" and recorded the song with the enthusiastic contribution of many talented vocalists and musicians. We were no strangers to doing such things as this core group of Canadians had donated their time and talents in the past for organizations such as Easter Seals and United Way.

What was sad, though, was that, due to financial issues, this fundraising event was canceled just weeks prior to the scheduled kickoff. We had a professionally produced "from the heart" inspirational anthem whose destiny apparently was just to lie on a shelf!

I couldn't help but agree with D that we now had the perfect message to help people come to grips with the pain and confusion they felt over the events of September 11. And I was blessed to have a pretty extensive reach on the Internet so we could successfully get our song of "healing and hope" to thousands of people who needed to hear it. So, there was *my answer*. However, it was just a small part of a much bigger picture.

D and I went back in the studio to upgrade the recording (after all, it was ten years old) while another good friend, Rozey Gean, went to work designing Web pages to house the song. The website and the song were completed within a week.

I then contacted all my "e-friends in high places," as well as the resellers in my four affiliate programs plus my newsletter subscribers. Almost immediately, we began to experience very heavy downloads. But more importantly, we received the most amazingly heartfelt replies from people who were positively impacted by our song!

As a result of a dream I had a week later, I decided to try my hand at creating a PowerPoint presentation for "We'll Be Victorious," which we uploaded and announced as an addition to our website. Then, out of the blue, I received an email from a long-time—but then unknown to me—subscriber, Rick Hunter, who after viewing our slideshow, took it upon himself to create a wonderful multi-media presentation that is also available to everyone now!

While all of this was happening, my dear friend and publicist, Anne Marie Baugh, silently set out a worldwide press release (not a minor undertaking by any stretch) about "We'll Be Victorious." Although it is hard to determine the impact it has had on people, we are sure that this song and our website will touch the lives of thousands from around the world!

What I Have Learned about Sharing Our Inspiration

Things don't always happen as we plan or expect them to. The universe often has its own schedule. The blood, sweat and tears of many talented people and weeks of studio work a decade ago seemed to have been all for naught, only to be resurrected at the "right time." Here is what someone wrote to me after listening:

> "God had a plan long ago to use you in this terrible tragedy.
> Your music will comfort many in their time of grief."

I bet like me, you were moved to tears when you witnessed the countless examples of selfless giving and utter heroics in wake of the terrorist attacks. The lines of another song I had written two decades prior come to mind. "The darkest nights will bring the brightest days."

It is my belief that these horrific events have served as the catalyst for the much-needed rebirth of spirituality and the making of a better and brighter world. I will go so far as to predict that from those people who were the most profoundly impacted by the senseless slaughter, the children of the victims, will emerge hundreds of noble leaders in all walks of life in this new world. They will all have one thing in common—they will give! Lots!!

My story is simply a great example of how utterly powerful and contagious the spirit of giving can be online. In our case, many caring individuals gave of their time and talents—singers and musicians, graphic artists, Internet citizens and e-business folks who took their time and often financial resources to help spread the word in order to help others at a most critical time. I know for a fact that even more caring individuals will come on board in the near future. Perhaps even you?

Debbie has named this chapter of her book "Internet with a Heart," and aptly so. The Internet is essentially a mirror of main street society in that there is good and bad. As is the case in the real world, the bad usually gets "the feature coverage." But there is **so** much good being done by **so** many people in cyberspace and it's time we start taking notice, and becoming a part of it.

Internet Toy Drive

Remember when I told you about our group of Canadian singers and musicians being no strangers to "giving"? Well, a song recorded by this same core of talented people that's even older than "We'll Be Victorious" is now at work in a large effort to help children and families in need this Christmas. And, remember Anne Marie, my publicist? Anne and I decided to put together the First Annual Internet Toy Drive in tandem with the official Marine Corps Toys for Tots program: www.internettoydrive.com.

Almost immediately and well before launching this, we began receiving serious inquiries from people asking how they could help. It didn't take long for the likes of NFL superstar quarterback Drew Bledsoe to not only pledge his personal support, but lay his powerful name on the line as a corporate sponsor.

Many of the same generous people I have mentioned above will be instrumental in helping raise funds to make Christmas a lot brighter for thousands of children who would otherwise **not** have a single gift under their Christmas tree! Even the simple act of letting family, friends and business contacts know about a worthwhile project, especially with the power of the Internet, can make a huge difference! I won't know the results of our efforts for awhile, but rest assured there will be many, many caring people getting behind this project!

As I wrote this story, just a few days before Thanksgiving, I was prone to become somewhat introspective on that holiday as well. The traditional meaning behind the word "Thanksgiving" and the holiday itself, is that we **give thanks for the many blessings we have.** Something most of us don't do often enough.

So, let me ask you this: *Have you ever been thankful for the opportunity to give?* Are we not only blessed because of the things we have in our lives but also for the things we have to give others to improve *their* lives? When we do give of ourselves to help others, is not the reward we receive but a blessing, and something we should be thankful for? Think about it!

I challenge you to first ask yourself, "What do I have to give to others?" You will find that the answer is lots! Your talents, your knowledge, your time and your "instinct to give" are among them. Then I challenge you to look around at **all** the places where you can give of yourself and be a positive part in the building of this new world. Again, you will find there are lots of places!

Lastly, I challenge you to take action. Get involved. Give, and give lots! I can also assure you, there is no better feeling in the world than knowing you have made a positive difference in someone's life!

Do Something Important

Doreene Clement

9/11/01—Tuesday: A friend, Patricia Steward, woke me with an early morning phone call. "Do you know what's happening?" she asked. "No." I replied. "Turn on your TV," she said.

I didn't know what to feel. Horror, shock, anger, fear! I was numb. Everything was surreal. I instantly thought that I wanted to do something to help, but I did not know what to do. As the day passed, I knew that I was going to do something, but what that *something* was, I had no idea just yet.

9/13/01—Thursday: I couldn't get it out of my head—it was in my every thought. Then it struck me. "We" would create a website to provide free tools and guides to help people heal from this tragic event. The idea for the site was now clear in my mind.

I instantly prayed with gratitude and gave thanks for the inspiration. Then I asked that the project be easy, and the path to creating it also be clear. The next step was finding the above mentioned "we."

9/14/01—Friday: Since I eat most of my meals out, I run into a lot of people I know. That is how the "we" came into the story. This morning I walked into one of my regular breakfast restaurants and there at the counter sat Kathy Marcil and Doug Licciani. As we talked I felt compelled to tell them my idea and ask if they would like to get involved.

They both instantly said "yes." I knew Kathy would be a great asset to the plan because of her extensive background as a counselor and her training in crisis management. Doug was another great person due to his experience in business, computers and the Internet.

9/15/01—Saturday: It was breakfast time and I was hungry for my favorite breakfast stop again. There sat Doug and his friend, Bob Lanzon. Doug asked me to join them and started up the conversation about our inspiring new project. As I began to update Doug, Bob was moved by the project and informed us that his wife, Marie, worked with children and with children's health issues. He suggested that she would love to get involved in the project too. We all agree to meet again the next morning, of course, at a restaurant.

9/16/01—Sunday: Marie joined up and was very interested. She instantly added her wisdom and ideas on what we could do to make a difference.

9/17/01—Monday: I talked to my friend and my doctor, Melenie Dunn, NMD, and asked her to join us. She easily agreed. I was thrilled since she is an expert in health and the connection of health to our physical bodies and emotions. A perfect addition to our team! Now we had the core of our project called www.DoSomethingImportant.com. Everyone had agreed to donate their time and expertise to the project.

9/18/01—Tuesday: We started talking to Web designers. Tom Simmons, of www.pointinternet.com, agreed to provide free web hosting.

9/20/01—Thursday: "We" met as a group for the first time and began to develop the mission and vision statements and to create content for the website. Working together has a flow and an energy that made this a dynamic group.

9/21/01—Friday: Charlie Davis, a friend and lawyer, agreed to join us to supply free legal advice. Dr. Val Farmer, Ph.D. agreed to be on our site and wrote an article for his column about the benefits of journaling and talking.

9/27/01—Thursday: I called a lot of people in search of a Web designer. Within five minutes of my call to him, Butch Clydesdale returned my call and plea for help. I was still on the phone looking for a Webmaster, when Butch called and left this message, "I'll do your Web design, but only if I can do it for free." Butch is a great Web designer and this project fit his personal desires to do something to help. He had been thinking of several projects to make a contribution, so my call was perfectly timed.

9/28/01—Friday: Butch, our new Webmaster and I meet to go over the website design. He endured several marathon weekends to get the website **up and live.**

10/05/01—Friday: Jill Davis, www.scrapbook.com, joined the website and created a series of age-specific scrapbook projects.

10/10/01—Wednesday: The site went *live* on the Internet! In just under one month, our dream turned into reality.

Since I wrote this story, wonderful people and incredible things are still happening with and around this project. I was humbled by what had taken place through this short amount of time. For me it has been a confirmation of faith, trust and belief that humbles me daily. I see that life can be easy. The path is clear. This was the answer to my original prayer and I am grateful and thankful to share this opportunity with the world with the magical powers of the Internet.

Special Websites Support and Help Others
Larry James

My business is built around helping and supporting others. Therefore, I feel my website must be helpful and supportive as well. This has not only helped others but has added great value to my website in return.

We have created special pages that are dedicated to causes that my organization and family believe in. I have had asthma and allergies most of my life, my sister is a breast cancer survivor and my mother died of Alzheimer's disease. These causes are important to us and we want to offer information that may help others. Each of these causes has a designated national awareness month: May—*National Allergy and Asthma Awareness Month*, October—*National Breast Cancer Awareness Month* and November—*National Alzheimer's Disease Month* and *National Family Caregivers Month.*

During these months we post an "attention grabber" on our home page with a link to several pages of information about each topic. We then submit these pages to the top ten search engines with appropriate keywords to reach more people in need of this information.

Holidays Are Always Special Times to Touch Hearts

People are always looking for sites that have information about their favorite holiday. Even though a holiday link may have little to do with our relationship site—with the exception of Valentine's Day—our holiday links bring us lots of visitors who venture on to other parts of our site.

We list 14 holiday links on our website, each with lots of information about that holiday and links to other holiday sites. We always look for tie-ins. For example: November (Thanksgiving) and December (Christmas) are months that typically bring to mind family and friends. It is often a difficult time for people who have lost a loved one through death, divorce or separation. Each of these holiday sections are linked to relationship books and several articles: "Rx for the Holiday Blues" and "A Sure Cure for a Hangover."

The next step is to offer to trade links with other similar holiday sites. This offers our viewers and endless stream of helpful information. I know that we have helped a lot of people with our charitable information and that warms our hearts and keeps us passionate about our website everyday.

The Dot Com with a Mission
Vivian Phillips

About three years ago I walked away from my dream job…or so I thought! It had all the trappings of grandeur, an executive title, a nice salary, an office filled with fine cherry wood furniture in an upscale downtown office building, travel and much notoriety.

But, something was missing. While I knew that externally my job had everything I dreamed of, internally I felt as if I were being suffocated. In order to maintain my mortal existence—for which oxygen is required—I left.

I knew that I had outgrown even my own dream of what would bring me total happiness and fulfillment. Somewhere along my journey I had unconsciously transitioned to another place of existence. What that meant, I did not know. Where my true place was, I knew not. But, I did know that until I found it I would not resurface to the world I had grown so accustomed to embracing.

Since that time I have had many encounters, some were life-altering and some were gut-wrenching, and I judge them not. Each step served as a guide to bring me to where I am today and for that I am eternally grateful. My life has evolved to a place of total joy, daily fulfillment, and a never-ending opportunity to do what I love—make a difference. I am shameless when it comes to sharing, showcasing or telling anyone about what I consider to be one of the most innovative and unique websites with a heart.

After much thought and a lot of work I have resurfaced as a power broker for charity. My vision for the website, is to share a lot of heart—a dot com with a lifelong mission. The goal is to lead the way for one million people to perform a charitable act (I am only beginning with the state of Arizona).

The website offers one of the most innovative and unique virtual methods to encourage, showcase and track charitable acts. It has redefined the art of giving by leveling the charitable playing field to make charitable activity accessible to everyone regardless of economic means, social status, educational background, religious beliefs, political preference or race. This dream fulfilled is part of an even bigger dream and that is to create a charitable phenomenon, on television, that revolutionizes that act of charity and creates calculated intention from every home in America.

As a recovering non-profit executive, small business owner and a product of a single-parent household each of these roles taught me you have to self-promote, even though I didn't recognize it as such, in order to get what you want or to accomplish your goals. It wasn't until the day I met Debbie Allen and attended her presentation, *7 Highly Effective Marketing Strategies for Under $500*, that I really embraced the essence of what that meant.

As Debbie spoke I listened intently. Her vibrant and shameless self-promoting demeanor had me coming out of my chair. I absolutely loved her! For me it was like meeting a kindred spirit who was more evolved. This motivated me to rise to a higher level. She was brilliant, captivating and sincere. Not to mention generous. It was that generosity that catapulted my website to the next level.

My mission had been to send the message that *a million moments of magic are possible when it begins with you*. While this statement proved to be captivating, it was not enough to get people involved.

It was Debbie's marketing strategy to *Create A Special Event Around Your Expertise* that really took me over the edge. This innovative marketing strategy ignited something inside of me that wouldn't rest until I had taken action on all of the ideas twirling around in my head.

Just a few days before attending Debbie's keynote presentation, my coach and I masterminded the slogan, *Commit-A-Charitable ACT™* which would become a nice enhancement for my website. When Debbie finished her presentation I couldn't get back to my office fast enough to *take action* on her advice and to utilize my new slogan. I created *Commit-A-Charitable*

ACT Month™—September. I believe that September will be the perfect month to engage people towards a charitable cause, since we will forever revisit the tragedy of September 11th, 2001.

Commit-A-Charitable ACT Month™ was founded, trademarked and featured in two major publications within a matter of days. It now stands as a prominent feature on the website and is also featured on every piece of collateral materials we send out. That's not the end of it—actually it's only the beginning. Because of that one action, our website will be promoted in a featured article in the *Inspirational Journal* and also on numerous radio and TV shows to increase awareness of this special event.

If I were to offer you an invitation to do one thing to platform your ideas, your business or your organization, it would be to read Debbie Allen's book, *Confessions of Shameless Self-Promoters*. I've always been a self-promoter, but since meeting Debbie and reading her book, I can truly say any residue stuck to me from people who don't understand the savvy and art of self-promotion is now gone. I am free in the truest sense of the word. This is truly something anyone can do and be, it's easy and it is soooooo much fun, try it you'll see. And, remember *the magic of a million moments is possible if it begins with you!*

A Mother and Daughter Team Up to Promote Kindness

Robyn Spizman

What do Michael Eisner, president of Disney; Dennis Haskins, TV star of *Saved by the Bell*; Neil Rudenstine, Harvard University president; Wally Amos, famous cookie-mogul Ahmet Ertegun, president of Atlantic Records; and Ali Spizman, an Atlanta teenager, have in common?

They are all advocates of saying "thank you!"

My daughter Ali, while only 14, wrote to these and other well-known people, including businessmen, actors, and politicians, to find out what they thought about the importance of saying "thank you." These individuals obviously thought Ali's message was worth their attention and wrote back to her with inspiring words of wisdom. Since many of these individuals were busy, Ali included her parent's e-mail in her letters. Some responses arrived via mail and many arrived through the Internet.

Their letters and other helpful thank you tips are included in Ali's book for kids titled *The Thank You Book for Kids: Hundreds of Creative,* and *Clever Ways to Say Thank You!*

As reviews began being posted online, people starting calling Ali's publisher for interviews. In fact, educators who discovered her book responded also and Ali was invited to be featured at many library events. In fact, Peggy Mages, a New York librarian commented: "Being an elementary school librarian, I originally bought this book as a reference for my students. I soon found, however, that it was a great inspiration to me personally. This book should be required reading for all ages!"

To connect instantly with other kids, Ali, who is a huge fan of the Internet and of chatting online with friends, immediately secured the domain name www.thankyoukids.com when she began writing the book. She designed a website and put the address on the jacket of her book. Her purpose in creating the website was to be able to share her ideas and suggestions for saying thank you and encourage other kids to express their appreciation. The Internet played an important role as most kids are online and seeing one of their peers doing something positive encouraged them to also check out her book.

The key ingredient in Ali's website and putting the Internet to work was to offer other kids a glimpse into Ali's mission and show how each kid could spread kindness. Her website features how-to suggestions for expressing thanks. But her mission has a heart, since Ali believes that a world of thanks is just a click away. The power of the written word and the ability to instantly thank someone can transform the Internet into a kindness connector.

Ali also used the Internet to research how to contact many of the famous people she wrote to, and her book has been featured and endorsed on many other websites, including www.usatoday.com, as recommended reading. She has been featured in *Time Magazine for Kids*, *American Girl*, and *Dr. Laura's Perspective Magazine* and across the country via a national satellite media tour. You may also have read about her in *The Atlanta Journal & Constitution*, *The Boston Herald,* and *The Chicago Tribune*.

The Internet played a key role in Ali's success since her website immediately positioned her book and her mission in a way that other kids could investigate instantly. The publisher's press release was also posted and that worked since once the press checked the website, they were able to get helpful information and write about the book without even talking to her. As kids logged onto her website, they also discovered a "real kid" and fellow teen who was doing something positive and making "thank you" cool. Thanks to her web website and the promotion done by her publisher, the media were able to instantly get a sense about her book and request copies and interviews.

The best part of having a website with heart is that Ali's book shows other kids how easy it is to express their appreciation and how good it makes people feel. Words are free and fabulous and she utilized the Internet to express that. One 13-year-old girl contacted Ali about interviewing her for a school report. Again, all of this happened through the Internet when the girl's mother contacted the press-room located on the website for media interviews. She thought Ali's mission to encourage kindness was great. This teenager even was inspired to have a "Thank You Letter Writing Party" at a veteran's hospital.

Sharing Kindness with the World

Ali's website now encourages kids from around the world to create kind acts and to express their appreciation by saying "thank you." Ali does this by offering visitors an opportunity to try a simple activity in their corner of the world. It's called The Thank You Kids Campaign, and kids are encouraged to take action and distribute blank greeting cards and writing supplies to others in need. Ali adds, "My goal is to also encourage other kids to join in and do something nice."

"The Internet is also a great place to send e-greeting cards to thank your friends for even the smallest kind deeds. No matter how big or small, when everyone is nicer to each other, the world's a better place. This is just my way to make a contribution."

So next time someone sends you a gift, does something thoughtful, or just needs a quick pick-me-up, remember that saying thanks isn't just child's play—it's the key to letting others know they are really appreciated and the Internet is a valuable tool for getting your message across.

> *Only work which is the product of inner compulsion can have a spiritual meaning.*
> —Walter Gropius

Chapter Thirteen

Even More Shameless Internet Marketing Stuff

*Always behave like a duck—keep calm and
unruffled on the surface but paddle
like the devil underneath.*
—Jacob Braude

Shameless Internet Promotion Step 13:
Create Multiple Streams of Online Success

Debbie Allen

Your continued education for online marketing is never done. The only consistent thing about the Internet is change and as soon as you think you have it all figured out—things will change. If you are serious about becoming more successful you must be a lifelong learner of this shameless Internet marketing stuff! If you want to achieve big dreams of making money on the Internet, you must think bigger that you ever have before. If you believe you can do it, you will be successful!

In my book *Confessions of Shameless Self Promoters*, I share with readers the three traits that highly successful self promoters possess. Let me share them with you again because they are extremely important for your online marketing success.

Highly successful self promoters **create their own style**. You can create your own style from your website and your e-mails by adding your very own unique twist and personality.

Next, highly successful self promoters look for opportunities and **position themselves to act upon them**. It's easy to position yourself in front of people on the Internet and you don't even have to leave your home to make it happen. You can do it from your home office sitting in your pj's.

The third trait of highly successful self promoters is **repetition**. Successful self promoters don't just say it once; they say it many times. They are persistent and refuse to give up no matter what. Keep trying and perfecting ideas, concepts and strategies presented in this book until you succeed beyond your wildest dreams. If you fall on your face a few times, that's okay, just pick yourself up and keep going. If you don't make mistakes and fail along the way you are not taking risks and you are not growing and learning. Consider failures simply lessons from your marketing mistakes—learn from them and move on.

This book is your ticket to achieving your Internet goals—but you must step on board the Internet train and go for the ride. If you don't, your competition will take that ticket, board the train and leave you at the station. The problem is that all your online customers will be on the Internet train with your competitors.

Your dreams of personal wealth and online success can and will be achieved when you *implement* these secrets and strategies. These valuable resources are here for the taking, yet many people will not take the *action* they need to be highly successful.

These are exciting times we live in! Take action today to implement the ideas you have learned from this book so that you can benefit from endless worldwide opportunities presented to you on the World Wide Web.

Let Your Mouse Do the Walking
Ken Arnold

The Internet is literally overflowing with information in the form of an unplanned, unwieldy Web of data. In fact, "web" might imply more structure than is actually found there. So how do you find anything on the Internet? There are two related methods for searching for information on the Internet: **index services** and **search engines**. Without these, the Internet would probably still be in the hands of a small group of techies.

Index websites are collections of websites or pages that have been culled from the Internet's vast collection of files and that are then categorized for you. One of the top index websites today is www.Yahoo.com. If you've visited Yahoo, you know what an index service looks like: categories such as Autos, Business, Health, Travel, etc., are each listed as a hyperlink to another index page of subcategories, and so on. You simply click the hyperlinks with your mouse, and start "drilling down" through Yahoo's web hierarchy. Other popular index websites include Lycos, AltaVista, Google, and Netscape. If you have an Internet service provider, such as America Online or AT&T, each one also has its own flavor of index services.

Search engines use software instructions that are adapted to the structure of information on the Internet. These instructions act as spiders that "crawl" through directories of files on the Internet to bring back specific results and store them in huge databases.

Searches are usually based on keywords contained somewhere in those files, but each engine operates differently. Some search engines index practically every keyword in the file. More commonly, they read the first few lines of a document file. Some search engines can also filter out the things you don't want in the results.

Search engines only categorize their results to the limits of the keywords and that the hits themselves were accurate and meaningful. Your search of the search engine database is equally serendipitous. The quality of the results from your search depends on how well the keywords you entered match the keywords in the database of files the search engine assembled when it searched through directories of files on the Internet.

Without this level of filtering, it would be nearly impossible to gather data from the Internet. Some Internet files that might be helpful but were not tagged as such, might be missed altogether. As a result, the concept of online self-promotion can make the overall Internet experience more fruitful. The more you volunteer about what your Internet document is about, the more likely it will generate accurate search hits.

What does this have to do with shameless internet promotion? If you understand how people search for you or your kind of business on the Internet, you can help them find you, and that's in *your* best interest.

Ten Strategies to Help People Find Your Website

1. Since all search engines collect keywords from at least the top of the document or Internet file that is where you should concentrate in order to maximize hits against your website. In HTML, this section of the file is under <<head>> and contains two main areas for you to drop in your keywords, the <<title>> and the <<meta>> tags. Some people still use a comment tag <<!>>, but if you do, don't forget to make it invisible to the web browser by including the exclamation mark. Otherwise, everything you type there will be displayed on the Web page, resulting in *shameful* online promotion!

2.   At a minimum, your website title page should include a keyword that names or describes your product or service, even if it is not part of your business name.

     However, don't load a ridiculous list of keywords in your title to attract search engines. For example, <<title>>Bonsai House Home Page, Bonsai, house, home page, plants, exotic plants, exotic bonsai, ...<</title>> might throw you into a results list of sex websites from someone's search. And don't put "sex" in your keyword list unless you *have* a sex website, and expect to be in the longest results list on the Web!

     You should also be aware that whatever is in the <<title>> tag will be displayed in the browser field containing the document title. So a ridiculous list of keywords will appear in the browser and also in your bookmark list—or list of favorite websites you select for easy access— if you happen to add this link to your favorites.

     Finally, don't repeat a keyword in your list expecting that the more times you write it, the more the search engine will pick it up. Such a practice is considered spamming (Think *irritating repetition*), and is not allowed by the search websites. A safe and reasonable example of the Bonsai list might look like this: <<title>>Bonsai House, Bonsai and House Plants Retailer<</title>> and then <<meta name="keywords" content="bonsai, house plants, plants, online bonsai retailer, interior decoration, Bonsai House...>> etc.

3.   Remember that each page of your website can and should contain all of your keywords again, plus anything unique to the page. More Web pages return search hits from your website, and so you look like an important website—shameless online promotion!

4.   Register your website with as many of the Internet search engines as you can. You can do this by going to each one and registering your account and pointing to your website address.

     Some index websites make it incredibly easy for you to do this. If you publish your Web page(s) on their website, they provide you the opportunity to list yourself in their website's index, in as many places as you can find to fit yourself. A few of them go further by letting you promote your website with them into a whole group of other search websites, all with one click of your mouse! How cool is that?

Bear in mind that business is business, and now some of the largest search websites, such as Yahoo, charge fees to be listed in their database. But there are still many free search websites, and you should get on as many of them as you can. Many free websites include nothing more than the URL for your website, e.g., www.hostdomainname.com/bonsai.html! Others ask you to enter keywords and find where you fit into the categories of their database. It's probably worth the investment to pay Yahoo and other pay-for websites to be listed in the database and then fit into appropriate categories.

5. Write a short description of what your website is all about and add it into your file's meta tags as well. You can also use this description when listing your website with the index providers. Always put the most important part of the description first because some search engines only capture the first line or handful of characters (maybe 25 words or so).

    Here's an example using the meta tag: <<meta name="description" content="bonsai, house plants for sale online and at store, other Asian indoor plants for decoration and atmosphere, special orders, Bonsai House online,...>>. The business name is less important than keywords, so it gets moved further down the list in case the search result cuts off some of the words.

6. Always include your e-mail and web addresses in any directories or other online advertising opportunities such as classifieds. Some professional organizations also provide vehicles for their members to promote themselves online. Check to see what your professional organizations can do for you.

7. Post your resume/curriculum vitae online at any of the Internet job websites, as well as professional organizations and industry resource websites. Always include your e-mail and web addresses on your resume.

8. Write a press release for your website and send it to friends, colleagues, clients, and even the media. Include your e-mail and Web addresses. Add your Web address to your e-mail signature file. This file becomes the close to every e-mail message you send. E-mail your press release to everyone you think might be remotely interested. One Internet guru, Joe Burns, even has parties before he takes websites live. It

generates interest and word-of-mouth publicity that can start growing as soon as the website is available.

9. Join a Web ring, such as the obvious one at http://dir.webring.com. Web rings are similar to index websites, except they are set up and promoted by people and businesses other than the provider (America Online, AT&T, and Netscape have similar services). You can join existing Web rings under appropriate categories, or create your own!

10. Last, but not least, find other websites that are related to yours by topic, and see if they will add a link to your website on their pages. Of course, you should also return the favor. Congratulations! You've just joined the World Wide Web and become a shamelessly successful Internet promoter!

With so many search engines (and so many businesses on the Internet), some companies in competitive (a.k.a. crowded) industries start to worry about how they fare on a daily basis. They worry about which search engines have the largest number of users on the Internet, and how they can make sure that their links come up more often and at the top of the results lists more often. Devising and implementing Web search strategies at this level, called Search Engine Positioning, become full-time jobs for skilled Web jockeys. Smaller businesses may not need to be this concerned (although a really shameless Internet promoter might be). If you are, hire a professional to help with this.

How to Build a Successful Affiliate Program
Yanik Silver

An effective affiliate program will help you extend the reach of your website in a way that will expand your ability to distribute your product to the marketplace and increase sales. What are the prerequisites for an effective affiliate program?

Good Product

You must have a good product. This goes almost without saying but I'll mention it anyway—you've got to have a good product that delivers on your promises. This is especially true if you want to attract "Super Affiliates" (the best of the best affiliates).

Sales Performance

You must have a website that sells! Unless you have numbers that prove your website sells you shouldn't move into marketing your affiliate program yet because you'll just succeed in getting affiliates upset at you.

Good Commission Payments

You need to pay good commissions. For most affiliates the bottom line is how much money they can make. It's about opportunity cost. For top affiliates there is a limited amount of space on their websites for endorsements, and a limited number of e-mails they can send out. If another program brings them $1.50 for e-mail and yours contributes only 25 cents—guess which one they'll pick. No contest!

I suggest you give as much as you can to your affiliates to help motivate them. This is much easier to do for a digital product than for a physical product. My affiliate program is a multi-tier program with two tiers. I give a 45 percent commission to my affiliates. On my second level or tier, I pay 5 percent. The program doesn't expand past the second level. For example, let's say Bob is my affiliate. Bob refers John. And John also becomes my affiliate. When John makes a sale, Bob will get paid 5 percent.

I place a heavier emphasis and commission on the first level because I want my affiliates going out and making sales instead of trying to recruit more and more sub-affiliates under them.

Provide Assistance

It is absolutely critical that you provide your affiliates all the tools and assistance they need to be successful. When most affiliate programs sign up affiliates they give them a couple of banner ads. However, the effectiveness of banners is fading. If you're lucky, you'll get only a 1½ to 2 percent click through rate.

Those who only give their affiliates banners are not giving them the tools that they need to sell. Remember that people are lazy, so you've got to give them everything they need. I created something called my "Affiliate Tool Box" for my affiliates to provide them with all the tools they needed to promote the program and be successful.

Announcing Your Affiliate Program

Start with your existing customer base and send out an e-mail announcing your program and providing a link to encourage them to sign up. I had a feeling my affiliate program would take off because I had received e-mails from customers asking if I had an affiliate program they could join.

Next, announce your affiliate program to the different directories of affiliate programs on the Web. I announced my new affiliate program to between 20 and 30 affiliate program directories. Here are a few Affiliate Program directories I'd recommend:

> www.associateprograms.com
> www.clickquick.com
> www.cashpile.com
> www.affiliatematch.com
> www.associatecash.com
> www.refer-it.com
> www.2-tier.com
> www.affiliatesdirectory.com

If you don't want to announce your program to all these websites there is a service called Affiliate Announce at www.affiliateannounce.com that will do it all for you.

Once you start getting affiliates signed up you'll begin to see a snowball effect as more and more affiliates join (especially if you have a two-tier set-up). Be sure to promote your affiliate program to every new customer and prospective customer.

What isn't tired won't work.
—Claude McDonald

Rich Resource Guide

Discover more about these famously successful online marketing experts. Visit their websites to learn even more about how to achieve online success.

Debbie Allen, *Who's Who of Marketing Experts*, is an internationally professional speaker, retail and promotional marketing expert. Debbie is the author of *Confessions of Shameless Self Promoters™* and *Confessions of Shameless Internet Promoters™*. To contact Debbie to present to your organization, sign up for her *Power Marketing* inner circle membership or sign up for her online newsletter, *Confessions of Shameless Marketing News* visit her website at www.DebbieAllen.com or her book's site at www.ConfessionsofShameless.com.

Dr. Tony Alessandra helps companies build customers, relationships, and the bottom-line. His audiences learn how to achieve market dominance through specific strategies applying Dr. Alessandra's high-tech and high-touch marketing, sales, service, and relationship-building skills. To learn more about Tony's presentations and/or book, view his website at www.Alessandra.com.

Jeremy Allen is the BNI International technology advisor Business Network International. He is also the founder of the Youth Excellence Foundation and a contributing author of the *New York Times* bestseller, *Masters of Networking* and the monthly journal, *Sales and Marketing Excellence.* Learn more about Jeremy and the Youth Foundation at www.youthexcellence.org.

Miguel Alvarez is Mexico's most well known Internet marketer. He owns over 30 successful direct-response websites, all of them focused on helping others achieve success online. His most recent venture is an incredible web hosting company called www.ThirdSphere.com.

Tom Antion is the publisher of the largest electronic publication on public speaking in the world. This dynamic publication brings in a shameless amount of profit each month. You may learn more about Tom's expertise and discover how to join his membership at one of the best websites in real world Internet Marketing Techniques at www.greatinternetmarketing.com.

Ken Arnold is a professional speaker, author, educator, business consultant, and Internet guru. Ken provides business consulting for global marketing through Internet/Web design and technologies, internationalizing small/mid-sized businesses, and import/export management. He is also an analyst for the computer software industry and an expert on the concepts of time and time management, business processes, and project management. Learn more at www.kennconsulting.com.

Rick Beneteau is the highly acclaimed author of three top-selling Internet marketing books. He is also the author of the record breaking www.WZ.com book, *Success: A Spiritual Matter*: www.interniche.net/ssm.htm. Rick invites you to join his brand new online community at www.PeopleBuildingPeople.com.

Ilise Benun is a national speaker and the director of Creative Marketing & Management, a Hoboken, NJ-based consulting firm that does marketing for designers and others offering creative services. She is also the author of *Self Promotion Online*. For more info, visit her websites: www.artofselfpromotion.com and www.selfpromotiononline.com.

Chris Bloor, The Walking Idea Machine, is one of Australia's most sought after direct response copywriters and president of the Quality Business Institute in Western Australia. Chris has generated literally millions in extra sales with his two and three page sales letters. Check out his website to learn more at www.bettermarketingcards.com.

Bonus: Simply mention that you read this book, and you will receive two **free** audio presentations with your order, *How to Create Display Advertising that Compel Prospects to Pay Attention and Take Action Now!* and *Ten Insider Secrets to Upsell More of Any Product or Service—Virtually Overnight*. These bonuses are valued at $98 each and mailed straight to your door anywhere in the world.

Alexandria K. Brown, *The E-Zine Queen*, is a marketing writer, consultant and author of *Boost Business With Your Own E-Zine*. It's a complete, step-by-step guide to planning, writing, publishing, and promoting a successful e-zine. The manual comes with *The E-Zine Queen Resource Report*, featuring more than 268 resources to help you gain thousands of subscribers. Learn more and sign up for her FREE biweekly newsletter at www.ezinequeen.com.

Rick Butts is an author, speaker, entrepreneur and owner of more than three dozen websites featuring a variety of marketing concepts. He is the founder of www.eBookSource.com—a new concept in e-book marketing of information, software and templates specially designed to bring authors and information seekers together in a one-stop resource. If you would like to have *The Easy Way to Create and Sell Your eBook in Thirty Days or Less!*—a free five day mini-course, just send an e-mail to: www.easyway@eBookSource.com.

Dr. Jeanette S. Cates, The Technology Tamer™, works with organizations who want to reap the rewards of their online technology and with professionals who want to reduce their technology learning curve. She is the author of *Online Success Tactics* and CEO of www.TechTamers.com. Jeanette welcomes readers of *Confessions of Shameless Internet Promoters* to send their trial signature file to Jeanette for a free review.

Doreene Clement has authored a series of craft instruction books and sold over 1 million copies. Doreene has vested the last two years in research, development, writing, and publishing *The 5 Year Journal,* a book offering a positive format for growth and healing through journaling. Kathy Marcil, MS is a licensed addition counselor, licensed professional clinical counselor and a critical incident stress debriefer with over 20 years of experiences. To learn more about this heartfelt website view www.dosomethingimportant.com.

Judy Cullins is a 22-year veteran publisher, book coach, and author of *Write your eBook or Other Short Book—Fast!* and *Ten Non-Techie Ways to Market Your Book Online*, as well as 30+ other books. Known as the e-book Queen, Judy helps people to market their products and services online. She publishes a free monthly e-zine called *The Book Coach Says*. If you are an author or aspiring author you may learn more and sign up online at www.bookcoaching.com.

Terry Dean publishes the Web Gold free newsletter along with running a membership site teaching step-by-step exactly how to market online with over 1,300 paid members. Terry has produced $33,245 in profits from his business in less than 72 hours in front of a live conference audience and has generated $7,976.00 before lunch in front of another audience. Both demonstrations were done with ZERO spent in marketing costs. To learn more about Terrry's accomplishments and receive his free e-book, *How to Start Your Own Traffic Virus* view his website at www.bizpromo.com.

Paulette Ensign's company, Tips Products International, supports booklet success for many companies by offering a menu of products and services. Paulette's home study kits take her client's step-by-step through the process of creating, producing, and marketing a booklet. Visit her *All About Booklets Discussion Board* and learn more about her presentations at www.tipsbooklets.com.

Joe Gelb, attorney and CPA, is the founder and President of Small Business Advisors, Inc. Joe is the author of *Building a Million Dollar Service Business and Tax Accounting for Small Business.* He regularly appears on radio and TV, and lectures to groups across the USA.

Eric Gelb, Joe's son, is a CPA, MBA, an investment banker and makes sales presentations to Fortune 1000 companies. Eric is the author of seven books including *Personal Budget Planner* and *Book Promotion Made Easy—Event Planning, Presentation Skills and Product Marketing* and the audio program *Promote Yourself and Your Business with Writing* (with Debbie Allen). To learn more, visit www.PublishingGold.com and www.SmallBusinessAdvice.com.

Dan Harrison worked his way through college as a professional magician and a pool cleaner. He stared Paramount Pools, which developed into the Virtual Pool & Spa Store. Poolandspa.com is now the largest pool and spa website in the world with over 3,000 pages and over 100,000 pool and spa related items. View this extensive online store at www.poolandspa.com.

Shel Horowitz, marketing copywriter and author of *Grassroots Marketing: Getting Noticed in a Noisy World* and several other books. Shel specializes in affordable, effective marketing strategies and materials for small businesses and nonprofits. Shel is the owner of www.frugalfun.com and www.accuratewriting.com.

Larry James is a professional speaker, relationship coach, Webmaster of his own site and author of three relationship books: *How to Really Love the One You're With, LoveNotes for Lovers* and *Red Hot LoveNotes for Lovers*. You can view his books and dynamic website at www.CelebrateLove.com.

Dan Janal has been a PR executive for 20 years. He has been involved in some of the biggest PR launches, including AOL, *Grolier's CD-ROM Encyclopedia* and GPS/Street Mapping software. He has authored six books, including Dan Janal's *Guide to Marketing on the Internet*, which has been translated into six languages. He is a frequent speaker on marketing issues around the world and is a former award-winning reporter and business newspaper editor. With his marketing and PR background, Dan created PR Leads to provide fast, easy and affordable publicity leads. For more information, view the website at www.prleads.com.

Bob Kish is founder of www.ezineADventure, a revolutionary program for online newsletter (e-zine) publishers to generate free advertising. Bob runs several additional websites dedicated to helping people make money on the Internet, including: www.AffiliateWinners.com, www.Zeenz.com, and www.EzineGoldmine.com. And, if you are looking for Free Powerball check out www.thelotterylover.com.

Dr. Jeffrey Lant is one of the most well-known marketing authorities in the world. Author of many books, including *The Unabashed Self-Promoter's Guide*; *Cash Copy: How to offer your products and services so your prospects buy them...now* and *E-Mail El Dorado: Everything you need to know to sell more of your products and services every day by e-mail without ever spamming anyone.* You'll find his catalog at www.jeffreylant.com. While you're there, pick up a *free* copy of Dr. Lant's 15th book *E-Money!: The Complete Guide to Using the Internet to Profit at Home NOW!* A $19.95 value, it's free to readers of this book!

Lenny Laskowski is an international professional speaker, author and expert on strategic Internet marketing. Lenny's book, *Success Via the Internet—How To Successfully Grow Your Business* and his live six hour seminar CD is available through his website at www.ljlseminars.com.

David McKenzie is founding editor of an online company in Australia. His websites are dedicated to helping people make money online and focus on affiliate programs and writing free articles. David is the author of two e-books entitled *How to Write Free Articles and Market them with a $0 Marketing Budget* and *The Facts You Should Know About Affiliate Programs*. You may view his websites and learn more about his e-books at www.brisney.com and www.1sthomebasedbusiness.com.

Merle (just Merle, thank you) is an experienced Internet Marketer/ Promoter Consultant. She knows what it takes for business websites to be successful. She has been online for over five years and has three websites to her credit: MC Promotions (www.MCPromotions.com); Merle's World (www.MerlesWorld.com) and E-zine Ad Auction (www.EzineAdAuction.com). Read Merle's free e-books, *Merle's Mission Anniversary Edition* at www.merlesworld.com/e-books/ merlesmission99.exe and *Secrets of Business in the New Millennium* at www.mcpromotions.com/ebooks/businessin2000.exe.

Dr. Ivan Misner is the co-author of the New York Times bestseller, *Masters of Networking* and the founder & CEO of BNI. BNI is the world's largest referral organization with over 2,200 chapters throughout North America, Europe, Asia, Africa and Australia. Dr. Misner teaches business management at Cal Poly University. To learn more about his organization view www.bni.com.

Thomas Murrell, MBA is an international business speaker, media consultant and award winning-broadcaster. His company, 8M Media and Communications, provides solutions to media, marketing and management issues to top 500 companies, government agencies and universities. He is the author of *How to Turn Your Big Marketing Idea into a Competitive Advantage* and *Web Marketing Essentials.* To learn more and sign up for *Media Motivators,* a free online media, marketing and management newsletter, visit www.8mmedia.com.

Gary Onks is a business consultant, senior advocate and author of *How You Can Reach & Sell the $20 Trillion Senior Marketplace.* His insights come from real-life, in-person sales to senior citizens. To learn more about gaining your market share with your online marketing, view Gary's website at www.soldonseniors.com.

Vivian Phillips, *America's Queen of Charity,* is the host of *The Vivian Phillips TV Talk Show,* a former Ms. Black Arizona and president/CEO of People in Motion, Inc. Visit her website at www.vivianphillips.com and find out how you can perform a charitable act and live your legacy instead of leaving one.

Karen Post, "The Branding Diva™," has been developing creative solutions and implementing innovative methods that cause positive action for nearly 20 years. Her work has benefited national and international companies and she has earned the respect and admiration of top executives, community leaders and industry professionals from around the country. Karen has co-founded and served as CEO of an Internet jewelry company and wrote a book about this venture and her experiences called *Lessons Learned—Dot.com or Not.com.* To learn more about her book and expertise view her website at www.karenpostbiz.com.

Stephen Renfrow is the director of Consolidated Investors Group, a private commodities investment firm since 1996. He is the creator of the Home Biz Network which helps others to succeed in the home-based business market. To learn more view his website at www.homebiznet.nu.

Jeff Rubin, a former newspaper reporter and editor, owns Put It In Writing, a full-service newsletter writing and design firm. He has spent the last 22 years helping companies effectively communicate with their clients and employees, writing and designing more than 1,300 newsletters. Jeff is a member of the National Speakers Association and speaks on writing, marketing and business integrity. To learn more view his website at www.put-it-in-writing.com.

Dan Seidman is a nationally recognized speaker, trainer and author of *The Death of 20th Century Selling: 50 Hilarious Sales Blunders and How You Can Profit From Them*. This unique book has been endorsed by top marketing experts including Seth Godin, Jay Conrad Levinson, Brian Tracy, Debbie Allen and many more. To learn more about Dan, view his website at www.salesautopsy.com.

Lee Silber is CreativeLee Speaking "Helping Creative People Deal with the Business Side of the Arts". In addition to being an award-winning trainer, Lee Silber is the author of ten books including *Self Promotion for the Creative Person* and *Money Management for the Creative Person*. He is also a popular radio talk-show host, accomplished graphic artist, and founder of five companies. To learn more about Lee, view his website at www.creativelee.com

Yanik Silver, at just 28 years old, has created several best-selling Internet projects, including instantsalesletters.com. You can find out more about Yanik and hear him in an online interview where he confesses his online marketing success secrets by visiting www.surefiremarketing.com.

Grady Smith is a copywriter who creates sales letters and ads for those who want to sell more, but are on a limited budget. He also offers tips and advice to help businesses write stronger sales copy. Visit his website and sign up for his free newsletter at www.cheap-copy.com.

Robyn Freedman Spizman, is a well-know television personality, previous consumer advocate for NBC's Super Shopper and The Gift Guru and author of *The Thank You Book*. To learn more about this book view Robyn's website at www.robynspizman.com. To learn more about daughter Ali and view her inspiring website, go to www.thankyoukids.com.

Joan Stewart, a.k.a. The Publicity Hound, publishes *The Publicity Hound's Tips of the Week*, a free weekly e-zine on how to generate free media publicity. Subscribe at her website at www.PublicityHound.com and receive a free by auto-responder the handy checklist *81 Reasons to Send a News Release*.

John Stanley is an international consultant, conference speaker, author, and retail expert based out of Australia. He started his business in 1976 and now works in 16 countries on five continents. John Stanley Associates operates successfully with only a four-member team due to his highly effective use of technology. To learn more about John Stanley and John Stanley Associates view his website at www.jstanley.com.au.

Natalie Buske Thomas is an author of mystery and children's books. Natalie owns and operates independent Spirit Publishing of Cannon Falls, Minnesota. For more information on her books and resources for entrepreneurs, contact Natalie from her website at www.independentmysteries.com.

Aaron Turpen is the proprietor of Aaronz WebWorkz, a complete service provider for small business online. Aaron has used a computer since early childhood and began his first website in 1996. View the website at www.AaronzWebWorkz.com.

Barry Urquhart is the managing director of Marketing Focus Perth, in Western Australia. He is author of six books including the two largest selling publications on service excellence in Australia. Each year he travels some 250,000 miles on five continents to deliver up to 150 conference keynote addresses. To learn more about Barry and his presentations, view his website at www.marketingfocus.net.au.

Joe Vitale is the world's first "Hypnotic Marketer." He is the author of way too many books to list here, including the best-selling new book *Spiritual Marketing*, the best-selling e-book *Hypnotic Writing*, and the best-selling Nightingale-Conant audio program, *The Power of Outrageous Marketing*. You can get his controversial new e-book, *Unspoken Marketing Secrets*, online at www.mrfire.com/Publications/ebooks.html Joe lives in the Texas Hill Country outside of Austin. He spends most of his time in his pool, or driving his new BMW Z3. But you can reach him directly at shameless@mrfire.com.

Mary Westheimer is founder of Book Zone.com, the Net's largest publishing community. BookZone has helped 3,500 publishing professionals with website hosting, development and promotion services. A former freelance writer, Mary has written for *Publishers Weekly*, *USA Today* and *Columbia Journalism Review*, among other publications. For more information view the website at www.bookzone.com.

Julia Wilkinson is a writer and nine-year veteran of America Online. Her book, *My Life at AOL*, is available via www.amazon.com, www.1stbooks.com, or via her website along with her e-book *What Sells for What on eBay*.

Index

Want a Dynamic Speaker?

Debbie Allen has been motivating and inspiring audiences from around the world for years. Debbie's contagious enthusiasm, wealth of knowledge and humor all team up to make her a dynamic presenter. To discuss hiring her for your next convention, meeting, tradeshow, or keynote presentation see the contact information below.

Keynotes, seminars and workshops include:

Marketing:

- ▼ 7 Secrets of Online Marketing
- ▼ Shamefully Successful Self Promotion
- ▼ 7 Highly Effective Marketing Strategies for Under $500
- ▼ Putting Personality Into Your Business
- ▼ Attracting Customers Like Crazy
- ▼ Retail Entertainment with Promotional Marketing
- ▼ How to Compete and Succeed Against the Retail Giants

Sales & Team Building

- ▼ I'll Take It!—The Science of the Sell
- ▼ Creating More Sales with Diversified Selling Strategies
- ▼ Creating Your Dream Team: Hiring, Training & Retaining the Best

Success & Customer Service:

- ▼ The Top 10 Business Strategies for Success
- ▼ Highly Effective Leadership Strategies that Build Success
- ▼ Ordinary to Extraordinary!

Want to Learn More Shameless Marketing Secrets?

Sign up for the free *Confessions of Shameless Marketing* e-newsletter on the book's website at www.ConfessionsofShameless.com. Keep up to date on Debbie's latest projects and complete travel schedule. View the pressroom and learn more from expert, Debbie Allen. In addition, you can link directly to your favorite contributing authors' websites. From this section you can e-mail the authors directly, order their books online, and view more information about their services.

Need More Marketing Help?

Debbie Allen is also a marketing consultant who can help you to skyrocket your marketing success both on an off the Web. To receive personalized and affordable consultation, personalized marketing critique certificates and monthly marketing success interview tapes discover Debbie's *Power Marketing Inner Circle Membership* online at www.DebbieAllen.com (click on Power Marketing Membership). Debbie's other services include strategic planning, radio and TV personality, MC for events, customized tele-seminars, and book signing events. For more details about how Debbie Allen's services can help you please, contract her at:

Debbie Allen, President
Allen & Associates Consulting, Inc.
P.O. Box 27946,
Scottsdale, AZ 85255-0149
Toll Free in US: 800-359-4544
International: 1+480-831-8090
Fax: 480-831-8334
E-mail: Debbie@DebbieAllen.com
Book's Website: www.ConfessionsofShameless.com
Author's Website: www.DebbieAllen.com

Give the gift of *Confessions of Shameless Internet Promoters*™ to your friends, family, and business associates. Check with your leading bookstores both on and offline or order here:

❏ YES, I want ____ copies of *Confessions of Shameless Internet Promoters* at $17.95 each, plus $3.00 S&H (throughout the U. S.)

❏ YES, I want to receive my FREE subscription to *Confessions of Shameless Self Promoters*™! e-zine.
My email address is listed below.

❏ YES, I am interested in having Debbie Allen speak to my organization. Please contact me with details.

My check or money order for $ _____ is enclosed.
Please make your check payable to Success Showcase Publishing

Please charge my:
❏ Visa ❏ MasterCard ❏ American Express ❏ Discover/Novus
Credit card # _____

Expiration date (month/year)   _____/_____

Name_____

Organization_____

Address _____

City_____State _____Zip_____

Phone_____Fax_____

Email (please print clearly)_____

Signature X_____

Return to:
Success Showcase Publishing
PO Box 27946
Scottsdale, AZ 85255-0149
Toll free ordering: 800-359-4544
Fax for ordering: 480-831-8334
Order online at: www.ConfessionsofShameless.com